NEWNES

COMPLETE PRACTICAL
WOODWORKING

NEWNES
COMPLETE PRACTICAL
WOODWORKING

Edited by

A. T. COLLINS

Managing Editor *Practical Woodworking* Magazine

NEWNES : LONDON

© George Newnes Ltd. 1966

First Published 1966

Made and printed in Great Britain by
Hazell Watson & Viney Ltd., Aylesbury, Bucks,
for George Newnes Ltd.,
Tower Hill, Southampton Street, London, W.C.2

CONTENTS

PREFACE

THIS book is intended to give the amateur who is – or is likely to become – seriously interested in practical woodworking all the necessary guidance on the choice and use of both tools and materials, and to provide suggestions and data for a wide range of inexpensive articles and fitments which are not difficult to make and would be useful and attractive in the modern home and garden.

Whilst it could be argued that the basic technique of woodworking alters only slowly, a glance through some of the older books on the subject will soon show that they have very little to offer the modern woodworker.

Woodworking has become a means to an end, rather than merely a pleasant pastime. Additions and improvements to the home, using all the new materials, call for designs which are substantially different from the types shown in the traditional books. New tools, new methods and a new approach to the end product are all reflected in this book.

What remains unchanged, however, is the pleasure of working with wood to create something pleasing, and the permanent satisfaction of seeing and using the results of your work for years afterwards.

Of course, if the finished work is to give satisfaction it must be well done, and this necessitates at least a certain minimum of equipment and a certain minimum of 'know-how'. In fact, surprisingly little of either is needed to begin with; you can put whatever you have of either category to profitable use, and add to them as you go along. 'Know-how' and your tool-chest will surely grow with every new job tackled.

It follows that you need not possess all the equipment shown here before you take up amateur woodworking; neither will you necessarily be able successfully to tackle all the projects collected between these covers if you do begin by buying all the equipment in sight.

The main purpose of this book, then, is to provide adequate guidance on what can be done, how it can be done, and what it can be done with. These three distinct functions are served by dividing the book into three separate sections.

The first of the three main sections deals with tools and equipment.

The range covers everything from handtools to power tools and includes toolboxes and workbenches. There is also a mine of information on timber (softwoods and hardwoods) and fastenings (nails, screws, etc.) in this first section.

The second section deals with methods, or how the tools and equipment of the first section should be used. After a complete coverage of wood joints – and almost everything that is made with wood requires jointing – there are such subsections as woodturning, construction, making-and-mending, veneering, french polishing, and working under difficulties with an absolute minimum of tools and facilities.

The final section contains a large number of things to make, complete with all the working details, constructional diagrams, photographs and full step-by-step instructions. These are all practical projects which have been planned to produce the maximum usefulness and efficiency combined with tasteful design in the modern idiom, based on simplicity of technique and economy of materials.

For convenience, the items to make have been grouped into the particular parts of the home concerned, such as bedroom (headboards, dressing tables, wardrobes, and other furniture), nursery and children's rooms (cots, toyboxes, desks and playtables), and so on, through the bathroom, hall, landing and loft, but with special attention to bright ideas for the living room and kitchen, and even the garden.

A glance through the index will show how comprehensive the work is.

Take glue, for example. Do you really know the difference between impact glues and epoxy resins? Or how to glue plastics? Do you know about glues that weld rather than merely stick materials together? Could you say what part the old-fashioned animal glues play in modern woodworking technology?

Or take finishes. Are dyes and stains the same thing? When would you use a chemical type in preference to a spirit, oil, water or tar derivative type? And when would you use a fitch brush as opposed to a polishing mop? When do you start fadding? And how do you go about pulling over or spiriting off?

Timber is, of course, very fully discussed (from Afara to Zebrano Satinwood) but modern composition boards are also fully described, including laminboard, blockboard, battenboard, chipboard, and so on.

And there are still over eight hundred other items in the index.

The title of this book is, therefore, fully justified.

'Complete' it certainly is, with full coverage of the entire subject. 'Practical' applies to the advice and guidance given, as well as to each project described.

And 'Woodworking', of course, is the *raison-d'être*!

SECTION A
TOOLS AND EQUIPMENT

TOOLS AND EQUIPMENT

HAND TOOLS

Toolmaking, even in these days of mechanisation, is still more of a craft than a trade, often handed down from father to son. That tools, and in particular those designed for woodworking, hold a peculiar fascination for many people in all walks of life is frequently demonstrated by the crowd that gathers round the window of a tool shop.

This section includes notes on how tools are made and how they should be cared for; types and uses of cutting tools—including chisels, saws, planes, spokeshaves, draw knives and gouges; boring tools—auger bits and augers, brace bits, gimlets and bradawls; screwdrivers, squares, and bevels; gauges, hammers and mallets; and sundry other useful tools.

TOOLMAKING

Because space does not permit a detailed description of the production processes of all tools, the evolution of a carpenters' chisel is taken as an example.

Power Forging

Most people are familiar with the craft of the blacksmith and how he shapes the glowing metal on his anvil. Modern methods have almost eliminated the use of the hand-forger in the tool industry, although a few do still remain. Most forging is done under power hammers.

Successful working of tool steel demands as fine and close a grain as possible, and the hammering on the anvil gives the chisel blade that close dense grain so essential in a good tool. That explains why good tools requiring a lasting edge cannot be moulded or cast to shape. The term 'cast steel' however, does not imply that the tool has been moulded or cast to shape, but that the steel has been cast or poured out of a crucible, instead of having been produced by an inferior and, incidentally, cheaper method. The carbon steel used for high quality woodworking tools is made by the crucible method, one of the earliest ways of making steel, because in no other way can the essential purity and consistency essential in tool steel be assured.

Carbon steel contains a percentage of carbon or charcoal in the raw iron, converting it with other constituents when heated up to a molten state into steel. Even within the limits of carbon steels, different analyses with varying carbon contents are necessary for different types of tools.

For example, the steel for a paring chisel demands a comparatively high percentage of charcoal in the raw iron to give it that property of holding a keen, lasting edge; whereas a mortise chisel, requiring a tougher and more resilient nature, calls for a lower carbon content.

Temper and Quality

The terms 'temper' and 'quality' of steel are often confused. Temper, the degree of hardness, depends upon the percentage of carbon. Quality is determined by the grade of iron and special alloys used in making steel. Good qualities of tool steel are made from high-grade iron.

Freedom from impurities can only be obtained by the use of pure iron, costly in proportion to its purity. Thus it behoves the tool manufacturer to insist on products of steel makers of repute.

After forging, the next process in making a carpenters' chisel is hardening, for after being forged the chisel blade is still in a 'soft' state and, if sharpened, the cutting edge would not last long. To make the grain harder and denser, tool steel is heated up to about 700 deg. C., at which temperature a structural change takes place. This is called the 'critical change' of steel. If cooled slowly, it returns to its previous state; but this hardness and denseness can be retained by sudden chilling. The application of cold air or immersion in water or oil are the methods used for this purpose, the two latter being the more usual.

Tool steel is extremely sensitive to differences in the water into which it is plunged. The purer and softer the water, the better will be the results. It may be of interest to know that Sheffield owes its reputation partly to its pure soft water flowing down from the Derbyshire Moors. Foreign manufacturers have even been known to go to the expense of shipping casks of Sheffield water abroad for hardening.

Tempered Steel

The contraction caused by the sudden immersion of red-hot steel in a cooling medium sets up certain stresses which must be removed or tempered. The hardened tool is therefore slowly heated up to a temperature of approximately 250 deg. C. When large quantities are involved this is usually carried out in gas—or electrically-heated furnaces, thermostatically controlled. In this way it is possible to reduce the brittleness of the steel to a degree suitable for the next process in the evolution of a chisel—grinding, or the removal of the black skin of oxide of iron by abrasion, and the formation of a cutting bevel.

For this process both machinery and hand-grinding are used. For some types of tools, no grinding machines are suitable, and the old method of hand-grinding is still employed.

The chisel blade is finally glazed or polished, a method serving a dual purpose. It closes the pores of the steel to assist in withstanding the action of rust, and it makes the tool easy and comfortable to handle.

CHISELS AND GOUGES

There are two points to look for when buying a chisel. In a good chisel, the face should be flat and true. This can be tested with a small steel rule laid across the blade on the face side (opposite the bevel)—bad grinding rounds the blade towards the edges. Next, test with the rule along the blade on the same side. The blade must be dead flat along the whole of its length, otherwise accurate paring will be impossible.

Chisels and gouges vary in shape, weight, and size according to the use for which they are intended. Sizes range from ⅛ to 2in. At one end of the scale is the heavy

Figs. A1 and A2 (left). Various chisels.

Fig. A3. Cutting a deep mortice with heavy chisel and mallet. If the chisel sticks—

Fig. A4.—as it may do when chopping deeply, an upward blow against the bolster will free it.

Fig. A5. Firmer (bevelled edge) chisel. The shoulder provides the driving power.

chopping chisel for the wheelwright; at the other end is the long thin paring chisel of the pattern-maker, or the delicate gouge of the wood carver.

The main types of chisels and gouges with their principal uses are shown in the photographs (Figs. A1—A6).

Chisels are dispatched from the factory correctly ground and set, ready for immediate use. In time, of course, the blade will need resharpening, which the user should be able to do quite easily for himself, once he has learned something about it. This is very necessary, for good work cannot be done with a blunt tool, no matter how high its quality.

Sharpening chisels and all cutting tools, gouges, plane irons, and so on, can be divided into two stages:

Grinding the bevel, i.e. obtaining the initial bevel to form the cutting edge, by use of a grindstone or abrasive wheel; and

Whetting, i.e., finishing the edge on an oilstone.

Grinding Chisels

For the grinding of chisels there is nothing better than a natural sandstone. It is much kinder to the steel and easier to use than an artificial stone or emery wheel, though the latter can safely be used if care is exercised and a sandstone is not available.

First, the stone or wheel must be running true, or satisfactory results cannot be expected. If it runs irregularly the chisel bumps. If there are grooves in the face of the stone, the face must first be retrued. For a sandstone (Fig. A7), this can be done by reversing the direction of revolution and holding a pointed steel bar or the tang of an old file firmly against the face and traversing it along the tool-rest backwards and forwards, after the manner of a turning tool. This should be done dry.

For artificial wheels a special dresser (Fig. A8) is made, consisting of a gang of hardened steel wheels in a holder, which is traversed across the face in a similar manner to the retrueing of a sandstone.

When grinding a hardened steel tool of any type it should be kept cool. If too much heat is allowed to generate by the friction of grinding, the hardness will be lost and the tool ruined. It is easy to tell whether damage has been done, because the edge becomes blue or purple.

Grindstones, artificial or natural, must be used wet. If possible fix a drip can (with a tap) on the hood, directing the stream of water on to the tool. If not practicable, then frequently plunge the tool in water to cool.

The edge of most chisels and plane irons should be dead square. Gently square up the edge of the chisel against the face of the stone (Fig. A9) and test with a try square (Fig. A10). With one or two exceptions, turning chisels

Fig. A6.   Paring chisel—work held by G cramp, left forearm supported for steadiness by work or bench top.

Fig. A7.   Re-trueing a sandstone.
Fig. A8 (*below*).   Harder grindstones such as carborundum, need a special dressing tool.

Fig. A9. Gently square up the chisel edge against the stone—

Fig. A10.—and check against a try square to ensure it is true.

Fig. A11. The cutting edge bevel of a chisel must be flat.

Fig. A14. The edge needs fairly frequent whetting on an oil stone.

Fig. A12. Grinding the bevel—do not rock the chisel.

Fig. A13. Working with a tool holder.

Fig. A16. Dummy wooden ends to protect the stone.

Fig. A15. Rubber studs stop the stone slipping.

GROUND BEVEL

CHISEL BLADE

WHETTED EDGE

for instance, the bevel of the cutting adge must be flat (Fig. A11) and never convex or rounded.

The angle of the bevel is also important and depends on the type of tool and the quality of the timber to be worked. For general work an angle of 25 deg. is recommended. Mortise chisels used on heavier work require about 30 deg. to give the edge the necessary support, while for paring soft wood, an angle of 22 deg. can be used (but such an edge would not last long on tough timber). A handy gauge can easily be made from a small piece of tin or sheet zinc scribed with the necessary angle from a protractor, and cut out with a pair of shears.

When grinding the bevel (Fig. A12), care must be taken not to rock the chisel. If the tool is held firmly at the correct angle square to the stone, a flat or slightly concave bevel will result, which is what is wanted. Any rocking motion, however, will produce that rounded bevel, which it is so necessary should be avoided. It may not at first be easy to do this successfully, but after one or two attempts the knack can be mastered.

For those who find difficulty in holding the chisel, a tool holder (Fig. A13) should be used. To use this the wheel should be rested lightly on the stone, with the handle of the chisel in the right hand, then with two fingers of the left hand placed lightly on the face of the blade towards the top, the necessary pressure can be applied. The chisel and the wrists should be traversed together right and left across the face of the stone, parallel with the axle, to ensure even wear and an even bevel, taking care not to press too much on one side.

As soon as the blunt edge produced by squaring the

blade has disappeared, a feather of steel of tissue-paper thickness may appear on the edge of the blade. The grind-stone cannot make it any sharper than this. With a piece of soft wood, this feather should be wiped away, down the cutting edge.

Water should never be allowed to remain in the trough of the grindstone, so that part of the stone is immersed. This will soften that part of the stone, or wheel, with consequent uneven wear. Unless in constant use, the trough should always be drained.

Whetting Chisels

The grindstone gives a correct bevel, but the edge of the chisel still requires a final sharpening by rubbing on an oilstone or a whetstone, as it is sometimes called. As with grindstones, there are both natural whetstones quarried from the earth, and artificial stones, which have the advantage that they can be supplied with medium grit on one side and fine on the reverse.

Whetting the edge (Fig. A14) is a more frequent operation than grinding the bevel and it has the same action of cutting the steel, but to a much finer degree.

One evidence of bluntness in a chisel is a thin bright line of reflected light along the cutting edge. The steel must be sharpened down still more, and when that line disappears, the edge is keen.

Firstly, the oilstone must be secured flat on a bench, up against a bench stop. Some carpenters drive a couple of small nails into the bottom of the oilstone case, which, with the heads filed off form non-skid studs, allowing the stone to be used anywhere on the bench top. The insertion of a series of rubber studs in the bottom of the

Fig. A17. The correct position for whetting a chisel edge.

Fig. A19 (*above*). At each subsequent whetting the handle must be raised slightly.

Fig. A20 (*left*). A special slip stone is used for an inside bevel gouge.

Fig. A18 (*left*). The wrists should move parallel with the stone.

Fig. A21 (*right*). When regrinding an outside edge bevel, do not grind too much from centre.

Fig. A22 (*below*). The right and wrong way of whetting an outside bevel gouge.

RIGHT

WRONG

case (Fig. A15) is an even better idea, as it avoids damage to the bench. Some carpenters fit dummy wooden ends to their oilstones (Fig. A16) to avoid slipping over the end. Having cleaned the oilstone with a paraffin rag, a few drops of thin oil should be applied and the chisel should be taken up in the right hand (Figs. A17 and A18). Then, with the left hand, bear down on the blade keeping the wrists rigid, swinging freely from the right shoulder and, bending the elbow, rub the blade backwards and forwards. The wrists must move in a line parallel with the stone and not be allowed to dip, or a rounded blunt edge will result.

The chisel, when it comes from the grindstone with a newly-ground bevel for whetting, should be held in position as in Fig A17, with the handle low down and the bevel almost flat on the oilstone. Each subsequent re-whetting necessitates the raising of the handle slightly, as in Fig. A19, positions (B) and (C), and so on, until the edge is so obtuse that the bevel needs re-grinding.

To avoid uneven wear on the stone, the chisel should be rubbed over the whole surface of the stone, occasionally reversing the stone itself. When the blade has been sharpened sufficiently and the thin bright line has disappeared, the blade should be turned over and laid perfectly flat on the stone. Then with a circular backwards motion, the wire edge that remains should be rubbed away; on no account must the handle be lifted, or the edge will be spoilt.

For a finishing touch, the blade can be stropped. A carpenter usually strops his chisels on the palm of his hand, but an old razor strop is safer. A good improvised strop can be made from a piece of soft leather, dressed with tallow and fine emery powder and nailed to a board. The blade should be pulled backwards only, or the leather will be cut. The chisel should now have a perfect cutting edge.

It is not generally known that the action of grinding steel is actually cutting. The natural sandstone, quarried direct from the earth and undergoing no other treatment than trimming to shape, is composed of minute particles of silicon, bonded by volcanic action millions of years ago, each of these particles being infinitely harder than steel. This is the ideal medium for grinding steel tools, because combined with water it cuts coolly, so lessening the chances of over-heating and softening the steel.

There are also artificial grindstones, an amazing product of modern science. Manufactured rock crystals, produced under terrific heat and bonded together by artificial means, constitute a grinding medium almost as hard as the natural product, with the advantage of control over varying grades of coarse and fine grit.

The same applies to whetstones. 'Washita' and 'Arkansas' oilstones are naturally quarried. 'Washita' stones do not cut so fast as the artificial, but are considered by some to give a finer edge. The 'Arkansas' is one of the hardest natural stones in the world and gives the finest edge, but on account of its rarity is very expensive.

Artificial whetstones are very popular with many carpenters. As pointed out, they can be supplied in a variety of grits to suit various types of work and are produced in many shapes and sizes, sometimes with a different grade of grit on each side. Emery is a compromise. Quarried from the earth, it is used for a range of abrasive purposes—artificially bonded into emery wheels, used as a powder, and applied to paper or to cloth.

To preserve the natural sharpness of the grit of an oilstone, the surface should be kept clean and wiped constantly with cotton waste to prevent the accumulation of oil and steel particles from forming a hard skin on the surface. Shavings should not be used for this because the dust will clog the pores of the stone.

When not in use, smear the stone with oil and replace the lid of the case. Even with careful use, the stone will become out of true with wear. Re-true the surface by rubbing on a flat stone or on the side of a grindstone.

The oil which is applied to a whetstone helps to wash away the particles of steel which would otherwise clog the pores of the stone. If, through neglect, the stone becomes glazed with dirt, it can be cleaned with petrol or paraffin. If that has no effect, spread a sheet of sandpaper on the bench, lay the stone face down and rub briskly.

Grinding and Whetting Gouges

The principles of regrinding and whetting chisels also apply to gouges, though the methods are slightly different. A gouge with an inside bevel is ground originally on a special stone, with a face made to fit the particular size and shape of the tool. Inside-bevel gouges are so rarely used in general work that the bevel provided by the makers lasts for many years. An occasional whetting, therefore, should suffice. This is done on a specially-shaped gouge slip, illustrated in Fig. A20.

The regrinding of an outside-bevel gouge is done on the grindstone, holding the gouge in the same position as you would a chisel. This needs some care and practice as the blade must be revolved. The inclination is to grind too much on the centre and too little on the outer ends, as shown in Fig. A21.

The same action should be used in whetting, rotating the gouge while rubbing up and down the oilstone (Fig. A22).

After whetting, the wire edge found on the inside can be removed with the gouge slip. With one hand, hold the gouge rigid against a corner of the bench, and with the other, gently rub the wire edge away (taking care to keep the slip flat on the inside surface of the gouge, or the edge will be turned.'

Finally, remember to wipe all edge tools with an oily rag after use.

SAWS

Though many types of saws are made for various woodworking purposes, they can be divided into the following broad classifications:—

Long cross-cut saws, for dealing with large logs and round timber;

Hand saws, with flexible blades for the initial cutting-up of the timber from the power-sawn plank or board;

Back saws, with stiff blades for more accurate work both on the bench and in the vice;

Special saws, for the cutting of intricate shapes.

Cross-cut Saws

Two-man cross-cut saws for use by two people (Fig. A23) have various shapes of teeth for different species of timber. Lengths range from 3 ft. 6in. to 7 ft. Shorter cross-cut saws, normally used by one person, have a supplementary handle which can be fitted for use by an assistant (Fig. A24). Lengths vary from 2 ft. 6 in. to 5 ft.

Hand Saws

Hand saws are divided into two main categories, 'cross-cut' and 'rip' saws.

Cross-cut Hand Saws: Cross-cut hand saws (Fig. A25) are designed for cutting across the grain, as in Fig. A26. The shape of the teeth is illustrated in Fig. A27 which shows a bevel filed on the inside edge of each tooth. The teeth are bent outwards alternately to right and left, to give clearance in the saw cut, otherwise the saw would jam or stick in the wood. The technical term for this is the 'set' of the teeth. In addition, the blade is ground, tapering to the back to give added clearance.

Fig. A28 shows the cross-cut saw in use, and there are three important points to note. First, the operator is aiming down the blade in much the same manner as one would aim along the barrel of a shotgun. This is to ensure that the blade is at right-angles to the timber. Secondly, the index finger is pointing along the blade, so helping to guide it on a straight line. Thirdly, the knuckle of the thumb is held against the blade to steady it until the cut is started. If, when aiming down the saw blade, you are not quite sure that the angle is correct, check this by placing a try square on the timber and against the blade (Fig. A29).

When starting the cut, use the heel of the saw and draw the blade slowly backwards. Use the thumb knuckle to steady the blade, and if the first cut is not deep enough, repeat the operation until it is. Fig. A30 shows the method of commencing the cut. Another point to observe is that the blade is at a very low angle when commencing the cut, as shown in Fig. A31. If this is done it will be found to be a great help when judging if the blade is in alignment with the pencil line on the timber. Having commenced the cut, the saw blade is gradually lifted to the normal angle, which is in the region of 45 deg.

Finishing off the cut is just as important as commencing it, and care must be exercised if the wood is not to splinter. The waste material must be supported, as shown in Fig. A32, when making the last few strokes. The left hand is brought over to hold the waste material, otherwise its weight will cause it to break away.

Rip Saws: Rips saws are designed for sawing with the grain, as in Fig. A33. The teeth are different from those of the cross-cut hand saw, the front of the teeth being vertical and backed off at an angle of about 60 deg. as

Fig. A23 (*above*). Two-man cross-cut saw.

Fig. A24 (*below*). One-man cross-cut saw, with detachable handle for second operator.

Fig. A25 (*above*). Cross-cut hand saw for moderately heavy work.

Fig. A26 (*right*). When cross-cutting, the wood is kept firm by the operator's knee and the cut piece supported to prevent the last few fibres breaking away.

Fig. A28 (*left*). The cross-cut saw in use.

Eye "aiming" down blade

Index finger pointing along saw blade

Saw blade

Knuckle of thumb against blade

Fig. A27. Close-up of cross-cut teeth.

45°   15°

Saw heel

Thumb knuckle against blade

Fig. A29 (*above*). Using the try square to check the cutting angle.

Direction of stroke

Fig. A30. Starting to cut.

Low angle

Fig. A32. Left hand crossed over to support waste material at end of cut.

Fig. A31. The angle of the saw when starting to cut.

Fig. A33 (left). Rip-sawing a board with or down the grain. The end may need support to prevent chattering.

Fig. A34. Close-up of rip-saw teeth.

Fig. A35 (left). Rip-sawing between trestles.

Fig. A36. Overhand ripping.

Fig. A37 (above). Starting the cut for overhand ripping.

Fig. A38 (left). Cross-cut teeth—eight per inch.

Fig. A39 (above). A back saw, used for tenons and dovetails, etc.

Fig. A41. Using the bow saw for curved work. Note the position of hands and fingers.

Fig. A40. The bow saw, showing tension wire.

Fig. A42. Nest of compass saws.

Fig. A44 (right). Using a pad saw to cut a curve.

Fig. A43. Pad or keyhole saw.

shown in Fig. A34. They are set alternately for clearance.

When 'ripping' a piece of timber it is best to support it on two trestles (Fig. A35). This may not always be possible, as not every workshop boasts a pair of trestles, but in such circumstances overhand ripping can be carried out as shown in Fig. A36. When carrying out this operation, the timber is clamped to the edge of the bench; the cut is commenced as shown in Fig. A37.

The size of a hand saw is determined by the length of the cutting edge of the blade in inches.

In addition, each size is made with varying sizes of teeth. The size of the teeth being given as the number of teeth or points per inch of blade.

Cross-cut hand saws and rip saws are made in sizes varying from 18 in. to 28 in. The most popular sizes are 24 in. or 26 in.; the sizes of teeth most generally used in cross-cut saws are 6 to 8 points to the inch (Fig. A38). Popular sizes for panel saws and small hand saws are 18 in. to 22 in. with finer teeth, 9 to 12 points to the inch.

The saws mentioned so far have thin flexible blades, made of high-quality steel, correctly hardened and tempered to stand bending with buckling. Handles are usually of polished beechwood, secured by inserted brass screws and nuts. although plastic handles, moulded on to the blades, are now available.

Back Saws

Back saws are smaller with the black of the blades stiffened with brass or iron (Fig. A39) and are designed for more accurate work, such as cutting mitres for picture framing, tenoning, dovetailing and so on.

Tenon and Dovetail Saws: Tenon saws range in size from 10 in. to 16 in., popular lengths being 10 in. and 12 in. Teeth vary from 18 to 22 points to the inch. Dovetail saws are shorter, usually 8 in. or 9 in. blades with smaller teeth, 20 to 22 points.

Special Saws

Although there is no end to the range of tools which could qualify for inclusion in this category, we are here concerned particularly with the narrow type of saws designed for cutting intricate shapes. The most common of these are bow, compass and pad saws.

Bow Saws: The bow saw (Fig. A40) or turning saw as it is sometimes called, is designed for curved work, as

the name indicates. It consists of a thin saw blade in a beechwood frame which is tensioned by a twisted cord, or by a looped wire stretcher, with a left- and right-hand threaded buckle. The round handles at each end of the blade permit the blade to be revolved to any angle. It is shown in use in Fig. A41.

This tool, unknown to many amateurs, has innumerable uses and is handy for roughing-away waste wood. Sizes range from 8 in. to 18 in. for normal work, 10 in. being the most popular.

Compass Saws: The compass saw is designed for cutting circles and curved work, starting from a hole bored through the wood. The long, thin, tapered blades range from 10 in. to 16 in. Some compass saws are made with three or more interchangeable blades of different lengths and are known as 'nests of saws'. (Fig. A42).

Pad Saws: Pad saws (Fig. A43) are made with a slotted beechwood handle, through which the blade passes. The securing screws in the metal pad at one end of the handle allow the blade to be adjusted to any length. Ideal for cutting keyholes and similar work, the blades range from 6 in. to 16 in. the most popular being 10 in. A pad saw is shown in use in Fig A44.

Saw Sharpening

A saw does not required sharpening as frequently as an edge tool, but when it does, it requires, if anything, more care and attention. The set of the teeth as they are sent out from the factory should suffice for the first two or three resharpenings.

Assuming that the teeth are set correctly, they can be sharpened. A saw blade is tempered to a degree that allows the steel to respond to a file.

The blade must be held rigid in a vice, the jaws being close up to the teeth to avoid chattering. A pair of clamps of timber, approximately 3 in. by 1 in. section, bevelled on two edges for clearance, and screwed together at one end, long enough to take the longest hand saw, can easily be made. Operations should be started with the saw handle to the right of the sharpener, as shown in Fig. A45.

First ensure that all the teeth are of an even height. To do this, lightly run a flat smooth file lengthwise along the points of the teeth until is has reached the point of every tooth. This is known as 'topping'.

The teeth are now ready for sharpening, which is carried out with a special triangular file known as a 'taper

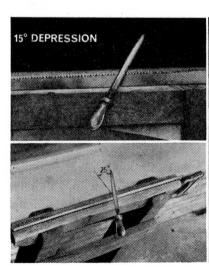

Fig. A45. Cross-cut saw with blade clamped for sharpening. Start to sharpen saw from left, handle on right. To file other side of saw, turn the blade in the vice to bring handle to left.

Fig. A46 (*right*).   A triangular file.

Fig. A47 (*far right*).   A hand saw-set.

saw file' as shown in Fig. A46.

When sharpening cross-cut hand saws, start at the end farthest away from the saw handle, i.e., to the left. File the teeth which are bent towards you. The valley between the teeth is called the gullet. The angle of the teeth is usually 60 deg., and the triangular taper saw file is most convenient for sharpening because all its angles are also 60 deg.

When starting, rest the file in the gullet on the left of the first tooth which is bent towards you. Then depress the file handle to an angle of 15 deg., and swing the handle of the file away from the saw handle, that is to the left, to an angle of 25 deg. Allow the file to cut on the push stroke only; in this way both the tooth selected and its neighbour, which is bent away from the operator, will be filed at the same time.

The next gullet on the right should be missed, and then the operation is repeated, keeping strictly to the angles mentioned and so continue on towards the handle end of the blade. Alternate teeth only must be filed.

Next turn the saw and clamps round in the vice so that the saw handle is on the left. Again, rest the file in the gullet to the right of the first tooth which is bent inwards; depress the file handle, and swing it away from the saw handle, that is to the right, and continue sharpening as before.

As explained earlier, there is no bevel on the teeth of a rip saw, so to sharpen this type of saw the file should be held horizontally and at right angles to the blade. It is still advisable to file alternate teeth, then reverse the saw and clamps and repeat, filing the teeth so far untouched, because this ensures that the burred edges from filing are evenly distributed.

When teeth are uneven through constant sharpening they must be reshaped. First comes the topping operation, then hold the triangular taper saw file horizontally and at right angles to the blade and bring the gullets down to a universal depth.

In dealing with extra large teeth which will be flat on top after topping, file away until half the flat has disappeared. Move on to the next gullet and continue until the flat has completely gone. The tooth should then be the correct size. After this, the teeth require resetting to give the saw the necessary clearance.

The teeth need bending outwards, alternately to right and left. The amount of set depends on several factors— size of teeth, type of saw, species of timber, and whether

it is wet or dry. Wet timber and coarse teeth demand a greater set to give a wider wider saw cut.

There are several methods of setting. The professional saw maker uses a setting hammer, working on a special steel anvil with a bevel edge. He works with remarkable speed and accuracy, but this is, of course, highly skilled and beyond the powers of the amateur.

The old-fashioned saw set (Fig. A47) is still much in use. It is simple and consists of a flat tool of hardened taper section steel, possessing slits of varying widths, to suit saw blades of corresponding thicknesses. It usually has a wooden handle, and the operator levers the teeth outwards, trusting to eye and experience.

Care must be taken to avoid bending more than halfway down the teeth, or a fracture may result. The plier saw set has been introduced to assist the inexperienced and is very popular. It consists of a tool resembling a pair of pliers (Fig. A48). The user decides the angle he considers correct for the job in hand. The closing of the pliers bends over the tooth and so makes it possible to obtain a consistent set throughout the whole blade.

PLANES

Planes are tools with a long ancestry; we know that early forms were used by the Romans, for example.

The present range of planes cover many uses; in addition to being used for reducing the thickness or width of a piece of wood, or smoothing surfaces, there are planes designed for special uses such as rebating, grooving, moulding and similar tasks.

Almost all planes are available in either wood or metal. Whatever they are made of, planes can be divided into two broad classifications—bench planes and special-purpose planes.

In considering the types, uses and care of planes, it will be most convenient to deal first with wooden bench

Fig. A49. Common jack plane.

Fig. A50. The correct stance for using the jack plane. The left hand bears down on the front end of the plane and the right arm brings the weight of the body to the work.

the longer lengths of wood. Its greater length of 22 in. or 24 in. gives more accuracy, necessary for jointing preparatory to gluing joints, and so on (Fig. A53).

Smoothing Planes: The smoothing plane (A54), about 8 in. long with a cutter varying from 1¾ in. to 2¼ in., according to size, is designed, as the name implies, to give the wood its final smooth finish. Its short body makes it more accessible to small surface or grain irregularities. It is shown in use in Fig. A55.

Component Parts: Beechwood is used for planes on account of its closeness of grain and hardwearing properties. The timber is steamed to facilitate drying and this process gives the wood the rich red colour which is characteristic of best quality planes.

A good plane block is cut 'on the quarter', i.e. with the medullary rays, which run from the centre of the tree to the bark, as near as possible at right angles to the sole of the plane, and the annular rings parallel with the sole (Fig. A56). This point should be borne in mind when buying planes.

Fitted in the beechwood body is a steel cutting blade or 'iron'. This iron is held in position by a wooden wedge and is adjusted by tapping with a hammer.

On the upper face of the cutting iron is a cap or top iron, adjustable and held in position by a screw.

The top iron serves the important duty of preventing

planes, then with their metal counterparts, and finally with various examples of special-purpose planes.

Wooden Bench Planes

Bench planes comprise three distinct types—jack, try, and smoothing planes, each of which will be considered separately.

Jack Planes: The jack plane (Fig. A49) is used for the initial smoothing of a rough-sawn surface, for squaring the timber and sometimes for shooting. It varies in length (14 in. to 17 in.) and in width of cutter (2 in to 2¼ in.). It is shown in use in Figs. A50 and A51.

The 'technical' jack plane is similar to the jack plane but smaller, being 14 in. in length with 1¾ in. or 2 in. cutter. It is designed for juvenile users in technical schools—hence its name. The handle is sunk, for economy in weight and greater control in handling (Fig. A52).

Try Planes: The try or jointer plane is used for trueing

Fig. A53. The try or pointer plane.

Fig. A52. A smaller jack plane.

Fig. A54. The smoothing plane.

Fig. A51. This view of the jack plane in use demonstrates how the left hand helps to keep the plane down.

Fig. A55. When using a smoothing plane, the right arm does the work, while the left hand steadies the plane.

Fig. A56. A good wooden plane block must be cut 'on the quarter'; beech is best. The 'rings' in the wood should run across the end.

STEEL FACE

IRON

Fig. A57. The cutting blade, part iron, part steel.

Fig. A58. The correct way to remove the iron and wedge from a wooden jack or try plane. Hold the plane steady against the body with the left thumb inside the plane throat for added rigidity.

Fig. A59. To remove the iron and wedge from a wooden smoothing plane, hold firmly in the right hand and with the left hand bring the plane down sharply on to the bench. A rubber pad used as shown avoids damage to the plane.

Fig. A60. A jack plane iron is slightly rounded while that of a smoothing or try plane is only rounded at the corners.

the iron from splitting the wood when planing, by breaking the fibres in the shaving immediately it is cut, and deflecting it out of the throat, instead of allowing it to curl round and choke the mouth.

The cutting blade is made of iron, on to which is welded a high-quality steel face (Fig. A57). This is mainly for economy, iron being much cheaper than best-quality steel.

Oiling the Block: A wood plane block should not be immersed in a bath of linseed oil and left to soak. The wood becomes sodden and so swollen that the iron and wedge will not fit, and when forced into position a split block may result. In addition, the hardwearing properties of the beechwood are impaired. A very occasional wipe with a rag soaked in linseed oil is all that is necessary; this is advisable, as it gives the wood a protective coat against the weather.

Dismantling: To remove the iron of a jack or try plane, the operator should hold with the thumb inside the throat. Repeated taps with a hammer will loosen the edge and allow the iron to be withdrawn. Take care to strike an even blow, or the face of the hammer will damage the surface of the block (Fig. A58).

A series of taps on the heel of a smoothing plane brought down sharply on the bench will have the same result (Fig. A59).

Grinding and Whetting Plane Irons: Before grinding the cutting iron, the top iron must be removed with a screwdriver. First, slacken the nut holding the two irons together and slide the top iron back until the screw head

can be slipped through the hole provided, taking care not to damage the cutting edge during the operation. With the top iron released, the grinding or whetting can start.

For the grinding of plane irons, as with chisels, there is nothing better than a natural sandstone. It is much kinder to the steel and easier to use than an artificial stone or emery wheel, though the latter can be safely used if care is exercised and a sandstone is not available.

The shape of the cutting edge varies to suit the work and type of plane in use.

The ordinary double-iron jack plane is used mainly for preliminary roughing work and so the edge should be somewhat rounded (Fig. A60). This roundness will not produce hollows in the work to such a degree as the illustration suggests; the cutting iron is not used vertically, but at an angle that will reduce the convexity by about one half.

Smoothing and try planes require a straight cutting edge with only the corners slightly rounded (Fig. A60). This lessens the chances of the mouth choking with shavings and avoids the possibility of leaving deep marks on the wood.

Reassembling: Having reground and rewhetted the iron to satisfaction, it is then ready for reassembly. Replace the top iron in the reverse order of that used when removing it, and slide it up into position. Care must be taken not to damage the cutting edge. For rough work the edge of the top iron should be about 1/16 in. to 1/32 in. below the edge of the cutting iron; for fine work about 1/64 in. Finally, tighten the screw.

When replacing the wedge, do not knock it in too firmly until the plane iron has been correctly positioned.

Using Wooden Planes: Some planing problems are:
Choking: This is caused by various factors:—

1 The cutting iron may be insufficiently rounded and is, therefore, cutting along the whole of its width. The shaving is caught by the sides of the throat, and jams instead of clearing itself.

2 The top iron may not fit quite flat on the cutting iron, so that the shaving is caught between the two irons. This can be rectified by filing the edge of the top iron.

3 Very occasionally, the mouth of a new plane may be found too small for certain classes of work; in other words, there is not enough clearance between the iron and the block for the shaving to pass through (Fig. A61). If it does pass through, it sometimes chokes. A thin piece of leather, ¾ in. wide, may be glued at the top corners of the bed underneath the iron, as in Fig. A61. This inclines the iron and automatically opens the mouth, without damage to the plane. Later when the sole has been worn a little, the leather can be removed and the iron restored to its original position.

Ridges: When small ridges appear on the planed surface, inspect the cutting edge of the iron. Probably it has been snicked by careless handling, or has come up against a hidden nail. It will have to be reground from the start. The slightest knock against a hard metallic object will damage the delicate cutting edge, so—when not in use—it is advisable to lay the plane down on the bench, resting on its side.

Sloping Grooves: When sloping grooves appear on the surface of the wood being planed, they indicate that the iron is fitted askew, and one corner is projecting too far. A tap on the appropriate side of the iron will rectify this fault.

Metal Bench Planes

The all-metal plane is designed to give a finer means of adjustment than is the case with wood planes, in which the iron or cutter is held in position by the knock-in tightness of a wood wedge. The adjustments of that type of iron are affected by judicious tapping with a hammer, whilst the metal plane is usually adjusted more precisely by screw or lever.

Each type has its advantages. Many older craftsmen prefer the wooden plane, contending that it is more comfortable to use, cheaper to buy, and does not break if dropped. The metal plane, which is usually made with a cast-iron body, will break if dropped on to a concrete floor. It is not suitable for the rough use of a jobbing joiner but, being more of an engineering proposition, appeals to the modern woodworker. With its capability of very accurate adjustment it is a delightful tool to use when its simple mechanism is correctly understood.

The 'X-ray photograph' Fig. A62 explains the more salient features which give such a wide range of adjustment.

Adjustments: The cutter can be fed in and out by rotating the milled adjusting nut and it can be aligned very quickly (adjusted laterally) by means of the side-adjustment lever.

An added advantage is the fact that the width of the mouth can be altered to suit varying types of work.

In principle the metal bench plane is no different from the wood bench plane described earlier. Sharpening and whetting of the cutter are dealt with in exactly the same way.

To remove the cutter, pull forward the lever which forms the cam holding the cutter and lever cap in position; this releases the lever cap which can be withdrawn over the lever cap screw, together with the cutter and top iron underneath.

To fit the cutter and top iron back into the plane, insert the sharpened end first, with the top iron uppermost. Allow it to lie on the frog, so that the protruding end of the centre-adjustment lever fits into the small slot provided in the top iron, and the roller of the side-adjustment lever coincides with the slot of the cutter.

The lever cap can now be replaced by being slid under the lever cap screw and snapped into position. If the cam is too tight, or too loose, adjust the lever-cap screw accordingly.

If the cutting edge is found to protrude too far, or not far enough, it can be adjusted with the milled adjusting nut.

Similarly, the cutter can be aligned with the side-adjustment lever, if it cuts too much to one side.

For rough work, a mouth wider than that necessary for fine-finished work is required.

The metal plane has the advantage of an adjustable mouth. To adjust this width, slacken the two adjusting screws. The frog can then be moved backwards or for-

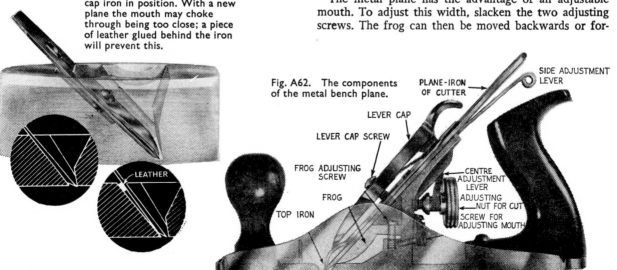

Fig. A61. Showing the iron and cap iron in position. With a new plane the mouth may choke through being too close; a piece of leather glued behind the iron will prevent this.

LEATHER

Fig. A62. The components of the metal bench plane.

PLANE-IRON OF CUTTER

SIDE ADJUSTMENT LEVER

LEVER CAP

LEVER CAP SCREW

FROG ADJUSTING SCREW

FROG

TOP IRON

CENTRE ADJUSTMENT LEVER

ADJUSTING NUT FOR CUT

SCREW FOR ADJUSTING MOUTH

wards by means of the screw provided. The top iron must also be adjusted for fine or rough work, as with wooden planes.

After a little practice the beginner will soon learn to appreciate the advantage of such easy methods of adjustment.

Metal bench planes can be supplied with corrugated soles, if preferred, which reduce the tendency to stick on resinous types of timber.

Metal planes range in size from 8 in. long with a 1¾ in. cutter to 22 in. long with a 2⅜ in. cutter, corresponding to wooden bench planes.

Smoothing Planes: The smoothing plane, shown in Fig. A63, is supplied in 8 in., 9 in. and 10 in. lengths with cutter widths of 1¾ in., 2 in. and 2⅜ in. respectively The most popular type of smoothing plane is the 9 in.

Jack Planes: The most handy jack plane (Fig. A64) is 14 in. long with a 2 in. cutter. The other popular size is 15 in. with a 2¼ in. cutter.

Jointer Planes: The jointer plane (Fig. A65) corresponds to the wooden trying or shooting plane. It is normally supplied in two sizes—18 in. or 22 in., both with a 2⅜ in. cutter.

Block Planes: Small metal planes, known as block planes, are designed for trimming and cleaning up, as well as close-quarter work. They are ideally suitable for end-grain planing, and single-handed work. There is no top iron; the cutter is set at a low angle and fitted in the plane with the sharpened bevel uppermost.

Two types of block plane are illustrated. Fig. A66 is 7 in. long with a 1⅜ in. cutter and has the added advantage of a screw adjustment to the cutter. Fig. A67 is double ended, 8 in. long with a 1⅝ in. cutter, and has two positions for the cutter, so that the operator can use the plane as a bull-nosed plane for close-quarter work if necessary.

Metal planes should be wiped with an oily rag before being put away. There are large unprotected areas of metal which will soon rust if exposed to damp.

Figs. A68 and A69 show typical all-metal planes in use.

Special-Purpose Planes

Apart from bench planes, there are many other patterns in wood or metal, each made for some special purpose. For instance, there are rebate planes, grooving and block planes, toothing, compass and moulding planes.

Then there are planes produced for craftsmen other than the carpenter. The cooper must have a plane of a special design. There is even a small spill plane for producing pipe lighters; the shaving curls out of the plane into a symmetrical spill.

Between the wars the demand for many types of special-purpose planes was decreasing before the advance of machine-produced mouldings and woodware. Since then, there has been a return to good hand-craftsmanship, both by the professional carpenter and by the practical householder who now does advanced woodworking as a practical and money-saving hobby.

Whilst some of the special-purpose planes mentioned are not likely to be required by the amateur carpenter, there is an intermediate range which should be understood, and used in the appropriate circumstances.

Rebate Planes: A rebate, or rabbet, is a slot or ledge cut out of the side of a piece of wood, as shown in Fig. A70. This may be required for various reasons, perhaps the most usual example being the ordinary door frame

which is rebated to accommodate the door itself. In this way the door can expand or contract with the weather—as all timber does—and yet remain a good draught-proof fit.

The rebate is used in carpentry in countless applications, some of them simple, some complex, as a glance around any room will reveal. There are several patterns of rebating planes in either wood or metal.

The simplest is the plain beech wood rebate plane. Fig. A70 shows that the cutter extends the whole width of the body. This pattern is made with either a square or a skew mouth. The advantage of the skew mouth is that it gives a shearing cut, with consequent greater ease in operation. These planes range in size from ½ in. wide cutter up to 1½ in., the most popular being 1¼ in.

With one exception (to be dealt with later) all rebate planes and most special-purpose planes possess single irons. In other words, there is no top iron.

Fig. A70 also shows how a strip of wood tacked or cramped on the work will guide the rebate plane. When the rebate is about ⅛ in. deep, the strip no longer becomes necessary, the plane following its own track.

Fence: A fence is a guiding gauge fixed on to a plane, usually adjustable, whereby the cutter is kept at an even predetermined distance from the face or edge of the work. The rebate planes mentioned so far are not fitted with fences.

Fillister Planes: When a rebate plane is fitted with a fence it is known as a fillister plane (Fig. A71). If the fence is not adjustable it is called a standing-fillister plane; this is made for special work and is only occasionally asked for today. The same plane with an adjustable fence is called a moving-fillister plane (Fig. A72).

If a rebate is to be worked across the grain, the wood fibres must be cut first. This can be done with a knife, a cutting gauge or a chisel. Better still, run a fine saw-cut down the whole depth of the rebate (Fig. A73).

To overcome this difficulty, however, a moving-fillister plane can be supplied with a tooth or nicker (Fig. A72), in front of the main cutter, which shears the fibres before the main cutter reaches them. An adjustable depth-gauge is also fitted to regulate the depth of cut.

There are occasions when it is necessary to have the fence working against the opposite face, as when rebating timber for window sashes. For this purpose, there is the sash fillister plane (Fig. A74). The fence is mounted on two long arms which slide through the plane body. When starting to plane a rebate, start at the end farthest away; after one or two initial strokes, gradually work backwards (i.e. start each stroke behind the previous stroke). Make steady, even strokes, holding the plane level and pressed firm against the fence (Fig. A75).

Bull-nose Rebate Planes: These are designed for fine single-handed work *in situ*, trimming rebates, making small adjustments in fitting mouldings and on countless other occasions where it is necessary to remove shavings close up to a stop.

The width of the mouth of the bull-nose rebate plane (Fig. A76) can be adjusted by slackening the screw and sliding the sole into the required position. The length of this plane is usually 4 in., with a cutter width of 1 in. The cutter is set at the normal angle and is fitted with the sharpened bevel underneath.

The bull-nose rebate plane with 1⅛ in. cutter shown in Fig. A77 has the added advantage that the cutter is adjustable by means of a milled nut. The cutter and bevel

Fig. A64. A handy-sized jack plane —14 in. long with a 2-in. cutter.

Fig. A67 (*above*). Double-ended block plane.

Fig. A66 (*above*). A block plane with screw adjustment to the cutter.

Fig. A65. An all-metal jointer plane.

Fig. A63 (*below*). All-metal smoothing plane.

Fig. A68 (*left*). A close-up of a metal smoothing plane in action. The position of the hands is important; note the index finger of the right hand.

Fig. A69 (*right*). A metal block plane in use; one hand is adequate for operating the plane, leaving the other free to hold the work.

Fig. A71. A fillister plane.

Fig. A70. A rebate or rabbet plane used for cutting narrow slots or grooves. The cutter iron is as wide as the plane body and a guide or fence may be needed to keep the plane true.

PLANE

REBATE

Fig. A72. In a moving fillister the fence is adjustable.

Fig. A73 (*below centre*). The sawcut made across the grain.

Fig. A74. A sash fillister plane.

Fig. A75 (*below*). How to hold a fillister plane.

Fig. A76 (*below*). Bull-nose metal rebate plane.

SAWCUT

Fig. A77 (*left*). Bull-nose plane with adjustable cutter.

Fig. A78 (*below left*). With the bull-nose plane it is possible to work right up to the end of the rebate.

Fig. A80. The coachmakers' plane used for cutting wider rebates.

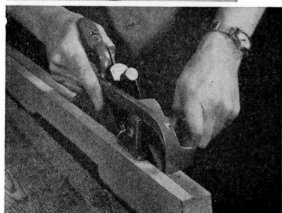

Fig. A83. A moving grooving plane.

Fig. A79 (*left*). Metal fillister plane in use; note position of hands.

Fig. A82 (*top*). A beech-wood fixed grooving plane.

Fig. A81 (*lower*). Work produced by a grooving plane.

cap are held in position by a tightening screw. When removing the cutter for resharpening, slacken the tightening screw until the lever cap is released. A twist of the cutter will allow it to be withdrawn from the plane.

This is a low-angle plane and the cutter is fitted with the sharpened bevel uppermost. The bull-nose plane is shown in use on a door rebate in Fig. A78.

The 8½ in. metal fillister plane shown in use in Fig. A79 is a modern tool embracing most of the features of a rebate plane and is an invaluable addition to every senior woodworker's tool kit. The methods of adjustment are simple and self-apparent.

The cutter, 1½ in. wide, has a lever adjustment, the plane being fitted with an adjustable depth gauge (which is detachable), a removable arm and fence which can be fitted to either side, and a spur for use when cutting across the grain. It is advisable to set this spur to the 'off' position when not required, since it is easily damaged.

For deep rebating, it will be necessary to detach the fence altogether after an initial ¼ in. or so of rebate wall has been formed.

Coachmakers' Rebate Planes: For heavier work, requiring wider rebates, there is the coachmaker's rebate plane (Fig. A80). This is similar in construction to a 14 in. metal jack plane illustrated earlier, but with the cutter extending the whole width of the body. The cutter, which has a top iron, resembles a jack plane in all respects of adjustment and assembly. There is one difference, however, in that a grey-iron body would be too weak. It is made, therefore, with the considerably more-costly malleable iron cast body. This is almost unbreakable and is capable of very hard wear.

Grooving: In carpentry, the groove (Fig. A81) ranks with the rebate in importance; if the modern carpenter has no means of cutting grooves he can achieve little. Perhaps the principle of grooving, or ploughing as it is sometimes called, originated from the early days when medieval workmen found that, whilst a plain piece of wood board shrank, split or warped in use, it kept its shape when inserted into grooved clamps of wood, and was permitted to expand or contract according to the humidity of the atmosphere. In this way panelling was evolved. Almost every piece of furniture today is grooved at some place in its construction, as also are doors and floorboards. As with bench and rebate planes, grooving planes can be made either of wood or metal. Wooden grooving planes are constructed with a steel plate in front of, and behind, the cutter. These plates are screwed-on integral with the wood body, and form the sole of the plane. The rear plate, in addition, forms the bed on which the cutter lies.

The fixed grooving plane (Fig. A82) is made for one job only, the cutting of a groove of a particular size. The most popular fixed grooving plane with a 3/16 in. cutter was much in use between the wars. It was designed for cutting the grooves in drawer bottoms, when 3/16 in. plywood was cheap and plentiful.

Moving Grooving Planes: More popular nowadays are the moving grooving planes, which are supplied with three interchangeable cutters of ⅛ in., 3/16 in. and ¼ in. These are made in wood (Fig. A83) or metal (Fig. A84); each type has its advantages. As the name indicates, the fence is adjustable in both types; with the metal plane, an adjustable depth gauge is also fitted.

Plough Planes: Plough is the name given to grooving

Fig. A84. A metal grooving plane with extending fence, showing some of the special irons available.

planes with a wider range of work. Plough planes, made in either wood or metal, have an adjustable fence of much larger capacity and are supplied with a set of interchangeable cutters, ranging from ⅛ in. to 9/16 in.

The wooden plough plane (Fig. A85) possesses a depth gauge operated from the top by means of a brass thumbscrew. The fence is mounted on two threaded stems which pass through the body of the plane, the adjustment being obtained from the wooden nuts which can be altered by hand.

Another pattern of wooden plough is made with plain stems which must be knocked-out with a tap from a hammer before adjustment.

The metal plough plane is similar in operation. The adjustable depth gauge is secured by a thumbscrew at the side. The fence slides on two steel arms which pass through the body of the plane. Adjustment again is obtained from two thumbscrews.

Fig. A85. A beechwood plough plane with screwed stem and depth gauge.

Tonguing-and-grooving or matching planes (Fig. A86) are made of beech, for the cutting of the 't' and 'g' joints on the edges of boards. Sold in pairs, one pair will be suitable only for one thickness of board. The size is determined by the thickness of the board, and ranges from ½ in. up to 1 in. board.

The easiest method of working mouldings on timber is with the wooden moulding plane, but it must be borne in mind that one plane can only produce one individual size and shape of moulding. English pattern moulding planes must be held at an angle to the work, as shown in Fig. A87.

Hollow and Round Planes: These are made of beech and in principle can be compared with matching planes (Fig. A88). For use in hollow and round joints they are sold in pairs. The size is determined by the thickness of the board and ranges from 3/16 in. up to 1½ in.

Router Planes: Router planes are used for levelling and smoothing the surface on the bottom of a groove, slot or cavity which is inaccessible to an ordinary grooving plane. The bulk of the waste is removed with a chisel or brace and bit, the router being used to finish off the groove to a uniform depth.

The oldest and simplest form of router is known as the 'old woman's tooth' plane (Fig. A89). It consists of a simple beechwood body, with a single cutter usually ½ in. or ⅝ in. wide, set at a high angle.

The diagram (Fig. A90) shows that the action of the cutter is to scrape rather than cut, and also that owing to the angle at which the cutter is set it can be operated in a very limited space, for instance in a small stopped housing. To start, the cutter is projected only a small distance and this is gradually increased as required by

Fig. A87. A moulding plane in use. Note how the operator holds the plane at the required angle.

Fig. A88. Hollow and round planes which resemble matching planes. They could be used to shape the mating edges of a table with its drop leaf, for instance.

Fig. A86. Tonguing-and-grooving planes, sometimes called matching planes. The insets show the shape of the cutters.

Fig. A89. An 'old woman's tooth' or router plane, used here for cutting a slot.

tapping with a hammer, until the correct depth of slot has been obtained.

Router planes made of metal are used for the same purpose, but are of rather different design (Fig. A91). The hardwood knobs are self-explanatory. The cutter is cranked to give a cutting action and works more easily than the old-fashioned type, but, of course, cannot be used in the same limited space. The cutter can be adjusted for depth very quickly by means of the screw adjustment.

The illustration shows a metal router plane with open throat. This permits the operator to view his work more clearly. A removable shoe is provided to close the throat if necessary, for added rigidity. Countersunk holes are also provided to allow the operator to screw wooden sole plates to the base to span a wide recess.

Fig. A90. Diagram showing the action of the cutter.

Fig. A91. Metal router plane with open throat.

Fig. A92. Beechwood spokeshaves.

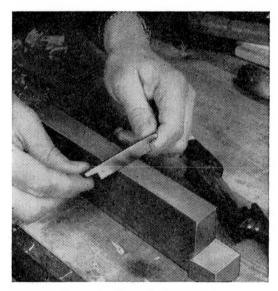

Fig. A93. Sharpening the spokeshave cutter on an oiled slipstone.

Fig. A94. Metal spokeshaves.

OTHER BLADED HAND TOOLS

In addition to chisels and planes, there are several other types of hand tool which depend on blades for their operation. Of these, spokeshaves, draw knives, Surform tools and scrapers are most likely to be useful for the amateur woodworker.

Spokeshaves

As was the case with planes, spokeshaves are available in either wood (Fig. A92) or metal (Fig. A93). Many workers prefer wooden spokeshaves on the ground that the resilience of the wooden stock, plus the fact that the iron (i.e. the blade) is set low, make it easier to use effectively. However, there are points in favour of the all-metal spokeshaves, too, so we will deal with the two types separately.

Wooden Spokeshaves: The spokeshave, originally a wheelwright's tool as the name implies, is also a tool of considerable antiquity. It is akin to a plane, but capable of following varying curves. When in good order it is a most useful tool, delightful to handle. It comprises two parts; a stock made of beechwood or boxwood and an iron or blade, with two square tangs projecting at right angles to the stock. The iron is forged from a solid piece of high-carbon tool steel, carefully tempered to take a fine cutting edge. The tangs are slightly tapered and the iron is kept in position by their knock-in tightness. Sizes are determined by the length of the iron on the cutting edge, and range from 1 in. to 3½ in. for normal work.

Spokeshaves are made with round or square fronts. The round fronted spokeshave can be used on curves of comparatively small radius. Its face soon wears under hard use, and some patterns, therefore, are made with an inserted brass plate to counteract this. A plain front (top) and a brass-plated front type are shown in Fig. A92.

The cutting edge of the iron should project only far enough to remove a fine shaving. A little practice will soon indicate to the user how important it is to work with the grain. Working with too much cutting edge protruding, or working against the grain, will only produce chattering accompanied by torn and jagged shavings. The spokeshave iron has no top iron with which to break the fibres of the shaving, as is the case with the bench plane.

As with all cutting tools, the iron must be kept sharp; to remove it for resharpening, hold the spokeshave in the palm of the hand and tap the ends of the tangs, alternately. Care must be taken, or the wooden stock will split at the mortised hole if the blow is too heavy.

Always sharpen a wooden-spokeshave iron from the inside. Two methods may be used—on an oilstone or with an oil slip (Fig. A93).

When the blade becomes loose through wear, glue a thin slip of paper, about ⅛ in. wide, in the holes on the end grain only. This will temporarily remedy the trouble.

All-Metal Spokeshaves: The metal spokeshave is used in the same way as the wooden type, and in construction resembles a plane even more than does its wooden counterpart. It is made in various patterns with a flat face for convex work or a round face for concave work.

The simplest type is that in which a single thumbscrew controls the position of the cutter. Adjustment is by slackening the thumbscrew and positioning the cutter accordingly.

The first metal spokeshave illustrated in Fig. A94 has

Fig. A95. Cutter holder for use when grinding.

Fig. A96. Working with the grain the spokeshave is pulled towards the user.

Fig. A97. Here the spokeshave is being pushed away from the user, but is still working with the grain.

Fig. A98. Showing how the cutter should work with the grain.

Fig. A100. Two types of draw knife.

raised handles and is 10 in. long. The cutter is 2⅛ in. The other is a fully-adjustable raised-handle metal spokeshave in which two adjusting screws control the position of the cutter, which is secured—together with the cap or top iron—by a thumbscrew. The dimensions are the same.

When sharpening the cutter, the same methods are used as for chisels and plane irons previously described. Being so short in length, the cutter is difficult to hold, but this can be overcome by making a simple cutter-holder as shown in Fig. A95. The cutter should slide into the slot with a friction-tight fit.

When using a spokeshave, remember to work with the grain as shown in Fig. A96 and Fig. A97, or the cutter will run into the wood (Fig. A98).

Draw Knives

The draw knife is another old and inexpensive tool but its many uses are unknown to many present-day amateur woodworkers. It consists of a flat blade, varying in length on the cutting edge from 8 in. to 14 in. (of which the most popular is 10 in.) and has a handle at each end, turned inwards. The tangs continue through the length of the handles, which are secured by riveting over small washers.

The operator pulls the knife towards him, using a shearing cut, and the wood can be pared away very readily to fine limits with a minimum of trouble. The carpenter uses it mainly for the rapid paring away of waste wood. It is easier and quicker than using a rip-saw, and is shown in use in Fig. A99.

The bevel of the cutting edge can be on top or underneath, as demanded by the direction of the grain. Two types of draw knife are shown in Fig. A100.

Sharpening a draw knife follows the same procedure as outlined previously for wood chisels. In whetting it is convenient to fix the oilstone in a bench vice, which gives the necessary clearance for the handles.

Surform Tools

Almost all woodworking tools have a cutting edge. Until recently, most tools had only one, or two at most, cutting edges—planes, chisels, drills for example—and these required careful use and maintenance to keep them in good working order.

A tool with multiple cutting edges naturally has many advantages over the single cutting edge, since the work is shared over a large number of blades. After a great

Fig. A99. Waste can be more accurately and quickly removed with a draw knife than with a saw.

Fig. A101. A Surform shaper plane with interchangeable metal and wood-cutting blades. *Stanley-Bridges Ltd.*

Fig. A102. Cabinet scraper blade.

Fig. A103. Using the cabinet scraper blade. Note the position of the thumbs pressing on the back of the blade, low down near the cutting edge; this bends the blade slightly, throwing the corners clear and avoiding any 'digging'.

Fig. A104. Method of sharpening the blade.

Fig. A105. How to burr the edge of a scraper blade with the scraper steel.

Fig. A106. An exaggerated view of the 'hooked edge' left after turning over the edge of a scraper blade.

deal of trial and research, an English firm found the right type of tool steel and manufacturing methods to apply the multiple-edge technique to so wide a variety of tools that working with wood, plastics, artificial boards and even with metals, has been almost revolutionised.

The Surform principle is basically a strip of hardened and tempered Sheffield tools steel with hundreds of ground cutting edges each with a controlled depth of cut.

Blades can be classified as 'standard cut' and 'fine cut' and are heat treated to make them suitable for working a variety of materials including wood, ferrous and non-ferrous metals, plastics and hardboard.

There is a wide range of different Surform hand tools available to suit different work applications, one of which —a shaper plane fitted with a wood-cutting blade and accompanied by an interchangeable metal-cutting blade —is shown in Fig. A101. Also there are two power tool attachments in the standard range of Surform tools— the 2 in. drum cutter and Surcut cutter disc. The drum can also be used with a planing and rebating attachment which can be used as a portable tool or fixed in a power tool bench stand.

Scrapers

The cabinet scraper blade consists of a piece of plain, flat, thin steel, hardened and tempered. It is much more important to the carpenter than its simple appearance would indicate (Fig. A102).

Properly sharpened, it will do the work of a fine-set plane. With cross-grained and curly-grained wood which cannot be planed, the scraper is the only tool than can be used. In effect, as the name implies, the scraper scrapes the wood, rather than planes it (Fig. A103).

When sharpening, hold the cabinet scraper blade in a vice; file the edge first with a smooth file flat and at right angles to the face (Fig. A104). Then smooth the edges on an oilstone to obtain sharp corners, still keeping the edge at right angles.

These corners are then burred or turned over, a special tool known as a scraper steel being used for this purpose. This steel consists of a piece of hardened round or oval steel inserted into a wooden handle. Any hard steel tool may be used, however, such as the back of an old gouge. The steel should be rubbed along the edge several times pressing the sharp corner over and starting with the steel at an angle of about 8 deg. and finishing at 15 to 20 deg. (Fig. A105). Considerable pressure is needed to turn, or burr, the corners. Finally finish off by smoothing the turned-over edge on an oilstone. The resulting hooked edge can pare away the rough grain or indentations left by a smooth plane (Fig. A106). An extra keen cutting edge can be obtained by filing the edge of the blade to an angle, similar to the bevel on a wood chisel. If this is done, the edge should be turned over as explained above. Some carpenters round the four corners with a file which gives added comfort in handling. Cabinet scrapers are made in varying sizes from 3 in. by 2 in. to 6 in. by 2½ in.

HAND BRACES, BITS AND DRILLS

For boring holes of ⅛ in. diameter and larger in timber, the tools normally used are a brace and bit. The interchangeable bits are made in a variety of patterns and sizes ranging from ⅛ in. up to 2 in. or more.

Hand Braces

The brace is fitted with an adjustable chuck which accommodates the square tapered shank of the bit. Fig. A107 illustrates the plain brace, but the ratchet brace (Fig. A108) is worth the extra outlay, for by moving the ratchet pawl, the crank can be operated in a confined space or a corner where the full sweep of the brace is not possible.

Centre Bits

The simplest boring bit is the centre bit; Fig. A109 shows this pattern with a plain pin, while the screwed pin is illustrated in Fig. A110.

This type of bit is used for thin work. To prevent the bit from breaking the timber on the far side of the board, boring should be stopped when the centre-pin has emerged. The wood is then reversed, the pin inserted, and the brace turned a few times, making a deep cut with the 'nicker' of the bit; this cuts through the final fibres. The work should then be reversed again so that boring may continue right through the wood. The result should be a clean hole, with a thin disc of wood falling out of the bottom of the hole.

Twist Bits or Screw Auger Bits

Auger bits are designed for deeper holes; some special patterns are made to bore up to 14 in. deep.

The jobbing joiner uses the Scotch screw auger bit (Fig. A111) or the Gedges pattern (Fig. A112) which are capable of standing rough wear. The Jennings pattern (Fig. A113) and the solid centre (Fig. A114) bits possess projecting spurs which cut the fibres before removing them, so producing clean holes.

The spurs are delicate and these patterns need care in storage. They are made in sizes from 3/16 in. to 1½ in.

Augers

The auger is used by the farmer and jobbing joiner. Approximately 24 in. long, instead of a square shank it has an eye welded on the shank which will take a wooden cross-hand or tommy bar and dispenses with the need of a brace. Sizes range from ½ in. up to 2 in. That illustrated in Fig. A115 is the Scotch pattern auger, the most popular.

Miscellaneous Bits

Other brace bits include the shell bit and spoon bit (Fig. A116) with sizes ranging from 1/16 in. up to 7/16 in.; the gimlet bit (Fig. A117), produced in sizes from ⅛ in. to ⅜ in.; and the square rimer bit, ⅜ in. (Fig A118). Other useful bits, not illustrated, are the octagon rimer bit, ⅜ in.; the half-round rimer bit, ½ in.; and the tape bit, with a range of ⅝ in., to 1¼ in.

Countersink bits are invaluable for countersinking a hole after boring. The snail-horn bit (Fig. A119) is made primarily for use with wood. The rose-head or countersink bit (Fig. A120) can be used on wood, but is designed primarily for brass, aluminium, ebonite, mild steel, and

so on. Sizes range from ⅜ in. to 1 in., the most popular being ⅝ in.

The screwdriver bit (Fig. A121) is self-explanatory. The dowel trimmer (Fig. A122) is available in a size of 9/16 in.

The expansive bit (Fig. A123) is a valuable tool because it overcomes the need for carrying a wide range of boring bits, particularly in the larger sizes. It is made in two sizes—small, for holes from ½ in. to 1½ in., and large, for holes from ⅞ in. to 3 in. A cutter can be supplied for the larger bit to bore up to 6 in. diameter.

Resharpening

After a period of use, bits will need resharpening. For this purpose a small file should be used; if a really fine edge is required, then it should be finished off with an oilstone slip.

Irreparable damage can be done to a twist bit if the cutting action of the spurs and cutters is not fully understood.

The main point to watch is clearance. The spurs, which cut the fibres and so form the wall of the hole, are slightly larger in diameter than the body of the bit, which is then permitted to follow the spurs without jamming.

The cutters remove the waste wood, which is automatically ejected down the spiral twist. The spurs should be sharpened from the inside or they will become less in diameter than the body. File the cutters from the underside and try to retain the original angle.

It is wise to bear in mind that bits should not be resharpened more than is absolutely necessary, for there is only a limited amount of material in the nose of a twist bit available for filing away.

Use a small fine cut file with a safe edge, to avoid doing any accidental damage.

The screwed pin of a rusty bit can be partially restored by the following procedure:

Hold a 1¼ in. thick piece of hardwood (beech or oak) in a vice and bore a hole about ¾ in. deep with the bit that is to be restored. Fill the resulting hole with a mixture of oil and emery powder. Insert the bit again and bore a little deeper, refill with the abrasive mixture and repeat several more times until the pin emerges. The treatment can be repeated with a piece of soft timber and dry emery powder.

Drills

Hand drills and breast drills are often used for boring woodwork as well as the bit and brace, although they are intended more for metal work. They, too, possess adjustable chucks, but these are made to take bits with a round shank. Twist drills are available in a wide range of sizes and are useful to the carpenter for a multitude of purposes.

The secret of the successful use of a brace or drill is to hold and keep it rigid with the bit at right angles to the works (Figs. A124 and A125).

Gimlets

The gimlet (Fig. A126) is a small brace bit fitted with a boxwood handle. The screwed nose draws the bit into the wood with less effort on the part of the user, but it must not be used near the edge or end of the timber, or the wood will easily split.

Bradawls

The bradawl (Fig. A127) is a useful little tool, and in-

Fig. A107.
The plain
brace.

Fig. A109
(left).
Plain centre
bit.

Fig. A110
(right).
Screwed
pin centre
bit.

Fig. A108.
Ratchet brace.

Fig. A113 (right).
Jennings
pattern.

Fig. A111 (left).
Scotch pattern
screw auger bit.

Fig. A112
(right).
Gedges
pattern.

Fig. A114
(left).
Solid centre
auger bit.

Fig. A115
(left).
Scotch
pattern
auger.

Fig. A122 (below).
Dowel trimmer.

Fig. A123
(below).
Expansive
bit.

Fig. A117
(below).
Gimlet bit.

Fig. A116 (below).
Spoon bit.

Fig. A120 (left).
Rose
(countersink)
bit.

Fig. A125
(right).
Using
brace
vertically.

Fig. A118
(above).
Square
rimer bit.

Fig. A119 (above).
Snailhorn bit.

Fig. A121 (left).
Screwdriver bit.

Fig. A124.   Using brace horizontally.

Fig. A127.
Bradawl.

Fig. A128.
A long
screwdriver
is less likely
to go out of
line and slip
than a short
one.

Fig. A130. Cross grind C is correct.
Grinding lengthwise as A, or filing
to a bevel B prevents a firm grip in
the slot.

90°

Fig. A129. The screwdriver tip
should not be allowed to wear
round at the corners.

Fig. A126.
Gimlet.

dispensable for all carpentry work for rapidly making small holes. To use it, hold the flat point at right angles to the grain, thus cutting instead of splitting the fibres. In this way a hole can be pierced quite near the end of the work without splitting the wood.

The best bradawls have the flat point slightly wider than the shank to give clearance.

When a bradawl becomes blunt with use, it should be touched up with a smooth file and finished off on an oilstone.

SCREWDRIVERS

A screwdriver blade demands a tough steel of a resilient nature, to withstand the rough usage which this type of tool encounters. If it were manufactured from steel suitable for a wood chisel, the point would fracture like glass. The steel for this type of tool requires a lower carbon content and a higher proportion of toughening metals such as vanadium and chrome.

There are many patterns of screwdrivers—or 'turn-screws' as they are often called in the trade—and they are made in varying sizes.

A wise householder should possess two or three screwdrivers to suit varying sizes of screws.

If working space allows, a long screwdriver is more easy to use than a short one, the reason being that in principle the blade should be held to coincide with an imaginary line from the centre of the screw (Fig. A128). With the effort of turning, the handle tends to move out of this line, and at a certain angle the tip will slip out of the screw slot. With a short screwdriver, the blade will be much more deflected from the true line of the screw than with a larger tool, and will slip out more easily.

Screwdriver Tips

The shape of a screwdriver tip is of paramount importance, for it is the business end of the tool. The point of a screwdriver should not be ground rounded (Fig. A129) for this will make it slip from the screw slot, and damage the screw as well. Neither should it be ground to a thin or chisel edge for it will then be so thin that it will break under pressure. This will also damage the screw.

A131

A132

A133

A134

A135

A136

A137

A138

Fig. A131. Carpenters' 'London' pattern.
Fig. A132. Carpenters' 'cabinet' pattern.
Fig. A133. Carpenters' round blade.
Fig. A134. Electricians' 'cabinet' screwdriver.
Fig. A135. Electricians' thin round blade.
Fig. A136. Electricians' moulded-handle screwdriver.
Fig. A137. Ratchet screwdriver.
Fig. A138. Spiral ratchet screwdriver.

The ideal tip is shown in Fig. A130 (C), the cheeks of the point are cross-ground perfectly flat, with the rounding of the tip eliminated. The series of tiny ridges left by the grindstone combines to keep the tip snugly home in the slot. The end of the blade is ground square, to coincide with the base of the slot. This skid proof feature should be looked for when purchasing a screwdriver.

If possible, a screwdriver should be used with the tip a fraction less than the width of the screw. If it is too wide and the corners project it will damage the wood, unless tilted, in which event it would be more likely to slip out and damage both the screw and the work.

Types of Screwdrivers

A carpenters' 'London' pattern with beechwood handle and flat blade is illustrated in Fig. A131. Length of blade ranges from 3 in. up to 18 in.

A carpenters' 'cabinet' screwdriver with oval beech or boxwood handle is shown in Fig. A132. Length of blade ranges from 3 in. up to 18 in.

The carpenters' round blade screwdriver (Fig. A133) is one solid piece of steel to form the blade, shank and head. Length of blade ranges from 3 in. up to 12 in.

The electricians' 'cabinet' screwdriver (Fig. A134) has an oval boxwood handle and thin blade. Sizes are from 3 in. to 10 in.

The electricians' thin round blade screwdriver (Fig. A135), with an octagonal boxwood handle, is supplied in blade sizes ranging from 1½ in. up to 10 in.

The electricians' moulded handle screwdriver (Fig. A136) has blade sizes ranging from 4 in. up to 8 in.

The ratchet screwdriver (Fig. A137) with blade made to revolve is produced in blade lengths from 3 in. up to 10 in.

The spiral ratchet screwdriver (Fig. A138) measures 13½ in. when closed and is supplied with 3 bits.

MARKING-OUT TOOLS

The carpenter traditionally uses a carpenter's pencil, which is a robust oval pencil with a heavy rectangular lead, for measuring and rough marking.

In fact a variety of more sophisticated tools are available for marking out, several of which are shown here.

Markers

For the accurate marking demanded by good-class work, the marking awl (Fig. A139) and the striking knife (Fig. A140) are used, while they are sometimes combined as one tool as shown in Fig. A141.

A pair of compasses, or dividers, are always useful to the woodworker. The pattern designed for woodwork (Fig. A142) is made with a wing and thumbscrew for rigidity and easy adjustment. Sizes range from 5 in. to 10 in. with the handiest size being 7 in.

Try Square

The try square (Fig. A143) is a tool used for marking out preparatory to sawing, etc., and for testing the squareness of timbers. The blade also serves as a straight edge for checking flat surfaces.

The square consists of a steel blade with parallel trued edges set at 90 deg. to a stock made of rosewood, ebony or metal. These two timbers are used in the best quality

Fig. A139. Marking awl.

Fig. A140. Striking knife.

Fig. A141. Awl and striking knife combined.

Fig. A142 (left). Woodworking compasses.

Fig. A143 (right). Joiners' try square.

Fig. A144. To test a try square for accuracy draw a line as shown, then reverse to square and draw another line. Both lines should coincide.

tools and are specially selected for their properties of withstanding the effects of the weather and the resultant danger of inaccuracy owing to warping. The inside edge is faced with brass to withstand wear.

The blade and stock are riveted together with brass inserts. The better quality squares have diamond or fancy-shaped inserts which give added rigidity as well as being decorative.

The try square should not be dropped, or thrown into a tool bag, as such rough treatment will soon cause it to lose its accuracy.

Fig. A144 illustrates a simple method of testing a try square; see also diagram Fig. 145. Take a piece of board

Fig. A145. Diagram showing the lines drawn in Fig. A144.

Fig. A149. Beechwood marking gauge.

Fig. A150. The way to hold a marking gauge.

Fig. A146. One type of adjustable bevel.

Fig. A147. Another type of adjustable bevel.

with one edge straight and true. Using the square in the normal way, mark a line with a sharp pencil, then reverse the square and repeat as near as possible to the first line. If the lines coincide, the square is still true.

Try squares are made with blades varying from 3 in. to 12 in. long for usual work; they are available up to 24 in. for special work. The most popular size is 6 in.

Adjustable Bevel

This tool (Figs. A146 and A147) comes into the same category as the try square. It also consists of two main parts, a steel blade, slotted for adjustment, and a rosewood or ebony stock, brass bound at each end.

The blade can be adjusted to any angle and is fixed securely into position by tightening the screw provided. Fig. A148 shows the tool in use. Adjustable bevels are made in varying sizes ranging from 7½ in. to 15 in., the most popular being 9 in.

Marking Gauges

In woodwork it is often necessary to mark a line parallel to a given trued edge. An example of this is when preparing to cut a rebate. The marking gauge is the tool

for this purpose and the trued edge can be used as a guide when marking the parallel line.

Plain Gauge: The plain marking gauge (Fig. A149), consisting of a head and a stem, is usually manufactured of beechwood. The head, often semi-circular in shape, is adjustable along the stem and is secured by a wooden or plastic thumbscrew. A hardened steel pin, fitted at one end of the stem, projects about 1/16 to ⅛ in. The head acts as a fence against the work as does the fence of a plough. The pin scores or scratches the line to be marked.

The illustration of the gauge in use (Fig. A150) shows how the half-round head fits the user's hand when correctly held. The main points to be borne in mind when using this tool are that the head should be held firmly against the edge of the work; the gauge should be pushed away from the body; three or four strokes are necessary.

Cutting Gauges: The cutting gauge (Fig. A151) is almost identical in action to the marking gauge, the main difference being that the pin is replaced by a thin steel cutter, held in position by a brass wedge. This tool is often used for the cutting of small rebates.

Mortise Gauges: When it is necessary to mark two parallel lines (before cutting a mortise and tenon joint,

Fig. A148. Adjustable bevel with thumbscrew, used here to set angle.

Fig. A152. A mortise gauge marks two parallel lines.

Fig. A151. A cutting gauge. Note blade and wedge.

Fig. A153. Warrington pattern hammer with cross-pein.

Fig. A154. Exeter cross-pein.

Fig. A155. Adze-eye claw hammer.

Fig. A156.   A wedge used to secure hammer heads.

for example) a mortise gauge (Fig. A152) is used. Made from rosewood or ebony, this consists of a head and stem and is operated like the marking gauge.

The stem is fitted with two pins, one fixed and one adjustable, the latter being carried in an independently movable brass slide housed in the stem. The head slide and stem are held rigid by the screw in the head. To adjust the gauge, the head screw should be slackened and the stem tapped into the required position.

In the more popular patterns, the moving brass slide has a thumbscrew means of adjustment.

HAMMERS, MALLETS AND PINCERS

Certainly one of the first tools invented by man, the hammer is today made in many different types, nearly every trade having a special pattern. The two principal patterns used by the carpenter are the cross-pein and the claw hammer. Even these are produced in various styles.

Pein Hammers: The 'pein' is the back part of the hammer head: in the cross pein type of hammer, the pein is used for starting small nails held between the fingers. This type is therefore most useful for light work, such as cabinet making. Two examples are shown, the Warrington (Fig. A153) and the Exeter (Fig. A154). Ball pein hammers, having a round knob at the back of the hammer head, are used in engineering and are not of much use to woodworkers.

Claw Hammers: For more general work, the carpenter finds the claw hammer most useful, because of its capability in withdrawing nails. The adze-eye pattern is the most popular in current use (Fig. A155).

When removing long nails with a claw hammer, a block of wood should be placed beneath the hammer head. This acts as a raised fulcrum, protects the work, and, by giving a more direct pull, enables the nails to be withdrawn more easily.

A hammer needs little attention. Occasionally the head works loose, but good hammer-heads are forged with a double taper at the eye, which permits the end of the haft to expand when the wedge is driven in. Spare steel hammer-wedges are stocked by most tool-dealers, hardware stores and ironmongers. Alternatively a home-made wedge of hardwood (Fig. A156) can be quickly made and inserted.

Hammers vary in weight, 16 oz. being a useful size for general work.

The following are a few hints on using the hammer.

1. Hold the shaft or handle at the end and not in the middle.

2. Make full use of the wrist, allowing the hammer head to fall freely in an arc (see Fig. A157).

3. Do not grip the handle too tightly.

4. When possible, something solid should be placed behind the work being nailed, even if this means temporary wood packing.

5. Keep the face of the hammer clean and free from oil and grease. Rubbing it on a sheet of emery cloth laid flat on the bench, or even on a concrete floor, is all that is necessary. A greasy hammer will slip off a nailhead, damaging the work—and the fingers!

Fig. A157.   Left, the wrong way to hold a hammer. The wrist can do none of the work and cannot guide the blow. Right, the correct way. The hammer can be easily guided to hit the nail squarely.

Fig. A158 (*top*). The tapered mallet.
Fig. A159 (*above, left centre*). Round head nail punch.
Fig. A160 (*above, right centre*). Square head nail punch.
Fig. A161 (*right*). Using a nail punch.
Fig. A162 (*above left*). A set of four nail punches.
Fig. A163 (*above right*). Carpenters' 'knob and claw' pincers.
Fig. A164 (*below left*). The correct way to use pincers—the wooden packing piece prevents bruising.
Fig. A165 (*below right*). Combination side-cutting pliers.

Mallets

A carpenters' mallet is made of beechwood and should be used in preference to a steel hammer for driving chisels with wooden handles. A mallet cushions the shock of the blow, whereas steel will split or bruise the wooden handles. If the user is not very skilled, he will find it much easier to strike an accurate blow with the larger surface (the side) of the mallet head.

The square tapered shaft is driven into a corresponding mortised hole from the top of the head, and the faces are cut at an angle to give a blow at right angles to the work (Fig. A158). An occasional wipe with a linseed-oil rag will help to preserve the beechwood.

The size of a mallet is determined by the length of the head. Sizes range from 4 in. to 7 in., 5 in. being the most popular.

Nail Sets

It is sometimes necessary to drive the head of a nail well below the surface and to fill the resulting cavity with putty or plastic wood. In outdoor painted work, the nail is thus insulated from the wet and consequent rusting. Nail sets, or nail punches, as they are sometimes called are designed for this purpose. A special tough shock-resisting steel is used, in either round (Fig. A159) or square (Fig. A160) section. The squarehead nail sets will not roll off the work bench. They are made with knurled finger grip and the points are cupped, i.e. concave, to lessen the chances of the punch slipping off the head of the nail. The method of using is shown in Fig. A161.

The points are made 1/16 in., 3/32 in., ⅛ in. and 5/32 in. in diameter to suit various sizes of nails. A handy set comprising one of each in a case is carried easily in the tool kit (Fig. A162).

Pincers

Pincers are designed for the extraction of nails and form an essential part of a carpenter's kit.

Made in various patterns, some pincers have sharp hardened steel jaws for cutting mild steel, wire nails, etc. Farriers' pincers (blacksmiths') possess this feature, for trimming both the horseshoe nails and parts of the hoof itself.

Carpenters' pincers range in size from 5 in. to 10 in.; the most popular in this country (Fig. A163) is known as the 'knob and claw' pattern, in sizes 6 in. and 7 in. As in the case of claw hammers, a piece of wood placed underneath the head of the pincers will protect the work and facilitate the extraction of long or obstinate nails. This is illustrated in Fig. A164.

Pliers

Although not strictly a woodworking tool, a pair of pliers is a valuable addition to the woodworker's tool kit. Many patterns are made to suit specific purposes, but combination side-cutting pliers are recommended for general use. Ranging in size from 5 in. up to 10 in., the most popular is 7 in. The three main characteristics of this pattern of pliers (as shown in Fig. A165) are (a) the hardened side-cutter suitable for cutting soft wire, electric cable, etc., (b) the shearing cutter at the joint for cutting hard thin wire, and (c) the jaws with a serrated hole for gripping round work. This is known as the 'burner' hole, deriving its name from the days when pliers with this feature were used in repairing gas burner jets.

An occasional wipe with an oily rag, and a drop of oil at the joint, will keep pliers and pincers in good order. Combination pliers can be obtained with heavily-insulated handles for electricians' use.

FILES, RASPS AND HACKSAWS

The file (a typical example is shown in Fig. A166) is a tool used by the woodworker as well as by the metal worker or engineer, and a handyman's kit should include several of the many different patterns of files that are made for various purposes.

The file—a scraping tool with raised teeth, working by abrasion—can be described under three main headings, all of which should be borne in mind when making a purchase; type, cut, length.

Type: The type of file is often defined by the section of steel from which the file is made, e.g. flat, square, round, half-round, three-square or triangular, etc. (see Fig. A167); or occasionally by the use for which it is intended—mill saw, reaper file and so on.

Cut: Cut denotes the kind of teeth; Fig. A168 refers. A single-cut file has one set of teeth, cut across the face at an oblique angle, but parallel to each other. A double-cut file has two sets of teeth, one crossing the other.

Most files for ordinary metal working are double-cut, for these cut more quickly and the teeth clear themselves

Fig. A167. File sections.
 l. = lengths
 s.c. = single cut
 d.c. = double cut

Fig. A166 (*right*).
 A typical file.

Taper saw file; *l.* 3–12 in.; *s.c.* or *d.c.*

Slim taper; *l.* 3–12 in.; *s.c.*

Extra slim taper; *l.* 4–8 in.; *s.c.*

Bandsaw blunt slim (parallel size); *l.* 4–8 in.; *s.c.*

Bandsaw blunt slim (parallel size) (also produced taper) similar to tapers of same inch, but with rounded corners. Used for saws requiring rounded bottom teeth; *l.* 4–10 in.; *s.c.*

Triangular double ender, tapers to each end; *l.* 6–12 in.; *s.c.*

Pitsaw file for pit or frame saws; *l.* 4–8 in.; *s.c.*

Mill saw file, for circular saws and brass finishing. Larger sizes used as lathe or shafting files. Can be parallel in width and length or tapered. It can have square or rounded edges or square and rounded; *l.* 4–8 in.; usually *s.c.* but can be *d.c.*

Cross-cut (parallel) file, used for sharpening cross-cut saws; *l.* 6–12 in.; *s.c.*

Cant-saw file for sharpening saws with M shaped teeth; *l.* 4–12 in.: *s.c.*

Flat rectangular engineers' utility file, tapered in both width and thickness, has teeth on both sides and edges; *l.* 4–20 in.; *s.c.*

Hand rectangular engineers' utility file, parallel in width with one safe edge, used for either roughing or finishing depending on the cut; *l.* 4–20 in.; *d.c.*

Half round double purpose file for flat and concave surfaces; *l.* 4–20 in.; *d.c.*

Triangular or three square file with angles of 60°, tapering towards point, used for cutting angular shapes and recesses; *l.* 4–20 in.; *d.c.*

Square, used for filing square recesses; *l.* 4–20 in.; *d.c.*

Round, used for filing circular and elongated holes and trimming radii, sometimes called 'rat tail'; *l.* 4–20 in.; *d.c.*

Pillar rectangular file, thicker than the hand file; *l.* 6–16 in.; *d.c.*

Knife—taper file having knife edge with broader back, used for filing acute angles; *l.* 4–12 in.; *d.c.*

Warding file used for cutting wards and lock making; *l.* 2–10 in.; *d.c.*

Fig. A167 (*cont.*)

Half round, wood rasps, tapers; *l.* 6–16 in.

Flat wood rasp, tapers; *l.* 6–16 in.

Half round lead float, also made in flat section, for plumbing; *l.* 6–16 in.

Half round wood file (also in flat section) for finer work than the cabinet rasp; *l.* 6–16 in.

Cabinet rasp, more shallow than wood file in section; *l.* 6–16 in.

Cabinet file of finer cut than the wood file; *l.* 6–14 in.

Shoe rasp (also in flat section), half file, half rasp; *l.* 6–10 in.

Horse rasp, supplied quarter or half file, half file reversed and with or without tang; *l.* 10–18 in.

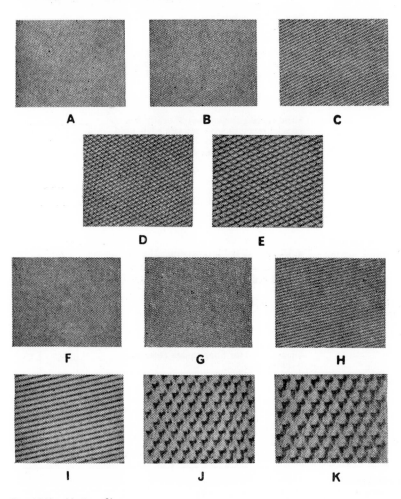

Fig. A168. Various file cuts

A. Dead smooth—double cut.
B. Smooth—double cut.
C. Second cut—double cut.
D. Bastard—double cut.
E. Rough—double cut.
F. Smooth—float cut.

G. Second cut—float cut.
H. Bastard—float cut.
I. Rough—float cut.
J. Bastard—rasp cut.
K. Second cut—rasp cut.

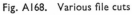

Fig. A169. The left hand on the file point prevents it rocking.

Fig. A170. Wire file brush, used to restore clogged teeth.

Fig. A171. Knocking a handle on to a file by banging it sharply on the bench.

more easily. Single-cut files are used more for accurate work including the sharpening of hardened tools, such as saws, hedge shears, cutters and so on. The size of the teeth is determined by the distance between the parallel cuts, the following terms being used in the trade to denote the respective sizes of teeth:

'Rough' cut for heavy work, leaving a coarse finish.

'Bastard' cut, not quite so coarse as the 'rough' cut and suitable for general work.

'Second' cut for fine work and for finishing after using a coarser file.

'Smooth' cut for extra-fine finishing.

Rasps are a type of extra-coarse file designed specially for woodwork, the teeth being punched individually and not in rows. They are used by plumbers on lead, by farriers on horses' hooves and by shoemakers on leather, as well as for timberwork. Carpenters' rasps are usually half-round in shape.

Length: The size of a file is determined by the length from the end to the shoulder, and does not include the tang which fits into the handle.

A useful set of files in a carpenter's kit might comprise the following: 10 in. taper flat bastard, double cut; 8 in. half-round bastard, double cut; 8 in. in both round and square bastard, double cut; 10 in. or 12 in. half-round wood rasp; 10 in. half-round cabinet rasp; 8 in. mill saw, single cut; 4½ in. taper saw, single cut.

Use: Accurate filing can only be attained with practice, the secret of accuracy being to keep the file on an even plane and not allowing it to 'rock'. The work must be held securely in a vice and the file gripped firmly, using both hands, if possible, as shown in Fig. A169.

It is better to cut on the forward stroke only, relieving pressure slightly on the return stroke, to avoid spoiling the teeth. The strokes should be made slowly and firmly. When the teeth become clogged with filings these should be cleared away with a wire brush or 'file card' which is made specially for the purpose (Fig. A170).

Made of a special high-carbon steel, a file is very hard and has not been tempered. It is, therefore, as brittle as glass and should not be used as a lever or a case opener, or a serious accident might result. Dropping on to a hard floor or being thrown on to a bench may chip the teeth. The cutting ability of the file will also be impaired if it comes into contact with oil or grease.

Handles for files are usually sold separately; when being fitted they should not be hammered on, because the hardened steel may chip and fly off. The correct method is to push the handle on to the tang. Gripping it firmly with the point upwards, the butt end of the handle should then be knocked sharply on the bench top as illustrated in Fig. A171.

To remove a file handle (see Fig. A172) grip it in the left hand and with the right hand strike the ferrule end with a piece of flat steel or wood, rubbing along the face of the file for guidance.

Glasspaper

Glasspaper, or glasscloth at an extra cost, is used for the final polishing of woodwork to remove the slight irregularities on the surface of the work left by the plane or scraper blade. Available in several grades of coarseness, the finest is called 'flour'. Glasspaper should never be held in the hand when working on a flat surface, for it is almost impossible to avoid rubbing over the corners, thereby losing the sharp clean edges left by the plane. It

Fig. A172. Removing a file from its handle by striking a blow towards the ferrule.

Fig. A173. Glass paper should be used round a cork rubber to avoid rounding the work.

is best used wrapped around a piece of cork rubber as shown in Fig. A173; it keeps the paper flat, and the resilience of the cork is an added advantage. It is better to work with the grain, thought this is not always possible. The usual size of cork rubber measures 4½ in. by 2½ in.

Hacksaws

The hacksaw, although this is also not strictly a woodworking tool, is another useful addition to the carpenter's kit. The two main parts are the blade and frame. The thin, narrow blades range in size from 8 in. to 14 in.; 10 in. being the most popular. These blades are usually made in four sizes of tooth: 14, 18, 24 and 32 teeth per inch. The frame is either made solid to take one size of blade only, or adjustable to accommodate all four sizes. Types vary from a pistol grip adjustable tubular-frame hacksaw frame (Fig. A174) to a bent-wire frame with smaller blade (Fig. A175).

The bent-wire type is particularly useful to the carpenter. It takes up little space in his case or tool bag and can be used in a confined space, or on work normally inaccessible to the ordinary hacksaw frame. It is so balanced that it can be used as easily with one hand as with both (Fig. A176). When no vice is available, the work can be held in the left hand and the saw operated by the other.

The advantage of the adjustable-frame saw is that it can take any of the standard size blades from 9 in. upwards. It cannot take the 6 in. blades used in the bent-wire type of hacksaw frame, since these blades are fitted

Fig. A174. Tubular frame, pistol grip hacksaw.

Fig. A175. A popular type of small hacksaw.

Fig. A176 (*below*). When using a small hacksaw, the work can be steadied with the other hand.

Fig. A177 (*below*). When using this type of hacksaw, a steady true stroke should be maintained. Note the steadying position of the right index finger.

Fig. A178. Hacksaw blade.

Fig. A179. To avoid breaking blades, at least two teeth must be in contact with the work.

 (a)

 (b)

with pegs which are sprung into slots cut in the frame, whereas standard blades have a hole at each end to engage on pegs fitted to the hacksaw frame.

Special developments of the hacksaw include sheet saws for cutting corrugated or sheet material. The blade in these is tapered in width and is gripped in a rigid back, like a tenon saw. They are useful when cutting an opening in the centre of a sheet of hardboard or metal.

The piercing saw resembles the coping saw and is used for shaping work in metals and plastic.

The following are a number of points to be noted when fixing or using a hacksaw : —

(a) When fitting the blade, the rake of the teeth should point away from the handle.

(b) Tension the blade by means of the wing nut, adequately but not enough to distort the frame.

(c) When sawing, use both hands, if possible, making slow steady strokes, not more than 50 or 60 per minute. Pressure should be applied only on the forward stroke, relieving the pressure slightly on the return stroke to permit the teeth to clear themselves (see Fig. A177).

(d) Straight, true strokes are essential. A hacksaw blade is hard and brittle; if the frame is twisted sideways or the blade is bent in the work, it will snap like glass.

(e) It is important to select a blade (Fig. A178) with the appropriate t.p.i. (teeth per inch) for the work in hand. Examples follow : —

14 t.p.i.: This coarse cut is for large sections and for softer metals such as cast iron and mild steel. The large

teeth clear themselves more easily than smaller ones.

18 t.p.i.: This size is for large sections of harder material, such as high-carbon tooth steel, and so on. If blades with finer teeth are used on large work, the teeth are apt to become clogged, and energy is wasted.

24 and 32 t.p.i.: These sizes are suitable for copper, brass, thin tubing, angle iron, and so on.

Many hacksaw blades are broken by the use of blades with teeth that are too coarse for the work in hand. Fig. A179 shows that two teeth at least must be in contact simultaneously with the work. If the blade is too course, the work is allowed to enter the gullet and so strip the teeth.

Fig. A179 (a) shows a piece of piping, the walls of which are thick, but the teeth cannot jam.

Fig. A179 (b) shows the work can enter between the teeth and so break them away.

Unnecessary wear is often caused by the operator sawing too rapidly and applying too little pressure. This causes the teeth to become polished and lose their sharp cutting edge.

SPIRIT LEVELS

A spirit level can be used for testing both horizontal and vertical surfaces. The tube is not straight, but is bent to a slight radius and is not completely full of spirit, thus allowing a bubble of air to flow to the highest point (Fig. A180). The curved tube fits into the body with the convex side uppermost, so that when the work surface is horizontal the bubble comes to rest at the highest part of the tube, i.e., between the two indicating lines. The liquid is usually colourless or tinted green, the latter being known as a 'green-line' or 'cat's-eye' tube.

Pocket levels range in sizes from 4 in. to 12 in., 9 in. being about right for general use. Fig. A181 shows a simple and cheap type of level. A very popular pattern, known as the 'boat' or 'torpedo' level and designed to slip easily into the overall pocket, is shown in Fig. A182.

The side openings in a level serve a dual purpose; the horizontal tube can, if necessary, be read from the side, high up above the user's head, while light admitted from the side refracts in the bubble, making it much easier to locate, even in a poor light.

The protecting plate of a level is usually made of brass and the ends of the level are often fitted with brass tips to avoid wear, while the body may be of metal or wood. Mahogany, boxwood, rosewood and ebony are the types of wood normally selected on account of their properties of resisting weather conditions.

The patent 'shockproof' spirit levels (Fig. A183) have their delicate glass tubes set in rubber mountings, which provide an efficient insulation against knocks and jars.

Fig. A184 shows how to obtain a vertical reading from a horizontal level, by using it in conjunction with a joiners' square, but most levels are now fitted with a small tube at right-angles to the sole. This is known as a 'plumb' tube after the old plumb-bob and line, which it has largely supplanted.

Bricklayers and builders require a longer level than the carpenter; the longer the base, the more accurate will the reading be, whether for horizontal or vertical use.

Fig. A185 shows a builders' spirit level with 'handy hold' finger grips, and Fig. A186 shows it being used for taking a vertical reading. The six-way level in Fig. A187 has six tubes fitted in such a manner that no matter how the level is picked up, it can be read immediately.

These long levels are apt to suffer as much rough treatment as any other hand tool. Often 48 in. long and 1 in. thick, they need to be made from carefully selected and seasoned timber. Almost invariably used outdoors, subjected to rain and sun, and in constant contact with

Fig. A181.   Pocket level, plain pattern.

Fig. A182.   Boat or Torpedo level.

Fig. A180.   Clear spirit level tube.

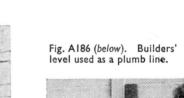

Fig. A186 (below).   Builders' level used as a plumb line.

Fig. A183 (below).   Shockproof level. The tube is set in a rubber mount.

Fig. A184.   A small level used with a straight edge or square can be used to check the uprightness of a wall or post.

Fig. A185 (below).   A longer level for builders' work. Can also be used as a plumb line.

Fig. A187.   A builders' six-way level.

Fig. A188.   Builders' aluminium level.

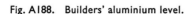

cement and mortar, they are still expected to remain accurate. In some patterns the tubes are set in special mountings, to enable the user to adjust the tubes periodically.

An occasional rub with a rag soaked in linseed oil will do much to preserve the wood, especially when constant use has worn away the initial coat of protective polish. For rugged use, an aluminium level has much to recommend it (Fig. A188).

WORKBENCH ACCESSORIES

There are a confusing mass of accessories available—some indispensable, some mere gimmicks. Here we deal with some of the most useful examples.

Shooting Boards

The 'shooting' or 'shuteing' board (Fig. A189) is used when the edge or end of a board is to be planed true and square along the whole of its length. The operator uses the plane on its side, and, with the work held firmly against the fence, a true edge can be obtained with a minimum of trouble. A typical use of the shooting board might be for preparing boards for gluing and jointing.

The wooden try plane and the metal jointer are the best planes to use for shooting, but a jack plane can be used if a larger type is not available. Illustrated in Fig. A190 is a mitre shooting board; it is usually made 18 in. or 24 in. long, and must be accurate. Of carefully seasoned beechwood, it requires no maintenance apart from careful storage and an occasional wipe with a linseed oil rag.

Mitre Templets

The mitre templet can be used both for scribing and for cutting a mitre with a chisel, as shown in Fig. A191. Templets are made in beechwood, brass, and (as in Fig. A192) malleable iron. When paring with a chisel, a fine cut should be used, gently tapping the templet back as required.

Bench Hooks

The experienced woodworker, whenever possible, ensures that his work is securely held. A piece of timber, loosely held with one hand on the bench, often means wasted energy, untidy work and even cut fingers. The bench hook (Fig. A193) is designed to provide this essential rigidity when using a tenon saw on the bench. It consists of a piece of seasoned beechwood, 10 in. long by 6 in. wide and ⅞ in. thick, with strips of wood at either end. The lower strip of wood is hooked against the front of the bench top, while the work to be cut is held firmly against the upper strip with the left hand.

Wood dowels are used to secure the strips because wood screws or nails might damage the teeth of the saw.

Mitres

The mitre block (Fig. A194) and the mitre box (Fig. A195) are used to cut picture framing and small mouldings at an angle of 45 deg. or, if necessary, 90 deg.

The mitre block is adequate for the smallest work. It consists of two pieces of seasoned beechwood measuring 10 in. to 12 in. long, which are either glued or screwed together (along the lengths) at right angles. The upright side possesses two saw cuts at 45 deg. and a centre cut at 90 deg. The block should be held securely on the bench with the left hand, the thumb keeping the moulding in position against the back. The saw cut guides the blade of the tenon saw to the correct angle (Fig. A196).

Larger mouldings need support for the saw on each side of the work and the mitre box is used for this purpose. The adjustable metal saw guides protect the saw cuts and give added support to the blade.

Two countersunk holes are provided in the base of the box for screwing to the bench top. It is wise to place a piece of waste wood between the work and the base of the box to protect the base from the saw teeth (Fig. A197). The front of the moulding should be held facing the user, so that the ragged edge left by the saw remains at the back of the work, where it will be less noticeable.

The next stage is assembling the frame, usually with both pins and glue. A corner cramp (Fig. A198) is almost essential for good work.

Bench Stops

When planing a flat board on the bench, a bench stop should be used, projecting above the surface of the bench. The end of the board to be planed is pressed against this, keeping it firm. The stop must not project above the top of the work, and it must be adjustable for various thicknesses of work, and removable when not in use.

The simplest form of stop is a thin piece of wood screwed to the bench top, but this is apt to get in the way since it is not readily removable.

Fig. A199 shows a malleable iron stop that fits flush with the top of the work bench. The hinged portion is adjusted with a screwdriver.

The rising-pillar bench stop shown in Fig. A200 is made of malleable iron with a steel pillar. It is adjusted by slackening the screw, tapping with a hammer and securing again by tightening the screw.

There are other types of bench stops but these are the most usual.

Cramps

Holding work in place, or cramping, is an operation frequently necessary in woodworking; cramps are made in a variety of patterns both for holding the timber while it is being worked and when putting together for nailing or gluing.

G-cramps (Fig. A201) are usually employed for holding work as shown in Fig. A202. Made of steel or malleable iron, with a steel screw, they are supplied in sizes ranging from 2 in. up to 18 in. The size is determined by the greatest thickness of the work to be held in the cramp.

Another type of cramp, used mainly for holding work, is the gluing cramp (Fig. A203). It consists of a steel bar with one serrated edge and has two arms, one fixed and the other adjustable, which can be moved instantaneously by pressure on the pawl that engages with the serrated edge. These cramps are made in a variety of sizes—to span from 4 in. up to 24 in.

The pressure of a G-cramp is rather concentrated and care must be taken not to damage the work. The hand screw (Fig. A204) distributes pressure over a wider area and the hardwood jaws are less likely to damage the work. Made of beechwood, the size is determined by the length of the jaws, which range from 6 in. to 18 in.; 10 in. and 12 in. are the most popular.

The hand screw consists of two jaws and two screws. Screw A shown in Fig. A204 passes through a plain hole

Fig. A189. A shooting board.

Fig. A190 (*right*). A try plane shooting a mitre on a mitre shooting board.

Fig. A191. A mitre templet used with a chisel for paring a mitre

Fig. A192. An iron mitre templet for squaring and mitring.

Fig. A194. Mitre block.

Fig. A193. Bench hook.

Fig. A195. Mitre box.

Fig. A196. Using a tenon saw the mitre block is shown in use.

Fig. A197. A thin piece of wood saves the base of the mitre box from damaging saw cuts.

Fig. A198. A corner cramp.

Fig. A199. Hinged bench stop.

Fig. A200. Rising pillar type of bench stop.

in the jaw nearest to it and screws into a threaded hole in the other jaw. Screw B screws into the end of the same jaw from the other side, and the butt end enters a plain recessed hole in the opposite jaw.

The middle screw A should be so adjusted as to hold the work comfortably tight. Increased pressure is then brought to bear by turning screw B, which has the effect of closing the jaws still further on the work. Fig. A205 shows a hand screw in use.

The threaded portion of the screws should be lubricated with blacklead, or a mixture of oil and graphite. An occasional wipe with a linseed oil rag over the remaining parts is advisable as a protection against the weather.

Other types of cramps include sash cramps (Fig. A206) for light work, such as cramping door frames and so on, made in lengths of bar ranging from 24 in. up to 60 in.; and joiner's strong cramps (Fig. A207), for heavy work, with a T-section bar which is made in lengths of bar from 3 ft. up to 7 ft.

When no sash cramps are available, cramp heads (Fig. A208) make a cheap and satisfactory substitute. A board of 1 in. or 1¼ in. thick, according to the size of the cramp head, can rapidly be converted into a bar.

The corner cramp (Fig. A198) is designed for gluing mitre joints, such as those of a picture frame.

Simple cramps, known as joiner's dogs, are often used by carpenters; for instance, in the making of a glued butt joint—that is the joining of two boards along their lengths. The edges should first be carefully planed straight and true; after applying ample glue to both edges, the boards should be rubbed together several times to fill the pores of the wood and remove surplus glue. A steel dog is then knocked in with a hammer as shown in Fig. A209.

Because of the marks left in the wood by the dogs, this method is only suitable for rough carpentry. An even better joint can be obtained by planing a little off the ends of the edges. The steel dogs are so designed that the

Fig. A201. G-cramp.

Fig. A202. A G-cramp will hold light work firmly and leave both hands free.

Fig. A203. Gluing cramp.

Fig. A204. Hand screw with wooden jaws.

Fig. A205. Using a hand screw, marking-out can be done on more than one piece at a time.

Fig. A208. Cramp heads can be fitted to a board of any length.

Fig. A206. Sash cramp.

Fig. A207. Joiner's strong cramp.

Fig. A209. Dog used to hold two boards together.

Fig. A210. Stamped dog.

Fig. A211. Forged dog.

Fig. A212. Method of building a leg vice.

Fig. A213. Steel bench screw used in leg vice.

Fig. A214. Woodworker's vice.

Fig. A215. Woodworker's vice for permanent bench fixing.

Fig. A216. Parallel jaw vice mounted on a vice holder.

ends of the boards are pulled together as the dogs are driven in. Joiner's dogs are made in a variety of sizes, ranging from 1½ in. up to 4 in. Fig. A210 shows a stamped dog and Fig. A211 shows a forged dog. The latter, simple in design, is much stronger than the stamped dog although breakage is relatively unusual with the latter.

Vices

The woodworker's leg vice (needed for heavy work) consists of a benchscrew that is assembled as shown in Figs. A212 and A213. The jaws must be kept parallel to the work, regardless of the width of the article to be held, or damage may be done.

The lower part of the vice, when it is anchored to the bench, must, therefore, also be adjustable. The adjustment is provided by the sliding steel bar, measuring 18 in. by 1½ in. by ½ in., which is cut with a series of slots ½ in. wide, to accommodate a lever ⅜ in. thick. This is fitted loosely across the bench leg and pivoted at one end.

If all these fittings work easily the lever can be raised by the foot and the capacity of the vice adjusted with one hand, an advantage on many occasions.

Instead of the steel benchscrew and leg vice, the woodworker might prefer the instantaneous grip vice, which is amply strong for most purposes (Fig. A214). With cast iron jaws and steel slides, this vice is screwed or bolted to the underside of the bench top with suitable distance pieces of wood between the vice and the bench. The back jaw is recessed flush with the front edge of the bench. The steel sliding bars of the instantaneous grip vice should be kept clean and oiled.

The instantaneous grip is operated by the small lever on the front jaw. Pressure on the lever disengages the nut from the screw and allows the front jaw to be moved in and out as desired. On releasing the lever, the nut is again engaged and the screw comes into operation once more. These vices are made in three sizes: 7 in. jaws with 8 in. opening; 9 in. jaws with 13 in. opening; and 10½ in. jaws with 15 in. opening.

A smaller vice made for amateurs, with 6 in. jaws, opening 4½ in., is useful for small work (Fig. A215). This type is made in two patterns, either for permanent fixing or with a thumb screw, for screwing to a table up to 2⅛ in. thickness.

The woodworking bench is not complete without a metal-working or mechanic's vice, for the woodworker's vice is unsuitable for many jobs that the carpenter has to tackle. If the bench is long enough, room can be found for a parallel-jaw vice on the right-hand end of the front. It should be secured with coach screws or bolts as close as convenient to the right-hand leg.

Some carpenters prefer to keep the bench top free of any obstruction. To overcome this difficulty they mount their mechanic's vice on a hardwood vice-holder, as shown in Fig. A216. The long leg of the tee can be held in the jaws of the woodworking vice and is rigid enough for a small vice. Parallel-jaw vices range from size No. oo with jaws 2¾ in. wide up to No. 6 with 6 in. jaws. No. 2 with 3¼ in. jaws is a useful size. When selecting a vice, it is best to err on the heavy side, for small work can always be carried out in a large vice.

Parallel-jaw vices can be obtained with an instantaneous grip, similar to the woodworking pattern. Small vices in different patterns are available for special work for model makers and watch makers. A small precision vice for clamping to the table can be bought with 1½ in. jaws. Another type, with 2½ in. jaws, has a swivelling base to lock at any angle; it also clamps to a table.

USEFUL ADDITIONAL TOOLS

Many small tools which can be made quite cheaply prove invaluable as additions to the tool box. The tools shown here take only a little time to make but can be labour-savers and make practical work so much easier.

Dovetail Templet

This is shown in Fig. A217 and can be made from mild steel or brass 18 s.w.g. (standard wire gauge) and a piece of 5/16 in. x 5/16 in. bar. The top is marked out and filed to shape. One end is square and the other has a slope of one-in-seven. The bar is then riveted to the top by marking out the position of the holes, and drilling and countersinking one of them in both top and bar. Locate, and lightly tap over, the first countersunk head

rivet, and then drill the second and third holes through the top and bar together. Rivet tightly together. Clean up and slightly chamfer the edges. This tool is a combined bevel and square, and is used to mark out the slope of the dovetail, and the lines to be squared across the grain. When working, cut the socket or hole first and then the tail, checking the scribed outline of the tail against the socket before you saw out. Work for a hand-tight fit—mallet-tight may split the wood. Practise on single dovetails first.

Depth Gauge

This is a useful tool to use when drilling blind holes (Fig. A218). It enables holes to be drilled to the same depth, which is very helpful when making dowelled shelves and racks. It consists of two pieces of wood 3½ in. × 1½ in. × ½ in. with shaped ends, and fixed

Fig. A218.

together with ⅛ in. bolts and wing nuts. In the centre of each piece a 'V' groove is cut and this enables the gauge to be tightened in any position on the bit. The required depth for drilling is from the underside of the gauge to the cutting edges of the bit. The bit shown is an auger bit, and is the type to use for deep holes. For shallow holes, use the centre bit without depth gauge.

Winding Sticks

These parallel pieces of wood (Fig. A219) are used as sighting pieces to see if there is any twist in the wood or job. If there is no twist they will appear parallel to each other. When making these strips, carefully gauge and plane two pieces of hardwood up to 13½ in. × 1¾ in. × ⅝ in. If a contrasting strip is going to be in-

Fig. A217.

Fig. A219.

COMPLETE PRACTICAL WOODWORKING

serted, a groove should be cut in one of the pieces and the inlay glued in place. It is easier at this stage, when the sides are square, to insert the strip, but it must be dropped in deep enough so as not to be planed out when the chamfers are planed. After chamfering, glasspaper and polish. Use them to check planks for warping; chair or table legs for length by levelling across the feet, so that they stand level.

Scratch Tool

The scratch tool (Fig. A220) is used for working small grooves and mouldings. It can be simply made from two pieces of wood screwed together. A cutter can be clamped between the two pieces at the required distance from the stock. A broken hacksaw blade can be made into cutters. The end should be filed square and then shaped. The action is one of rubbing backwards and forwards and the

Fig. A220.

stock must be tightly pressed up against the work. To make the scratch tool prepare two pieces of hardwood 4½ in. × 1½ in. × ½ in. Screw them together with three brass ¾ in. No. 6 countersunk head screws. Mark out the 'L' shape and carefully saw away the waste. Round the corners and clean up and polish. Make the cutter from an old hacksaw blade, forming the required shape by file or grindstone. Loosen the screws and insert the blade at the correct distance from the stock. Tighten the screws and the scratch tool is ready for use.

Spokeshave Blade Holder

To make the tool shown in Fig. A221, prepare a piece of wood 3½ in. × 2¼ in. × ¾ in. and at one end make a saw-cut 1¼ in. deep. This saw-cut will hold the blade of

Fig. A221.

a metal spokeshave, and sharpening is so much easier. All corners should be rounded so that the holder fits snugly into the hand. You can also use this for sharpening a cabinet scraper—the tool used to remove plane marks—or to hold the scraper when working. Since scrapers are sharp on all four edges you may need a wider holder than for spokeshave blades.

Rounding Cradle

The rounding cradle (Fig. A222) is used for shaping square wood, e.g. chamfering and shaping table legs and for rounding square wood for turning. The wood is placed in the cradle and then the edges can easily be worked. Plane up two pieces of hardwood 18 in. × 2 in. × ⅞ in.

Fig. A222.

Mark out a 45 deg. chamfer along the edge of each piece. Then glue and screw the two pieces together so that there is a 'V' trough in the centre. When the glue has set, let in, one inch from one end, a ¾ in. × ¾ in. stop. Clean up and polish.

Diagonal Strip

This strip (Fig. A223) is used when gluing up carcases. It is used to test the diagonals. The pointed end is placed in one corner and the length of the diagonal is ticked off

Fig. A223.

with a pencil. If the diagonals are not the same, then the cramps should be adjusted until they are. Prepare the wood to the sizes shown in the diagram and glue on an end. When set, shape, plane, and glasspaper.

Dowel Plate

This is a mild steel plate 6 in. × 2 in. × ¼ in. with various size holes drilled through as shown in Fig. A224. The wood to be made into dowels should be pared

Fig. A224.

roughly to size and then forced through the plate with a hammer. The main purpose of this tool is to make short lengths of dowel in a particular wood, for use as cover buttons to hide screw heads, and for shaping round tenons.

Chamfer Gauges

These small wooden gauges (Fig. A225) can be made as single, double, or triple markers, and will prove very handy when chamfers have to be marked out. Prepare a piece of hardwood 2 in. × 1¼ in. × ½ in. Make a

Fig. A225.

stock by removing a piece from one end ½ in. × ¼ in. and at this end cut 'V' grooves to finish the required distance from the stock. This double gauge enables parallel lines to be marked ⅛ in. and ¼ in. from a given edge.

Oil-stone Case

If you are going to keep your oil-stone in good condition then it should be kept in a case (Fig. A226). This can be simply made as follows: on a base 10 in. × 3 in. ×

Fig. A226.

½ in., strips are nailed and glued to house the stone. Each end of the stone should be protected by small strips. These strips stop the ends of the stone from crumbling when the tool being sharpened is passed along its length and occasionally overshoots the ends. It can be made from a hardwood such as mahogany, although plywood is suitable. A top made in the same way affords further protection.

Planing Aid

Very often, when planing up a wide piece of wood, the wood swings around the bench stop and shoots off the bench. This can be prevented if the bench stop can be lengthened. The planing aid (Fig. A227) does this. In itself it is not strong enough to be planed against, but if

Fig. A227.

it is placed in the vice and supported by the bench stop it then becomes a rigid and efficient fixture. Prepare a piece of wood 9 in. × 3 in. × ⅝ in. and one piece 11 in. × 1½ in. × ⅜ in. The two pieces are housed, glued and screwed together at right angles. When the glue has set, clean up and polish.

WOOD-TURNING TOOLS

A full set of good quality turning tools can be very expensive, but the eight basic tools shown here, together with notes on their uses, will meet the needs of most jobs. These tools are, in fact, all very necessary if a reasonably wide range of turning has to be attempted. Others can be made for special jobs or as the general need dictates. Old files can be ground to the required shape and serve admirably with a new handle on the tang. Old or surplus chisels may also be utilised for this same purpose. New handles can easily be turned. Beech is the best wood to use; a suggested shape is shown inset in Fig. A228. It is made from 2 in. × 2 in. stock and finished with carnauba wax. The ferrule is a ⅝ in. length of ⅝ in. brass, copper, or aluminium tube.

Old files should, ideally, be 'let down' and re-tempered, since in their natural state they are too brittle for wood turning. 'Letting down' entails annealing the file in a forge to soften it. It may then be ground to the required shape and the cutting end re-hardened by heating to red heat and quenching in oil or water. Scale should then be removed with emery cloth to enable the tempering colours to be observed; the correct colour is light straw. When the file is in the soft annealed state, the teeth can be ground off and the length of the file cleaned up, if desired, but this is very laborious work. Accidents with unprocessed files are most likely to occur when they are allowed to dig in and there is a wide distance between the cutting edge and the tool rest, which acts as a fulcrum. If the tool rest is kept well up to the work, this danger of breaking files is greatly reduced.

There are two kinds of lathe tools: cutting and scraping. There is a definite knack to the former, whilst scraping is the usual technique of self-taught amateurs. Both techniques have their place.

Skew Cutting Chisels

These vary in width from ¼ in. to 2 in. and more. For most work, one about 1½ in. wide is recommended. Fig. A228 shows the shape of the chisel and the method of use. In cutting, the chisel is held at an angle and cuts tangentially. The corner A should be kept well clear and only part B–C allowed to cut. The bevel should be allowed to rub on the work and the handle of the chisel then slightly raised until shavings appear. Sideways movement may then be effected. With practice a very smooth finish will result. Until this technique is perfected, the beginner may finish with a ribby spiral. This fault can be remedied by moving the handle of the chisel sideways, thus reducing the width of the shaving. If corner A is allowed to drop, it will dig in with disastrous results. Practice on scrap wood is the only way to master this particular skill.

Scraping, Fig. A229, is easier and gives a better result on hardwood than on softwood, in which the fibres tend to tear out. The tool is held at centre height. Try the cutting technique on half of a test piece and the scraping technique on the other half, and notice the difference in finish! Hardly any glasspapering will be necessary on the cut half to produce the final finish and this can effect saving in time and costs.

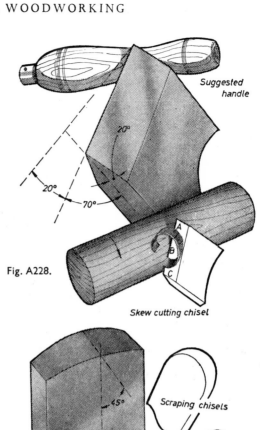

Fig. A228.

Skew cutting chisel

Scraping Chisels

An assortment of these chisels is very useful; examples are shown in Fig. A229. They should vary in width from about ⅜ in. to 1¼ in. and the ends may be square, slightly rounded, or even semi-circular, according to the work undertaken and the shape desired. Left- and right-hand skew scraping chisels are also very useful. In all cases they are bevelled on the underside at 45 deg., the top remaining quite flat. An oilstone or slip should be used for touching up and the burr which is normally removed may be left on with advantage, since it helps in the scraping action. In scraping, keep the tool rest well up to the work and hold the tool horizontally, or, if anything, trailing a little; that is, sloping slighty downwards—the handle being higher than the cutting edge. If the cutting edge is held high it will tend to dig in, and this is to be avoided.

Scraping chisels

Fig. A229.

Parting-off Tool

This tool, shown in Fig. A230, is invaluable for narrow work and, as its name implies, parting off. To assist in the latter operation the cutting edge of the tool is wider than the rest of the blade, thus preventing binding. It is a good thing to part off to within ¼ in. and then, with the lathe stopped, to screw off the nearly parted piece with a twisting hand action. Alternatively, the tailstock centre should be slackened when nearly through; the work may then be slightly pulled towards the operator and the parting off completed. This action of slackening the tailstock and pulling the work slightly out of line gives more clearance on the parting tool and the left hand is available to catch the finished work as it is detached.

Side Cutting Tool: The side and end of this tool, which is illustrated in Fig. A230, should be ground to about 85 deg. and bevelled on the underneath of these sides at 45 deg. It is intended for the inside of match holders or biscuit barrels, etc., allowing the inside corner to be cleaned out. Furthermore, in accurate fittings, such as a rebated lid, a job can soon be spoiled by taking another cut from the face, whereas the side-scraping action of this tool will alter the diameter only fractionally by using very light pressure.

Egg Cup Tool: As shown in Fig. A230, a radiused end replaces the two distinct cutting edges of the previous tool. It enables egg cups to be cleaned out neatly, and to

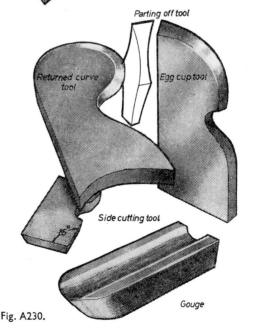

Parting off tool

Returned curve tool

Egg cup tool

Side cutting tool

Gouge

Fig. A230.

some extent ensures that successive cups are identical, the tool acting as a pattern. (Most egg cups are turned far too small; the inside diameter should be 1¾ in.).

Returned Curve Tool: Where the sides of a bowl 'return', as they may well do on a sugar bowl to help prevent spilling the contents, this tool (Fig. A230) is designed to clean out that awkward interior. When these last three tools are being ground to shape, care must be taken not to make the 'necks' too narrow, thus weakening them unduly and encouraging a rolling action when in use. Increased pressure sideways tends to make the tool roll anti-clockwise since the tool rest is usually under the narrow neck.

Gouge: This group of tools, an example being shown in Fig. A230, has been left to the last because, although they are of prime importance to the professional craftsman, most amateurs can well do without them. However, one round-nosed gouge about ¾ in. wide and bevelled at 35–40 deg., should be included, if only for roughing cuts. It is used in a similar manner to the cutting chisel, the bevel being allowed to rub on the revolving work and the sides of the gouge doing most of the work. A scraping action with the tool held horizontally and the tip doing the cutting is also possible and, indeed, to be recommended whist the work is still irregular, a true cutting action being undertaken when the work becomes cylindrical.

General Tips on Wood Turning

Make sure all work is securely mounted; rotate by hand before starting up the motor.

Move the rest before glasspapering and let fingers trail in the direction of rotation.

Brush polish (6 oz. orange shellac dissolved in 1 pint of meths.) will help to produce a better finish. After glasspapering, apply the brush polish and leave to dry. Re-glasspaper until the swollen grain is again perfectly smooth and then polish with carnauba wax.

When turning between centres, squirt two or three drops of oil on to the end grain touching the tailstock. This reduces friction and possible burning.

Never use a hammer directly on the fork centre to fork it into the end grain. This forms a burr which will prevent the efficient working of the Morse-tapered headstock.

Use a felt or plywood washer between the headstock spindle and face plate. This helps to prevent seizing in the contact of metal to metal and makes for easier removal.

Olive oil may be used as a finish for salad bowls.

Many timber merchants supply miscellaneous bundles of off-cuts suitable for turning. Make enquiries locally; 10s. worth will provide materials for many hours' interesting work.

POWER TOOLS

Power tools, either combination bench units or electric drills plus accessories, should show any householder a profit on what they cost. They can do this by saving time (and so enabling more work to be done) and by imparting a professional accuracy which allows more important jobs to be tackled with confidence.

Electric Drill

The portable electric drill is, perhaps, the first power tool the handyman will handle, probably when undertaking some job around the house or on the car; or, if he is lucky, as a gift from his wife who anticipates getting some of the outstanding jobs done around the house!

First of all then, let's have a look at the drill itself. It's always a wise man who knows something of the tool he is using.

On the market today are various makes of drills—and they are usually listed as having a chuck capacity of ¼ in. to ½ in., the most popular being the one having a chuck capacity of 5/16 in. or ⅜ in.—that is, it will take a normal metal twist drill of that size. Of course, its drilling capacity on wood will be considerably more, depending on the type of drill used and providing the shank will fit the drill chuck.

A typical portable electric drill is shown in the diagram Fig. A231. It is powered by a small universal (A.C./ D.C.) electric motor, which is located in the body of the drill and geared to drive the chuck at a speed between 2,500 r.p.m. and 3,200 r.p.m.; some have a choice of two speeds, the change of speeds being effected by a small lever at the front of the drill. This naturally gives the tool

greater flexibility in use. From the mechanical point of view, very little maintenance is required, although it is a good idea to unscrew the gear box and repack with grease, should the drill be doing a great deal of work. On the electrical side, a certain amount of regular inspection is necessary to keep the drill in running order. The main shaft of the motor carries the armature; fitted to the end of this is the commutator, which consists of a number of copper segments, to which are connected the windings of the armature. In most modern drills, these connections are welded, but in many earlier types they were soldered, and this is where trouble can occur. Making contact with the commutator are two carbon brushes, which allow the electric current to pass through the windings of the armature. Should these carbon brushes wear or become loaded with dust and dirt, excessive sparking will occur. This will cause the motor to heat excessively and in drills with soldered connections a disconnection may occur on the commutator, the centrifugal force throwing the solder out. Greater sparking will follow and eventually complete stoppage or a burn-out will occur. With the welded motor this is not likely to happen.

Another thing which will cause sparking and overheating is overloading—forcing it to overwork. If a drill jams in a hole, switch off and free it manually. Investigation of various complaints about electric drills invariably shows that the fault has been with the user. If the drill is used in the manner for which it was designed, it will give very long service.

Many of the drills on the market require only two connections and can be plugged into a normal electric

Fig. A231. A typical portable electric drill.

A. Switch   E. Field Coil
B. Armature   F. Gears
C. Commutator   G. Chuck
D. Brushes   H. Cooling Fan

Fig. A232. Drill points.
Above—Drill points for various materials. **A** for general use up to medium steel. **B** for hard metals and plastics, slow cutting. **C** for cast iron, hard copper, fibre. **D** for soft materials, wood, aluminium, etc. (Note small angle of **B**.)

Below—Bits for wood. **A** Jennings pattern; spurs at X and cutters at Y. **B** centre bit for large holes. **C** metal-working bit ground solely for woodworking. **D** flat quick-bore type.

lampholder, because the electric motor is completely insulated from the case and handle. These are usually advertised as being double-insulated. On types which are not double-insulated, a third wire, the earthing wire, is provided and this must be connected to a three-pin plug and socket which is correctly earthed. Failure to do this can render the drill dangerous in use, particularly in wet situations, or when used out-of-doors.

Drilling Holes: Before drilling holes in metal, centre-punch the point where you wish to make the hole. This will prevent the drill from wandering. Apply only sufficient pressure with the drill to enable the drill to cut. If your metal drill is correctly sharpened, this will not be too difficult. If too much pressure is applied, particularly with the drill running between 2,000 r.p.m. and 3,000 r.p.m., the resultant heat will spoil the drill point and probably damage the electric drill itself. Always use lubrication on the point of the drill when drilling any metal except brass; soluble oil, paraffin or turpentine would be suitable. If you are using a large drill, to the maximum capacity of the drill chuck, do not apply continuous pressure, but ease off the pressure slightly from time to time to avoid overloading. A steady pressure *is* required, however, when using a masonry bit, otherwise the bit will rub and quickly lose its cutting edge; and

remove the bit completely from the hole to clear away dust and chippings, at intervals. Never use a lubricant for drilling masonry.

When drilling glazed tiles, in lieu of a centre-punch, place the drill point on the spot to be drilled and apply pressure before switching on the drill. The point will then penetrate the glaze and will not skate across the surface when the drill is switched on.

Drilling holes in wood, of course, is a simple matter, providing you are using the correct type of bit. For small holes, ordinary metal drills can be used, providing the tip is ground to a point or spur. Another good boring bit is the flat type, which has balanced cutters and which scrapes rather than bores. The big advantage of this type is that it only cuts whilst pressure is being applied.

Sharpening Drills: It must be emphasised that to enable the work to be done efficiently, and to minimise the damage to the power drill, all bits and cutters must be kept sharp and clean. Drills for metal cutting are made of high tensile steel and must be sharpened on a grindstone, maintaining the original angle and shape of the cutting point. Fig. A232 shows drill points for various materials. It will be seen that for hard material the point of the drill differs from that for soft. Accurate drill grinding is quite an acquired skill, but the average reader will be able to make a reasonable job of it, along these basic lines.

Wood-boring bits must have different treatment. One of the first essentials is to keep the bits clean and well polished. If this is done, the chips of wood will be easily ejected, whereas if the bit is rusty or dirty the chips will clog and burn and, in large diameter holes, cause considerable overloading of the power drill. Steel wool will keep the bits clean and bright and a wipe over with thin oil will keep them in good condition. Also shown are

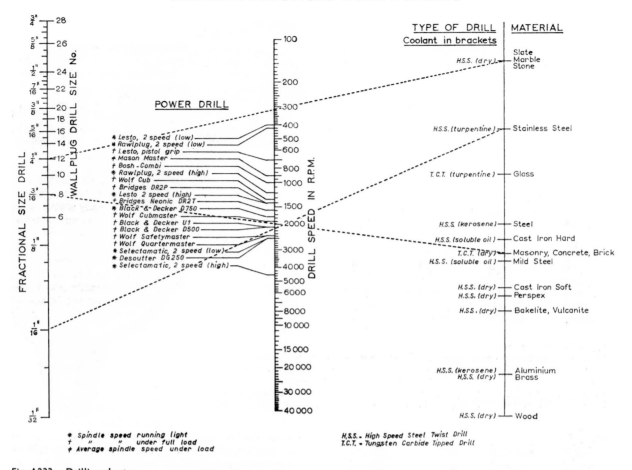

Fig. A233. Drilling chart.
N.B. Not shown in the above table is the GrenCo 2 speed drill, with no-load speed of 4,500 and 2,500 r.p.m. and low speed capacities of up to $\frac{5}{16}$ in. in steel and $1\frac{1}{4}$ in. in wood with suitable spindle attachment.

several typical wood-boring bits and their various uses. Sharpening is done by filing, as the metal is mild steel and comparatively soft. A small half-round file and a small square or triangle file will do the trick.

The two points which must be sharpened are the spur and the cutting tips. For just touching up the cutting edge, the filing is done on the inside of the flutes; if they need complete sharpening, the outside or top of the cutting edge is filed, making every endeavour to maintain the original edge. The spurs on the auger or Jennings-type bit must be sharpened on the inside, not on the outside, otherwise the overall diameter of the bit will be reduced at the cutting point. Scraper bits, such as the speed-bore type, are very easily sharpened but it is important to maintain the original cutting angle. Some of these bits are of hardened steel and may have to be ground to shape.

Do not try to drill holes above 1 in. in diameter, in wood, unless your drill has a variable speed to give slow shaft-speed. With a normal direct-drive drill of 2,500–3,500 r.p.m. the speed is too great for large-diameter boring, and it would be preferable to use a hand brace. This is also true for the drilling of, say, a ¼ in. hole in slate or marble, as will be seen from the chart, Fig. A233.

Drill Chart: This chart gives some useful information on the use of drills, and shows the rated speeds of a number of power drills. To obtain the correct speed for drilling any material lay a straight edge across the chart be-

tween the drill size on the left-hand scale and the material on the right-hand scale. Read off the optimum speed from the centre scale. One dotted line shows, for example, that to drill a 1/16 in. hole in stainless steel the ideal drilling speed is just over 2,000 r.p.m. It also shows that a high-speed twist drill is required, and that the correct coolant is turpentine.

Similarly, another dotted line shows that to make a hole in concrete or brick to receive a No. 8 Rawlplug, a 3/16 in. tungsten-carbide tipped (masonry) drill, rotated at about 2,000 r.p.m. and used dry (without coolant) would be correct.

Of course, no fine control is provided over the speed of the drill; but speed is by no means critical in other than repetitive factory processes. Thus, any of the small power drills on the market could be used effectively in either of the examples cited. If you have a speed-change attachment for your drill, however, you have a wider range of speeds and you can choose that nearest to the theoretically-correct one.

Where very low speeds are required—say below about 500 r.p.m.—it is often better to use a hand brace unless a special type of power drill is available.

The commercial twist drill is tempered for average conditions and can handle the great majority of drilling jobs giving good results on either hard or soft materials, but to get the maximum efficiency and full life its speed would be determined by the material and the drill size. The cutting edges break down quickly with too much speed, whereas insufficient speed greatly increases the risk of breakage.

Tungsten-carbide tipped glass drills should only be used for drilling glass, china, pottery, vitrolite and the like; tungsten-carbide tipped masonry drills are for drilling all types of masonry, brick, concrete and so on.

Drilling Mortices: Cutting mortice slots in wood with the drill is pretty straightforward without a morticing attachment, although, naturally enough, it is simplified if you are lucky enough to possess a drill stand such as manufacturers supply for their drills. The procedure is as follows. First of all, mark out the mortice with a pencil or a marking gauge. Then, preferably with a wood-boring bit the diameter of which is equal to the width of the mortice, make a series of holes along the length of the mortice. Hold the wood in a vice whilst boring the holes. The slot is then cleaned out with an ordinary woodworkers' chisel. If all the mortices are marked out together, holding them in a vice enables you to do all the boring at once.

This raises an important point with power tools. To get the maximum amount of use from any power tool, it is advisable to follow an organised system of working. When your tool is set up for, let us say, drilling ¼ in. holes, do all the ¼ in. holes you have to do. One of the big disadvantages of any tool which relies on attachments for its flexibility is the time consumed by the changing-over process—so do all similar jobs at one time. A little elementary time-and-motion study will lead to an efficiently-run workshop.

Power Saws

In any home workshop, the most useful light machine the handyman can instal is probably the circular saw. It may be as an attachment to the portable electric drill or combination woodworking machine, or even a self-powered machine tool. Whatever the arrangement you have or propose to have, the basic principles of using and maintaining the tool apply, so first of all, let us consider the requirements.

When choosing a circular saw, buy the best you can afford, and preferably one of reputable make. You will then have no trouble with after-sales service and obtaining spares and accessories.

The first essential is a substantial table which is perfectly flat and rigid. It must have a rip fence which is easily adjustable and which can be securely locked in any position. Some of the better makes of saw benches have a micrometer adjustment to the fence which facilitates very accurate sawing. It is preferable, if the fence is adjustable in alignment, that it is always parallel with the saw blade. There is also the question of having either the table or the saw blade adjustable to a tilt of 45 degrees. Usually the combination of fixed saw table with a tilting blade is more expensive than a tilting table with a fixed blade, but the extra expense is justified because the working surface of the table, always remaining level, permits full control over the work at all times.

The next requirement will be a mitre and mitre-groove, thus enabling you to cut at any angle and to make such things as picture frames quite easily. Just one point here : though the mitre fence is calibrated in degrees, and although this should be accurate, it is always advisable to check it with relation to the saw blade, with a set square and protractor. Small discrepancies don't really matter a lot for rough work, but if, for example, a pic-

ture frame is being made when four angles or mitres of 45 degrees have to be cut, then should there be an error of 1 or 2 degrees on your mitring you will seee daylight through the corners of your picture frame. To minimise any error with your rip fence and mitre gauge, set your saw bench up in the following manner and all will be well.

First of all, set your mitre fence at zero and place an engineer's square against the mitre fence and saw blade, then adjust the position of the table, which is usually bolted to the saw table frame, so that the saw blade and mitre fence are at exactly 90 degrees. When this point has been established, securely tighten up the holding-down bolts or screws of the saw table. Next to receive attention is the rip fence which, as already stated, must be parallel to the saw blade. Most rip fences are bolted or screwed together, so if any adjustment is needed, just slacken off these screws and, with a parallel piece of wood or an ordinary wooden rule placed between the fence and the saw blade, tighten up the fence so that it is touching the straight edge along the entire length and at the same time holding the straight edge lightly against the saw blade. Now all is set up; if you refer to Fig. A234 you will see the main points covered.

Saw Blades: Now what about the saw blade itself? There are three blades which you will most likely come across. They are the rip, cross-cut and novelty or planer blade. Fig. A235 shows the profile of these three. The most common type fitted to saw benches and drill attachments is the rip saw which, as the name implies, is designed for cutting with the grain of the wood. The teeth are so designed that they easily clean the sawdust from the cut or, to name it correctly, the kerf. This type of blade is easily maintained in serviceable condition, because with a relatively small number of teeth it is easily and quickly touched up with a saw file. Always remember to maintain the original shape of the teeth when sharpening. The cross-cut saw has teeth arranged very similar to a normal handsaw, and as there are more of

Fig. A234 (*above*).

Fig. A235 (*below*).

Fig. A236.

SET OF SAW

TEETH SHARPENED IN DIRECTION OF SET

Fig. A237. Rip-sawing using a push stick.

Fig. A238. Cross-cutting.

MITRE GAUGE CLOSED POSITION

MITRE GAUGE OPEN POSITION

Fig. A239. The mitre gauge.

Below left—The gauge used in the closed position. Note the position of the hands and how the saw cuts with the grain.

Below right—Gauge used in the open position.

them than in the rip saw, it cuts much cleaner but slower. In sharpening this blade, both the back and the front of the teeth are sharpened, and to maintain the correct cutting edge, the teeth are filed with the file pointing slightly upwards or at about 80 degrees to the face of the blade. Fig. A236 shows the correct tooth slope after sharpening. Although used for cross-cutting, this does not mean that you must keep on changing over blades whilst setting about a particular job. Naturally enough, if you are doing just general rough sawing the rip saw will be found the best, but if your work requires a finer cut then use the cross-cut saw. For really fine work, where a perfectly smooth cut is required, the novelty or planer blade should be used; but unless you have a lot of use for this type of saw blade, you may not think its extra expense is justified. It is not usual for drill attachments to use this type of blade and they are very seldom supplied with one. This only briefly covers the three main types of blade; there are others, some being slight variations of the rip and cross cut.

Maintenance and Usage: The circular saw, owing to its speed, cuts a large amount of wood in a short time, so frequent touching up with a file is very important. Sooner or later the blades will require gulleting and setting, but if you have a fair amount of patience this can be carried out quite reasonably. Saw-set pliers can be used for the cross-cut and planer blades to renew the set, but the rip saw is best done with a gate-type saw-set and saw-set gauge as these teeth are spring set.

Now, what about using the saw? Having set the machine up as described, take a piece of wood and commence to cut it down its entire length. This is where caution is the watchword, so mind your hands. Make yourself a push-stick as shown in Fig. A237, or a number of different shaped push-sticks for special jobs. Use these to push the work past the saw blade. With long lengths of wood, use your hands up to the edge of the saw bench only; then take a push-stick and finish the cut. When cross-cutting, hold the wood securely with both hands on each side of the blade (Fig. A238), keeping your thumbs out of the way at the back of the work, the fingers holding the front of the work pulling slightly outwards, so that as the cut nears completion, there is no tendency to trap the saw blade. To cut pieces of wood at right angles, or at any other angle, use the mitre gauge. The gauge is first set to the angle required and the work held against the mitre gauge with both hands; that is, both hands will be to the side of the saw, keeping the rip fence well out of the way. Now follow through with the cut. For cutting angles of say 45 degrees, the mitre gauge can be used in either the open or closed position, as shown in Fig. A239. In the open position the saw cuts against the grain, and in the closed position it cuts with the grain, which is really the best position. When using the mitre gauge, there is a tendency for the work to creep towards the blade, so hold the work securely and advance the work to the saw slowly.

If the saw is fitted with a guard, use it wherever possible. There are cases where the nature of the work will not allow it, such as when cutting tenons, so watch those hands and use a tenoning jig, which is one of the gadgets and attachments you can make at home (details are given later; Fig. A248 refers). If you wear a tie, make sure it does not hang out over your work—tuck it in your shirt or take it off. Always carry through with the cut, don't pull back half way through a cut, particularly with small pieces of timber. You will probably trap the blade and find your hand dangerously near the blade. Don't allow odd pieces to accumulate on the saw table; they will vibrate gradually towards the blade, then 'ping', an odd piece may whizz past your ear, or worse.

Operation: Now, just a word or two about the saw speed. A lot is written about theoretical speeds in feet per minute, but most of us have to put up with the speeds we have. If you are an electric-drill user, you will be governed by the drill speed, which will probably be a long way from the theoretical speed at which the saw should run. This cannot be helped as sawing is only one of its uses, so keep the saw blade sharp and don't force the saw to cut. Where variable speed is available, as with a belt-and-pulley-driven saw, an 8 in. saw should run at about 2,500 r.p.m. for the best results, although this is only about half of the theoretical speed.

A Simple Project: The home handyman is always very anxious to put his tools to work to make something useful, so here is a simple project which will be found very easy to make and can be completed in an evening. It is a pair of 'antique' wall brackets as shown in the illustration (Fig. A240).

For these, which are best made in oak, scrap pieces will do; say from old beams, as they will look fine in the natural old oak colour. First of all, cut up some pieces 1½ in. square. For the single bracket, one piece 4½ in. long and for the double bracket, one piece 7½ in. long and one of 3½ in. Now from some 1 in. or ¾ in. stock, cut two pieces for the back plates, 3 in. × 6 in. Finally, for the lamp holders, out of some 2½ in. × ½ in., cut three pieces of 2½ in. square. Fig. A241 shows the parts for the double bracket. To cut the back plates and lamp holder pieces use the mitre gauge as already described.

Holes are now drilled in the back plates as shown. In each plate drill two ⅜ in. holes half-way through followed by two ⅛ in. for fixing screws and dowel plugs. In the centre, drill one hole of 1 in. diameter. Now drill a 1 in. hole in the centre of the 7½ in. piece, and two ½ in. holes at either end, as shown. These last two holes can be cut with a slot mortiser bit as shown in Fig. A242, if you have the equipment. Similarly, the 4½ in. piece should have a ½ in. hole drilled at one end to a depth of about 1 in.

Using a 5/16 in. or ¼ in. wood boring bit, drill the 7½ in. piece from both of the ½ in. holes to the 1 in. centre hole. This is to take the flex. The 4 in. is also drilled along through the centre to meet the ½ in. hole. Drill also a 5/16 in. hole from end to end through the centre of the 3½ in. piece. The three 2½ in. square pieces are drilled in the centre to 5/16 in. to take the brass pillar nipples for the lamp holders, and two ⅛ in. counter-sunk holes on either side for fixing to the arms. You will notice that when your tool is set up for drilling holes, you drill all the holes required in the various parts. Similarly, all the sawing is done together. Time and motion study, again!

The fitting of the arms to the back-plate may call for some improvisation. You could turn a 1 in. pin on the lathe at the end of the 4½ in. piece and at both ends of the 3½ in. piece; but, of course, you could cut it by hand or even sand it to fit. Or, depending on your equipment and know-how, mortice and tenon could be used. The next job is to sand all parts smooth (Fig. A243) and put on the 'antique' look. This latter can be done with a hand chisel, **or** as shown in the illustration (Fig. A244)

Fig. A240. Single and double antique wall brackets.

Fig. A241. Double bracket parts.

Fig. A242. Cutting a hole for the flex with a slot mortising bit.

Fig. A243. Cleaning up the back plate on a small sanding drum. The drum is a turned wooden disc about 4 in. dia. with sandpaper cemented to the outside.

Fig. A244. Putting in the 'antique' effect.

Fig. A245. The double bracket showing the parts before and after assembly.

Fig. A246. Height of saw is adjusted to give a depth equal to tenon.

Fig. A247. A wide piece of timber screwed to the fence helps to steady the work.

using a small sanding drum made from wood. The sandpaper is stuck on with impact glue.

Assembly is simple. Fig. A245 shows the parts for the double bracket before and after assembly. Run in the flex and screw on the lamp plates, having first fitted the brass pillar nipples. Glue the single arm into the back plate, the 3½ in. short arm into the 7½ in. arm (threading the flex through), and finally glue into the back-plate.

Apply one coat of dark oak stain; allow to dry. Then apply one coat of sealer, and sand when dry with number O glasspaper. Finish with dark oak wax polish or shoe polish applied with a brush, and there you are—'antique' wall brackets.

Cutting Tenons: Let us assume that you are making a small table or stool and you wish to cut the tenons in the four rails (the horizontal members between the legs). The tenon on all four pieces will be the same length and width, so it is only necessary to mark out one piece of wood. This is done with a pencil and square, the depth and thickness of the tenon being marked at each end of one piece of wood. The saw is then adjusted to give a depth of cut equal to the length of the tenon (Fig. A246).

This will mean either adjusting the height of the table or the height of the saw, depending on the type of saw bench you have. With the type of equipment most handymen have, it generally means adjusting the table. Next adjust the position of the rip fence so that the saw will cut on the waste side of the marked tenon. Now here's where we can do with a slight modification to the rip fence. It will be found much easier to hold the work against the fence if a wide piece of wood is first screwed to it, as shown in Fig. A247. This will give the wood added support as it is passed vertically over the saw blade.

Should you want to get a step further and make yourself a tenoning jig, then the set up shown in Fig. A248 will come in useful for all sorts of sawing jobs. Having cut the first half of the tenon, carry on and cut the remaining three pieces of wood. Then reset the position of the rip fence or tenoning jig for the second cut and carry on as before. If the tenons are in the centre of the ends of the wood, no particular order of cutting is required, of course.

The next stage is to cut off the shoulders (Figs. A249 and A250). Here again it is a good idea to cramp a parallel piece of scrap wood to the rip fence with a G-cramp, extending from the front of the saw bench to a point about an inch or so past the front edge of the saw blade. This will prevent the off-cuts being jammed between the fence and the blade and causing injury. Now set up the rip fence to give your correct cut-off position between the saw blade and the piece of wood which is clamped to the fence. Set the height of the saw to give you the correct depth of cut and pass the wood over the blade using the mitre fence set at 90 degrees or zero, both hands holding the work firmly to the mitre fence.

Although the whole operation of cutting tenons can be carried out on the saw bench as described, some people prefer to cut off the shoulder with a tenon saw, and for very fine work this is to be preferred, as the circular saw tends to tear out at corners.

Wobble Saw: Should you desire to do rebates and grooves on the saw bench you will need a wobble saw. With most drill attachment saws, the ordinary saw is

Fig. A248. A tenoning jig.

Fig. A249. First stage in cutting off the shoulders of a tenon.

Fig. A250. Second stage in cutting off tenon shoulders.

Fig. A251. Passing the work over the blade when rebating.

Fig. A252. Follow through with a push stick.

Fig. A253. A combing jig.

Fig. A254. First stage of comb jointing.

Fig. A255. The first cut in comb jointing.

Fig. A256. One end of work completed.

Fig. A257 (left). Starting to cut the matching side.

Fig. A258 (right). Completed joint.

used with tapered washers to give the blade the required wobble. One slight disadvantage of using an ordinary saw blade is that it tends to flex, particularly when cutting wide grooves in hardwood. The wobble-saw used with other saw benches is a much stiffer affair and has tapered washers which are graduated, thus simplifying the initial setting up. Let us now assume that you want to cut a rebate in a length of wood. First of all, set the blade by slackening off the fixing nut and adjusting the wobble washers to give 1/32 in. more than the finished width of cut. Adjust the height of the saw to the required depth of the rebate. Now screw a sub-face of soft wood to the working side of the rip fence, to prevent damaging the saw blade against the fence. Bring up the fence so that the saw just commences to cut into the wooden sub-fence. This is why 1/32 in. extra is allowed in the wobble of the saw. The work is then passed over the blade, making good use of a push-stick, Figs. A251 and A252. One further point here is to run the saw at a slower speed than for normal cutting, because of excess vibration set up by the throw of the saw blade. Of course, if you are using a saw powered by an electric drill with a fixed speed, you will just have to exercise a little more care.

For cutting grooves in such wood as multi-ply panels, the procedure is exactly the same as for rebating with the wobble-saw. If you haven't a wobble-saw and you wish to cut rebates, etc. the ordinary saw will do. The rebate is cut by first setting the saw blade to the required depth, and the fence to the width of the rebate; a single cut is then made down the length of the work. The rip fence is then brought a little closer to the blade and a second cut is made. Carry on like this, until the whole of the rebate is cut. Grooving is carried out in a similar manner.

Box Combing: The next exercise with the wobble-saw, and one that is a real time-saver, is box combing. This process enables you to cut all the joints for a drawer or box in next to no time, once you have got the idea. If you have watched handicraft demonstrations, no doubt you have been fascinated by the speed and ease with which this is carried out by the experts. Well, once you know the knack, there is nothing to it. First of all we must have a combing jig. Different manufacturers vary their products slightly, but the principle remains the same. The accompanying illustration shows the method carried out on a Coronet Minorette, but the Stanley-Bridges attachment is very similar.

Let us now look at the attachment itself and see how to set it up, referring to Fig. A253. A small insert of wood, A (called a shear block), is provided to prevent the work splitting out when passed over the saw. B, and C, are adjustable fingers, which are for setting the width of the cut and the distance from the face edge of the work to the beginning of the cut. To make the joint, we will assume that the cut is to be 5/16 in., which is a fair average for this type of work. It is suggested that two pieces of scrap wood are used for the initial setting up. The wood for the work is prepared to the required lengths and the ends cut absolutely square. This is most important. When cutting to length, allow an extra 1/32 in. on each piece for the final sanding. Now set the wobble-saw to the required width; in this case it is to be a 5/16 in cut. Check this with a trial cut on a scrap of wood. Adjust the height of the saw above the bench to the thickness of the wood, again allowing 1/32 in. for sanding. Next, adjust finger C, so that the distance between

it and the saw is equal to the width of the cut. The wobble-saw must be turned so that it is leaning towards the finger C, of course. Now place the trial cut over B and C, and adjust B so that the two fingers are a snug fit in the cut. The combing jig is now set up for work (Fig. A254).

Before commencing to comb the joints on your box or drawer, mark the opposite sides. With one of the pieces of wood held firmly to the jig and against finger C, commence the cut (Fig. A255). Place the first cut so as to embrace fingers B and C and make a second cut. Now carry on until the entire width of the work is combed (Fig. A256). To comb the other end of this piece turn it end-for-end, Keep the face edge towards the finger, C, and proceed as before. Repeat this operation on the piece of wood that is going to the opposite end of the drawer or box. To make the mating sides to those already combed, reverse the first piece of wood so that the first cut that was made embraces fingers B and C, and bring the mating piece to it as shown in Fig. A257 face-edge to face-edge, and continue to comb this latter piece. Repeat this with the opposite end, turning it end-for-end. The final piece of wood is completed in a similar manner. If the jig is set up correctly, the joints should be a good tight fit (Fig. A258). Finally, sand all round, particularly the ends of the work. If a combed joint is well made it should not be possible to pull it apart without a good blow from a mallet. The foregoing instructions hold good for a four-sided frame where all the sides are of the same thickness, but in the case of a drawer the front member should be of slightly thicker material. In this case, allowance will have to be made to cut one end of each drawer, with the length of the combs equal to the extra thickness of the cut member. To facilitate this, the height of the saw will have to be adjusted to cut this extra length

Another Project: Instructions have already been given for making a pair of antique wall brackets. To complete the set, here is a fairly straightforward four-arm chandelier to match (Fig. A259). First of all, cut one piece of wood, preferably oak 12 in. × 2 in. × 2 in., four pieces 8½ in. × 1½ in. × 1¼ in., and plane them square. Now cut four squares 2½ in. × 2½ in. out of a piece of ⅜ in. × 2½ in. wood and finally four pieces 6 in. × ⅝ in. × ⅝ in., cutting the ends of these to 45 degrees with the circular saw and mitre fence.

Now take the 12 in. piece and cut a 1½ in. mortice on each of the four sides at a point about 2 in. from one end. Cut these mortices right through, or at least arrange for them to meet in the centre. Now drill a 5/16 in. hole down from the top through the centre to meet at the centre of these mortices to take the wiring. You will find that a parrot-nose bit, which is obtainable up to about 12 in. long, will do this job quite easily if care is taken in starting off the drilling operation. Now drill another hole, 1 in. in diameter, from the centre of the bottom end again to meet the mortices. This is to facilitate making the electric connections.

The arms, which are made from the 8½ in. pieces, have to have a tenon cut at one end. It need only be about ½ in. long but make it so that is a tight fit in the mortices already cut in the centre column. Now at a point 1 in. from the opposite end to the tenon, drill a ½ in. hole to a depth of 1 in. and also a 5/16 in. hole through the tenon and the centre of the piece to meet it. This drilling business is simple if you apply the work to the drill which must be held securely in the vice or stand. If the wood

Fig. A259. Components of an 'antique' candelabra.

5/16" CENTRE HOLE

CENTRE COLUMN 12"X2"X2"

4 PIECES 2½"X2½"X½"

ARMS MORTICED AND TENONED TO CENTRE COLUMN

4 ARMS 8½"X1½"X1¼"

4 STRUTS 6"X⅝"X⅝"

1" DIA HOLE

SMALL PLATE TO COVER HOLE

Fig. A260. Rabbeter attachment in use with a two-speed drill.

ADJUSTMENT SCREW

SAW BLADE

REQUIRED DEPTH OF CUT

GUIDE PLATE

REQUIRED DISTANCE OF CUT FROM FACE OF WOOD

WOOD IN POSITION FOR FIRST CUT

Fig. A261. First stage in cutting a rebate with rabbeting attachment.

ADJUSTMENT SCREW

SAW BLADE

FIRST CUT

WOOD IN POSITION FOR SECOND CUT

Fig. A262. Second stage in cutting a rebate.

is rotated slowly whilst drilling you can soon see if you are drilling straight or not; this may sound a bit like Heath Robinson, but it works quite well. The four 2½ in. square pieces are next drilled as follows: a 5/16 in. hole in the centre of each piece to take the pillar nipple for fixing the lampholder, and two ⅛ in. holes countersunk on either side of this for fixing to the arms.

The next stage is to scallop the edges of all the pieces to give that 'old' look including the four mitred pieces. This can be done with a sanding disc or by hand with a gouge. To assemble, screw a brass nipple in to each of the 2½ in. square pieces and one into the end of the centre column, to which is added a ½ in. female hook. You can get these from a electrical shop or handicraft store. Thread flex in to each of the arms, glue them into the mortices of the centre column and allow to set.

Next screw on the four lampholder plates to the ends of the arms, threading the flex through as you do so. A 2 ft. length of flex is then passed through the centre column and connected in parallel to the four arms with a small 2-way electric connector (all the reds together and all the blacks together). The 1 in. hole in the base will facilitate this.

The four mitred pieces are then pinned to the arms and centre column to give a more pleasing effect. If preferred, these pieces can be fixed with screws which are recessed, the screw heads then being covered with small wooden pegs. All that remains now is to fit a small square of wood, which has had the corners sanded off, over the 1 in. hole in the base of the centre column to cover the electrical connections.

Finish the project with a coat of dark-oak stain followed by a brush coat of shellac sealer when dry. When the sealer coat in dry, give a light rub over with number o glass paper and polish with a good wax polish. If you have made the fitting from different types of wood, you will find a water stain will give a more uniform colouring. As woods vary a lot in texture, an oil stain, such as Colron, will darken softer woods more that hard ones. On the other hand, all woods will accept water stains since water is natural to all woods. Water stains will raise the grain somewhat, so further sanding will be required before applying a sealer coat.

Rabbeter Attachment: We have already discussed the cutting of rebates and grooves using a wobble saw. For those whose sole power unit is an electric drill there is a very useful attachment which will do this job very well. It is the Arcoy Rabbeter (Fig. A260) which consists of a very small saw blade set in a holder and adjustable for cut by the insertion of wobble washers which are supplied with the attachment to give various widths of cut; because of the small diameter of the saw there is no tendency for the blade to flex when cutting grooves, etc.

To set the attachment for cutting grooves, first of all set the saw position to the desired depth of cut, then set the saw guide until the saw is the desired distance from the edge of the wood, as shown in Fig. A261. Make a second cut as shown in Fig. A262 and the rebate is completed. Should you want to make a slot in the wood to take a thin plywood panel it may be done in a similar manner, except that the position of the saw blade from the saw guide will have to be adjusted after each cut until the desired width is cut. For any groove of ⅛ in. and over, use the saw with the wobble washers.

Also available for this attachment are a variety of moulding cutters which will make easy work of putting a fancy bead on your wood. When using moulding cutters it is advisable to adjust the position of the cutters

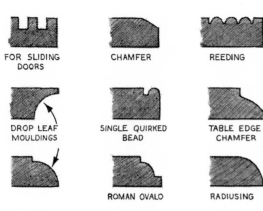

FOR SLIDING DOORS CHAMFER REEDING

DROP LEAF MOULDINGS SINGLE QUIRKED BEAD TABLE EDGE CHAMFER

ROMAN OVALO RADIUSING

Fig. A263. Mouldings produced by the Arcoy series of moulding cutters used in the attachment.

Fig. A264. Components of a planing machine.

FENCE

REAR TABLE FRONT TABLE

ROTOR WITH THREE CUTTERS

so that only light cuts are made. Several cuts are made along the work, each time adjusting the position of the cutter until a point is reached when the moulding is completed. Fig. 263 gives you details of various types of mouldings, cutters for which are available for this particular attachment; providing your electric drill gives you a speed of over 2,000 r.p.m. a professional finish will result.

Planers

Having had a reasonable look at saws and what you can do with them, the next obvious choice for a power tool is the planing machine. No workshop is really complete without these two items. If you are a weekend woodworker you may think that the expense of a planing machine is not justified, but once you have tried one you will soon appreciate its uses. There are two distinct types of planing machine to be considered—the stationary type, and the portable machine, which is really a powered hand plane. The cutting principle of both machines is the same. First, let's have a look at the stationary machine and see how and why it works.

Stationary Planers: The cutting capacity of a planer is dependent upon the width of the blade; for amateur use, one of $4\frac{1}{2}$ in. or 6 in. will cater for most of the work you will want to take on. The business end of the planer is the cutter head, which consists of a rotor running in ball bearings. Mounted in the rotor are two or three cutting blades which are either clamped or bolted in position. The latter fixing is preferable because bolted cutting blades will not fly out should they become loose. The rotor is driven by an electric motor through a vee-belt driven at a speed which will give about 12,000 cuts per minute. That is, a three-cutter machine will have to rotate at 4,000 r.p.m. and a two-cutter at 6,000 r.p.m. This speed is obtainable by mounting a suitable pulley on the electric motor.

To find the size of the motor pulley, first divide the desired r.p.m. of the rotor by the motor speed. If the motor speed is 1,440 r.p.m. and the rotor has to rotate at approximately 4,000 r.p.m. then the motor pulley will have to be approximately 2.7 times the size of the rotor pulley, that is:—

$$\frac{4,000}{1,444} = 2.7$$

We can call this 3.

Now if the pulley on the planer is 2 in. in diameter, then the pulley on the electric motor will have to be 6 in. in diameter. A simple equation for this is as follows:—

$$\frac{\text{Rotor Speed} \times \text{Rotor Pulley Diameter}}{\text{Motor Speed}} = \text{Motor Pully Size}$$

So much for the cutters. Now let's have a look at the rest of the machine. On either side of the cutter are two adjustable tables; the one leading to the cutter is known as the front table and the other the rear, as shown in Fig. A264; and they should have perfectly flat surfaces.

To set the planer up, first adjust the rear table so that it is exactly level with the tip of the blades. This can be done by holding a straight-edge on the rear table and adjusting the table so that the straight edge is just touched by the cutters when they are rotated by hand. The front table is adjusted to give the desired depth of cut. If these preliminaries have been carried out the planer will cut nice and true. Now take a piece of wood and, with the planer running, pass it over the cutters, carefully observing the following precautions:

Never have either hand directly over the cutters or allow your fingers or thumbs to trail behind on the table: a push-stick should always be used.

These common mistakes showing how planing should *not* be done are illustrated in Figs. A265 and A266.

The wood should first be held with both hands pressing it down on the front table and advancing it on to the cutters, as in Fig. A267. As soon as about 2 in. or 4 in. have passed over the cutters, the left hand is brought over to hold the work down on the rear table and at the same time continuing the forward movement with the right hand, in which is held the push-stick (Fig. A268). If the cutters are sharp, very little effort will be required. Should it prove to be rather hard going, this is some indication that the cutters need attention.

Before commencing to plane any wood always look at the direction of the grain and always endeavour to plane with the grain. Planing against the grain will give a rough finish and tearing will result with some woods. Sometimes planing against the grain cannot be avoided, so in this case advance the work slowly across the cutters. One thing which is most dangerous is planing very small pieces of timber and end grain. Woods which are difficult to plane with a hand plane, such as mahogany and African walnut can be planed quite easily with a machine plane.

If, when planing, the finished work appears to be slightly tapered, this indicates that the rear table is just a trifle too high; on the other hand, if after passing the work over the cutters the end is slightly gouged out, this indicates that the rear table is a shade too low; so before you get down to serious work with your machine, try out few scraps of wood, examine your work for these simple faults and rectify them before getting on to some serious

COMPLETE PRACTICAL WOODWORKING

work. If your work has a slightly wavy finish on the surface this indicates that you have planed the work too quickly. Remember that a planer makes a series of cuts rather than a continuous slice as with a hand plane.

Fitted to the planing machines is an adjustable fence, which should be set at 90 degrees to the tables; although a protractor may be fitted to facilitate this, it should always be checked for truth with a set square. The fence is also adjusted in a horizontal plane; for safety's sake it should be placed so that the work is just covered by the cutters. Besides planing wood flat and true, there are other adaptations to which the planer can be put; for example, cutting straight tapers, tapered legs for tables or chairs. To do this, the front table is lowered to a position equal to the amount of taper required. For instance, if a 2 in. square leg has to be tapered to 1½ in. over the entire length a ¼ in. will have to be removed; that is from zero to ¼ in. at the end of the work. The front table is then lowered to give a ¼ in. cut. This is easily measured if a straight edge is placed on the rear table and the distance between it and the front table noted. The machine is then started up and, with one end of the work resting on the rear table and the other on the front table, the work is then pushed over the cutters using a push-stick (Figs. A269 and A270). If a pencil mark is made on the rear table where the cut is commenced, all four sides of the work will be the same. It must be remembered that as the work progresses over the cutters, the amount of waste removed will increase, so proceed with care and at a slower rate-of-feed to avoid splitting and tearing. For long work it is advisable to fit extension rollers to the machine. For short work which has to be tapered, a small block of wood clamped to the front table will also help to get the tapers all the same length.

Sometimes it may be necessary to stop the taper short of the end of the work to form a foot; in this case the cut is stopped at a marked point on the work as shown in Fig. A271, or, if preferred, at a small wooden stop clamped to the rear table. Care must be taken when lifting the work off the machine; it is advisable to push it back towards you before doing so. Yet another facility is the making of stopped chamfers; here we have to adjust both front and rear tables to give the desired amount of cut. To do this accurately, small wooden stops should be clamped to both front and rear tables to coincide where the chamfer commences and finishes; the stop on the front table will also prevent the work kicking back.

The cut is commenced as follows. The work is placed with one end against the stop on the front table and gradually lowered on to the cutters and then advanced over the cutters until it reaches the stop on the rear table. Chamfers are usually done for decoration on the corners of the work so the fence will have to be canted to 45 degrees. Fig. A272 shows the chamfer being commenced and Fig. A273 shows the completion. Note the use of the push-stick. Don't disregard this repeated reference to the use of a push-stick; it is most important with powered saws and planes to take all safety precautions.

You will notice (in the illustration) that the cutters

Fig. A265.   How *not* to plane—fingers too near cutter.

Fig. A266.   Another how *not* to do it— thumb in danger.

Fig. A267.   How to commence the pass —hands well back.

Fig. A268.   The left hand is carried beyond the danger zone; push stick follows.

Fig. A269.   Cutting a taper—note block of wood clamped to front table for starting all cuts.

Fig. A270.   The final pass in taper cutting—note hand positions and push stick.

Fig. A271 (*above left*). After tapering, work can be done on the foot.

Fig. A272 (*above centre*). Beginning a stopped chamfer; rear table is lowered as well as front to cut depth.

Fig. A273 (*above*). Completing the stopped chamfer; hands clear.

Fig. A274 (*far left*). A self-powered portable planer.

Fig. A275 (*left*). With a planer upside down straight-edge can be used.

Fig. A276 (*below*). A simple project to make.

guard has been removed. This has been done only to illustarte the cutting details more clearly. Wherever practicable, all guards must be fitted when machining.

Rebating: This is another very useful application of the planing machine and the procedure is very simple. It will be noticed from the accompanying illustrations, which, incidentally, are of the Coronet Minorette, that the front table has an extension, which is known as the rebating table. To cut a rebate, first adjust the front table to give the required depth of cut; adjust the position of the fence to give the width of cut; then proceed as for normal planing.

Portable Planers: Another type of planing machine which the home craftsman will find most useful is the portable type of planer which, as already mentioned, is a powered hand-plane (Fig. A274). The cutting principle and general construction is very similar to the bench

version. If the portable plane is turned upside down, the similiarity will be noticed. There is a front table which is adjusted to give the desired depth of cut and a rear table which is set so that it is on the same plane as the cutters. Fig. A275 shows the underside of the planer; with a straight edge resting on the rear table, the actual depth of cut can be measured.

In use the unit should be adjusted to give a cut of about 1/32 in. and the machine switched on before it is put to work. This is most important. Failure to do this will put considerable strain on the driving motor. Once again, if the machine is passed too quickly over the work, the resulting surface will have a wavy appearance. With all planers the condition of the cutters is most important, but the amateur may find the sharpening of cutters a laborious job. With the portable planer such as the Arcoy planer illustrated, a sharpening kit is available which consists of a carborundum stone and a hand guide for holding the cutters. With the bench or stationary machine the cutters can be kept in reasonable condition as follows. Lower the front table to a point where it is level with the bevel of the cutting blades. Now take a medium-grit oil stone and wrap it with a sheet of newspaper, leaving about ½ in. unwrapped. With the stone held down on the front table in such a position that the unwrapped portion will make contact with the bevel of the cutters, lightly hold the cutting blade in contact with the oil stone, by means of the driving pulley, and at the same time move the stone sideways across the front table. In this manner quite a reasonable job can be made. If the cutters are really badly worn then it will be much easier if they are removed completely and taken to the saw doctor at your local saw mill, who will do the job expertly for a few shillings.

A Simple Project: Now, to put all this theory into practice, here is a one-evening project you can make.

Fig. A276 shows the constructional details of a small hanging kitchen cupboard, which, if bought finished, would cost quite a bit, but can be made very cheaply. The sizes shown need not, of course, be adhered to. Perhaps the best material for the amateur to use is plywood or blockboard, although you may prefer solid wood. Using ¾ in. blockboard or ply, cut the two ends 12 in. long, 10 in. wide at one end, tapering to 7 in. at the other. With your planer or circular saw, cut a ⅜ in. rebate in each of the two end pieces, the width of the rebate being equal to the thickness of the wood. Next cut the two boards for top and bottom. They will be 23¼ in. long; one of 10 in. wide, the other 7 in. wide.

Now with the wobble saw set to give just over 3/16 in. cut, cut two grooves ⅜ in. deep in the front edge of the top as shown, and two in the bottom ¼ in. deep. These grooves are to take the doors.

The doors could be made out of 3/16 in. plywood; or better still have them cut out for you from frosted glass, 12 in. square. If they are to be of glass, have a small thumb-hole ground in the face side of each panel. For the back, cut a panel of hardboard 24 in. × 12 in.

Assembly is straightforward. The sides are pinned and glued to the top and bottom. The back is secured with panel pins, and two mirror plates are secured to the top for fixing to the wall. The doors are first lifted up into the top grooves and then lowered into the bottom ones, the top grooves having been made deeper for this purpose. Finally, give a good sanding all round before painting.

TOOL BOXES

A good workman is a man who looks after his tools, but what does the average amateur do with them? He throws them in an old box, and when he wants a certain tool that particular one is always at the bottom. And rummaging through doesn't do them any good either. So why not make a proper toolbox? It's easy and won't take long.

Tool Box No. 1

For the box shown in Fig. A277, start by making up a frame of ⅝ in. × 9 in. prepared timber. Don't forget that timber merchants measure timber before planing; so ⅝ in. × 9 in. will in fact finish about ½ in. × 8¾ in., which is just what we want. Dovetail the sides and top and bottom together as in Fig. A278. Now screw a piece of ¼ in. ply on either side; countersink screws for neatness. No particular sizes are given as these depend on the amount of tools you want to store. As a guide though, the prototype is about 18 in. high and 24 in. long. When you have assembled the box, mark the ends as indicated. Saw along these lines until the two pieces are separate.

You now have two trays as shown. These trays will be hinged in their original position and retained at the top by two case-clips. It is advisable to reinforce the plywood edge with a piece of batten, say ¾ in. × 1 in. prepared (finished size ⅝ in. × ⅞ in.) and screw the hinges on to these pieces of timber.

Now fix a shelf under the top of the box, as wide as the piece that is left.

Drawers: Divide the space in two equal parts to accommodate two little drawers. These are accessible from both

Fig. A277.   The finished tool box.

SHELF FOR DRAWERS

DRAWERS

BASE

STRENGTHEN THIS EDGE
WITH A PIECE OF ¾"X1" BATTEN

PARTITIONING OF
¼" PLYWOOD

Fig. A278.   Component parts of tool box No. 1.

sides. The drawers are easily made from ½ in. × 2 in. prep. or similar material. Make a small frame dovetail, honeycomb, or even ordinary screw and glue fixing will do. Glue a piece of plywood inside this frame to act as a bottom and the drawers are ready. A small piece of batten will do for handles; glue a piece on either side of the drawers.

When all this has been finished, divide the tool box in half by putting a piece of ¼ in. ply in the position shown.

You now have four surfaces on which to fix all your tools with spring clips. Chisels, screwdrivers, pliers, hammers, etc., can all be fixed closely together in the two trays and on the partition. Heavy tools, such as planes, mallets and G-clamps will find a place in the bottom with plenty of room left for the odd tin or box. The two drawers will hold all your drills, bits and other small stuff.

Tool Box No. 2

Another style of tool box is shown in Fig. A279. Sizes may be altered at will and the inside fitted out according to personal preferences.

Good quality, selected materials should be used.

Carcase: This is the cutting list for the carcase: 2 @ 24 in. × 6½ in. × ⅝ in. (finished sizes) softwood; 2 @ 14 in. × 6½ in. × ⅝ in. (finished sizes) softwood; 2 @ 24⅛ in. × 14⅛ in. × ⅜ in. plywood (9mm); 4 @ 3½ in. × ½ in. × 5/16 in. oak (drawer runners).

Figs. A280 and A281 show details of the carcase joints. Either dovetails or a corner housing may be used. The latter is quicker and easier, but the former is much stronger and nothing looks better than a well-cut row of dovetails—but remember, also, that nothing looks worse than a badly-made set of dovetails!

Having made your choice, bear in mind that the cut-away portion of the box (that is, the lid or 'door') demands special attention. It is a good idea to mark the vertical line on the box ends, and, if a housing joint has been chosen, space the nails carefully as shown in Fig. A281 to allow for the saw cut. The top dovetails need a specially-wide pin through which the saw-cut goes. This pin should be at least ⅝ in. wide at its narrowest edge and the slope for dovetails in softwood should be 1 in 6.

Clean up the inside of the box, glue-up and cramp. Check for squareness. If housing joints have been used, cramp vertically and nail as soon as the cramps have pulled the carcase square.

When the glue is dry, clean off the two edges of the box and then fasten on the plywood sides using glue and 1 in. oval nails at about 2½ in. intervals. Clean up the outside of the now closed carcase and mark out the portion to be sawn out.

The sawing out must be done with a very fine-toothed tenon saw. This is laborious, particularly going down the grain of the soft-wood, but must be done with great care. Clean up the sawn edges with care.

Fig. A279. Tool box No. 2.

Fig. A285. Details of brass corners.

Figs. A280 and A281 (*above and below*). Details of the carcase joints.

Fig. A284. Dimensions of handles.

Fig. A282. Details of the drawer construction.

Fig. A283. Side of cabinet showing position of runners.

Sand the sawn-out lid back in place on doubled layer of glasspaper which should restore the top to its original flatness. Now fix the three butterfly hinges using 4 BA nuts and round-headed bolts. Insert one bolt at a time in successive hinges and feel with the finger tips to ensure that the hinged lid is meeting up squarely with the carcase. Six bolts will do for the time being.

Fix a good quality leather handle (suitcase type, which lies flat) with 3/16 in. bolts. Fit a brass box lock. Lock-fitting is not difficult but does require care.

Drawers: Here is the cutting list for each drawer: 1 front ½ in. thick; 2 sides ¾ in. thick; 1 back ⅜ in. thick; 1 bottom ¼ in. (6mm) ply.

Sizes should now be taken from the carcase and the drawers made to fit individually. Fig. A282 shows one method, although there are several others. A simple housing-jointed box is made up, but the sides are grooved to ½ in. × 5/16 in., as shown, before glueing. Strips of wood are screwed to the inside of the carcase, Fig. A283, and the drawers slide in and out on these runners. The back of the top drawer should be ⅜ in. narrower than the back of the bottom drawer to allow clearance when passing under the ends of the bolts securing the handle. Alternatively, the appropriate parts of the top edge of the back of the top drawer may be cut out to provide sufficient clearance.

The drawer joints and the plywood base are glued and nailed. Before doing this, it's a good idea to fix on the handles by means of two 1 in.× No. 6 screws from the inside of the drawer front—these screws are awkward

to insert after the drawers are glued up. Suggested handles are shown in Fig. A284. Fill up all nail holes.

Finishing: The finished job could well be painted black, or you might prefer a varnish-type finish. Dissolve 3 ozs. of brown shellac in ½ pt. of methylated spirits. Stir well and allow to stand over-night. Remove the handle and hinges and glasspaper the whole box. Appy an even coat of the prepared solution with a clean paint brush (1½ in. or 2 in.). This solution is know as brush polish—it is an excellent grain filler and leaves a nice colour. Wait an hour for this to dry and then smooth off with flour grade glasspaper. Give a second coat of brush polish. When applying brush polish make sure that no runs or double thicknesses build up. Rub down the second coat with steel wool. Now apply one coat of Ronseal. This should result in a fine, hardwearing finish. Refix handle and hinges.

Protective Corners: Eight 2¼ in. squares of 18-gauge brass are required for protective corners. Draw diagonals and remove one quarter as shown in Fig. A285. Bend on remaining lines and silver-solder the meeting edge. Clean up, bore holes in each side near to the edge, emery cloth and then buff or polish. Fix in place. Four rubber feet screwed on under the box complete the job.

Tool Hold-all

Jobs about the house and the garden vary a great deal. Equipment of all sorts is wanted. Often one has to return to the workshop many times for some tool or other—for longer nails or larger screws. This hold-all, designed to carry a wide assortment of general necessities, can be taken to the job to save a great deal of time and exasperation.

Figs. A286 and A287 show the hold-all closed and open respectively. You can carry it in one hand and open and shut it in a moment; it is reasonably dust-proof, strong

Fig. A286. The tool hold-all.

HOLE 3⅜"X 1⅜"

CARRYING HANDLE 11"X 2⅛"X ⅝" (PLYWOOD)

CARRYING STAY 10¼"X 1½"X ⅝" (DEAL)

LID SHOWN DOTTED

METAL HANDLE AT EACH END

BASE SLAT

½" THICKNESS SPACER BLOCK FOR BOX CLEARANCES

BASE SLAT

STRÀPS ½"X ⅛" IRON OR MILD STEEL

METAL BOX CORNERS

Fig. A287 (*left*). The component parts.

Fig. A288 (*above*). The cutting layout.

and compact, and has large carrying capacity. Nails, screws, small bolts, nuts, washers, etc., occupy the four 8 in. × 8 in. boxes, while the bottom 16 in. × 8 in. box will hold most of the smaller tools such as tenon saw, hammer, pincers, screwdriver, pliers, two-foot rule, tin snips, pencils, small square, scissors, chalk line etc.

It can, of course, be made to any size to suit individual taste; the one being described measures 16 in. long, 8 in. wide and 7 in. deep excluding carrying handle.

Nearly all essential details for construction can be obtained from the sketches. The drawing (Fig. A288) shows the plan dimensions of the various component parts.

Materials

About 16 ft. prepared deal 2 in. × ½ in.
Two pieces deal each 10¼ in. × 1½ in. × ⅝ in.
One piece ⅝ in. plywood 11 in. × 2⅛ in.
Hardboard about 33 in. × 20 in.
Two metal handles 4 in. × ½ in.
Twenty metal box-corners 2 in. × 2 in.
About 6 ft. iron or mild steel ½ in. × ⅛ in.
28 off 1 in. × 3/16 in. Whitworth R/H bolts
2 off 2 in. × 3/16 in. Whitworth R/H bolts
8 off 1 in. × No. 6 csk wood screws
4 off 1½ in. × No. 8 csk wood screws
A quantity of ½ in. R/H pins
A quantity of ½ in. panel pins
A quantity of 1½ in. panel pins

Boxes: There are five boxes—four 8 in. × 8 in. × 2 in. outside measurement, and one 16 in. × 8 in. × 2 in. These are butt-jointed, glued, and pinned with 1½ in. panel pins at alternate slopes—iron dovetails. Bases are hardboard (smooth side uppermost) glued and pinned with ½ in. panel pins. Bore small holes in the hardboard to receive the pins, otherwise they may bend when being hammered home, as hardboard really is hard. The metal box-corners are fitted with ½ in. round-headed pins.

On the bottom box—the long one—two slats 8 in. × 2 in. × ½ in. are fixed; these act as a base for the hold-all to stand on, conserve the under surface of the hardboard, and also lend support.

The hardboard lid is slightly larger all round, and has two notches cut, top right, to clear the side handles. Opening the hold-all automatically releases the lid which, however, remains quite a firm fit when the boxes are closed.

Handle: The carrying handle is composed of three parts—the handle itself and two side stays. The handle is cut and shaped from ⅝ in. plywood. Obtain a nice smooth finish, particularly to the oval hand grip—it will be uncomfortable to carry if there are any sharp, rough edges. The two stays, each 10¼ in. × 1½ in. × ⅝ in., have a slot cut in the top to carry the handle; these slots are ⅝ in. full wide and 1 in. deep. Through them, and the handle, are bored 3/16 in. holes to take the screws which fasten the two together.

Two filling blocks, each 2 in. × 2 in. × ½ in., are required and are placed between the inside of the stays and the outside surface of the bottom box; these serve to throw the stays away from the boxes and thus give clearance to the steel pivot straps when the hold-all is opened

and shut. The feet of the stays overhang the base of the bottom by ⅜ in.

Divisions: The divisions are entirely arbitrary and should be put in after consideration of what the boxes are intended to hold. We divided the top two boxes into four for an assortment of French and oval nails from 1 in. to 2½ in. The two intermediate boxes were each divided into three, one holding 3 in. and 4 in. nails and odd Whitworth bolts, nuts and washers, the other various wood screws, Nos. 6 and 8 from ¾ in. to 1½ in. long.

The bottom (long) box is best not divided at all since it will contain a variety of the most-used tools.

The divisions can be made from hardboard (not allowed for in the list of materials required), and grooves about 3/16 in. deep should be cut in the sides of the boxes to receive them. Where they cross each other, as in the two top boxes, they should be halved by cutting ⅛ in.-wide slots halfway down each and interlocking them.

The steel pivot straps are, in effect, hinges, and when the side handles are pulled away from the centre, the boxes rise slightly and also move outwards; when fully open they come to rest one on top of the other.

All are made from ½ in. × ⅛ in. mild steel or iron; the shorter ones (eight in number) are 4½ in. long, the longer ones (four in number) being 8 in. long. Round all the ends for the sake of appearance.

A certain amount of care must be taken when drilling them, and also in positioning the corresponding holes in the boxes. If they are not accurate and correctly aligned the boxes will not swing smoothly. All the holes are drilled 3/16 in.

In the boxes, the holes are drilled centrally as to vertical height and 1 in. from each outside edge, but note that the two top boxes have no holes towards the outsides. The centre holes in the four small boxes are 3 in. from the outside ones—mid-way across the box. Similarly, the second holes in the long box are 3 in. from the outer ones.

On the short straps the two end holes are bored 3 19/32 in. centres, and the three holes on the long straps at the same distance. It is not a bad plan, however, to omit the central holes on these long straps until a trial assembly, in which case their correct position can be marked with an awl passed through the appropriate holes in the boxes. A further first check may also be made before drilling any of the holes by measuring the relevant distance between the holes already made in the boxes, but take care that they are all lying perfectly one above the other.

With the boxes correctly aligned, pass a bolt through one hole in the strap, thread on a washer, push the bolt through the hole in the box, thread on another washer and nut, and tighten up. Repeat this process until the whole is assembled, leaving the central holes in the long straps until last. The boxes should now ride upwards and outwards with a smooth, slightly tight motion. If jerkiness or forced 'jumping' is experienced, try to locate the faulty alignment between strap and box and, if necessary, slightly enlarge the holes in the box.

If all is well, dismantle and give a coat of good quality matt paint. When dry, reassemble and, with a hammer against each screw head in turn, tap over the ends of the bolt; this will prevent the action of constantly opening and shutting the boxes causing the nuts to become unthreaded.

WORKBENCHES

Essential to any craftsman or home handyman is a well-made bench. The kitchen table, although it may stand up to a certain amount of knocking about, is no substitute for the solid surface of a workbench.

Table-type Workbench

What you are actually making is only a strong table. No fine work is needed. It can be easily made from inexpensive wood with the simplest of tools. All you have to do is cut the materials to length and width and join the whole group of pieces together. If you build the bench described, it will fit into a average shed; or, if you want to, you can enlarge it to be used in a larger workshop.

Frame: Make up the two identical leg frames using the joints shown in Fig. A289—stopped dove-tails at the top; through, wedged tenons at the bottom. The wedges should be of hardwood. On the bottom rails there is an allowance in length of ¼ in., i.e., ⅛ in. of tenon to project at each side until the glue has set; this is then planed-off flush. The bench stop may now be made and fitted to one of the leg frames by means of the 5/16 in. bolt and wing nut as illustrated. The hole for the bolt should be bored 3 in. from the outside of the leg. The slot in the stop, which allows vertical adjustment, should be approximately 1¼ in. long and should begin about 2¾ in. from the top end.

The two bottom stretcher rails are fitted by means of a simple housing or notch joint. After drilling the top part of the hole, place the stretcher rails in position, G-cramp them to the legs and then drill the lower part of the holes. A ratchet brace, or electric drill, is necessary for this lower hole. Chamfer these stretcher rails where thought necessary, and bolt together so that the underframe is now complete.

If two pieces are necessary for the well, all four long edges should be planed true. The mating edges of the boards in the original bench were joined by means of four secret slot-screws. This makes an excellent joint and prevents gaps appearing or one board sagging below the other when weighed down. Alternatively, wooden dowels may be used to locate the two edges or a couple of battens can be screwed across underneath the join.

Fig. A289. The table-type workbench with constructional details.

Materials

Legs: 4 off 29 in. × 3 in. × 2 in.
Bottom rails: 2 off 19¼ in. × 3 in. × 2 in.
Top rails: 2 off 18¼ in. × 3 in. × 2 in.
Stretcher rails: 2 off 4 ft. 1in. × 3 in. × 2 in.
Front apron: 1 off 4 ft. 3 in. × 8½ in. × 1 in.
Back apron: 1 off 4 ft. 3 in. × 6 in. × ¾ in.
Well: 1 off 4 ft. 3 in. × 12½ in. × 1 in.

Softwood planed. All sizes nominal, i.e. before planing. One or more pieces to make up in width. The following two items in hardwood planed.
Bench stop: 1 off 6 in. × 2 in. × 1¼ in.
Bench top: 1 off 4 ft. 3 in. × 8 in. × 2in.
Coach bolts: 4 off 5½ in. × ⅜ in.; 4 off 4 in. × ⅜ in.; 1 off 4½ in. × 5/16 in.
Steel countersunk screws: 8 off 2¼ in. × 12; 6 off 2 in. × 10; 6 off 1¾ in. × 12; 4 off 1½ in. × 10.

The end view shows how an unusual feature has been introduced. The back edge of the well overlaps the legs by 5/16 in. This overlap is housed into a back apron which contributes enormously to the important factor of stability. The back apron could be built higher to carry tool clips, if desired. Four 1½ in. × 10 screws from the back secure the well in the back apron housing. The rear apron is firmly screwed to the back legs, using six 1¾ in. × 12 screws. The well also is screwed down at this stage, using six 2 in. × 10 screws.

After shaping the front apron this can now be screwed in place using eight 2¼ in. × 12 screws. Care should be taken to get these screws home tightly since this board is of paramount importance in stiffening.

Bench Top: Finally, and most important of all, comes the bench top itself. Well-seasoned hardwood is essential, and beech is the traditional choice. However, much of today's beech is home-grown and cannot be relied upon to stay flat. If not fully seasoned, this will certainly lead to trouble. Keruing—a Malayan hardwood—is an excellent alternative and was used in the bench described here. By virtue of its distant habitat, this wood is a better gamble than beech with regard to seasoning.

Notice from the end elevation, inset, how the inside edge of the top is rebated to fit in over the well. The size of this rebate will depend on the thickness of the well and apron and the finished section of the bench top. Remember that 8 in. × 2 in. finishes at 7¾ in. × 1⅞ in. after planing, and the 3 in. × 2 in. underframing will become 2¾ in. × 1⅞ in.

Mark the position of the bench stop and chop out this mortice to a snug fit. Most of the waste can be bored out with a 1 in. twist bit working from both sides. When in place and satisfactorily fitted, bolt down the top using two 4 in. × ⅜ in. bolts at each end. Bore the recessed hole first which takes the head of the bolt (as shown inset) and then the ⅜ in. shank hole. Bolt up, and remove all sharp edges with glass-paper.

Vice: Apart from fitting a vice, the bench is now finished and should last several lifetimes. Depending upon the type of vice required, it may be found necessary to remove the top and do some chopping out and 'a bit of fiddling here and there'! With the top off, the apron can be shaped with a bowsaw to house the vice screw and slides. To preserve the maximum strength, the minimum

of materials should be removed from the apron.
Further refinements worth considering are:—

1 Block up the bolt-head holes in the top with pieces of dowel, glued in and then planed-off flush.
2 Board over the stretcher rails to provide extra storage space under the bench.
3 Fit a bench holdfast at the opposite end to the vice. For some jobs these holdfasts are more useful than a vice.

Foldaway Workbench

This is a suitable design for use in a garage, since it can be folded away to take up only one foot of valuable space when not in use. It was made several years ago; as you can see from the photograph (Fig. A290) it is no longer new, but the fact that it has stood up to regular use for so long proves the soundness of the design.

The dimensions may be adjusted according to the individual, but for the purpose of description let us take them as 4 ft. 6 in. long; 3 ft. high, and 1 ft. 11 in. wide.

Working Top: For this, select a true piece of pine 11 in. × 3 in. and plane the top clean and square. Also clean up a piece of 3 in. × 2 in. for the back rail and find a couple of boards ⅝ in. thick, preferably tongued-and-grooved, for the well, which should be 9 in. wide. Place all on one side whilst you prepare the bearers.

Take two pieces of 3 in. × 2 in. and square off the ends down to the full width of the bench—i.e., 1 ft. 11 in.

At one end of each, cut a half-lap as shown in Fig. A291 (back). This is designed to fit into the slot in the rail on the wall (Fig. A292).

At the other end, cut into the 2 in. side, 2 in. down and 2 in. deep, and from the end to meet it, as in Fig. A291 (front). This leaves a 2 in. × 2 in. cutout, and a 2 in. × 1 in. nose. NOTE: This cut in the other bearer should be the opposite way on.

These bearers lie with the 3 in. face to the underside of the bench, whilst the legs show the 2 in. face to the front. See Fig. A293. Hence the cutout of the bearer leaves a shoulder to give added support to the leg at the hinged top.

Now drill and screw (one only at first) the bearers to the underside of the bench top, the outside edge of the bearer being 3 in. from the bench end, and the nose of the bearer flush with the front.

Similarly, screw the back end of each bearer to the back rail and fill in the well with the tongued-and-grooved. Ensure that all is tight and square, then insert additional screws from the underside into the working top, and from the top side of the well into the 3 in. × 2 in. The working top is shown in Fig. A294.

Wall Support: This is perfectly straightforward in that the back rail of the bench sits on an equivalent rail firmly fixed to the wall with the 2 in. face to the wall and 3 in. out. For added strength this rail is supported by two vertical pieces which need not run to the floor, but may if you wish. See Fig. A292.

At 'A' and 'A' 3 in. from each end a slot is cut 3 in. × 1 in. to take the half-lap cut in the end of the bearers (Fig. A292). These should be a good fit, neither tight nor sloppy. This enables the two rails to fit snugly, and the half-lap joint prevents movement of the bench when in use.

Before plugging to the wall, slot these two rails into position, and, holding them together with a couple of

Fig. A290. The foldaway workbench in operational position.

Fig. A296. The bench folded away.

Fig. A291.

Fig. A292.

Fig. A295.

Fig. A293.

Fig. A294.

73

Materials

Apart from the top which is 11 in. × 3 in. × 4 ft. 6 in. long, and the well-base which is of ⅝ in. tongued-and-grooved, the bench is built entirely of 3 in. × 2 in.

Wall support: 1 off 4 ft. 6 in.
Wall support: 2 off 1 ft. 3 in.
Back rails: 1 off 4 ft. 6 in.
Bearers: 2 off 2 ft. 0 in.
Legs: 2 off 3 ft. 0 in.
Leg rails: 2 off 4 ft. 6 in.

cramps, drill a 9/16 in. hole right through both rails, at the slot. These take ½ in. bolts, without nuts, which are dropped into position when the bench is up.

Now carefully mark on the wall the position of the supporting frame, adjusting it to the correct height, and ensuring that it is level. Plug the wall in several places, drill the timber, and fix with four 6 in. nails or screws. It will stay there for ever!

Legs: Take the two leg pieces and square off the ends 3 in. shorter than the overall height of the bench. Cut the rails 6 in. shorter than the length of the bench. As already mentioned, ensure that this frame is built up with the 2 in. face front and rear. The bottom rail should be 3 in. up, and the top rail 4 in. down. the purpose of this is to keep the hinge at the top clear of the mortice.

Mortice the rails into the legs—or dovetail them. If you mortice, go right through, and wedge.

The top of each leg is now sawn out (as shown in Fig. A293) 2 in. down and 2 in. in.

In preparing this leg frame it is most important that it fits the slots in the front ends of the bearers.

Assembly: The legs are now hinged to the top with 2 in. square steel hinges. Turn the bench top upside-down on the floor, and place the leg frame upside-down in position. Make sure that the fits are both good before setting the hinges. It will be observed that this particular type of joint distributes the weight on to the leg partly direct from the working top, partly through the bearer, and the nose at the side of the bearer adds a little rigidity to the hinge. Furthermore, the hinge is set back 2 in. from the edge, which gives it a firmer seating.

The bench can now be dismantled again to fit the vice, and to mortice out a neat, square hole for a planing block, which should be of beech, and such a true fit that it is adjustable by the tap of a hammer. Alternatively, saw the block diagonally lengthwise, to make two wedges. Place the wedges in the hole and give the wide end a tap with a mallet to tighten them.

The 'back leg', which is the front leg farthest from the vice, can be drilled at intervals with ⅞ in. holes to take a peg to support longish timbers when held in the vice.

To Stack: Assuming the bench to be up, lift out the bolts (no nuts required). Now place one foot on the bottom rail, and grasp the bench top with the fingers of one hand over the back edge of the working top. The other hand can hold the vice-bar. Draw the bench away from the wall; lower gently against the legs; place toe under the rail and lift back to the wall. This position is illustrated in the drawing (Fig. A295) and in the photograph (Fig. A296).

To Raise: Draw the bench away from the wall about two feet; hold leg frame down with toe on bottom rail; lift top to horizontal; drop into slots in wall-rail; drop bolts into holes. Finally lift front of bench and ensure legs are vertical.

Believe it or not, they will not kick under while you are working.

Always brush the workbench down after use, and ensure that the wall rail and slots are free from sawdust.

If soundly constructed, this bench, like its prototype, should last a generation.

Tool Cabinet Workbench

This is an easy-to-build workbench in which rigidity is achieved by its being braced in all directions with panels of fir plywood (Fig. A297). A cabinetmaker's vice can be mounted on either front corner of the solid double-thick plywood work surface. The tool cabinet, with hooks and shelves for safe, convenient tool storage, mounts on the wall behind the bench.

Cutting: In Fig. A298, the cutting diagrams are given for two 8 ft. × 4 ft. panels and one 4 ft. × 4 ft. panel of fir plywood. The two larger panels are ¾ in. thick and the smaller panel is ¼ in. thick. The dimensions of each cut piece will be found in the Parts List. The parts A, B, C, D and E in the left-hand panel make up the tool cabinet. The parts in the centre and right-hand panel are required for the workbench. If you prefer to construct the workbench alone, and postpone construction of the tool cabinet until later, the left-hand panel will not be required at this stage.

Construction: The step-by-step instructions which follow, together with Fig. A299, cover the construction of both units.

Use a straight edge and square and lay out the parts of the plywood panels as shown in the cutting diagrams. Remember to allow for saw kerfs.

Fig. A297. The tool cabinet workbench.

Two pieces 3/4" plywood glued
23 3/4"
1" 1 3/4"

Fig. A299.
Constructional details
of the tool cabinet
workbench.

2"x4"
1/4" Plywood
back
3/4" Plywood
22"
23"
2"x4"
9"
21"

60"
36" 24"
8 1/4"
E
C
13 1/2" D
A
E
C
6 3/4"
E
B
7 1/2"

23 3/4"
60"
6"
both
ends
H
I
H
G
1/4" Plywood
end
2"x4"
48"

A
B B
C C D E E

F F
G

I
H H

Fig. A298. Cutting
diagrams. The above
from 3/4 in. ply and on
the left from 1/4 in. ply.

Materials		
Tool Cabinet Back :	1 off 34 1/2 in. × 58 1/2 in.	coded A
Tool Cabinet Top, Bottom :	2 off 4 3/4 in. × 60 in.	coded B
Tool Cabinet Sides :	2 off 4 3/4 in. × 34 1/2 in.	coded C
Tool Cabinet Shelf Standard :	1 off 4 in. × 34 1/2 in.	coded D
Tool Cabinet Shelves :	3 off 4 in. × 34 1/2 in.	coded E
Workbench Top :	2 off 23 3/4 in. × 60 in.	coded F
Workbench Bottom Shelf :	1 off 19 3/8 in. × 48 in.	coded G
Workbench Sides :	2 off 21 in. × 25 7/8 in.	coded H
Workbench Back :	1 off 22 in. × 44 3/4 in.	coded I

The main frame needs about 33ft. of 4 in. × 2 in., or
as required.

Saw out these parts, then smooth the cut edges with
medium sandpaper wrapped around a block. Also saw
4 in. × 2 in. for bench framework to the lengths given
in the sketches, notching one end of each 4 in. × 2 in.
leg for cross rails as shown.

Assemble the 4 in. × 2 in. lower shelf framing with glue
and nails. Nail and glue the 3/4 in. plywood shelf (G) to
this frame, after ensuring that the two front-edge notches
will accommodate the 4 in. × 2 in. legs correctly. Then
set up the legs, the cross braces and the top rails. Nail
and glue the 1/4 in. plywood back and end panels to the
4 in. × 2 in.

Glue the two 3/4 in. plywood panels for the top, back-
to-back, using clamps around the edges and screws at
other points driven into the underside until the glue sets.
Then true the edges of the top, rounding the corners
slightly, with medium sandpaper or a block plane. Fasten
the top to the bench framework with glue and wood
screws. Counterbore and plug these screw heads.

To assemble the tool cabinet, glue and nail the side and end strips to the back panel. Bore holes for chisels, screwdrivers, etc., in one shelf before fitting the vertical divider and shelving.

Painting the understructure of the bench and the tool cabinet gives worthwhile protection and makes cleaning easier. After filling nail holes and sanding with fine sandpaper, prime the wood with enamel undercoat or resin sealer. Then apply two finish coats.

EQUIPMENT

The more equipment you have, the more versatile you can be. And you can make a lot of equipment yourself. For example, a saw stool—cheap and easy to make—would be useful for cutting long lengths of timber, sheets of hardboard, corrugated sheeting, pipes and so on. A door can be gripped in a vertical position for edge planing, etc., and pieces of wood can be planed smooth against the dowel stop. With a pair of stools and a scaffold board decking, a convenient scaffold can be made for work on ceilings. Here are two patterns which are well worth making.

Saw Stool No. 1

To make the stool shown in Fig. A300 you require 2 ft. 6 in. of 3 in. × 2 in. timber and an 8 ft. length of 2 in. × 2 in., preferably planed finish. Square off both ends of the body piece and mark out for the 'V' cut at one end. From one end, measure along the centre of the width for 3½ in. Scribe a line off each edge on the end with the gauge set at ⅜ in. Draw lines to connect the scribe marks to the point on the face and drill a ¾ in. hole on the point. The wedge shape can be cut out by making the two cuts towards the hole.

Mark out for the ¾ in. hole at the other end, 8 in. in and central. This can then be drilled, not forgetting to stop drilling as the worm of the twistbit protrudes on the back. Reverse the timber and complete the hole from the other side. A 3 in. length of dowelling can be inserted later to provide a stop for use when planing.

At one end of the 2 in × 2 in. timber, square a line across two faces adjoining. Mark one face with an 'S' and the other with an 'E' to denote the angle when looking first from the side of the stool and then from the end. Repeat these symbols at intervals so that a pair will appear on each leg position.

On the 'S' face measure ⅜ in. off the squared line towards the timber length, at the farthest edge from the other squared line. This will form one angle for the cut

Fig. A301. The leg housing.

Fig. A300. Constructional details for saw stool No. 1.

and a bevel can be set to it. Alternatively a template can be made from plywood or hardboard.

On the 'E' face measure ½ in. away from the squared line off the farthest edge as before. Set another bevel or template to this angle. Mark the lines across and cut the waste off the end. Measure along the timber 1 ft. 10 in. and repeat the markings of the level or template in exactly the same direction. Cut off the first leg on these marks. The same cut can be used for one end of the second leg and this can be marked and cut off to serve as a diagonal partner on the stool. For the second two legs, which must pair up with the first two, turn the bevel over and work off opposite edges of the timber but using the same symbol faces.

Shouldered Haunches: The shouldered haunches can be cut next at the tops of all four legs. To mark out, scribe a line central of the timber thickness off the 'S' face at the end which has the blunt angle. The sharp angle is for the foot of the leg. Square a line down at each side of the scribe marks for 1⅞ in. or ⅛ in. less than the finished thickness of prepared timber. Use the 'E' face bevel to mark the shoulders off this point, parallel with the top cut angle. Then use the 'S' face bevel on the reverse of the 'S' face to join up the return lines. The haunches can now be cut off, using a tenon saw for accuracy.

To mark out the leg housing (Fig. A301), square a line across the 3 in. face of the body piece, 5 in. away from the end. Use the 'S' face bevel to mark the angles on the edges of the timber. Square the marks across on the underside. Measure the exact thickness of the leg timber and mark this size square off the angled marks. Once again, return the marks across both 3 in. faces. Do exactly the same, in reverse, at the other end and set a gauge to ½ in. Scribe between the sets of marks on the top and underside of the body piece, working off the edges. To ensure a tight fitting joint it would be better to cut inside the marks with a tenon saw. Using a firmer wood chisel, the housings can be chopped out on the bench. When completed, drill the 3/16 in. holes in diagonal pattern, to follow the direction of the top bevel cut. The legs may now be screwed into position, using 2 in. × 10 countersunk steel wood screws.

For rigidity, the end straps ought to be fitted across the legs. Mark off the two pieces of 6 in. × 1 in. and cut the compound splay cuts at each end. Drill and countersink three 3/16 in. holes at each end and fix with 1¾ in. × 10 screws. With heavy usage or shrinkage of the timber after assembly, a rocking movement may develop in the stool. This is easily put right by re-tightening the screws or replacing them with slightly longer ones.

Saw Stool No. 2

This is an alternative design which does not require splayed legs and which includes pockets for screws and nails. Fig. A302 shows a perspective view. There is the usual 'V' cut for holding a door or sash frame; a bench stop could easily be added as described for saw stool No. 1.

The stool is quite simple to make, with no complicated joints. It can be fastened together with nails only—or the perfectionist might care to use part nailing and part screwing. Although the height is a standard 1 ft. 9 in., it can be varied without any alteration to the design, to suit the individual. Using prepared board of the nominal sizes

Fig. A302. Details of saw stool No. 2.

Fig. A303. Dimensions of the prepared parts.

Fig. A304. Details of the V-cut and brace fixing.

illustrated in Fig. A303, all the parts can be cut prior to the assembly. To avoid the complication of setting out for the brace mitres, these could be cut after part assembly of the other pieces. It is important that the ends of the legs are cut square, otherwise the completed stool will not stand straight. You may like to mark out and assemble in the following manner.

Lay the bottom piece on to the underside of the top piece. Measure all round the margin and equalise them, to get the smaller piece centralised on the other. Using the finger on the edge as a guide for a pencil, mark the continuation of the 4 in. bottom piece for 1 in. or so at both ends. Mark the termination of the ends and square a line across each mark. These channel section markings show the position that the legs will occupy. Measure the centre of the top piece in length and square a further line across. This is where the braces will meet. At this stage the 'V' cut can be marked out at one end as in Fig. A304. The hole is drilled first, followed by the cutting of the wedge at each side.

Legs and Top Rails: On the legs now, in pair, mark up 2 in. from the base and square a line across the width. Then 12 in. up from the base, square a further line across for the brace positions. Using 2 in. oval brads for the fixing or 2 in. × 10 countersunk screws, join the bottom piece between the two legs with the underside to the marks. Stand the 'U' shape erect and fix the top piece to the channel section markings; then, having a piece of lath handy, measure the diagonals of the frame and position them to get equal distances. Tack on the lath temporarily from corner to corner. Rest the brace timber on edge across the marks so that the top end straddles this mark equidistant of the timber thickness, and the bottom underside is in line with its mark. Mark off the angles with a pencil. Square the mark across at each end and make the splay cuts. Offer the brace into position and, using a square off the top piece, continue the central mark on to the edge of the brace. Square this across the width and cut off the waste to form a bird's beak shape. Do the same in reverse for the other brace and then both can be fixed into position. The lath can be dispensed with.

The top rails can be fixed to the legs, tight up to the underside of the top piece. Then each one can be rested on the edge of a bench for nailing the top to them, or they can be housed into the legs with a shoulder formed to give extra support. The bottom rails are nailed on next and the two or more dividers can be positioned to make the pockets required. Whether the previous parts have been nailed or screwed into place, the feet should be screwed on with 1½ in. × 10 countersunk steel wood screws, making sure that they are perfectly square across the base of the legs. It may be found more convenient to fix one by the square and the other by sighting a parallel across between the two. This will avoid undesirable rocking movements.

Drilling Table

This is an easy-to-make drilling table which will enable you to tackle more jobs in less time.

It can be used for most of the other purposes for which a power drill is so useful—morticing, grooving, sanding, grinding, polishing, reaming, shaping, routing, and so on. It can be constructed by any handyman in a few hours, and need not be expensive; the prototype was constructed from wood obtained from an old chest of drawers, the

only outlay being for angle brackets, bolts and wing nuts, and a few inches of strip metal. Adjustments in use can be made in a few seconds with accuracy. It is essential that all edges and corners are square. The dimensions are to suit a Black and Decker drill and the maker's stand. In the case of other makes, the only alteration needed is to adjust the position where horizontal and vertical bases meet, to suit the height of the particular stand. A wooden stand can be made to fit your drill easily enough—a nose clamp and a locking bolt at the rear are the main items.

Base: First cut out the horizontal base, a piece of 8 in. × ¾ in. wood 18 in. long; the vertical base is next cut from 8 in. × ¾ in. wood 15 in. long, and fixed to the horizontal base, allowing 3¼ in. to project. Drive two 2 in. wire nails into the joint, first sharpening the points with a file to give them a good grip of the end grain. Fit two 3 in. angle brackets underneath, about 1 in. in from each edge. Fit two more at the top, on the edges. These will have to be recessed below the wood to allow the drill carrier to slide freely (Fig. A305).

Drill Carrier: This is a piece of ½ in. plywood, 8 in. wide and 12 in. long. With a fretsaw, cut two slots, 3/16 in. wide, 6 in. long, 6⅛ in. between them, and 1¾ in. from the front end. Make sure that they are parallel. Clean them out with glass-paper wrapped round a knife blade. Place this piece on the top of the horizontal base. Mark through for the bolts which should be positioned 7½ in. back from the vertical base. Drill two 3/16 in. holes and insert two 2 in. × 3/16 in. bolts. Ensure that the carrier slides freely, then put on two large washers with 3/16 in. holes and two wing nuts (Fig. A306). The drill stand is now fixed to the carrier. Horizontal adjustments are made by sliding the carrier along the base. This allows the use of a fixed fence, which of course is more rigid than a movable one.

Table: First cut out the table carrier, ½ in. thick, 6½ in. wide and 9 in. long. Using the fretsaw, again cut two 3/16 in. slots but only 3 in. long. These should be situated 1 in. from the edge and 2¾ in. from the top. Sandpaper the slots as before. Cut the table top from 4 in × 1 in. wood 6½ in. long. Glue and screw the table carrier to the side of the table top, leaving a projection of 1 in. This forms the fence. The table support is cut from a rectangle 4 in. × 6 in. by sawing across from corner to corner. Glue in central position, screw through the table carrier into table support, but screw through the table support into the table top and do not let the screw protrude (Fig. A305). Now place this assembly against the vertical base and mark for the bolts. Drill two 3/16 in. holes, to just clear the top of the horizontal base. Fit bolts, washers and wing nuts. Make sure that the assembly will slide the full length of the slots.

Cut guide plates from ½ in. wood, ¾ in. wide and 6 in. long. Glue and screw one at each side of table carrier. These plates prevent the table from jamming sideways when the cam is rotated towards the top of the rise.

Now fit a ¼ in. drill in the chuck, put the drill in the stand, slide up the table until the fence meets the drill, and mark for the cut-away in the fence (Fig. A305). Remove drill and saw this cut-away right down to the table with a coping saw.

Cam: Fig. A307 shows how to lay out the cam. Using a protractor, draw the lettered lines at 45 deg. intervals. Mark off on line A, ⅜ in. from the centre; on line B, ¾ in.; on C, 1⅛ in.; D, 1½ in.; E, 1⅞ in.; F, 2¼ in.;

Fig. A30 5.   Details of the drilling table.

TABLE TOP

DRILL CLAMP

DRILL STAND

BENCH FIXING

TABLE CARRIER
FENCE

THE DRILL CARRIER

BASE

WING NUT
WASHER
GROOVE FOR MAXIMUM
CARRIER MOVEMENT

BRACKETS

GROOVE

WING NUT
AND WASHER

TABLE GUIDES

TABLE SUPPORT

CAM

BASE

BENCH FIXING

Fig. A306.   Details of the drill carrier.

3/4"

8"

12"

TO SUIT DRILL STAND

7½"

18"

8"

H

G

A

F

B

E

C

D

Fig. A307.   Lay-out of the cam.

METAL STRIP

ABOUT
2"

Fig. A308.   Details of
a rest carrier.

G, 2⅝ in.; H, 3 in. Trim up the dots in a smooth curve. Draw this on a piece of ½ in. ply. Drill the centre hole to suit 1¼ in. × 8 round-head screw. Cut out with a fretsaw and finish with file and sandpaper.

If your first effort doesn't look so good, screw it to the inside of your bench leg to raise and lower a bench stop, and make another one—it is important that the cam be accurate.

Now slide the table right to the top. Place the cam in position with point H (Fig. A307) uppermost. Screw in position. The whole unit is attached to the right hand front corner of the bench with a single screw through each of the two bench fixing points shown in Fig. A305.

As a refinement the table and fence side may be covered with sheet alloy or plastic laminate. If a longer table is required, the guide plates should be 2¼ in. lower.

Using the Table: In order to take full advantage of the possibilities of this versatile piece of equipment, adjustments should be made as suggested under the appropriate headings.

Mortices: Fit a ¼ in. twist drill or router drill in the chuck. Slacken off all wing nuts. Place the work on the table, rotate the cam until the edge of the drill is level with the line on the work. Camp up table wing nuts (a steel rule laid against either the top or bottom of the drill is a help to height setting). Now move the drill carrier until the drill protrudes past the fence to the required depth. Clamp up wing nuts.

Stand behind the drill, switch on, pull the work on to the drill; when most of the waste has been removed, move slowly from side to side to make a clean edge. For a deep mortice, do half the depth first, then the other half. Keep the table clear of debris.

Grooving: Insert the size of drill required. Set for height and depth. Move the wood slowly along as when finishing the mortice.

Sanding: Move the drill carrier to the forward position, insert the sanding plate in the chuck. Raise the table until it is just clear of the plate. Move back the drill carrier until the plate is just clear of the fence.

Grinding and Buffing: To make a rest carrier for grinding we have to construct a part that is really a version of the table carrier, made to carry rests instead of a table.

Cut from ½ in. wood a piece 6½ in. wide and 11 in. long. With the fretsaw cut two 3/16 in. slots, 3 in. long, 4⅛ in. apart and 2¾ in. from the bottom. Remove the mortice table and try on this part. Make sure it fits snugly to the guide plates, and moves freely from the cam. Remove, and cut a portion from the centre of the top, 1½ in. wide and 2 in. deep. This allows the chuck to protrude.

Take a piece of mild steel ½ in. wide, 3/32 in. thick, 9¼ in. long. Bend as shown in Fig. A308. Drill 3/16 in. holes in each of the ends. It can then be bolted to the rest carrier about 1 in. from the top. This will suit a 4 in. grinding wheel. Any number of these rests can be made in varying sizes. Those made longer could have the tabs cranked inwards, and those shorter could have longer tabs to allow the use of the same pair of holes in the rest carrier. For grinding twist drills, a small piece of metal can be riveted to the rest, and bent downwards to produce the correct grinding angle (59 deg.).

Turning: Turning on the face plate can be carried out with the aid of these rests. In the case of repetition work (such as small wooden toy wheels), notches can be filed in the rest, to mark the main dimensions.

If fairly heavy turning is to be carried out, a metal support can be fixed to the centre of the metal strip and carried down to the bottom of the grinding table and fixed by a screw.

Tee Square and Drawing Board

It is obviously advisable to plan your work before you start it, and a good tee square and drawing board are indispensable items. Today they are expensive to buy, yet they are cheap and easy to make. Once made, they will give you a lifetime of service, provided they are well handled and cared for. The 'half imperial standard', as used in schools and colleges, is the most useful size for the home workshop.

Tee Square: The best quality manufactured squares are made from mahogany with ebony working edges. These ebony edges look very attractive but the reason for them is a practical, rather than an aesthetic one. Ebony is a close-grained, very hard, hardwood. It works to a silky finish which is ideal for use as a straight-edge. It is less susceptible to bumps than mahogany although every effort should be made at all times to protect the square from such treatment. Since ebony is difficult to obtain in suitable strips we must be satisfied with the alternative hardwoods. In this instance a combination is very effective, in appearance and in practice. Mahogany may be used for the stock and oak for the blade. Since the blade must be accurate we require a piece of first-class timber— quarter-sawn Japanese oak is ideal—this timber being most likely to remain true.

Prepare the stock to the sizes given in Fig. A309, rounding two corners as shown and bevelling the working edge. This edge must be perfectly straight.

The blade should be planed to 3/16 in. out of ¼ in. or 5/16 in. material. The wood must be well seasoned and could with advantage be planed down in two or perhaps three stages with an interval of a day or two between stages.

If it is going to 'move' slightly then the amount of 'move' in the timber will be catered for by the time its final thickness is reached. The blade is then tapered and the lower right-hand corner rounded. Three inches from the end, bore a ⅜ in. hole by which to hang the square when not in use. The working edge is then bevelled to approximately 1/16 in. thick.

Screw together the stock and blade by two diametrically opposite steel screws. Before inserting the second of these screws check that the two working edges are at right-angles. Once the steel screws have formed the threads they can be replaced, one at a time, by the brass screws. The latter will then enter easily and their slots will not be damaged enough to detract from the finish. Before replacing these two screws glue the centre of the common areas of the blade and stock with a non-waterproof glue. If too much glue is used the surplus will be squeezed out; try to avoid this. The remaining screws can now be inserted—steel first, then brass.

Apply several coats of brush polish, rubbing down between each with fine glass-paper. Successive coats should be slightly thinned each time with methylated spirits.

Should the blade be damaged in subsequent use and need re-edging, remove the screws and hold the glued joint over the spout of a kettle from which steam is emerging. In a few minutes this will soften the glue and the two parts may be prised open gently. Re-plane the

Fig. A309. Dimensions of a tee square. (*Inset*). Section of stock and blade.

Fig. A310. The perspective inset shows how the batten is chamfered to prevent the board collapsing in use.

damaged edge and reassemble as before after lightly glass-papering the glued areas.

Drawing Board: The best quality boards are made from ¾ in. softwood—usually yellow pine. A thin ebony strip is grooved into the working edge along which the stock of the tee square slides. Underneath are two battens (slot-screwed to allow for expansion) to keep the board flat. Such boards are not difficult to make although prime quality, knot-free timber is essential and three or four rubbed joints are necessary to obtain the usual width of 16 in. It is simpler to make the board by the following method: First, obtain a piece of ⅝ in plywood 23 in. × 16 in. (Make sure that this really is flat! Badly stored

plywood often twists in spite of the theory that plywood remains flat.) Radius the corners; plane and glass-paper the edges; fill the edges with one of the many grainfillers obtainable; smooth again with fine glass-paper and then paint the edges. Many such boards are being manufactured.

A further refinement to give a sloping surface would be to hinge two pieces of tapered plywood underneath the board (Fig. A310). They would lie flat when not in use and when opened would lift the front edge of the board two or three inches. Two 2 in. brass butt hinges are used to hold each 'ramp' and when open the ramp fits up against the batten for support.

FASTENINGS

In former times, woodwork was held together with wooden pins and dowels, but today machine-made nails and screws have taken the place of the older (and, incidentally, highly-skilled) method.

Nails

The nails most generally needed are shown in Figs. A311 and A312 to help you to identify them.

Types and Uses: The popular wire nail, with flat or countersunk head, is widely used for all kinds of work, such as making fences and gates, tool sheds and shed doors, etc. It is readily obtainable in lengths up to 10 in. Oval nails are easily driven so that their heads are flush with the wood, or even below, and are less liable to cause splitting of soft wood. The headless, or 'lost head' nail

has a somewhat similar general application, but gives a neater appearance than does the popular wire nail with round head.

Hollow domed nails, both plain and twisted, are used to secure corrugated iron, and in similar circumstances where a waterproof joint and a large bearing surface are required. Twisted and serrated types hold best, and are driven so that the head conforms to the contour of the material secured. Very heavy driving may break the heads, however, so care is recommended.

Iron nails stamped from sheet are also termed floor brads or clasp nails. Oval wire nails are sometimes used instead of floor brads. The clasp nail suits rough work such as fences, etc.

Cloutheaded nails have large heads, and are useful for

securing material which would tear away from a small head. As 'felt nails' they are employed for laying roofing felt. They should not be hammered in so far that the head cuts into the felt, which may tear, or let in water.

Panel and veneer pins are slender, with small, well-shaped heads, and are used to secure mouldings and panels, etc., in good-class carpentry and joinery. They do not split thin wood, and can have very small heads which can be punched below the surface, and afterwards concealed with filler.

Headless sprigs can be used to secure the backs in picture frames, or to hold glass in window frames before puttying outside. In greenhouses, where no outside putty is employed, such sprigs will retain the glass in position.

Headed tacks are used to secure chair webbing, and for many odd jobs. Their sharp points usually allow them to be started with thumb pressure.

The chair nail often has a polished brass head, though it may be copper finished, or ornamented. The nails should be used close together, equally-spaced and in a straight line.

The larger brass-headed or ornamented nails can be used to hold carpets, matting, etc. As with the chair nail, the heads are of good appearance so that no attempt need be made to conceal them. Staples, in various sizes, are popular for securing wire netting, for which they are particularly intended.

Methods of Nailing: When nailing two pieces of wood together, it should be remembered that the holding power of the nail is determined by the amount of the nail projecting into the second piece, and this should, if possible, exceed the thickness of the first piece of timber.

For added security and when nailing on to the thinner piece of wood, the nail can be 'clenched'. This is done by selecting a nail which extends by $\frac{1}{4}$ in. to $\frac{1}{2}$ in. the combined widths of the pieces of timber being joined. Having driven the nail through, the work should be reversed with the nail head resting on a steel plate, and the point knocked sideways with a hammer.

The same result can be achieved on work that is *in situ*, by holding the face of a large hammer firmly against the nail head in one hand, and knocking the projecting nail over with a small hammer in the other hand.

Fig. A313 shows how a dovetail effect can be obtained with nails driven in obliquely, giving increased rigidity. Practice will soon show what liberties may be taken with different species of timber when nailing at such a vulnerable spot, near the end of the board.

Softwoods, red deal, pine and so on, will not split easily, but when working with hardwoods, such as oak, chestnut, mahogany, etc., it is usually essential to make a pilot hole, slightly smaller in diameter than the nail but large enough to cut the fibres of the wood. This is easily done with a bradawl.

When nailing boards together as shown in Fig. A314 the nails should be staggered so that one particular run of the grain is not overladen.

When a neat finish is required, the nail heads are often punched below the surface. Oval or lost-head nails, or panel pins with small heads, are most suitable for this. In cabinet work and similar jobs, the holes are made up with filler and sanded flush when dry, as mentioned. When varnishing or staining is in view, the filler can be toned to suit the finish. Or a filler which will take stain, such as plastic wood, may be used.

For garden sheds, and similar work, visible nailing is often employed. Two nails for each board, staggered to reduce chances of splitting, will usually be sufficient. The nails should be slightly shorter than the combined thickness of boards and horizontal bearers. Common wire nails will be fairly conspicuous, so oval or headless nails may be preferred.

In the interests of appearance, concealed nailing may also be used. Tongued-and-grooved boards may be fixed in this way, as shown in Fig. A315, oval or headless nails being driven well in and punched flush. This type of nailing is easier with tongued boards of the shape shown at 'A', but the ordinary tongued-and-grooved boards will be satisfactory if the nails are given a good slant, and kept as far from the edge of the tongue as possible. This method is used for floors, but is not very suitable when much pressure has to be resisted, as may be so with fences. No nails are visible, of course, when the work is completed.

Corrugated iron is quite often used for roofs, because it offers a watertight, durable roof; hollow dome nails are best to secure the sheets. The nails should pass through holes in the ridges, to obviate leakage of water which would result from nailing in the valleys. Thin-gauge galvanised iron can be pierced by the nails, or by a pointed steel punch. Alternatively, if the noise is objectionable, holes may be drilled. At least 3 in. overlap is necessary and overlapping to the extent of two ridges is preferable, but not essential. In localities where strong prevailing winds are experienced, the overlap should face away from the wind, so that rain is not driven between the sheets.

Corrugated asbestos or plastic sheeting will have to be drilled; piercing would crack or shatter the sheet. It is wise to keep holes at least $1\frac{1}{2}$ in. from the edges of the sheets, as the material is brittle. Lead or composite washers should be used under hollow dome nails, and hammering should cease when the head is firmly down. Owing to the risk of breaking the sheets, screws may be used instead and, indeed, are preferable.

For wire netting, $\frac{1}{2}$ in. staples are usually suitable. They are spaced regularly along the mesh, the wire being kept tight and even. The distance between the staples depends on the size of mesh. At the cut ends, appearance is improved if the ends are turned in as shown. Stapling can be on these turned ends, if preferred.

For roofing work, copper, alloy or yellow-metal nails are best, because of their durability. Failing these, galvanised nails are recommended. Copper and brass-dipped nails are also made, but are less durable than the solid copper or alloy type.

Non-rusting nails are also best in positions where failure due to rusting may be experienced, or where rusting will stain decorations. The rusting or iron or wire nails may easily cause patches in bathrooms, or with built-in kitchen fitments. Galvanised or zinc nails are not recommended in coastal areas, where corrosion may be rapid.

Aluminium alloy nails may be obtained, and are particularly suitable for securing aluminium flashings and sheets. They can also be driven into hardboard, plasterboard, and other materials normally nailed; they resist sulphurous and coastal atmospheres.

Sizes and Weights: Small tacks, pins and sprigs may be bought by the ounce and larger nails may be had by the pound. When a fairly large job is in hand, it is useful to obtain a fairly accurate idea of the weight of nails which will be required. This can be done with reasonable accuracy by noting the number of nails per board, multiplying by the number of boards, and then consulting

WIRE NAIL

OVAL NAIL

HEADLESS OR LOST HEAD

HOLLOW DOMED

IRON NAILS

CLOUTHEADED

PANEL PINS

HEADLESS SPRIG

HEADED TACK

CHAIR NAIL

BRASS HEAD

STAPLE

Figs. A311 and A312. A selection of nails in general use.

Fig. A313. Nails driven in obliquely for a dovetail effect, to give increased rigidity.

INCORRECT

Fig. A314. Nailing boards together.   CORRECT

CORRECT

CORRECT

Fig. A315. Nailing-tongued and grooved boards.

the table. With the latter, it must be realised that the exact number of nails obtained in a pound will vary somewhat, according to the actual gauge of the nail. However, the figures given will usually be a sufficient guide.

As an example, assume that 80 ft. of garden fence, with three boards per ft., has to be erected. With three horizontal bearers, six nails will be required per board, or 18 per ft. (6 nails per board × 3 boards per ft.). The total will thus be 80 × 18, or 1,440. If 1¼ in. wire nails are used, at 300 to the pound., then 5 lb. (1,500) will be required.

For small jobs, or when using small sprigs and pins, no calculation need be made. But the larger nails do not run very many to the pound., and a rough check is then worth while.

Length of Nail (inches)	Number of Nails per Pound		
	Wire Nails	Headless Nails	Aluminium Alloy
1	850	1,000	—
1½	300	450	650
2	175	225	400
2½	100	150	130 } hollow
3	60	90	120 } domed
4	30		—

Screws

The invention of the woodscrew must rank with the invention of the wheel as one of the greatest brainwaves of all time. The thread cut on the centre shank forms a continuous inclined plane and as it rotates it worms its way in, cutting its own thread into the material into which it is driven.

In theory, what goes in must also come out, when needed, simply by turning the screw in the opposite direction. Unfortunately, there are often many reasons why theory parts company with practice. The screw may have rusted, so welding itself to the material, or at least greatly increasing the friction that has to be overcome to get it out. The slot may be badly damaged or, most probable of all, the screwdriver blade has worn to the wrong shape.

Correct Screwdrivers: This is very important, and when neglected is nearly always the cause of wasted time and damaged screw heads. Fig. A316 shows the shape usually resulting from long-term misuse, the end of the blade being far too rounded and locating only with the top edge of the slot. As a result, when the screwdriver is turned, the blade rides out and in so doing distorts the sides of the slot. Consequently the tendency is to apply excessive downward pressure which means that energy is wasted keeping the blade located in position instead of turning the screw. Ultimately, the blade rides out so many times, and the wear on the slot becomes so great, that it is impossible to remove the screw by normal means. This condition can be prevented by ensuring that the end of the blade is correctly shaped.

In Fig. A317 the usual shape is illustrated showing how the end of the blade is normally ground to a taper, but the disadvantage is that the blade is not an exact fit and, depending on the angle of the taper, it may not locate to the full depth of the slot.

For most efficient results, the shape shown in Fig. A318 is the best. The blade tapers down normally but then reaches a shoulder which has been formed by grinding or filing the end to a flat of the same thickness as the width of the screw slot.

It may appear that if the blade is shaped to fit the slot exactly, each different screw size will require a reshaped blade. In fact, if the slot widths of different screw sizes are checked it will be found that **certain groups have the same slot width :—**

Screw Size	Slot Width
4 to 7	1/32 in.
8 to 12	3/64 in.
13 to 16	1/16 in.

This means that for screw sizes in this range the handy-man requires three differently-ground screwdrivers, which is not unreasonable because with an increased screw size a stouter screwdriver will be required in any case. It should be noted that the depth of the slot also increases with screw size, but is not greater than 3/32 in. in the range of sizes mentioned.

Another point regarding the shape of the blade is also illustrated in Fig. A318. The end must be ground perfectly at a right-angle to the length, otherwise when the screw-driver is located in the slot it will be leaning away from the axis of the screw, with the result that when the blade is turned, the user will tend to keep it upright causing it to ride out, further damaging the slot. Normally, with the blade ground to locate correctly, many 'impossible' screws can be withdrawn.

Rust and Paint Bonds : However, rust and paint bonds sometimes retain the screw against all efforts and an attempt should always be made to break the bond before endeavouring to turn the screw. The effect of the rust bond will be aggravated if the screw is securing some ferrous metal object such as a hinge. Usually, the rust bonds form as shown in Fig. A319. Application of paraffin oil will usually soften the rust sufficiently to allow the screw to respond to normal treatment, but the softening action of paraffin usually takes some time to react, so a

reasonable period of time must be allowed to elapse before further attempts are made. If the rust still remains firm, the use of a liquid rust solvent is advised.

A paint bond sometimes forms round the circumference of the screw, this is shown in Fig. A320. In some cases if the screw was inserted whilst the paint was wet, a paint bond will also have formed under the head as shown. The bond can usually be broken by smartly tapping the screwdriver in the screw slot.

If, after the foregoing suggestions have been observed, the screw still refuses to budge, the end of the screwdriver should be located in the screw slot and gripped in an adjustable wrench which can then be used as a lever. This method should be attempted very carefully because, due to the great leverage available, it may easily result in a snapped screwdriver blade or broken screw head.

Screwing Procedure : Finally, much time and trouble can be avoided if a few points are considered when originally inserting the screw.

The screw can be considered as a cramp, the screw thread and the underside of the head supplying the cramping action. As an example, consider a screw fixing to-gether two pieces of wood. To facilitate the cramping action, the shank of the screw must turn freely; to ensure that this is possible, a hole of the same diameter as the screw shank should be drilled through the top piece.

The cramping action is provided by the screw thread cutting into the wood; to ensure that this action can occur easily a pilot hole is drilled in B to facilitate the entry of the screw. In addition, the pilot hole also removes the wood which would normally be displaced by the entry of the screw and thus prevents the possibility of the wood splitting. The diameter of the pilot hole is of course, governed by the size of the screw thread, which in Fig.

Fig. A316. Worn and rounded blade which will slip out of slot.

Fig. A317. Chisel point. Does not fully engage sides of screw slot.

Fig. A318. The correct driver shape; actual point ground square and parallel to make a close fit in the groove.

Figs. A319 and A320. Rust bonds a screw along its length with the wood in which it is driven. Paint bonds it round the head.

Fig. A321. A screw holds by a clamping action, so the shank must turn freely to allow the head to bear.

Fig. A322. The proportions of the standard csk. wood screw.

A321 is shown, together with required clearance hole in full outline.

Before inserting the screw it is usually advisable to coat the thread lightly with grease which, by preventing the formation of a rust bond, facilitates the later removal.

With the holes drilled as described, the screw can be inserted easily and little effort is required until the under-side of the head meets the surface of A. A few strong turns then supply the cramping action for which the screw has been designed.

As a final guide, the general relative dimensions of the wood screw are shown in Fig. A322. Note that the head diameter is twice that of the shank and that the angle of the head is 90 deg. which determines the depth of the head as half the shank diameter. Normally, the threaded portion is approximately two-thirds of the total overall length.

Hinges and Door Springs

The practical householder will frequently meet jobs on which hinges and similar fittings are needed. There is a great variety of types and patterns and care should be taken in selecting suitable designs to meet the particular job in hand. Hanging a door or gate should not be taken as needing just 'a pair of hinges'; we should decide what is really needed and make a decision accordingly.

Hinge Types: For instance, Fig. A323 shows a typical cellar-flap hinge. As will be seen it is long in the strap and there are ample screw holes to secure it, having regard to the rough usage a cellar flat is subjected to. This type is made either of malleable iron or wrought iron. Fig. A324 shows a similar hinge for trap-doors; it has plenty of screw holes. Notice that it fits flush with the floor. These are usually in sizes 6 in. × 2⅜ in. to 8 in. × 2⅝ in. or thereabouts.

Fig. A325 shows a back-flap hinge, usually available in five sizes, the smallest being 1 in. and largest 2½ in.; they are made in either brass or steel. Not quite the same is the steel butt hinge shown in Fig. A326, available in six sizes from 2 in. to 6 in. Two not-so-familiar hinges are shown in Figs. A327 and A328. The table flap design is not often used, but it is useful and should certainly be re-membered, whilst the 'Parliament' hinge finds use with shutters of one sort or another.

The 'H' and 'HL' hinges shown in Fig. A329 are very useful, but the latter is often forgotten. These are in sizes 3 in., 3½ in., 4 in., and 5 in., their finish being bright steel.

An example of the rising butt hinge is shown in Fig. A330. It is a very useful fitting—as the door opens it rises a little to clear the carpet, but it needs to be well fixed by the eight screw holes shown. It is made in sizes 3 in., 3½ in., 4 in. and 5 in.

The 'T'-hinge, one example of which is shown in Fig. A331, is probably the most common of all hinges. It is in sizes from 3 in. to 24 in. long, possibly larger. It finds use in numerous cases. The two holes marked 'A' are provided to make good fixing at that point, most of the stress being taken up there. Chest and strap hinges are shown in Figs. A332 and A333, these being in sizes from 4 in. to 10 in.; chest hinges are measured from the joint, and strap hinges are measured when closed. Fig. A334 shows three examples of the heavier pattern hinges. When ordering 'Collinge' hinges, don't forget that in a pair one is right and one is left hand, and you must state if they are to be hinged to wood, stone or brickwork. The rever-

Fig. A323. Cellar flap hinge.

Fig. A324. Trap door hinge.

Fig. A325. Back-flap hinge.

Fig. A326. Butt hinge.

Fig. A327. Table flap hinge.

Fig. A328. 'Parliament' hinge.

Fig. A329. The H and HL hinge.

Fig. A330. Rising butt hinge.

Fig. A331. The 'T' hinge.

Fig. A332. The chest hinge.

Fig. A333. The strap hinge.

Fig. A334. Heavy duty hinges: *top*, the 'Collinge'; *centre*, reversible; *bottom*, hook-and-rider.

Fig. A336 (*below*). Internal spring door hinge.

Fig. A335 (*right*). Various 'special' hinges; *From top*, cabinet, antique, trestle and another type of antique hinge.

Fig. A337. Door closers. *Above*, light duty, and *right*, heavy duty.

Fig. A338. Wheel action door closer.

Fig. A339. Coil door spring.

Fig. A340. Floor-fitted door spring.

Fig. A341. Patent door check.

sible hinge gets over the right- and left-hand trouble. The hook-and-rider hinge has the advantage of the door being readily lifted off its frame. There are, of course, other variations of these types of hinges.

Fig. A335 shows a group of special hinges which would fall under the heading of 'various'. There are many more in this category, but space will not permit them all to be given.

Springs: Fig. 336 shows a single-action helical-spring hinge—this will close a door quietly. Made in japanned iron or polished brass, it is made in a variety of sizes.

Turning now to door-closing springs, Fig. A337 shows two patterns. Usually the strength of the spring can be adjusted by increasing or decreasing its tension, by a single mechanism. In the wheel door-spring shown in Fig. A338 the arm pushes on a plate screwed to the door, the wheel making rolling contact between the arm and plate. These are in sizes 12 in. to 14 in. and are usually japanned finished. The coil door-spring shown in Fig. A339 is probably the simplest of such fittings. The longest size is about 14 in. This finds use on garden gates, etc., and is quite cheap.

One form of floor-fitted door-spring is shown in Fig. A340. These are made in very-light, light, medium and heavy patterns. They need care in fitting and the makers' instructions should be strictly observed.

Lastly, Fig. A341 is one example of a patent door check. As can be seen, it is fitted to the top of the door and its frame. This example is for closing doors which open inwards, but is also made for doors opening outward. The suppliers always need full details of the working conditions to enable the best fitting to be offered to you.

Fitting and Maintenance: Hinges and springs need care in fitting and maintenace. The correct number and size of screw should always be fitted and tightened up properly. The moving parts need lubrication from time to time, with special reference to outdoor fittings and patent door checks. Hinge pins of a set of hinges should most certainly be in one straight line, or binding (sometimes very small and unnoticeable) will cause undue metal wear, noise, and possibly binding of the door in its frame. The broad distinction is between the butt hinge, or butt as it is often simply called, and the longer strap hinges. The butt is intended for concealed fitting, being let into the thickness of the door and the door frame. It is thus suitable for ordinary house doors and cabinet work.

Doors made of wood too thin to take a butt hinge, such as braced-and-ledged doors, must be given a hinge with a long strap such as the T-hinge, while heavy gates need a hinge of the Collinge or similar type. The traditional materials for hinges are cast iron, steel and brass. For cabinet work, nylon hinges are available which need no lubricating.

TIMBER

While whole books have been written on the vast subject of timber, it is hoped that the following notes will help you to buy timber economically and at the same time obtain the right type of wood for the job in hand.

The hundreds of different species of timber are divided into the two main groups of hardwoods and softwoods. These names must not be taken too literally, however, as they apply only to the structure of the wood and not to its degree of hardness or softness in the usually-accepted sense. For example, Parana pine, though officially classed as a softwood, is, in fact, much harder than, say, obeche, which is officially classed as a hardwood. Both these timbers are much used by handymen as they are obtainable in wide pieces and are free from knots. Finally, we must consider plywood and composition boards.

Softwoods

This group which can generally be described as consisting of the coniferous types growing fairly widely in the more temperate climates, can be divided into three main groups. These are: redwood, whitewood and Canadian softwoods. Of these, redwood is probably the best known and most used for joinery work and is a suitable all-purpose timber for amateur or professional use. It planes and works easily to a good shiny finish and is available at all timber yards and handyman stores.

Whitewood differs very little in appearance from redwood, but, while equally good for constructional work and floorings, it is more difficult to plane to a smooth finish.

Probably the best known Canadian timbers are Douglas fir (Columbian pine), hemlock and Western red cedar. With the exception of cedar, these woods are harder to work than European softwoods and may be identified by their light to red-brown colour and bold graining. This graining is very attractive for decorative effect when a varnish finish is required but can cause trouble by showing through on a painted finish unless care is taken. An extra coat of paint will often help to minimise this danger.

Special Uses: With so many types of timber to choose from, some will obviously be more suited to certain jobs than others, and expense can probably be spared by starting off with the correct timber. Western red cedar is being used increasingly for outside work due to its inherent resistance to decay. No painting or preservative treatment is required as the natural oils contained in cedarwoods are sufficient to keep it in good condition for many years. These same oils, however, prohibit the use of ordinary iron nails or screws, which would stain the wood

and rot away in a very short time, and it is advisable to use galvanised sherardised or brass fastenings when working with cedar. Cedar is not strong, and should never be used for structural work, but it is very stable, and will not swell, warp or shrink as much as most timber, even in the worst conditions.

Douglas fir, on the other hand, has many special uses owing to its great strength/weight ratio, and has the advantage of being obtainable in clear grades which, though expensive, are almost entirely free from knots and other defects. A typical use for this timber is in the making of ladder sides.

Choosing Sizes: While timber may be cut to almost any size, large or small, it is not possible for a stockist to keep every size required, so in planning a construction it is advisable to work to the available standard sizes even to the extent of altering the specification slightly. If, for example, a non-standard size such as $1\frac{1}{8}$ in. $\times$ $4\frac{3}{4}$ in. is asked for, it is likely that this would be cut or planed from $1\frac{1}{4}$ in. $\times$ 5 in. and this latter size would be charged for, plus the cost of the machining. Thus it will be seen that money can be saved by using imported thicknesses of timber which are in general supply. These are $\frac{5}{8}$ in., $\frac{3}{4}$ in., $\frac{7}{8}$ in., 1 in., $1\frac{1}{4}$ in., $1\frac{1}{2}$ in., 2 in., $2\frac{1}{2}$ in., 3 in., and 4 in. Widths progress in increments of $\frac{1}{2}$ in. up to 6 in. wide and 1 in. increments thereafter. Softwood is normally only obtainable up to 12 in. wide, but, if the works permits, it will generally be cheaper to buy two narrower boards to make up the desired width because 9 in. to 12 in. boards cost more per sq. ft.

Machining: A good selection of sizes is obtainable already 'planed square-edged' (P.S.E.), but it must be understood that this timber will not measure up to full size. The British Standards Specification allows 3/16 in. for planing, but it will be found that most planed-up timber will be only $\frac{1}{8}$ in. under size. Thus 1 in. $\times$ 2 in. P.S.E. will actually finish $\frac{7}{8}$ in. $\times$ $1\frac{7}{8}$ in. Floor boarding (P.T. & G.) and matchboarding (P.T.G. & V.) conform to this rule but the actual laid width of these will be $\frac{1}{2}$ in. less than the normal size to allow for the tongueing-and-grooving.

If a fine finish is required, machine-planed timber must be planed again with a hand plane to remove the marks which are always left by the circular action of machine cutter blades. Heavy sanding will also remove these marks, which appear as very faint lines across the width of the piece. Good machining will leave approximately fourteen marks per inch.

Defects: Most of the faults are cut out of the timber before shipment to this country. Knots, splits and wane are left, varying in quantity with the grade of timber offered. Knots (which are usually only found in softwoods), if they are sound and tight in the wood, do not present much difficulty, and affect only the strength of the timber. Splits, on the other hand, are liable to cause trouble by lengthening as the timber dries out, and all such splits should be cut out. Wane is part of the bark of the tree and, if present, will appear on the edges of the piece. This is the sign of a lower grade of timber and will be less satisfactory in use owing to the large proportion of sapwood which will be present. Sapwood is not as durable as the heartwood and if there is any likelihood of insect or fungal attack this usually develops first in the more susceptible sapwood.

If timber is used in damp conditions or to replace pieces which have been affected by rot or insect attack, it is essential to make use of one or other of the preservative treatments which are available. Some of these may be bought in liquid form and applied by brush or spray; this may be adequate, but complete protection can be given by pressure impregnation carried out at special plants throughout the country. This is not an expensive process; some timber merchants carry treated timber in stock. A similar process can now make timber virtually fireproof.

Some timbers, particularly Douglas fir, contain small pitch or resin pockets, and these will probably not be apparent until the wood is planed. If such small defects are on a surface which is to be painted or varnished, the resin should be carefully scraped out and the resultant depression levelled off with filler. If this is not done, the resin will work out to the surface and spoil the finish. Discoloration is often to be found when timber has been stored outdoors, but this is usually in no way detrimental, and when planed up even the blackest-looking piece will be seen to have a bright, clean appearance. Redwood, however, will occasionally be discoloured by sap stain. This will cause the sapwood to turn a green-blue colour which cannot be removed by planing; but, while altering the appearance of the timber, this has little effect on the strength or other properties.

Dryness and Seasoning: The use of wet or unseasoned timber can often lead to disappointment, for wood may twist when drying out and spoil an otherwise perfect job. A great deal of the softwood imported into this country is kiln-dried before shipment; or otherwise, where kilns are not used, the timber will have been air-dried and is therefore seasoned and ready for use. Wood is an hygroscopic substance and thus will pick up moisture from the air, or, more directly, by being left out in the rain. However, wet timber is not necessarily unseasoned as any such surface wetness will quickly dry out in warm conditions without any adverse effect other than slight swelling and shrinking. This, of course, is the cause of sticking windows and doors in winter. Ideally, all timber should be thoroughly acclimatised to the conditions in which it is to be placed, though this is seldom possible. Always allow wet softwood to dry out in a cool, dry place for a few days before use. Hardwoods require thorough seasoning, as will be discussed later.

Hardwoods

Compared with the relatively few species of softwood which are in general use, the available choice of hardwoods would seem to be almost bewildering in number and type. A complete list would probably include more than six hundred different kinds of hardwood, compara-tively few of which would be of interest to the handyman. Approximately fifty species are commercially available in this country, and of these only a handful will be of use to do-it-yourself enthusiasts, though all too often only the ubiquitous oak, mahognay or walnut are considered.

While it must be admitted that these three hardwoods are very satisfactory, there are other suitable woods which give an unusual effect and finish. However, it will be as well to discuss oak, mahogany and walnut first.

Oak: Most of the better class of oak on the market at present is imported from Japan. This is available in a very wide selection of sizes and grades, and prices, too, vary a great deal. Plain sawn oak is very much cheaper than the more exotic prime quarter-sawn stock with its distinctive graining. As well as our native English species (Quercus Robur), oak is also imported from several other countries, but none of these is as readily available or as useful to the handyman. Really dry English oak is ideal, but it is seldom obtainable as most of this wood is sold unseasoned straight from the saw, and in this condition it is only suitable for use as fencing, gate posts, etc. Oak takes many years to become air seasoned, so unless kiln dried stock is obtained it must be assumed that the material will be only partially seasoned. This means that some shrinkage may take place and there will be danger of the wood twisting slightly if used in warm, dry situations. In this respect quarter-sown oak is worth the cost, for it is less liable to shrink.

Japanese oak is fairly easy to work; with care, and the use of a scraper, a very fine finish is possible.

Mahogany: The largest imports of mahogany are from West Africa, but British Honduras mahogany is also in demand, particularly for shipbuilding, owing to its fine even texture and easy working qualities. It is, however, much more expensive than the African varieties. There are several timbers collectively called African redwoods, which are much akin to mahogany and which are often sold to the public as mahogany, but this is presumably a case of mistaken identity for there is little or no price advantage. Two of the most common of these timbers are sepele and utile both of which are like mahogany in appearance, though utile is a little heavier, while sapele is well known for its stripey graining. For the purposes of this article it may be assumed that where mahogany is mentioned the same remarks will apply to sapele and utile.

Mahogany also is obtainable in a variety of sizes; boards over 24 in. in width are occasionally available. Very little lumber under 1 in. thickness is imported, and thinner boards will be hard to obtain—or be considerably more expensive. It is as well to bear this in mind when planning the woodwork in hand. Mahogany seasons much more quickly and easily than oak and does not usually show a tendency to cracking or twisting. Indeed, most of this timber offered for sale will be seasoned sufficiently for interior use. A good smooth finish is easily obtained, though here sapele may prove an exception, for the handsome and distinctive striped grain in this timber is caused by interlocking of the fibres. This means that the grain of the wood runs in opposite directions along the length of a plank and this necessitates planing each narrow stripe the correct way. If this is not done, the fibres will 'pick up' and it will not be possible to obtain a good finish as even heavy sanding will not remove the marks. For this reason it is not always wise to machine-plane sapele, for unless the cutters are set exactly, this effect of planing against the grain can produce marks which are virtually impossible to remove by hand. Incidentally, sapele is used for building fire engine bodies because it resists charring.

Excellent substitutes are the crabwoods and pearwoods —and Honduras cedar. The latter is fairly soft and has great use for furniture drawers and linings, as it is naturally moth-repellent.

Walnut: Walnut is much favoured in decorative furniture making, because of the beautiful effects obtained with its veneers. The traditional types are in short supply —but there are many other excellent types available, such as Queensland walnut (which is much stronger but rather hard to work), Nigerian (which has a natural golden-brown finish accented with dark streaks), and the American black (a walnut that is very hard and durable but quite pleasant to work). Marsonia is also favoured because of its attractive purple-brown colouring.

Other hardwoods which are occasionally used for furniture are beech, birch, ash, elm and lime; but their unusual properties mean that they are more suitable for special purposes and are consequently available only in comparatively small quantities.

The naming of some of the lesser known hardwoods can often be confusing and many species have several names, some of which may be misleading. For example Rhodesian teak is not teak at all and a better name for this timber would be Rhodesian redwood. Another hardwood with more than one name is idigbo. This timber is also known as emeri or African yellow oak. It has no botanical connection with oak, but looks very much like flat sawn European oak, though perhaps more yellow in colour; where the finish is to be stained or varnished idigbo makes a good and much less expensive alternative.

All thicknesses are imported from ⅝ in. up to 4 in. and very wide boards are available. Idigbo seasons quite easily, and even the thinnest sections show little tendency to warp or twist. Some interlocked grain similar to that in sapele is occasionally present, but as idigbo is a softer timber this is easier to smooth down. If this wood is planed and then allowed to stand for a few days the surface will take on an attractive pink sheen, but this will disappear if planed or sanded again. Idigbo is not suitable for use as draining boards or similar articles which are in contact with water, for like real oak it will quickly become discoloured and black.

Sycamore: This is one of the best hardwoods to use for draining boards, being a good substitute for the more expensive teak. There are a few other timbers which are marketed as a substitute for genuine teak and of these afrormosia is probably the most satisfactory. Sycamore is also useful in having a very white colour which lends itself to attractive contrast with darker woods, but it has little visible graining.

With so many hardwoods obtainable, from abura to zebrawood, it is only possible to give brief notes on some of the special uses and most common defects of the better known species.

Ash and beech deserve mention, if only because they are used for the handles of most tools. Both are very suitable for turnery work, and ash in particular is extremely resistant to shock loads such as sudden bending or hammer blows. Mansonia, imported from Nigeria, is another timber which will turn easily to give a good finish.

East Asian Hardwoods: Many of the East Asian hardwoods are very hard-wearing and durable. Two of these are yang and keruing, which are a dark reddish-brown in colour and very evenly grained. They are rather hard to work with hand tools but where toughness is the prime requisite they are ideal, and keruing is relatively cheap. Probably the cheapest imported hardwoods are sold as 'mixed Malayan' and while this term may include as many as six different species, this is a good buy where a quantity of lower grade hardwood is required, for, say, joisting, etc.

Grading and Seasoning: Hardwoods are graded in a totally different way from softwoods and the terms used are more easily understood. The best grade in hardwood is prime, which may also be called 'F.A.S.' (firsts and seconds). After this come 'selects' and then the various 'common' grades. From the handyman's point of view it is worth the small extra cost always to use prime grades for joinery work, as this grade includes the best textured and thus more easily worked timber.

It is very seldom that knots are found in hardwoods; besides a few defects which have already been mentioned, the main difficulty to be found is in the seasoning, or perhaps the lack of it. Very little kiln-dried stock is available except to special order, and the air seasoning of most hardwoods is a very long process. The most usual defect is, therefore, twist caused by the wood drying unevenly. This can be minimised by gradually acclimatizing the timber to its situation, and by the use of good joints and plenty of fastenings. This twisting will become very apparent if small sections, say ½ in. × ¾ in. or smaller, are cut from a larger board for if they are left for only a short time they will twist and curl so much as to be almost useless. If such small pieces are needed for cover strips or the like, they should be cut and then pinned or glued in position at once, when the fastenings will hold them straight.

Worm holes, often not apparent before the wood is planed, are occasionally found, but as a general rule these do not mean that the wood is infected.

Plywood

Present-day plywoods are extremely versatile and most attractively surfaced. Purpose-made ply is available for constructional work, concrete formwork, interior and exterior decoration, etc. The sheets which make the plywood are literally peeled from the log on special machines. The sheets are glued and pressed together in layers with the grain running alternately in horizontal and vertical fashion. The commonest ply is better known as three-ply; above that number of laminates the material is known as multi-ply.

The plies are usually of birch, and the decorative veneer types have facings on one or both sides in oak, mahogany and so on.

Before buying plywood the following five points must be considered: thickness required; length and breadth and direction of grain on face side; whether the plywood will have to withstand steam, moisture and/or water; the kind of finish to be applied; the quality or grade required.

Thicknesses: Never ask for 'three-ply' or 'five-ply'. Ask for the actual thickness required. Three-ply can be 1/16 in. or ⅜ in. thick! Fig. A342 shows the make-up of two types of plywood which are virtually identical in thickness.

Fig. A342. The make up of plywood in Finnish Birch and Douglas Fir.

Fig. A343. The length and breadth should always be given to denote grain.

Grain: Always give the length and breadth to show the way of the grain, e.g., 24 in. × 12 in. = long-way grain; 12 in. × 24 in. = short-way grain (see Fig. A343). Unless you wish to buy by the sheet, which is cheaper, and then cut as required, ask for the actual size needed or the nearest offcut size, as small offcuts can usually be obtained at reduced prices. When cutting, use a fine-toothed saw at a low angle and always cut on the face side, taking care not to strip the face veneer at the end of the saw-cut.

Weather-resistance: It is important to know if the plywood will have to withstand moisture or long exposure to weather. The easiest way is to ask for 'interior glue' or 'exterior glue' when buying. Some glues are only moisture resistant whereas glues which are guaranteed as 'W.B.P.' will be proof against long exterior use and actually remain unaffected by boiling in water. Particular attention should be paid to protecting the edges of plywood used outside, with a good lead paint or sealer; although the plywood will not delaminate, moisture can be absorbed and run along the plies between the glue lines, thus giving an uneven surface or blister caused by the swelling of the plies.

Finishes: Will the finished job be varnished, stained and polished or painted? This will affect the type of plywood required. A cheap sanded plywood is excellent for painting, even if plugged. For treatments where the grain of the plywood is to be brought out, much depends on the personal preference of the buyer and whether you are matching existing articles. Points to watch are a well-sanded surface, joints in the face veneers, whether plugs can be allowed and the general pattern of the grain.

Grades: Grades of plywood vary. With glue, the number and type of knots, splits, plugs, etc., all count If only one side of the plywood will be visible, it is com-

mon practice to use a grade with knots on the reverse for cheapness, but if only a small quantity is involved this may not be worthwhile.

Regarding knots, these should be sound and free from rot. A tight knot should not exceed in diameter one-fourth the greater transverse dimension of the piece unless so situated as not to impair its strength. In addition it should be noted that where such a knot is enclosed within the thickness of the piece, its width should not exceed one-third of the thickness. A loose knot or knot-hole should not exceed in width one-half the greatest width permitted in the case of a tight knot, unless it is situated as not to impair the strength of the piece. A knot cluster or a knot-hole cluster is measured as a single knot.

It is worth bearing in mind that although thin plywood has been superseded in many cases by hardboards, there may be only a small difference in price; a polished door panel in plywood, for example, may be cheaper in the long run than a hardboard one painted every few years. Consult your timber merchant or handyman's shop about your exact needs to make certain you get the correct material for the job.

Composition Boards

These boards are an interesting development initiated by the timber industry in order to eliminate waste and to meet the increasing demand for good but cheap timber.

Today these 'man-made' timbers, as they are called, are commonly used and often preferred because of their high quality, strength, superior finish and stability. The commonest is blockboard. The core consists of regular squares or rectangles of wood up to 1 in. wide which are glued together and glued again between a sandwich of timber 'skin' or veneer. The boards consequently offer a very wide surface area, unimpaired by joints, and are ideal for normal joinery or constructional work. Often these boards are specified with a lipped edge; this means the boards give the appearance of a solid piece of timber. When both edges are lipped, as in the case of doors, they are in great demand for the popular 'flush' appearance, various finishes being available. Laminboard is a rather more expensive development of the principle whereby long, narrow strips of wood are glued together to give an immense vertical strength.

One of the timber industry's greatest gifts to the builder and handyman has been particle board. The material consists principally of small chips of wood mechanically bonded under pressure with resin, to give a solid board with virtually no inherent vices. As plain chipboard it is used extensively by the building and shop-fitting industries; as a finished material with plain or exotic veneers, finished both sides, with one, two, or all edges veneered, it is offered in standard accurate sizes for the professional and handyman to use in most projects which can be undertaken with normal timbers. The material is finished to a high degree and finds a ready market in the handyman field.

Probably the only cautionary word to be offered regarding the use of this material is that it must be jointed and worked according to the manufacturers' instructions.

METHODS

METHODS

METHODS

Having dealt with the various types of tools and equipment available, we now consider the methods of using them. From 'what to do it with' we now turn to 'how to do it'.

JOINTS IN WOODWORK

Almost everything that is made with wood requires jointing—and joints are the weak link in the chain of construction. If they are not fashioned correctly, the finished article will not give good service. A good design for a joint must be such that all the stress and strain imposed upon it will be equally distributed about the whole. At the same time, account ought to be taken of the unstable nature of the material used, with some effort made to help retain it in a true plane. And, of course, with the bare minimum of cutting—especially across the grain in places where a weakness would occur.

Framing Joints

There are accepted standard joints to cover almost every sort of framing that you are likely to make. The ones dealt with here are in most common use for holding the corners together of various types of framing.

Door Frame Joints: Fig. B1 shows a mortice-and-tenon joint used on a door frame of solid timber. There may be a weight above to be carried and therefore the mortice is cut in the head piece with support given from below by the shoulders of the tenon. Cramping the joint together would be difficult so it is usual for draw-boring to be used instead. This is done by the following method. Enter the tenon fully into the mortice and tap home. Start drilling a $\frac{3}{8}$ in. hole central across the mortice about $\frac{1}{3}$ up from the shoulder of the tenon. Stop drilling when the point made a mark on the tenon, and withdraw the joint. Continue drilling the hole through the other wall of the mortice. Place the point of the twistbit on the tenon about 1/16 in. nearer to the shoulder and drill the hole right through. Re-make the joint using a waterproof adhesive, and tap the tenon fully home. An inch longer piece of $\frac{3}{8}$ in. dowelling can be pointed at one end, coated with adhesive and then hammered through the hole. This draws the two members together very tightly and holds them

there. The excess of the dowel can be cut off flush at both sides. Wedges can be used to fill the fine gaps at the ends of the mortice to squeeze the tenon really tight. The door stop fitted to the inside of the completed frame is joined at the top with a scribed joint. Cut the top piece tightly between the two jambs and fix into position. The uprights are then squared and scribed to fit around the section where they join. The overhanging horn can be shaped for building into new brickwork or it may be cut off for fitting the frame into a prepared brick opening.

For some internal doors, especially on lath-and-plaster partitions where there is already a rough timber frame, a prepared lining is used instead of a solid frame. This is made of boarding of about 1 in. nominal thickness and to the width of the plaster faces at either side. In Fig. B2 you will see that the tongue joint had been used, the main purpose of which is to prevent warping of the boards. The joint can be screwed, but more often 2 in. oval brads with a strong adhesive are used to fasten it together. Linings for a trap door to the loft can be made in the same way. The tongue need only be about $\frac{1}{4}$ in. wide and project for the same distance into the prepared groove.

The half lap depicted in Fig. B3 is again for use on boards but particularly where the showing of the fullness of the end grain would be objectionable. The joint is non-load bearing and is considered more suitable for cabinet or joinery work of a non-structural nature. If it would help the design, the end grain of the lap can be made into a pencil round so that in effect it would not show at all on the end. The thickness of the overlap can be $\frac{1}{4}$ in. and nailing is done in both directions for extra strength. This joint can be used for joining the corners of box framework like shaving cabinets, etc., also for the top board of a set of book shelves and the like—in fact for almost any whitewood furniture of boarding construction that is to have a painted finish.

Joints for Drawers: Drawers require a joint that can withstand tension. The dovetail joint is ideally suited to prevent the sides parting company from the front and back when the drawer is in heavy use. Industrial drawers can have the dovetailing extending through to the front for a stronger joint. In these types of drawers the strength is more important than the finish. But for all other than these strictly utilitarian drawers are lapped type of dovetail joint featured in Fig. B4 is used. At the back, where the finish is not so important and where the wood is thinner, the dovetail is cut for the full thickness. The best way to make this joint is to mark out and cut the tails on the drawer sides first. The front is then gauged up for the projection and the thickness of the sides, off the ends. By clamping the front in a vice, the side is rested into position for the pins to be marked with the tip of the dovetail saw or a penknife. Square the thin edge of the pins down to the other scribe mark and the housings for the tails can be chopped out with a bevelled-edge wood chisel on a firm flat surface. If an accurate fit can be managed, the joints can be fitted together with a strong adhesive only. Otherwise panel pins can be used as an extra fixing providing they are punched well below the surface.

The halving joint, Figs. B5a and B5b, is easy to make and is in regular use for jointing battens and quarterings together. It is not very suitable for joining boards. Other variations that may prove serviceable for certain work incorporate the dovetail shown in Figs. B6a and B6b. This type of joint is mainly for use when part of the frame is in tension and there is a drag on the joint.

Mitre Joints: For joining any two pieces of timber together at right angles, where the outer sides are exposed and a finish is required, the mitre joint is ideal; but as there are no interlocking or overlapping parts the joint is weak and not much use for structural work. There is, however, a great field in both cabinet making and some joinery work where it is almost indispensable. The simplest form is the glued mitre, nailed from both directions. Where nailing is not suitable, the joint is glued and a small angle block is glued into the corner for strength. Cramping is most desirable for this method of mitring. For specialised jobs where a mitre is essential but where some extra bonding is necessary one of the joints shown in Figs. B7a, b, c or d could be employed. Fig. B7a shows dowels being used for the bonding.

The simplest way of making this joint is to cut and plant the mitre accurately, then hammer a 1 in. panel pin at 2 in. intervals along one mitre for the central positions of the dowels. Position this part in a vice and cut off the panel pin heads to leave a 1/16 in. projection. By accurately placing the other mitre and tapping it into position, a corresponding set of impressions will be made. Withdraw the panel pins to leave two sets of marks into which the point of the twistbit can be entered for drilling the dowel holes. Fig. B7b is a sound form of the combined mitre joint, but it does require a high degree of skill in making. There is little room for adjustment once the parts have been cut. Only one of the mitres can be planed properly; the other can be partly planed with a bullnose plane and then pared with a bevelled-edge chisel. Fig. B7c is an easy joint to make where a power tool can be used to form the grooves. The mitre is trued accurately first and the grooves are cut square off the faces. Before gluing the joint together, a loose tongue of short-grain plywood is fitted and the joint cramped dry for a test run. Fig. B7d is a most complex joint that requires a fair degree of skill to fashion properly. Nowadays it is a joint mainly for the perfectionist. It consists of the basic mitre with an internal set of dovetails and pins similar to those shown in Fig. B4. A further version of the strengthened mitre joint is illustrated in Fig. B8; this time veneers are glued into sawcuts.

One of the most common joints in regular use is the haunched mortice-and-tenon shown in Figs. B9 and B10. The haunch is necessary to position the tenon away from the end of the stile and, by fitting into a prepared groove, it prevents the outer edge of the rail from curling. Doors, top and bottom rails of sashes, backing frames for hardboard, are some of the articles that can be constructed with this type of joint. Fig. B9 shows the one generally used for joinery work, with the end grain of the tenon showing on the edge of the stile. Wedges, with sometimes a panel pin, are tapped into the dovetailed space at the sides of the tenon for clamping.

Polished cabinet work requires the stopped tenon in the illustration Fig. B10. Providing that there is a fixed panel set into the grooves, no further aid other than glue is necessary to hold the joint firm. A system of foxtail wedging is an advantage for frames that have a loose panel or a glass pane inserted. Either one or two wedges can be employed into prepared sawcuts away from the sides of the tenon. To allow for the expansion that takes place automatically when the joint is cramped, the mortice must include a dovetail shape at one or both sides. This must be sufficient to house the tenon fairly accurately in its expanded state because the joint cannot be parted for adjustment once cramping has commenced. Where possible, tenons ought to be cut for one-third the total thickness of the material used, where both parts being joined are of equal thickness.

Another kind of dovetail joint is the one featured in Fig. B11. It is very simple to make and once again is favoured where one part of a frame has a pull exerted, such as the meeting rail of a lower sash in a pair of sliding sashes.

A straightforward dowel joint is depicted in Fig. B12. This can be used on a variety of framework, but the weakness is the comparative ease with which the joint could be parted, as only the small area of the dowels is effective with the gluing. Often, the dowels are pinned into position for extra stability. Better still, use this form of jointing on a framework that is being covered with some form of sheeting material such as plywood. Fig. B13 shows the use of corrugated fasteners to make a simplified joint.

Other Joints

So much for joints suitable for corner construction of framework. Some of these could be utilised or adapted for many other jobs. Providing a joint is well designed, the strength is mainly determined by the accuracy. Therefore it is important to remember, especially where there is a limited skill, to cut to one side of all scribe lines and, if need be, complete the cutting with a paring chisel.

Housing Joints: The housing joints in Fig. B14 are popular for a variety of work because of their simplicity. In cabinet making, they are ideally suited to the joining of shelves to ends, and for partitions. Joint *a* is better for use where the joint has to be self-bonding or where there seems a positive danger of an end being parted from the shelf.

Joints for Shelving: An example is a longish end-piece with only a central shelf. If desired it could be stopped short of the front, as in joint *c*, for a neater finish. In that case the fitting is by gluing and sliding the shelf into the dovetailed housing from the back. Joint *b* is the more common form, especially for softwood that is to be painted. Glue and oval brads can be employed to hold the joint firm. Polished work demands that the housing be

Figs. B1–B13.

B1. Mortice and tenon of the type used for door frames and window surrounds.

B2. Tongue joint, as used for door casings.

B3. Half-lap joint. This is not a load-carrying joint but is used where neatness is more important than strength.

B4. Lapped dovetail; often used to join drawer front to side.

B5. a, b. The halving joint can be used either on edge or flat.

B6. a, b. An improvement on the plain halving joint is this 'dovetailed' halving.

B7. a, b, c, d, show methods of overcoming the tendency of mitred joints to pull apart.

B8. Veneer slips inserted to strengthen picture frame joints.

B9. Wedged through mortice and tenon.

B10. Stopped mortice and tenon with fantail wedge.

B11. A through dovetail is commonly used in the lower sash of a window.

B12. Double dowel joint—glue must be used.

B13. A gusset or fish plate will strengthen a plain joint, as also will corrugated nails.

not visible from the front, as in joint c. Naturally, nails would spoil the finish so the stability relies upon a strong adhesive. To cut the housing, mark out the position with scribe lines and gauge the depth, about ¼ of the thickness. Nail hardwood guide battens to the scribe marks or clamp them down, then work the tenon saw along the edge until the full depth is reached. The waste is then pared out and trued with the aid of a 'grannie's tooth' tool. Quicker ways of making the sinking are with a special routing tool or with a routing attachment for the power tool.

Figs. B15 and B16 show some uses for the housing joint in carpentry; joint a depicts the usual method of joining studding to both the floor and ceiling plates of common work. The sinking is made for ¼ in. to ⅜ in. deep and fixing is by skew nailing through both sides of the stud. A better class work sometimes requires a tenon, either stub as in joint b, or full length with draw bored dowelling. The stub tenon that is formed with four shoulders instead of the two is called a joggle joint.

Floor Joist Joints: A further use for the stopped housing is to join trimmed floor joists to a trimmer as in Fig. B16. Because these timbers are load-bearing, the joint must be designed to suit the timbers in use. You will note the formulae for the depth that can safely be cut away from both parents. The sinking into the trimmer can be made by drilling with a brace and bit within the boundary markings and then chopping the remainder accurately with wood chisel and mallet. For maximum stability, or where the joist cannot be fixed through the back of the trimmer, a dovetail housing can be formed as shown in Fig. B14a.

The three types of joint that you see in Fig. B17 are really all housings in the reverse procedure: a and b are straight-forward notchings used to join floor joists with wall plates so that the top edges are kept in a true plane. The less-used cogging joint (c) serves the same purpose but has the advantage of gaining a full depth bearing of the joists on the plate. In no case ought more than 1/16th the depth of the joist be cut away to form the notch.

Whilst still on with floor joists, mention could be made of other joints which are often used on or to a trimmer. Fig. B18 gives the accepted ratios for the design of a tusk tenon. This is an exemplary joint in that it is fully self-bonding. A hardwood wedge is employed through a slot cut in the centre of the tusk for ⅓ the timber thickness. A similar joint, without the aids to bearing strength, has been used for many years in furniture making, especially for tables. Fig. B19 shows another method of making the joint between joists and trimmer. More often it is utilised on ceiling joists that are to be fixed to a central beam, but there are many other applications for this worthwhile joint. To avoid having the fillet of too large a dimension, screwing should be central of each joist position along the length for a direct bearing. The ends of the joists are then gauged from the underside for the notch to be sawn out.

Fig. B20 illustrates just two of the ways that timbers can be lengthened. B20a is the common lap joint used for floor plates and, in some cases, self-supporting head pieces that are to carry no imposed weight. The length of the lap will depend on the purpose it is to serve. Where the timber cannot be secured at or near the joint to the floor or another timber, the lap can be up to six times the timber thickness. Elsewhere it may only be necessary for it to be as long as a single timber thickness. Sometimes it may be an advantage to incorporate a dovetail shape into the length of the lap to provide some extra resistance against tension along the length. Use stout-gauge screws for the fixing. The scarf joint is more suitable for load-bearing timbers, Fig. B20b. The length can be found by marking out the splay-cut at 15 deg. off the edge of the timber. For light constructional work, two or more carriage bolts with nuts and washers are sufficient to clamp the joint firmly together. Timbers over 2½ in. thick and over 5 in. deep, where there is a heavy load to support, ought to have staggered bolts, with perhaps a mild steel fish plate at either side extending past the joint at both ends.

The bridle joint in Fig. B21 has a variety of uses. Where two timbers join at an angle in the same plane (such as a strut to a beam or a ledger) this joint is employed to prevent the strut from twisting out of alignment with its parent timber. Fixing is square off the face of the strut, with nails, screws or bolts—depending upon the strength required. Facially, the heel joint in Fig. B22, used on ledged-and-braced doors, is very similar. Although there is no reason why the complete bridle joint ought not to be made, especially on first-class work, it seldom ever is. In any case, the parent timbers are clench-nailed fast to the face boarding and there is little likelihood of a twist occurring in the strut only. The setting out for both the bridle and the heel joint are the same as shown in the inset to Fig. B22.

Joints for Door Frames: Mortice-and-tenon joints are the standard for all panelled doors. But as a tenon ought not to be wider than about 5 times the thickness, a different type is required from the one featured earlier for narrow rails. Centre rails (or lock rails as they are called) are often 8 in. to 9 in. wide. Therefore, two tenons are made as detailed in Fig. B23a, with a haunch between to prevent the rail from twisting. Not so much used these days, but shown as a matter of interest, is the double tenon in Fig. B23b. The prime purpose of this joint is to allow for a deep mortice lock to be fitted to the door without weakening the joint unduly. Both forms extend through the full width of the door stile and are wedged from the outer edges. Bottom rails can be made the same as Fig. B23a with the inclusion of a small haunch on the bottom edge to keep the first tenon inward from the edge. Where it is necessary to join a timber to, and between, two other fixed timbers, the chase mortice (Fig. B24) will be found invaluable.

As there is a partial amount of excess cutting required which will be visible when the joint is completed, the chase mortice is mainly used for work between ceiling and floor boards or in other covered positions. A bare-faced stub tenon is formed at each end of the spacer, and a mortice is cut to receive one end. The other mortice is cut in the form of a continuous chase with a square end.

Joints in Moulded Work: By cutting the end of one tenon to fit the angle of the chase, and widening the mouth of the normal mortice, the spacer can be set obliquely into position and tapped into place. Normally there will be sufficient spring in the side timbers; but should they be firm, the diagonally-opposed ends of the tenons and the shoulders must be eased to facilitate entry. Where moulded work of joinery is joined at internal angles, the correct joint to use is a scribed joint. One part of the woodwork is allowed to finish square into the corner. The other part is mitred to the correct angle and,

Figs. B14–B25.

B14. (a) dovetail housing; (b) through housing; (c) stopped housing.

B15. Methods of joining uprights to floor plates; (a) housing; (b) stub tenon.

B16. Housing used for floor joists at fireplaces, loft trapdoors, etc.

B17. Fitting floor joists to wall plates: (a and b) notching; (c) cogging.

B18. Tusk tenon joint.

B19. Notched joint with screwed fillet.

B20. Joints for lengthening timber: (a) lap joint; (b) scarf joint.

B21. Bridle joint.

B22. Heel joint as used on braced and ledged door.

B23. Door joints at lock rail: (a) the usual two tenon and haunch; (b) a double tenon used on heavy doors to accommodate a mortice lock.

B24. Chase mortice.

B25. (a) cutting a scribe joint; (b) mitre butt joint.

Fig. B26. Four popular types of tapered legs.

Fig. B27. A simple tapered leg commencing at the lower rail edge.

Fig. B28 (above). Chipping away the waste between saw cuts (straight-grained wood).

Fig. B29. A taper carried right through requires both a top and bottom rail.

with a coping saw, the profile is cut to shape. It will make a better fit if this cutting is undercut so that the back edge does not foul. An alternative method is to mitre the moulded section on both parts to be joined and then to cut the flat part square, or at an angle, to form a butt joint. Fig. B25a (with saw) is the scribe joint and Fig. B25b the mitre butt joint.

Naturally, there are many more joints that have not been dealt with but the reader will find that the more common ones in most demand for everyday work have been featured.

Making and Fitting Tapered Legs

Amateurs often experience difficulty when fitting legs set to compound angles. This is how to tackle the various problems.

The choice of timber is important in many respects when making tapered legs. A taper may be easily chopped out with a chisel where the wood is straight-grained since there is no possibility of cutting against the grain. However, many of the best timbers, particularly African and other tropical hardwoods, have interlocking grain, and great care is required if splitting into the surface is to be avoided.

Tapered legs may conveniently be divided into four groups (Fig. B26); those of square section and fitted parallel, square section again but fitted splayed, and rectangular section, which are almost invariably splayed, in both straight and curved forms. It is not intended to consider round-section legs here, which involve the use of a lathe.

The tools required to tackle tapered-leg work are probably already in the kits of most workers. A bevel for fitting the splayed types, and a coping saw and spokeshave for cutting out curves, are all that are required above the usual selection of chisels, saw and plane.

Square Legs: The construction of type A (Fig. B26) is perfectly straightforward and produces the effect shown in Fig. B27. The legs are fitted by means of the usual mortice-and-tenon, the taper commencing at the point adjacent to the lower edge of the rails, the latter thus having square-cut shoulders. If the taper were carried through to the top of the legs, the rail shoulders would have to be marked with the bevel, and true parallelism of the legs when assembled would be more difficult to attain.

The tapering, which is applied by cutting away the two inside surfaces of each leg, may be carried out by making a number of cross saw-cuts at intervals of approximately 1 in. and of such a depth that about ⅛ in. is left for planing. The waste wood between these saw-cuts should be chopped away with a chisel working across the grain, i.e. sideways if there is any danger of splitting, although the method shown in Fig. B28 is quicker with straight-grained wood.

In the splayed variation (type B of Fig. B26) the tapers are produced in the same way, the taper commencing, as before, from the lower edge of the rail. The ends of the legs are, in this case, marked out with the bevel set at an angle which may be ascertained by means of a paper pattern, or a trigonometrical method. Any slight error in this respect is not likely to matter since the only effect would be a greater or lesser degree of splay. Generally, the best angle is such that the bottom ends of the legs are apart by an amount equal to the width of the table top.

The objection raised against carrying the taper through to the top of the legs in type A does not, of course, apply to type B. However, if the taper were carried through to the top, two different bevels would be required; one for the rail shoulders, and another for the leg ends. Made as suggested, one bevel setting will serve throughout and the work is simplified.

The taper may be carried right through to the top of the legs in a design that requires both a top and lower rail (Fig. B29), since in this case a second bevel will have to be determined anyway. Furthermore, if the shoulders of the top and bottom rails are mutually parallel, accurate marking and cutting will be facilitated. Of the two bevels, that for the joints is of greater importance, since any slight error in the bevel for the leg ends may be corrected after assembly by trimming.

Splayed Legs: When cutting mortice-and-tenon joints for the splayed types of leg it must be remembered that the mortice should be cut into the angle of the bevel (Fig. B30). This operation is not particularly difficult if, when making the final cuts, the bevel is held against the chisel as a guide.

It will be necessary to cut out some wedges for use when cramping the joints where the legs are splayed. Parallel legs may, of course, be assembled in the normal manner.

Rectangular, Curved Styles: The styles C and D of Fig. B26 are very suitable for small occasional tables such as that shown in Fig. B31. They may usually be cut from 1 in. thick boards and are tapered across both the width and thickness. It is necessary to cut out the shape and also cut the joints before tapering through the thickness, in order to avoid the necessity of holding the tapered part in the vice. The inside curve in type D is sufficiently shallow to be cut with a flat-faced spokeshave, set, perhaps, a little coarser than usual. This technique results in a very smooth curve, which almost forms itself if the waste wood has been cut away fairly accurately with the coping saw.

A convenient method of joining this style of leg to the table top is by means of an ordinary through mortice-and-tenon to a small block, the tenon being wedged from the top side as shown in Fig. B32. The assembly is then screwed to the underside of the table top.

The last operation before assembly is applying the thickness taper; in this case the waste wood is cut away from both sides. The amount to be removed is usually so slight that the work may be carried out quite easily with the plane. Marking out may be effected by flexing a steel rule round the curved surfaces.

The angle of the splay is slight, as shown in Fig. B26, but if for any reason a considerable amount of splay has been introduced it would be wise to leave the bottom end of the leg square cut until after the tapering is completed, otherwise some difficulty would be experienced in keeping the leg firmly against the bench stop.

The assembly shown in Fig. B32 allows the legs to be placed independently, and is thus very suitable for kidney-shaped tables. For small round or square tables, however, the method shown in Fig. B33 may be used. The legs could be fitted to the crossed rails by simple open mortice-and-tenon joints, for with a fair amount of overhang in the table top the joints would hardly be seen from normal standing or even sitting positions.

The joint at the centre of the crossed rails is a simple cross-halving, and fixing the top is effected by screwing right through from the underside. Timber 2 in. × 1 in. would be a suitable size for a small occasional table.

Suggested Dimensions: The various types of leg may,

Fig. B30. Cutting a mortice into the angle of a bevel for a splayed leg.

Fig. B31. Attractive tapered legs for an occasional table.

Fig. B32. Wedges are used in this mortice-and-tenon joint for the legs shown in Fig. B31.

Fig. B33. Assembly for a small table. The centre joint is a cross halving; the table top is attached by screwing through from the underside.

of course, be of any dimensions to suit the work in hand, but the following are given for guidance. The legs on the table in Fig. B27 are 3 in. × 3 in. at the top, tapering down to 2 in × 2 in. at the bottom, and those on the kitchen stool in Fig. B29 taper from 2 in. × 2 in. at the top to 1½ in. × 1½ in. at the bottom. The curved legs on the kidney-shaped table in Fig. B31 are a little under 3 in. across the top and 2 in. across the bottom, the thickness tapering from 1 in. at the top down to ½ in. at the bottom.

WOODTURNING

In all types of turning where comparatively large amounts of wood are removed, some change of shape will be experienced. Round bowls became oval, the extent depending upon the dryness of the timber. In a bowl this is not as serious as in a lidded box, because whilst the former will still hold fruit or nuts, the latter may have two parts which no longer fit together. If, however, turning can be done in steps, roughing out and then finishing after a lapse of time, this trouble will be greatly obviated. Any 'movement' of the timber can be remedied in the finishing movements of the chisels.

For shallow boxes, the lid should fit inside the lower part. If cigarette barrels or similar tall boxes are envisaged, the lid can fit outside the box. An outside-fitting lid on a shallow box looks very cumbersome. On a tall box it is quite permissible, indeed it is better, because the ends of the cigarettes are not crushed.

An axe handle is an example of oval turning which has to be steamed to shape after the lathework is completed. It is not a process the amateur woodworker is likely to use often, though it has its uses. Some woods, such as walnut, will steam fairly easily, and this is how gunstocks are bent. Boatbuilders also often steam planks where an awkward shape is involved. Chairmaking occasionally involves a difficult bend, when steaming will help.

Bowl Turning

When turning a bowl, many amateurs simply screw on a metal faceplate and then shape up the outside and the

inside of the bowl at the same time. Faceplates are usually too large for this and/or the headstock casing is in the way and prevents chisel manipulation. The result is a heavy and mis-shapen bowl. Among the advantages of the wood-chuck method are the following points:

1. Inside and outside shapes are done separately with full freedom of movement.

2. Bowl bottoms can be much thinner because no screws are used for holding the bowl.

3. No risk of running into screws with consequent damage to tools and bowl.

4. No baize needed to hide unsightly screw holes.

5. General improvement of design.

Wood Chuck Method: This is illustrated in Figs. B34–B38. It is best described by a step-by-step account.

Step 1 (Fig. B34): Screw the faceplate on to the disc and turn the outside shape. Note that a ring foot is left on the bottom of the bowl.

Apply one coat of brush polish all over, paper down when dry and then finish with carnauba wax or other polish. Do not wax or finish-polish the underside of the ring foot, i.e. the surface on which the bowl stands.

Step 2 (Fig. B35): Remove bowl and screw a ⅞ in. softwood disc on to the faceplate. From the face of this, turn out a recess into which the ring foot of the bowl fits snugly. Glue the bottom of the recess and cramp the bowl in position. Leave to set. The grain of the bowl should be placed at right angles to that of the softwood.

Step 3 (Fig. B36): Remount in lathe and screw up the tailstock centre. This helps to take some of the weight in the preliminary turning of the inside. Turn out the majority of the waste, leaving a centre pillar for the tailstock. Remove tailstock and complete the inside turning. Brush polish, paper down when dry and finish in accordance with the outside.

Step 4 (Fig. B37): Unscrew the faceplate and split off the wood chuck by chiselling the end grain. Very lightly glasspaper the bottom of the ring foot to remove any traces of glue. Polish the ring foot by hand and the bowl is complete.

Step 5 (Fig. B38): If a flat-bottomed bowl is required, a solid stub instead of a ring foot should be left to locate into the wood chuck. In glueing here, a paper disc should be inserted when fastening the bowl to the chuck. When the bowl is removed from the chuck, the stub can be planed off and the bottom polished by hand.

Oval Turning

Take a piece of rectangular timber (ash is ideal for this purpose) and mark the centre lines on both ends. The size of timber is not important—2 in. × 1½ in. is used in this example, about 9 in. long. On the shorter centre lines mark two points A and B about 5/16 in. from the edges (Fig. B39).

With A as centre and AD as radius, mark an arc. With B as centre and BE as radius, mark the opposite arc. With C as centre and CF as radius, mark two opposite arcs which complete the oval shape. Centre-punch all six centres. Mark the corner waste and plane off as much as possible. This will make the actual turning much easier.

Using a fork centre in the headstock and, if available, a ring centre in the tailstock, securely mount the piece of wood on centres A. The work will revolve somewhat alarmingly at first, but with steady, controlled tool pressure the curve through D will be formed.

Change to centres B and form the curve through E. Finally, mount on true centres C and form the two remaining curves through F and G.

The corners are now rounded off with glasspaper and a pleasing oval shape results. In practice, oval turning has a somewhat limited use apart from handles and shafts, etc., but as a novelty and a turning exercise it does have its own value.

It may be found safer to leave the end inch or so unturned. The fork centre in the headstock may tend to slip if placed too near the outside. These end pieces are easily removed by a parting tool after glasspapering.

Rebated Lid Turning

Pill-box type articles are very attractive and have the advantage of using up small ends of squares and other off-cuts. They require a certain degree of accuracy, but apart from this precision no special 'know-how' is necessary. For this type of turning, a woodscrew faceplate is used.

Several kinds are now on the market, but all are of the same principle. A better holding power is obtained by screwing into side grain. Whether screwed end- or side-grain, the tailstock should be used wherever possible

to take some of the weight from the single holding screw (Fig. B40).

Step 1: Mount the work and turn into a solid cylinder. Remove the tailstock and turn out the underside of the lid and the rebate. Polish the inside of the lid then part off with a parting tool until approximately ¼ in. remains. Stop the lathe and 'screw' off the top.

Step 2: Turn out the main box and lower rebate so that the lid is a snug fit. Should the lid be too loose, turn off the lower rebate and form a new one to obtain a good fit. Polish the inside of the box.

Step 3: Fit on the lid and hold in place with very light tailstock pressure. Using a slightly-rounded scraping tool, even-up the outside of box and lid. A small bead may be cut on either side of the joint to disguise the joint if required. If this is cut too deeply the lower rebate will be parted-off! Remove the tailstock and slightly dome the top of the lid. This is where a good fit becomes essential for the lid is held merely by friction. Glasspaper lightly and polish. In parting-off, remember to stop short of the screw and to allow a sufficient thickness for the bottom. Undercut the bottom slightly so that there is no chance of the box rocking on its base. 'Screw' off when ¼in. remains and clean off the central nub with a chisel.

Figs. B34–B38. The five steps in the wood-chuck method of turning.

Fig. B40. Rebated lid turning.

Fig. B39. Marking for oval turning.

Fig. B41 (*above*).   Turning a leg.

Fig. B42.   Leg and block wedged and glued.

Turning Legs

Modern techniques and contemporary design have ousted traditional methods of construction in many fields —particularly for home handymen. For those who wish to make a coffee table 'in an evening' the method shown here will avoid lengthy mortices-and-tenons, under-framing, etc., and will only be a fraction of the cost of buying ready-made legs.

Four blocks of hardwood (size will depend upon the length of leg and the table dimensions, but should not be less than 3½ in. × 2¼ in. × ¾ in. for the smallest legs) have a ¾ in. hole (possibly larger) bored centrally. A 3/16 in. hole is bored at each corner and countersunk underneath for fixing to the underside of the table.

Turning: The legs are then turned as in Fig. B41. Notice that the round tenon should be at the tailstock end, which enables the tenon to be tried in the hole of the block and fitted to a nicety. If the legs are to be painted and have the 'brass end' appearance a slight nick should be made 1½ in.

or 2 in. from the end. This enables the leg to be painted black and the extreme end to be done gold and yet retain a crisp meeting edge.

Painting: Painting is best done in the lathe. To reach all parts of the leg it can be rotated easily by hand turning the headstock. This is a very clean method and solves the problem of what-to-do-with-it after painting.

The first leg is the easiest to do. The other three have to be identical copies of No. 1, which should be marked as the pattern.

Saw down the round tenon, glue-up, and then wedge firmly across the grain as shown in Fig. B42. When the glue is dry, plane-off the top of the block to give the required splay to the leg. Wide variations of splay angles are now possible by rotating the positions of the blocks under the table top, which should be not less than ½ in. plywood or some similarly suitable material. The various stages are shown in the photographs, Figs. B43–B46.

Fixing: The legs should be fixed temporarily by two

Fig. B45 (*above*).   Block and dowelled end.

Fig. B46 (*below*).   Ready for fitting to the top.

Fig. B43 (*above*).   The round tenon at the tailstock end.

Fig. B44 (*below*).   The first leg, pattern for the others.

Fig. B47 (*above*). Simple
construction for thick wood, and an
alternative bottom-fitting method.

Fig. B48 (*above*). Joint (B) is much stronger
than joint (A).
Fig. B49 (*below, extreme left*). Cabinet for
which a hardboard back is suitable.
Fig. B50 (*centre left*). The hardboard back
has a stiffening effect like a repair plate.
Fig. B51 (*centre right*). Battens provide
support for screwing hardboard-backed
cupboard to wall.
Fig. B52 (*below right*). Butt-jointed frame
member (*top*) would support hardboard, but
the lower member gives greater dependability.
Note halving joints.

screws; when you are satisfied that the splay angles are
correct, the top surfaces of the block should be glued and
all four screws inserted. Note that two different sizes of
screw will be necessary for each block, one being approximately ¼ in. longer than the other—or perhaps one
could be countersunk a little deeper.

Fittings: It may be difficult to purchase the brass,
thimble-like ferrules separately—but the pad end type
which is simply fitted in a universal socket should be
readily obtainable.

CONSTRUCTION

Box Units

Sooner or later the need arises for some item which,
because of size or special purpose, is not available ready-
made nor included among published designs. It is then
that the handyman benefits from knowledge that enables
him to work out his own ideas. It is particularly helpful
to be familiar with boxes, for the box structure is the
basis of at least half of the furniture we own or make. In
fact, if you can build a box, you can build furniture!

Simplicity Saves Time: A rigid box can be made as
simply as that of Fig. B47A provided you use a substantial
material and good modern glue with nails or screws to aid
assembly. This construction will make several sturdy
pieces of furniture which will survive years of service
without any trouble. The traditional joints—dovetails, for
instance—have been fully described elsewhere, but ade-

quate strength for many purposes can be achieved by
quick and simple methods. Plain, straightforward joints,
well made, often prove to be more efficient than complex
ones which have inaccuracies due to lack of the time
needed to cut and fit them really well.

Cut the panels clean and square—a saw table with your
electric tool guarantees this—and assemble with gap-
filling synthetic glue, and you can be sure of good results.
If necessary in a large job you could add fillets in the
angles where panels meet, to increase the glue area; these
will be useful, too, for screwing at points where the panels
present end-grain. Much of the strength in a box structure
of this type is in the support each panel gives to its neigh-
bours. They act as a sort of mutual-aid society.

The arrangement shown in Fig. B47A is all right where
the box rests on floor or table, or has legs under it. There
is a modern trend to the idea of fitting the legs to side
panels, and some examples are very attractive. But this
leaves the bottom unsupported with the weight of the
entire contents to bear; the joints are prone to strain and
might fail. The wily constructor can reduce the risk by
arranging for the joint to take the strain in 'shear' instead
of 'tensile'. The simple re-arrangement, shown in Fig.
B47B, joints the bottom panel within the sides instead of
under them. An explanation of the improved strength is
given in Fig. B48, in which (A) has only a very small area
of the joint in opposition to the strain, while in (B) a much
greater area is in the direction of thrust. Consider it as a
matter of effective joint thickness—the thickness as it

Fig. B53 *(upper).* A solid bottom panel with framing for hardboard sides.

Fig. B54 *(lower).* Construction of a simple drawer, shown bottom-upwards.

appears to the load; then (A) will always be small while (B) can have a thickness of anything up to 1 in.

You will notice also that the screw in (A) could be forced out by downward pressure, while the other arrangement permits it to be fitted through the side, a position in which it is virtually immovable by the force we are considering. The principle is an important one to be kept in mind for large jobs where utmost strength is of great importance. It is not an invariable rule, but one to apply according to the expected conditions of usage. If the contents are to be light and a bottom panel of thin plywood or hardboard is to be used, the jointing method shown in the first drawing is better because of the greater glue area.

Plan for Economy: When boxes are stood on edge, as they are for cabinets (Fig. B49), one of the narrow panels becomes the bottom and, in accordance with Fig. B47, is arranged to be stood on legs and to bear the weight of the entire structure and the contents. The largest panel is now at the back and carries no weight at all; clearly the expense of thick material is not justified and hardboard is good enough. Often it can be nailed or pinned in place during the last stage of assembly—or screwed for easy removal, if required. It can, however, serve a most useful structural purpose. Glued in position so that it is unable to flex in any direction, its edge-stiffness gives more rigidity to the assembly than one might expect. The effect is exactly the same as that obtained by using triangular steel assembly plates (Fig. B50), for the corners.

Taking this as a hint we can use an accurately-cut hardboard panel as an aid to assembly, for it can square the four panels to which it is screwed or nailed and glued, and hold them while the adhesive sets, after which its stiffening effect will be permanent. Choose a good dense hardboard rather than the papery variety which tends to laminate and break away from the joints.

The hardboard back is suitable for any free-standing piece of furniture but cannot be expected to support weight, as when a cupboard is fitted to a wall by screwing through to plugs. Reinforcement can be added in the form

of timber battens, as indicated in Fig. B51. These should be firmly jointed into the wood side panels before the hardboard is fitted.

Framework Not Essential: You will have noticed that (except for the back panels) the arrangements described so far call for the use of thick material such as blockboard or multi-ply. According to the strength required, you could substitute a good grade of chipboard; this would enable you to retain the simplicity of jointing that is one of the advantages of substantial material. Even so, many constructors will want to investigate the use of a cheaper product. Hardboard would seem to be the answer. However, much depends on how much time is available for cutting, jointing and assembling the considerable footage of good quality carcase timber that must be used to support it, and particularly on the additional cost of it.

There is no point in quoting prices here because they vary from district to district, but let us take an example on which you can table your own comparison based on local costs. Suppose a box such as that of Fig. B49 measures 2 ft. 6 in. high, 1 ft. 6 in. wide and 1 ft. 3 in. deep; for four solid panels (say, 1/2 in. or 5/8 in. thick) you would need 10 sq. ft. of plywood, blockboard or chipboard; the back would require 3¾ sq. ft. of hardboard. For the all-hardboard construction the total area would, of course, be 13¾ sq. ft., and in addition it would be necessary to obtain (allowing for off-cut scrap) at least 22 ft. of straight seasoned wood, say 1½ in. × 1 in. There will be differences in the costs of surface treatments. Thick material can be bought veneered; hardboard may require painting or covering with one of the plastic treatments, or can be purchased at higher cost with its own melamine decorative surface. Edge treatments must also be taken into account. Fill in the costs, at local prices, against the following table and compare them.

Solid Material	Total £ s. d.
10 sq. ft. blockboard (or alternative) @	
3¾ sq. ft. hardboard @	
Surface treatment @	
Total	

Hardboard and Carcase	Total £ s. d.
13¼ sq. ft. hardboard @	
22 ft. carcase timber @	
Surface treatment @	
Total	

Bracing for Strength: Even if the thicker material adds up to a higher total, the difference may be rather less than expected. Many busy men would write it off as a fair exchange for saving labour and time.

Nevertheless, framed hardboard is very popular among handymen. It has the advantage of lightness, and strength adequate for almost every purpose can be achieved so long as the skeleton is accurately-made and rigid. Nothing more complex than the halving joint is needed with an efficient glue. A difficulty is that this joint is not easily adaptable to accommodate the three directions from which the frame members meet at each corner. Arrange for the halving joints to carry the largest panels and fit the third carcase piece as shown in Fig. B52. It braces the edge of the narrow panel, but the butt joint with the frame is not renowned for its reliability. Another factor improves things a little however—the hardboard which, when glued in place, spans the joint and helps to bind the points together. In the direction in which the joint is most likely to part, the hardboard exhibits the most phenomenal strength. For complete safety we suggest one or two supplementary pieces of wood jointed into the carcase at points clear of the three-way union, as shown in Fig. B52, to tie front to back securely and accurately.

Thickness Gives Strength: The panel that will have to carry the weight of the intended contents must be well reinforced and something substantial has to be provided at the points to which the legs are to be fitted. Supplementary carcase pieces could be jointed in, but a cabinet with legs would be all the better for a thick bottom panel even if the remainder were of light construction. This can be united with the main skeleton in the manner illustrated in Fig. B53.

This is a typical example of the way the astute handyman adapts his technique to suit each need, borrowing from all methods—mixing them where necessary—but tied rigidly to none.

Your box may have to be divided by partitions or shelves. Often, in both professional and amateur work, these are loose-fitting and removable, but there is much to be said in favour of accurately-fitted permanent ones, for they brace and stiffen the other panels. This is good engineering, in which every part provides its contribution to the overall rigidity. Large hardboard main panels that are prone to be a little flabby or drummy become much stiffer when the attachment of shelves divides their areas. The shelves must have support, of course, and this can be supplied by cross-members jointed into the carcase in just the same way as already shown in Fig. B52. So we find that shelves, by introducing additional carcase members, bring a further contribution to structural strength.

For the shelves themselves you will find hardboard rather too flexible, except for really small sizes. Plywood, from ¼ in. to ½ in. thick according to area and load, is the most satisfactory material.

Lids and doors are not really structural parts of the boxes to which they are attached, and receive none of the mutual aid to which we have referred. The material for these must, therefore, be flat and inherently free of any tendency to distort. This rules out the use of any natural wood. We suggest plain pieces of plywood with nothing added except edge decoration and the usual door fittings. The thickness should not be less than ½ in. for furniture; for items as large as wardrobes 1 in. would not be too thick, and as warping becomes very obvious in large areas the plywood should be selected with very great care. The odd bit of fire or flood salvage simply will not do for this type of job.

Now to the boxes within boxes—drawers. Except for the very heavy contents of a workshop tool-drawer, the load is generally kept reasonably light by the limit to capacity imposed by the depth. Hardboard can stand up to the average weight and makes a cheap bottom panel, but it must be protected from any of the rub of the drawer action. Make the sides of rigid plywood, because there must be no risk of bulging, which could lead to jamming. The front, always subject to push and pull strains, must be as substantial as possible.

Drawer Construction: Drawers are the parts of furniture most prone to wear. One that has become sloppy can be more of a nuisance than a stiff one, for it wanders and binds in the most infuriating ways. The internal wear shows in the outward appearance of the furniture when the once-immaculate nest with neat parallel lines sags rather sadly into tilted rectangles showing uneven gaps. It is advisable to fit hardwood wear-strips to resist the effect of the sliding action. These, fitted under the bottom panel in the first assembly stage, give another benefit, for, as Fig. B54 shows, they form a base to which the other parts can be pinned and glued. It is, of course, necessary to provide corresponding hardwood runners in the cabinet so that wear is minimised there as well.

Enthusiastic householders who simply bristle with good ideas do sometimes run into difficulties when they come to practical interpretation. Yet most of our problems can be reduced by various combinations of simple basic principles; some of the most elegant furniture is basically of box design, or comprises a number of boxes. With a working knowledge of this basic unit many furnishing ideas can be put into practice and emerge from the workshop as useful and attractive household articles.

After the simple type of drawer, we must mention the orthodox construction. The fitting—'running and guiding' —conforms to tradition but is not very easy. (Figs. B55 and B56).

Contemporary Drawer Construction: Nowadays, with flush effects and other contemporary design demands, there are modern methods which render the making somewhat simpler. The increasing production and use of man-made board materials, such as veneered chipboard and blockboard, makes the modern box-like carcase of special appeal to the spare-time cabinet maker. The professional has, of course, widely adopted it for a long time past. Carcase ends, which are flush inside and out, permit quite different ways of drawer fitting than when end framing is used for panelled or slabbed ends. Initially the material may be dearer but the saving in time and labour will make it well worth while. A typically modern piece of furniture, with the drawers the main feature, is shown in Fig. B57 and the illustrations B58 to B61 show how the general effect can be varied by different drawer and handle arrangements. In one or two (B57 and B59), veneered drawer fronts are shown, but these are not imperative although they do improve the finished piece. In some, the drawer fronts lap over the ends and show no drawer rails. The lap permits the running to be done in various simple ways, and also saves slipping the ends as they are not exposed. Drawer rails, if any, can be concealed by the drawer fronts and can be of softwood.

The stopping of the drawer is done for you as it meets the ends, rails or runners. The drawer sides are dovetail-grooved (B62) into the drawer fronts, somewhat simpler than the usual lap dovetailing. Plastic runners and channels are shown in B63 and B64; the drawer base in B64 is fastened to the lower edges of the drawer sides and protrudes to run in the channels. This simplifies the construction as the sides and front do not need grooves to take the base.

In B60 and B65 the drawer fronts themselves act as handles. If wood bar-type handles are used and fixed at the bottom edges of drawer fronts, the bases must be kept up far enough to permit them to be screwed from the inside of the fronts beneath the drawer bases (B66). Simple metal pull-type handles (B67), made from aluminium or brass about 1/16 in. thick are shown which are quite easily

Fig. B57. Metal pulls.

Fig. B55 (right). Simple basic principles.

Fig. B56 (below). Orthodox drawer construction.

Fig. B58. Metal knobs.

Fig. B59. Wood bar handles.

Fig. B61. Hand holes cut in drawer fronts.

Fig. B60. Moulded drawer fronts.

Fig. B62 (left). Drawer side dovetail-grooved into drawer front.

Fig. B63 (right). Plastic runner and channel.

PLAN VIEW

Fig. B64 (*below*). Drawer base protruding to form runner.

Drawer side

Drawer front

End

Plastic channel

Drawer side

Bottom

Small gap between side and channel. The bottom guides not the sides.

Drawer front

Bottom

Fillet glued to front and bottom. (Stopping at outside of drawer side).

End

Fig. B65 (*right*). Handle is part of drawer front.

Handle moulded on bottom edge

Front

Bottom

Fig. B66. Wood handle secured from beneath drawer bottom.

Drawer front

Top rail

Top drawer front. (normal locking)

Concealed drawer rail

Drawer bottom

Lock plate screwed to rail

Lower drawer fronts

Fig. B67. Easily-made metal pulls.

4"

2½"

3½"

PLAN
(Approx. measurements)

Fig. B68. Locking plate arrangements for drawers overlapping concealed rails.

Plate to take lock tongue

Fig. B69. Channels and runners in hardwood or plastic.

¼" hardwood runner fastened to drawer side

Side

Front

A

B

Runners

C

Drawer front laps top fillet

D

End

or channels

ABCD hardwood fillets on end.

made and fixed. If we use drawer fronts which lap over the concealed rails, locking involves using plates as shown in B68 screwed in the undersides of the rails. The upper drawer front must be recessed at its lower edge to pass over these plates. When metal or wood handles are positioned at top edges of drawer fronts, the lock, if any, must be offset, beside the handles as shown in B57.

The illustrations are self-explanatory and various combinations of the ideas are possible. In all, some previous thought and careful marking out will permit the runners to be fixed to the ends prior to assembly of the carcase, and this saves the awkwardness of working, at a later stage, within a restricted box. Some of the suggestions may make your next job look contemporary and yet be easier to construct than a more traditional design.

Wood runs very smoothly on plastic and an orthodox drawer runs very well indeed if the runners have narrow strips of plastic on them. The runners may then be of softwood and even over the course of years the sides will not grind into these runners.

The method shown in Fig. B69 can have hardwood or plastic channels and hardwood or plastic runners fixed to the top edges of drawer sides.

Of them all, the simplest method for the amateur is probably that shown in Fig. B64. Here the drawer bottom projects about ½ in. at each side and runs on plastic channel or between wooden guides. If this method is adopted, the best material for the drawer bottom is a good grade of plywood, not less than ½ in. thick, and preferably ¾ in. thick for large drawers. The need for accurate fitting is reduced, since it is easy to sand-down the projecting edges until the drawer is an easy fit in the grooves. The drawer front can be dovetailed, grooved or screwed-and-glued to the sides, the bottom being screwed-and-glued to the sides only.

FIXING AND FASTENING

Screwing-and-Gluing

Most of our older crafts have developed excellent techniques over the centuries by a process of trial and error, and it is only in comparatively recent years that we have studied the why and wherefore of materials and methods, old and new. More often than not the rule-of-thumb of the old craftsmen is shown to be founded on sound principles, so we ought not to dismiss old techniques or materials just because they sound old-fashioned.

How Joints Hold: A nailed or screwed joint takes its strength from the grip which the wood fibres get on the shank of the fastening, plus the hold of the nail- or screw-head. This grip can be broken if sufficient force is applied —as in drawing a nail with a pair of pincers. There is little or no adhesion between the two joining surfaces, except the friction or compression caused by the nail or screw as it is driven home.

In a glued joint the two surfaces will be bonded together over the whole area that has been glued. However, it is a surface effect, so the strength depends mainly on two things—the strength of the glue and the strength of the wood (especially the adhesion between the surface layers and the interior of the board). It is quite possible to take a pair of boards, glue them together, and then apply sufficient force to tear the boards apart, leaving the glue line intact. This is a particular problem with plywoods, veneered chipboards and similar materials, and you can

see that there is no particular advantage in having a glue of far greater strength than the material it joins.

Hence a combination of screw-and-glue is often used to combine the deep anchorage of the cores with firm bonding of the surfaces. A metal fastening concentrates the stress at one point, while a glued bond spreads the stresses evenly over an area. The bonding of the surfaces eliminates leverage and the squeaking movement which follows. So, unless you are doing well-fitting dovetail or mortice-and-tenon joints, when screws are superfluous, always consider the advisability of screwing-and-gluing.

The Glue Must Suit the Material: While timber is still one of the most useful and attractive materials, we now take for granted many man-made substances and often want to stick them together. Many of them can be stuck with normal wood glues, but sometimes a special adhesive is necessary. The reason is that adhesion depends on the 'polarity' of the materials (i.e. the degree to which they absorb or repel solvents such as water) and the ability of the adhesive to 'wet' the surfaces. That is why a substance like polythene (which is of low polarity and repellent to almost all solvents, including water), presents a very difficult adhesion problem. It must also be possible for the solvent (water or other chemical) to get away after the joint is assembled, and this can be very difficult with non-porous substances such as metal and certain plastics.

Timber and related materials are sufficiently porous for all but the most viscous solvents to disperse; with water-based glues, full drying-out presents no problem. Wetting of the surfaces is not normally difficult. It is as well to be sure the surfaces are smooth but not polished or 'case-hardened'; if the fibres are folded over and are not cleanly cut, the glue will not penetrate and the minute bubbles of entrapped air will undermine the strength of the joint. So when gluing materials which have been under great pressure, such as chipboards and certain qualities of plywood, it is well to sandpaper lightly and then remove all traces of dust. Figs. B70, B71 and B72 refer.

Another case where sanding is advisable prior to gluing is when using one of the greasy timbers, of which teak is the best known. Glue up immediately after sanding as otherwise the grease will come up to the surface again. An alternative method of de-greasing is to use Teepol, strong detergent or ammonia—remembering, of course, to clean this away before gluing.

Not Too Much Pressure: While still on the subject of gluing timber and the like, a word on the subject of pressure will not be out of place. Basically, pressure is applied to hold the surfaces in intimate contact while the glue gets a grip; if the joinery is accurate very little pressure is needed.

If the joinery is not so good or the surfaces are large, the pressure is applied to force the faces into contact, but do remember this is the reason for the pressure and it is not required to make the glue stick. As the pressure is increased, some glue is forced further into the pores, and this is beneficial; but greater pressure-increase forces the glue out of the joint and away from the place where it is required to do its job, and a starved joint (with poor adhesion) may result. This applies particularly to some of the synthetics which are of low viscosity anyway, and become thinner, owing to the heating effect of the added hardener, when the joint is first closed. (One interesting exception, industrially, is when radio-frequency heating is being applied to the glue line; in this case great pressure is put on in order to raise the boiling point of the glue and thus prevent trouble due to steam or frothing.) Therefore, apply what pressure is necessary and no more. Use just the right amount of glue, too. Not so little that it has dried or soaked in before the joint is closed, and not so much that it is almost impossible to get the surfaces into contact.

Gluing Plastics: Now let us have a look at some of the non-porous adherents such as laminated plastic sheets. When a plastic sheet (e.g. Formica) is to be stuck to (porous) wood or something similar, the water-based glues are entirely successful as the water can get away quite easily. Pressure need not be heavy, but must be evenly distributed so that contact is secured all over the area. Select the glue (Animal, Casein, P.V.A. or Urea) according to the job in hand (e.g. a water- and heat-resisting glue if water- and heat-resistance are required), but remember that in this climate timber 'moves' with humidity and in its movement exerts a mighty force, so if you use a rigid-setting synthetic glue in February you may get an inexplicable failure if the job is exposed to the full heat of the summer sun. The timber dries and shrinks; neither glue nor plastic move, so something must give, and you will get a bowing effect or, at worst, a split panel.

If it is quite impossible for a solvent to get away from the closed joint there are two alternatives; one is to use a synthetic glue which sets without giving up solvent, the other is to get rid of the solvent before the joint is closed. The first alternative uses the rather expensive epoxy resins (e.g. Araldite) and the second an 'impact' glue (e.g. Evo-Stik).

the type, and has given rise to the terms of impact or contact glues. We can, therefore, understand the method of use; the glue is spread on both surfaces, thus ensuring the physical wetting mentioned earlier, and in ten to twenty minutes the solvent evaporates and the glue feels dry, or at least not tacky. When the two glue films touch they immediately grab and no shuffling is possible. This brings out two points. First, keep dust away from the drying films; second, ensure absolutely accurate alignment before the surfaces grab. One further point which sometimes escapes attention; the two films unite under pressure, so get as much pressure on as is practicable and you will get a more dependable and stronger bond.

Glues That Weld: There are a number of glues on the market which do not fall into the classes already discussed but have their own special uses. These can be classed as solvent glues as they tend to be based on a chemical other than water. The specialised adhesives such as Perspex and polystyrene cements are solutions containing the material. When applied, the solvent softens the surfaces to be adhered, and as it evaporates some of the same material is desposited in the joint. This can be considered a weld rather than a glued joint, and will normally have the strength and characteristics of the original material.

These specialized glues often give a fair result on materials for which they are not primarily intended, and may be considered along with the general solvent type. The chief merit of this type is that, being based on a volatile solvent, they dry very quickly, and where speed is more important than ultimate strength they can do a

Fig. B70. Much-magnified section of freshly-sanded wood surface, ideal for gluing. At this scale of magnification, no surface is really smooth.

Fig. B71. Much-magnified glue line showing normal irregular surfaces with all gaps filled with glue, giving good mechanical adhesion and allowing full play to inter-molecular forces.

Fig. B72. Much-magnified section showing fibres bent over by great pressure or a blunt knife. Trapped air and inadequate glue penetration inhibits good adhesion.

Epoxy Resins: The epoxy resins are quie remarkable and highly complicated substances and have many uses in their different formulations. As adhesives they will stick almost all materials, are unaffected by most chemicals and climatic conditions, set solely by chemical reaction and are dimensionally stable. For metal adhesion and many other uses they are quite invaluable, but at times, of course, their very rigidity is a disadvantage. When using an epoxy resin it is always worthwhile getting some warmth to assist curing; a really hot summer day, or an oven at low heat and with the door ajar, are good curing conditions.

Impact Glues: With impact glues we go from the completely-rigid to the completely-flexible. These glues are based on synthetic rubber and other resins in a solvent which is often inflammable, and they depend for their effect on the power of two films of rubber to unite under pressure even when superficially dry. Correct formulation ensures an increase in the initial 'grab' characteristics of

useful job. For light repairs or a quick make-do, for small areas of non-porous materials, on china, or on surfaces which might be susceptible to the solvent, they meet a need. On wood, however, they are not recommended, because their tensile strength is rarely adequate for the strain likely to be imposed.

There is a great deal of overlapping of the several types so that personal preference or advertising claims tend to determine the choice. Most modern glues are so good that they often give a reasonably satisfactory result on jobs and materials to which they are not really suited; but if you want the maximum strength and durability it is worth giving the glue a moment's thought and getting the one which is best for your immediate purpose.

Animal Glues: Nothing said above should be taken as meaning that the traditional animal glues are obsolete. They are still in wide use today, for jobs where they are suitable. They are called animal glues because they are made from animal bone or blood, fish residues, etc.

The cheapest and most widely used animal glue for general carpentry purposes is popularly known as Scotch glue.

It is unsuitable for use where damp and other extreme conditions prevail, being neither heatproof nor waterproof – but it is still widely used in the trade. It is available in cake or pearl form—the pearl form is a more convenient buy, although it costs a few pence per pound more. The advantage is that the pearls can be used to the precise amount required and they are more easily prepared for use.

Cake requires breaking under a cloth or paper and soaking in water overnight. Surplus water is poured off the following day and the jelly mass placed in the inner container of the glue kettle. The outer part of the kettle is partially filled with water, the whole being brought to the boil when the kettle is then allowed to gently simmer until the glue becomes hot and free-running.

It is important that the right viscosity is attained; if too much water is left in the glue after soaking, the hot glue itself will be thin and runny, making a very poor joint. Similarly, if too thick the glue will be hard to use and spoil accuracy and strength of the joint.

To test, dip the brush in the hot glue and lift it above the pot. The glue should run steadily and consistently.

Plywood is available both in the animal glue and in the resin glue form.

Everyone must have seen plywood de-laminated (come apart) after exposure to damp. If you built a boat with this plywood the results might well prove disastrous! So do ask for resin-bonded plywood which is glued with synthetic resins. This won't come apart, even if you boil it. But, of course, it will cost you more and so you use it only where it is necessary, for garden furniture, garage doors, kitchen or bathroom fitments and so on.

Plywood is not the only form of wood in which a glue is used as a bonding agent; wood-particle board or chipboard is an agglomeration of small fragments of wood, mixed with a glue (usually a synthetic resin) and formed into sheets under heat and pressure. A further use of adhesives may be made if the appearance of the board is improved by veneering, possibly on all faces. They are excellent materials, now widely used, and (provided a suitable grade is selected for the job) will perform as well as natural timber. If you intend to use glue when making up furniture with these materials, treat them as non-porous.

Wall Fixings

The primary household fixing need in the house is usually on the service side—shelves and cupboards in the kitchen. The first requirement will be wall fixings.

Basically the principle remains the same for all wall fixing, but in kitchens and bathrooms (particularly in kitchens) the periods to which the contents of the room are subjected to varying atmospheric conditions—steam, moisture and heat—affect room contents much more than in other parts of the house; timber will swell, then shrink and swell again. Ferrous metals used in fittings and fixings will soon rust unless well preserved; paintwork will deteriorate more quickly.

Fixings in the kitchen and the bathroom will therefore have to withstand a great deal of strain and stress—so the best and proper method will be the only acceptable way.

Type of Wall: The construction of the wall is a most

Fig. B73a. Plugged hole equals full screw length.

Fig. B73b. Pressure of screw threads expands plug.

Fig. B73c. Plug retains its properties when screw is withdrawn.

Fig. B74. Lath-and-plaster walls require bearers across studs for heavy loads.

important consideration when making heavy load-bearing fixings.

Much will depend on the age of the house; modern houses will usually be of the two-skin construction on outside walls—the outer wall being of facing bricks, then the cavity, and an inner wall of bricks or blocks. Usually the interior wall surface is made immediately to the inner skin wall so that there is no space between plaster, rendering and breeze or brick. The partition walls are usually of breeze or hollow blocks, again with plaster and rendering placed directly on the material.

With these, the wall fixing can be plugged directly into the wall, the only condition being that the fixing and the wall itself are strong enough for the load.

The load, of course, will have to be borne by the actual base material, not the plaster, or other rendering.

Fig. B73 shows a typical and popular method of plugging and fixing with the familiar Rawlplug. At A the hole is seen to be drilled deep enough to take the full length of the plug—with no load at all borne by the thin skin of plaster. At B the screw is partially turned home and the plug expands and grips the side of the hole. With the screw withdrawn at C one can see how this type of plug retains its properties without mechanical breakdown of the jute fibres.

Fig. B75. Detail of bearer across studs.

Fig. B76. Aggregate in concrete may trap a drill. A jumping tool will break up the obstruction.

In older properties, householders may find themselves faced with an entirely different type of wall construction.

This will be the old traditional lath-and-plaster, which is mounted on regularly-spaced wooden studs which run vertically on the inner face of outside walls, or on a wooden framework in the case of interior walls.

Fixing in such places can become something of a problem. The first job is to determine the location of the studs so that fixing may be made into them. In the case of heavy objects, such as a water heater, intermediate support between the studs may be required. Bearers in the form of stout pieces of batten screwed across the two studs, as shown at A and B in Fig. B74, will serve the purpose. The plaster in this illustration is left out to show how the wall is constructed.

Generally, it is best to remove the two small areas of plaster so that the bearers can be fixed in the manner shown in Fig. B75.

Where it is necessary to fix large areas to a wall, the problem of condensation requires the circulation of air behind the fitment. In such cases vertical grounds can be screwed over the studs, as shown at C in Fig. B74.

Locating Studs: Initially it may seem a difficult task to locate the studs beneath the plaster. It can be done quite simply, however—and all that is required is a sharp bradawl with a sound boxwood handle.

First, with the bradawl reversed, tap the handle on the wall and travel in a lateral direction for a foot or so. The wall will sound hollow until you reach a stud when the sound will become dull and flat. Now slowly tap downwards to make sure that it is not simply a lath that is deadening the sound.

Satisfied on this point, turn the bradawl round to the business end and drive the point firmly and slowly into the plaster. If the point suddenly shoots in without resistance after about ¾ in. of resistance you have missed the stud and will have to try again. When the stud is found you will have resistance all the way—and you can

make similar points left and right of the first to establish the exact centre of the stud. Now you have found your anchor point and can assume that at 16 in. centres you will find other studs.

This type of fixing, of course, requires no plugging, as screws can be driven straight into the wood.

Drilling holes in masonry requires special tools. They are not at all expensive and, naturally, the right tool for the job is the best. The choice lies between the older type of jumping tool, in which the hammer is used to drive the tool into the wall, or the modern and efficient carbide-tipped drill. With an ordinary hand brace or a low-geared electric drill these tools will cut an accurate hole in brick or masonry with surprising ease.

Generally a Number 8 and a Number 10 drill will meet all the handyman's requirements—for a few shillings.

The higher-grade types of drill will last for a large number of holes before regrinding is necessary and they will drill equally well in concrete, although this use is not to be recommended where the size of the aggregate in the cement is unknown. The drill will cut through stone in the concrete providing it meets it squarely—but if it strikes the stone at an angle or gets trapped between two stones, as shown in Fig. B76, there is a risk of breaking the brazed-on tips. If this happens, it is better to break the trap with a jumping tool before proceeding with the drilling.

Plugging: There are various ways of plugging, ranging from the home-made plug of wood to the proprietary brands of plugs such as Rawlplugs, plastic inserts—which can be quite good providing the correct sizes are chosen —or Philplug, an asbestos wool compound containing its own cement. When this is wetted and plugged into the hole it will dry out and form an integral part of the wall itself. An advantage with this material is that it can be used on the most irregular holes.

Remember, when fixing outdoors and indoors where steam and condensation are conditions to be met, always to use brass or cadmium-plated screws and fittings.

Shelf Fixing Without Brackets: It is sometimes desired to fit a series of small shelves in staggered formation in order to break up a large expanse of interior wall where, since their purpose is more ornamental than practical, brackets of any kind would be out of place and would detract from the neatness of the feature. The only solution to this problem, therefore, is to make use of invisible brackets. In others words, to fit metal dowels partly into the shelf itself and partly into the brickwork. The effect of this secret fixing is well worth the extra patience called for, and arouses no little interest in friends when they see the shelves without any visible means of support!

The material for this type of shelf is usually 1 in. × 4 in. deal, rounded or splayed at the ends as required. The edges must be finished off before final fixing, unless, of course, it is intended to put a cover beading along the edge, in which case this will be the last operation.

The first step is to mark off the dowel positions on the back edge of the shelf. Two dowels to each shelf is about all that will be necessary as these shelves are never very long. Let the mark show on the top surface of the shelf as you will need to transfer these positions on to the wall, placing the shelf in its finished position and marking round it. Suitable dowels can easily be made from pieces of ⅜ in. mild steel rod.

If a ⅜ in. masonry drill is not available for drilling into the brickwork, one of the smaller and cheaper drills could

Fig. B77. Knock the ⅜ in. steel dowels into the holes in the wall. Cut dowels to the required length.

Fig. B78. Drive the shelf on to the dowels, mating holes having been pre-drilled in the wood. Protect edge with scrap.

Fig. B79. Over radiators, fix aluminium sheet to form a deflector.

Fig. B80. Typical situation calling for a ragbolt. Jacks are usually required, as shown.

be used and the hole enlarged with a conventional drill of the correct size. This will, of course, take a little more time, as the drill may need sharpening after each hole. For drilling into the back edge of the shelf a sharp, clean centre bit is the ideal tool, as you won't be troubled so much by raggy edges round the hole. After the holes have been drilled, the pieces of dowel should be driven home and the surplus metal cut off. Check each one for length with its corresponding hole in order to avoid trouble in getting the shelf back to the wall when you come to tap it gently into position, using a piece of scrap wood to protect the edge (Figs. B77 and B78).

This same idea can be adapted to a more practical use when a smoke shelf over a radiator is required, as brackets are awkward to fix once the radiator is in position. The method of fixing is just the same but the back edge of the shelf should be let into the plaster, to stop the air current rising behind the joint when the wood shrinks due to the heat.

Alternatively, a strip of thin gauge aluminium—about 22g.—can be fastened under the shelf to form a deflector. It will need to be cut about 1 in. wider than the shelf itself, fastened at the front underside and then pushed gently upwards to give it the necessary curve (Fig. B79).

In the case of radiator shelves it is essential to allow plenty of length past each end of the radiator in order to stop the haze creeping out at this point.

A point to bear in mind when making these shelves is that they must be finished before fixing. The overall presentation is very much better than attempting to paint or polish afterwards, as marks on the wall would spoil the clean line and detract from the impression of invisible support.

Floor Fixings

The usual types of plugs can be used with normal domestic floor fittings—with the possible exception of household machinery such as fixed washing machines and refrigerators when vibration may be expected. Radiators in central heating systems and hot pipes will also need special fittings, as the high temperatures may cause normal plugs to deteriorate.

For this there are a number of 'ragbolt' types of fittings available which can be used on solid or cavity floors. Most ironmongers carry stocks and are willing to advise when such problems arise.

When using these fixings, jacks are also necessary to secure the object, such as the washing machine shown in Fig. B80.

Outdoor Fixings

On the few occasions that the handyman requires material for outdoor fixings he must bear in mind that apart from varying conditions, the fixtures will be buffeted by the elements.

Important points will be the need for a perfectly sound bearing-surface and the correct fixing.

Quite often some of the stronger plugs will be serviceable—but generally the special bolt fitting with an expanding insert is best.

Hinge Fitting

Many home woodworking projects call for hinges, but omit details of their fitting—it is taken for granted that every woodworker knows all about hinge fitting. For the benefit of those who somehow never got around to the subject, the following notes have been compiled.

Butt Hinges: The most common of all hinges is the butt, which is required for cupboards, sideboards, wardrobes and in fact almost all doors. These hinges vary in size, but the method of marking-off and fitting is similar in all cases.

Like any other woodworking job, marking-off in an accurate manner is essential if neat workmanship is to be achieved. The marking-off can be divided into three operations, the tools required being a marking gauge, a sharp marking-knife, and a try-square.

The first operation is illustrated in Fig. B81, which shows at A the fence of the marking gauge set tight against the end of the hinge wing while the marker is positioned in the exact centre of the pin. The measurement thus obtained is then marked-off on the edge of the door as indicated. Note that the actual hinge recess is cut in the door, and not on the door frame or carcass.

In the second operation, the gauge is altered to give the depth of the recess. In this case the fence is set against the outer face of the wing and the marker is again placed in the centre of the pin as shown at B in Fig. B81. This dimension is then transferred to the outer face of the door edge, as seen in Fig. B82. Do not make these marks longer than necessary as they will disfigure the timber.

For the third operation, the marking knife and try-square are required. With these tools the two lines already in place are joined up as seen in Fig. B83. The 3 in. measurement shown in this drawing is the actual length of the hinge, and will, of course, be altered to suit the hinge in question.

Cutting the Recess: The recess in which the hinge will sit is now cut; this part of the work is commenced with a fine back-saw. The first cuts are made close to the lines made with the try-square and knife; these lines should remain visible after the sawing, but only just. A series of saw cuts are then made to cut up the grain of the timber, so the operation will appear as in Fig. B84. Notice the angle at which the saw is operated, because, of course, a straight cut cannot be made; and take care that saw cuts do not project beyond the gauged lines or else the timber will be disfigured.

The waste material is now removed with the chisel held at a slight angle, as much as possible of the waste being removed in this manner. The ends of the recess are next cut, and it will be remembered that these lines were left visible during the sawing. The downward cuts are made exactly on these lines, and similar cuts are made on the two gauged lines also. This will give four sharp edges to the recess, the bottom of which can now be levelled off.

One very important point concerns the shape of the bottom of the recess. This should taper slightly, being deeper at the front than at the back. Because of this the chisel work should be done in conjunction with the actual hinge which, when in the closed position, should sit flush with the timber.

Fitting: At this stage the hinge should be fitted into the recess by two screws only, and the door set in place in the carcass or frame. The door will, of course, be planed to size before the hinges are fitted. It will be necessary to have a small amount of clearance between the bottom of the door and the bottom of the carcass and this can be achieved quite easily by setting the door on two small pieces of cardboard or glasspaper. When the door is in place, the hinge positions can be marked off with the aid of a try-square as illustrated in Fig. B85. However, do not use the marking knife for this as the lines must be removed before finishing; pencil lines are best as these can easily be removed.

When the hinge positions have been marked off on the carcass front, the door is removed and the lines continued around the edge of the timber to the inner face of the carcass; this is shown where the top corner of the door is cut away.

At this stage it must be decided whether the hinges are to be fixed direct to the carcass or frame, as can be seen

in much of the less-expensive items of furniture, or if another recess is to be cut. The extra recess provides a bed into which the wing of the hinge will fit and also gives a little additional support.

If the recess is to be cut, the marking gauge is again used as shown at A in Fig. B81. However, this only applies if the door sits flush with the carcass. If it is to be inset by, say, ¼ in., then the measurement will have to be increased by this amount.

This recess is not sawn; the work is carried out with the chisel and mallet. Particular attention is drawn to the fact that no material is removed at all from the front edge of this recess; thus the bottom of the recess is on a slope running from front to back. The depth of the recess at the back is equal to the thickness of the hinge wing.

Even if no recess is required, the marking out should still be done as this will indicate the position of the hinges for fixing to the carcass.

Fig. B81. The two measurements required when marking off for a butt hinge.

Fig. B82 (*above*). The two measurements transferred to the door edge.

Fig. B83 (*right*). The two lines joined up.

Fig. B84. Cutting the recess.

The door is now replaced, but in this case in the open position. The hinges are opened, and located in the recesses or lined up with the marks, and secured by one screw only in each case. The door can now be tested, and any minor adjustments carried out. Drive in the remainder of the screws and the finished job will appear as in Fig. B86.

Faults: One of the common faults is using wood-screws which are too large in the head. This means that the door will not close properly because the screw heads act as packing between the hinge wings. The fault can be elusive as the screws cannot be seen when the door is closed; the remedy is obvious.

Another fault is the binding of the door when closed, and if pressure is applied this will have the effect of springing the hinges out of place. This fault is caused by sinking the recess too deep, and the only remedy is to use packing in the form of veneer or cardboard.

A third fault is the binding of the door edge against the edge of the carcass when the door is opened beyond 90 deg. The fault here is that the hinge centre has been set too far in, and the only cure is to reposition the hinge. Careful marking-out will prevent this fault.

Drop Leaf Hinge: When making a hinged joint for a drop leaf table—often known as a rule joint—there are special points to remember. In the first place, you don't use an ordinary hinge, but a hinge specially designed for the job, with one long and one short wing and with the countersinking for the screws on the opposite side to the knuckle. The long wing is fixed to the underside of the fixed leaf and the shorter wing is attached to the drop leaf. When making a table of this type remember that the actual joint is marked-off in conjunction with the hinge.

Figure B87 shows how such a hinge is fitted; notice that it is an inverted view. A recess is cut to house the hinge knuckle, in addition to the usual recess which houses the hinge. The first recess in which the hinge fits is cut with the chisel and mallet, and then the knuckle recess is cut. The centre line of this recess must line up with the edge of the top fillet; this is why the joint must be made to suit the hinge. The centre line is drawn to mate up with the top fillet in the illustration.

The recess for the short wing is cut in the usual manner, and again the bottom is sloped. The recesses should be cut and the hinges tried in place to ensure that they are flush with the timber when fitted.

T-Hinges: A very common hinge used mainly for shed doors and gates is the T-hinge (Fig. B88). This hinge is quite simple to fit, but there are one or two points which should be remembered.

The first, and perhaps this is the most important, is the actual location of the hinge. In the case of a ledged-and-braced door, the hinge should be positioned on top of the ledge. This allows the maximum length of screws to be used, and consequently a stronger job results.

Another point concerns the positioning of the hinge; note that the hinge knuckle is positioned in line with the small clearance between the door and the frame.

Box Hinges: Fig. B89 illustrates a box hinge. The top edge of the box must be recessed to house the hinge; this measurement is shown in the drawing. The width of the notch is dictated by the hinge width at this particular point. The insert in the drawing shows the hinge in position.

Rising-Butt Hinges: These hinges automatically lift the door as it opens, thus increasing the clearance between the door and the carpet. When closed, there is no draughty gap under the door; and—if fitted accurately and kept well-oiled—the hinges allow the door to close automatically.

When purchasing rising-butt hinges, the important point to remember is that they are made in different 'hands' and are not interchangeable. To discover the correct hand, stand outside the door—that is, have the door opening away from you. If the existing hinges are to your right hand then right-hand hinges are required, and the opposite is the case if the hinges are fitted to the left-hand side of the frame.

Each hinge is supplied in two parts. One part is fitted with a fixed pin, and this is secured to the door frame. The other part, in which there is a hole to fit over the pin, is fitted to the door. A typical hinge of this type is shown in Fig. B90.

We have already seen that the opening of the door will cause the door to rise, but a little clearance is necessary at the top of the door to prevent the door catching on the frame. This clearance is provided by lightly chamfering the top edge of the door, as seen in Fig. B91.

It is impossible to say with any degree of accuracy how much chamfer will be required, so trial of the door in the frame is the best method of finding out the correct amount.

The chamfered edge will not show when the door is closed as it will be hidden by the rebate into which the door closes, as also shown in Fig. B91.

Storing Fixings

Have you noticed how screws, nails, rivets and small parts always seem to disappear when they are wanted? Keeping them in an accumulation of odd-shaped tins, packets and boxes (some labelled, some not) is a fruitful source of frustration. What is wanted is a simplified storage fixture.

The revolving stand shown in Fig. B92 is the answer to the problem, using glass jars to show at a glance what you are looking for. The complete assembly can be varied to suit the number of containers and their size. If you want to standardize, you can use old screw-top honey-jars. They are a neat size, 3½ in. deep with a 2 in. diameter. Should you have a larger or smaller jar then the unit can be adjusted accordingly.

In addition to the jars you will require the following items: a length of electrical conduit; a circular solid base of 1 in. board or chipboard; a short length of tubing which should be a sliding fit on the conduit; metal washers; self-tapping screws; circular plywood or chipboard discs for shelves.

First, cut out the 12 in. diameter base circle and drill the centre hole to take the conduit. If the hole is drilled with a bit the exact size of the conduit, or a shade smaller, the screwed end will make its way in and give a tight and firm joint. If it is at all slack, dip the conduit in glue first.

Cut the short length of tubing into a number of pieces about ¾ in. long and drill a hole in the centre of each to take a self-tapping screw. This acts as a set screw to lock the sections of piping on the conduit, where they act as spacers for the revolving shelves.

Screw the lids to each of the circular shelves, evenly spaced around the outside edge. In the arrangement

Fig. B85 (*left*). Hinge positions marked off and recess cut.

Fig. B86 (*inset*). Hinge in position.

Carcase

Hinge positions marked off

Door

Carcass

Door

Recess for hinge knuckle

Top fillet

℄ of recess

Fig. B87. A drop leaf hinge.

Clearance

Door

Frame

Ledge

Fig. B88. A T-hinge.

Door frame

Clearance

Door

Fig. B91. The top edge of the door chamfered away for clearance.

Box hinge

Depth of notch

Fig. B90. A rising-butt hinge.

Lid

Box

Fig. B89 (*above*). Details of a box hinge.

Fig. B92 (*right*). Revolving storage stand for fixings.

Fig. B93. Details of the assembly.

Shelf

Washer

S.T. Screw

Section of tube sliding fit on conduit

Conduit

shown, seven lids were used per shelf. Two large tacks in each lid are sufficient to fix them securely. Screw a jar on to each lid. Place a collar of tubing on the centre tube, with a metal washer, followed by the shelf with the jars hanging beneath. Fig. B93 illustrates the assembly.

Leave enough clearance between the base and the jars so that they can be unscrewed and withdrawn easily, then tighten the set screw in the collar. Fix the remaining shelves and jars in the same way. You can make and add as many shelves as your centre rod will accommodate, but the higher the stand, the larger the base must be.

By standing the complete unit in a handy location near your work bench, any jar can readily be swung into position for detaching and replacing. You can label each jar if you like, but the contents are easily seen. Should you later decide to use larger or smaller jars, just alter the position of the collars and shelves on the centre rod.

MAKING AND MENDING

In the home a little maintenance goes a long way. A little money and a little time spent on small jobs about the house keep down the future inconvenience and build-er's bills which are bound to come if necessary work is neglected or postponed too long.

Fig. B94. Stiles and outer linings cut and removed.

Fig. B95 (below). Flat steel angles screwed on to casement.

Fig. B96. Renewing worn treads.

Most of the small jobs can be done with the usual tools in a handyman's kit, though for best results it is essential that the tools should be sharp. A sharp tool is less danger-ous than a blunt one, is easier to control and gives a better finish to the job. If you haven't the knack of sharpening your own, it pays to have them done—but full instruc-tions will, of course, be found in Section A.

Windows

Windows are usually the most vulnerable spots in the house. Moisture seeping through a joint in the woodwork will cause decay which, if not cut out, will spread in time throughout the whole window. Meanwhile, decorations are spoiled.

In the common sliding sash window, the part to keep an eye on is the wooden outside sill. Although the window may be regularly painted, water always seems to find a way to soak in through a fault in the cement pointing, drive in under the sill, or seep through an open joint or crack in the paintwork. Under the paint film, the rot sets through the sill, making way for following damp and draughts.

Sill Replacement: Replacing a rotted window sill may seem a tricky piece of repair work, but it can be done *in situ* without even cracking the plasterwork.

First of all the materials should be got together. Measure the length of sill needed between the masonry or brick-work, and add the length of each side which protrudes into the jambs. Removing the sash weight pockets will allow this to be measured. While the pockets are out, measure the thickness of the pulley stile (shown at A in Fig. B94).

It is a good idea to make a cardboard template of the sill's cross-section to ensure buying the correct type from the timber merchants. Besides a sill, about 2 ft. of pulley-stile material and 3 ft. of outside lining (B) should be pur-chased. All the timber is, of course, planed to the required breadth and thickness.

Having obtained the necessary materials, see that the new sill is well creosoted on its underside and allowed to dry. The pulley stile material is then prepared to match the existing stiles.

Begin by marking the position of the draught bead on both edges of the inner lining (C). The draught bead on the new sill must coincide with these marks when the sill is in place. About 9 in. from the top of the sill draw a mark square across the pulley stile (B). Then, 9 in. higher than this mark, square another mark across the outside lining. Repeat this with the other side.

The stiles and the outer linings can now be cut and removed as in Fig. B94, and the rotted sill chopped and split out with a heavy chisel. If it is in good condition the draught bead grooved on the top of the sill can be re-used.

By working carefully it is possible to cut the old sill completely out without disturbing the inner linings or the window board.

After cutting out the old sill and cleaning out the rub-bish and chippings, trim the new sill to its size, allowing ¾ in. clearance from the masonry or brickwork at each end of the sill. Place it in position and level it into place with waste wood or chippings. Mark-on the positions of the pulley stile grooves and the cut-outs for the inner and outer linings.

With a saw and chisel, cut out the housings and grooves. The prepared sill is then bedded on the stone sill with a lime or cement mortar, and can be repacked to its finished position. The inside sill or window board is usually tongued into a groove at the back of the wooden sill—this helps to position the new sill.

The new pieces of pulley stile can now be slipped into place, and nailed through the inner lining and into the new sill with oval-headed nails. Then fix the outer linings, making all the joints in thick paint to prevent the ingress of water.

The top sash can then be re-hung, the parting-rods inserted, and the bottom sash replaced. It may be necessary to refit the bottom sash to the new sill. The easiest way to do this is to coat the top of the sill with paint and bring down the sash on it. The paint will show the places which need planing off to ensure a tight weatherproof fit.

To finish the job, the new timber should have a priming coat of paint as soon as possible, and the sides and sill should be freshly pointed.

Sliding sash windows have an annoying tendency to jam. This is usually due to successive coats of paint being brushed on while the window is shut, and can only be temporarily cured by easing the sash with a chisel. The only sure cure is to strip off the excess paint.

Never plane too much from the edge of a sash, otherwise it will rattle. A clearance of the thickness of a halfpenny on each side is sufficient. A glance at the meeting rails may show that their ends are binding against the parting-rod, in which case a saw cut will give the necessary clearance.

In wooden windows of the casement type, the frame usually drops at the bottom corner of the opening edge and makes opening and closing difficult. Fig. B95 shows the answer to this problem—flat steel angles screwed into the corners of the casement.

If possible, it is best to remove the sash and place it on a bench or table for handiness. The sash must first be squared by making the diagonal measurements equal. To do this it may be necessary to remove the glass to avoid breakage. After the sash has been squared, the steel angles are sunk into each outside corner of the sash and screwed firmly. The sash can then be re-glazed and refitted.

Stairs

Houses which have passed through the hands of several owners usually show some wear on the stair treads. Fig. B96 shows in progressive steps how worn treads can be renewed.

The worn part is chiselled out to its limits—but no deeper than is absolutely necessary, as shown on the second step—with the sides of the cut-out tapering very slightly inwards. The patch is cut with a corresponding taper, driven right in and glued or nailed as the third step shows. Finally, the edge of the patch is rounded off to match the rest of the tread.

Squeaking stairs can be very annoying. The trouble can sometimes be cured if it is possible to get at the underside of the flight. An examination here may show a loose wedge or a slack glue-block. If there is a strip of moulding under the nosing of the tread, the squeak may possibly originate from a loose moulding sliding slightly down the riser when weight is applied to the tread.

Doors

Doors are frequently subjected to rough treatment, and

Fig. B97. Repairing damaged door edges and panels.

the edges are usually the most vulnerable parts. Fig. B97 shows progressively how a damaged door edge can be made good.

It is always more convenient to remove the door from the frame before starting work on the door. Any unwilling screws can be persuaded to turn by tapping the handle of the screwdriver with a hammer—with the blade in the screw slot, of course.

Patching Edges: After marking out the patch on both sides of the door, cut down the angled cuts with a saw, preferably of the fine-toothed tenon or dovetail type. When chiselling-out the damaged timber, work from both sides of the door towards the centre. This will give a clean, tidy joint when the patch is in place.

The patch is cut slightly wider and thicker than the edge of the door, as shown at E, and glued into position as in F. If the cut-out and the patching piece are tapered slightly from one side of the door, the patch can be tapped home to a really tight fit.

The surplus timber can be planed off after the glue has dried or after the patch has been pinned by one or two oval-headed nails (G). Any open joints can be filled with plastic wood or a glue-and-sawdust mixture. When dry, the patch is rubbed down with sandpaper and painted or stained to match the rest of the door.

This method of patching can be used for numerous repairs throughout the house, such as window-frames, shelving or damaged furniture. When repairing stained woodwork, a little care in selecting a patch to match the grain of the timber results in a very inconspicuous repair. Square cuts across the grain should be avoided as they show up more easily than an angled cut.

Panel Renewal: Replacing a split door panel presents little difficulty. In Fig. B97 are shown the three most common types of door panel fixing. In H, the panel is retained by a heavy moulding on each side of the door. By gently prising off the moulding from one side, the damaged panel can be taken out and replaced.

In J, the panel is grooved into the door stile and the joint hidden by a moulding. Here, also, the moulding must

Fig. B98. Fitting a lath to a door.

Lath

Glued surfaces

be lifted out, but the damaged panel will have to be cut out. The groove must then be filled up and the replacement panel held in by refixing the mouldings.

K shows how the panel is retained by a door stile with a moulded edge. Here, all the moulding on one side must be pared off with a sharp chisel and a new quarter-round beading glued and pinned back after the new panel has been inserted.

Locks: Often the only trouble with a stiff lock is an accumulation of dust and dirt inside it. To take a rim lock off for cleaning, remove the knob spindle and unscrew the lock from the door. On the reverse side of the lock the retaining plate is held by a small screw. After unscrewing this screw, lever off the plate. Remove the dust and old oil with a paint brush dipped in petrol, and allow to dry before re-assembling.

Mortice locks can be removed by unscrewing the plate on the edge of the door after withdrawing the knob spindle. Unscrewing this plate will reveal the screws which secure the lock in the door.

A lock should be oiled only very sparingly because an excessive amount of oil tends to collect dust.

Correcting Binding: The top opening corner of a door sometimes drops and binds against the door post. The

trouble may be caused by loose screws at the top hinge. Remove the door and plug the existing screw-holes with wooden plugs or plastic wood. Re-hang the door, using slightly larger screws. If the trouble persists, remove the hinges from the door and plane the hinge side to a very slight taper, enough to lift the dropped corner and clear the door-post. Never be tempted to plane the offending edge; on a painted or varnished door the bare wood will be difficult to re-finish.

Draughts underneath a door can be cured by fixing a hardwood threshold on the floor and refitting the underside of the door to the hardwood strip. An alternative method is to lower the door to give the minimum clearance from the floor. The resulting space at the top of the door is filled in with a strip of timber. Remove the door stops and architraves and fix this false lintel on the underside of the existing lintel. The stops and architraves can then be refitted to hide the alteration. Although this entails more work, the finished job shows no signs of the repair.

Badly-shrunk doors are often a problem in old houses. Apart from draughts, the locks seldom function properly owing to the space between the bolt and the receiver. The expense of fitting a new door can be circumvented in the following way.

Take the door off its hinges and remove the lock. Using a marking gauge, scribe a line along the face of the stile approximately ¼ in. from the edge; this will serve as a guide for planing. Before planing, however, examine for tacks or small nails, either drawing them out, or, if this is not possible, punching them well in with a nail punch.

Plane down to the gauge line with a jack plane, making sure the edge is dead straight and square with the face of the door. This will ensure that there are no rounded or bruised edges to show up on the finished job.

The next step is to provide a straight lath of the required thickness and which is at least as long as the door. If it is rather wider than the thickness of the door, so much the better. Note that in Fig. B98, which illustrates this, the door has been stood on its long edge.

Prepare plenty of thin, hot glue, and apply by brush to the edge of the door and to one face of the lath. Work fast, as glue thickens easily, especially in cold weather. Now lay the lath in position and push it backwards and forwards using pressure. This will work out the surplus glue from the joint, leaving only a thin line showing. At the end of this process the lath will be quite immovable, which indicates that you have completed this part of the job. For further security, fix the lath firmly with panel pins, and allow the glue to set.

If the door is an outside one, use one of the waterproof glues. In this case start work early in the morning, so that the door can be back in place before night-time. When the glue has set, lay the door flat and plane both edges of the lath down to the level of the door-face.

The door can now be placed temporarily in position, with the hinge-stile hard against its post. While it is held firmly in position ask an assistant to pencil a line down the edge of the lath where it touches the rebate in the door-frame. This will indicate how much must be planed off the lath to ensure a good fit.

Turn the door on edge with the lath uppermost and punch the panel pins well below the surface. Plane down almost to the pencil line, but keep an eye on the panel pins or your plane will suffer badly. Punch them down slightly more if necessary.

Try the door in its frame and mark the tight spots. Ease these carefully with a smoothing plane until the door fits in closely. Replace the hinges and the work is complete.

Finally replace the lock, remembering that the thickness of the lath will bring it forward. It may be necessary to plug the hole in the door and bore a fresh one.

Sliding Door Gear

How many doors are there in an average three-bedroom house? You could hazard an immediate guess—and probably be quite wrong.

Count up the total number of room doors, add cupboard and wardrobe doors, furniture doors, and so on—and you will be astounded.

In one ordinary home we checked, there were 44 hinged doors!

The kitchen alone accounted for 16 of these—and the doors were so badly located that six of them opened against each other with consequent mishaps and damage to paintwork.

These days, of course, there is a simple answer to all these problems—sliding door gear. Furniture manufacturers are installing sliding doors in furniture, and among the first to do so were those who make kitchen furniture. In this aspect one of the most important considerations is safety. Overhead-type wall cabinets with hinged doors are a positive danger in small kitchens, and sliding doors eliminate the danger completely, and make access to and activities in the kitchen much more efficient, since there is no need constantly to open and close doors while standing at a working base.

Sliding doors are by no means new—but one cannot compare the old type, usually made on the job with timber sliding in a felt-lined timber channel, with the efficient purpose-built units widely available today. In humid atmospheres the timber swelled and doors were frequently jamming. Apart from this, quite an amount of effort was required to slide the door which generally bore entirely along the bottom edge, presenting a considerable frictional resistance.

Today's modern units are effortless in action, highly efficient, safe and decorative. Their efficiency is brought about by a number of factors—experience, research, design and materials. Their application is very versatile, not merely for cabinets and wardrobes, but also for room dividers, french windows, garages and even the gigantic aircraft hangars at airports.

Suspension Principles: Broadly speaking the method of suspension can be divided into two categories, the top-hung type (in which the entire weight of the door is carried by the top channel) and the slide type (in which the top of the door 'floats' in its channel, whereas the bottom rides in the base channel on wheels or gliders).

Various components are used to make movement easy. The track, channel, and bearing glides or wheels can be aluminium, brass, phosphor-bronze or nylon. Such materials, of course, offer two inherent virtues—they are rotproof and self-lubricating. Where steel is used, generally with wheels, it is suitably protected against corrosion.

Installation: Fitting is not such a problem as would at first appear. The selection of proprietary brands reviewed in this article are all sold with data and fixing instructions. Perhaps the main points to bear in mind when constructing are that sliding doors must have a 'passing' space, or be erected in pairs of equal width; that due allowance must be made, when designing the carcass or adapting an existing fitment, for easy action of the doors; and that door knobs or finger pulls go on the outside of the door opposite to the opening action of the slide.

Types of Gear: The choice of gear ranges from the comparatively simple and cheap track-and-slide type to the more expensive type with track, rail, wheel gear and so on. All are extremely efficient and selected appropriately for the type of fitment and usage.

Fig. B99 shows a serving hatch application of the 'Wispa' range of cupboard tracks made by Geo. W. King Ltd. The track, available in 4 ft., 5 ft., and 6 ft. lengths, is drilled in 6 in. intervals. This is an overhead-suspension type, with a channelled top track in which runs the nylon slider, while the base of the door is grooved to run over the simple angle-shape nylon guide fitted to the base of the opening. The diagram in Fig. B100 shows how very simple operation and fitting are. Provided instructions are followed, the system is highly efficient and foolproof.

'Wispa' will carry doors up to 30 lb. in weight. You can buy track only or a pack containing two slides, one guide and a set of woodscrews. There are two other types of gear in the range, basically the same in principle, categorised as 'Mini-Wispa' and 'King-Wispa'.

Fig. B99 (*above*). Functional, unobstrusive and efficient serving hatch using Wispa cupboard tracks.

Fig. B100 (*right*). The simple mechanics and easy fixing arrangements.

Another well-known brand of door gear is that made by P. C. Henderson Ltd. They manufacture a wide range from the simple nylon slide type to heavy roller suspension patterns. This type of gear is particularly suited for heavier doors, from wardrobes upwards. The type of application is shown in Fig. B101, which shows a neatly-enclosed wardrobe in a boxroom. This arrangement could be made with Henderson's 'Single Top', a new type of suspension gear, the mechanics of which are illustrated in

Fig. B102. Detail of Single Top gear, showing the adjustment slots in the hanger and the end stop (*left*).

Fig. B103b. Detail of Double Top gear. The left leaf has opened to pass the right leaf (seen from inside).

Fig. B101. Single Top gear fitted inside a wardrobe; suitable for a single door or two doors opening against each other.

Fig. B103a (*right*). Double Top gear for double passing doors, fitted in a typical situation.

Fig. B104 (*below*). Simultaneous action is a real boon. These partition doors, geared to each other, are on Marathon gear.

Fig. B105 (*above*). One of the many practical components available in the Zed range.

Fig. B106 (*above*). The method of hanging Coburn Zip gear.

Fig. B107 (*right*). The simple Zip components as they are supplied.

Fig. B110. Bottom-action rollers, mortice-fitting.

Fig. B111. Face-fitting units. Both have nylon wheels.

Fig. B108. One-Two, another Coburn system but with wheel operation.

Fig. B109. The stout components of the Coburn One-Two system.

Fig. B112. The Marley Regal folding partition, on a pantograph frame.

Fig. B113. The Marley Princess folding wall-door. Both Marley types are centre-hung on glide wheels operating in a U-track.

Fig. B102. Note that the track centre is in one single line and therefore unsuitable for double passing doors, although non-passing double doors can be hung providing there is room for door retraction on both sides. This gear is retailed in standard sets including track, hangers, guides, stops, pulls and screws. Weight capacity is 60 lb. per door.

The 'Double Top' version for passing doors is shown in use in Fig. B103a; the mechanics are shown in Fig. B103b. Weight capacity is the same as 'Single Top'. Set sizes are 4 ft., 5 ft., 6 ft. and 8 ft. Another of Henderson's popular mechanisms is the 'Marathon' simultaneous action unit for bi-parting sliding doors, as shown in Fig. B104. On sliding one of the pair open or shut, the opposite door is linked by gear to operate simultaneously. These doors are well within the capacity of the handyman to hang and are ideal for dividing doors, patios, sun lounges, etc.

There are, of course, other types in the Henderson range—but of real interest to the home cabinet-maker is the 'Zed' range of tracks, sliders, channels, bolts and finger-pulls. A component in this range is shown in Fig. B105.

Another comprehensive range of door gear, well-known to the trade, is made by Coburn Engineers Ltd. One of their latest additions is the 'Zip' gear, shown in Fig. B106. This is a top-hung gear with extruded aluminium top track and nylon gliders, slides, etc., as shown in Fig. B107.

This gear is sold in popular retail sizes up to 8ft of track, and fittings for one door, including two sliders, two guides, one flush pull, all screws and instructions, are included in a complete polythene pack.

Another simple-to-fit gear in the Coburn range, specially designed for wardrobes and larger cupboards, is shown in Fig. B108. This is the 'One-Two' gear which will take up to a weight of 50 lb. per door. Also a suspension type, it consists of metal top hangers with nylon wheels and galvanised steel track; the latter is supplied in standard sizes up to 8 ft. Polythene packs of fittings for a single door consist of two hangers, two nylon glides, one flush pull and screws and instructions, as shown in Fig. B109.

Coburn are constantly improving their products, a recent modification being in the well-known Cubbard range. The rollers within the steel casing are of solid nylon and available in two versions, 'M' for mortice fitting (Fig. B110) and 'F' for face fitting (Fig. B111).

The track is galvanised steel and as the rollers (which bear up to 50 lb.) are bottom-mounted, the running rail is a T-section of extruded aluminium.

Partition Doors: In modern houses with through-lounges and dinette-kitchen arrangements, the social activities of parents and teenage children are likely to clash. For more seclusion when multiple activities are taking place in the same large room, complete privacy can be obtained in a few seconds with a sliding partition.

Handymen who wish to construct their own partition doors can do so with the heavier grades of gear described; but for a custom-built job which is supplied ready for hanging and finished in a tough, washable and hardwearing vinyl covering, matched to existing decor, the Marley 'Space-Saver' doors are hard to beat. Although truly sliding in action, the principle is somewhat different to the suspended frame structure which complements the type of gear previously described. The Marley units are complete folding partitions, which consist of a number of narrow panels sandwiched between vinyl which fold concertina-wise into a remarkably small space. The maximum 8 ft. model (standard range), for instance, will stack to 14½ in., although it has 24 folds or pleats.

Sizes range from 2 ft. 3 in. (to replace normal room doors) to special order sizes. The doors are supplied with catches for closing; two types of mechanism are shown in Figs. B112 and B113.

Furniture Repairs

Sooner or later the home handyman will be called upon to repair furniture around the home, so the following notes should be of interest.

Chair Legs and Frames: Perhaps one of the most common faults is the broken chair leg, which can be repaired by dowelling. The break usually occurs close to the end where the leg tapers off. In order to ensure that both parts mate-up when fixed, the following method of drilling is suggested. The broken part is set in place, taking care that a neat fit is obtained, and held in this position with the aid of a splint. The splint is a short length of straight timber which is held by cramps (Fig. B114).

The centre of the leg is then marked off and a hole drilled to receive the dowel. By drilling through both parts in this manner the two holes will be in line. A length of dowel rod is then glued into the hole and trimmed off flush with the leg end, and the splint retained until the glue has set.

It sometimes happens that the tenon of the mortice-and-tenon joint breaks in a chair frame, and in such cases a dowel joint can be used. The first step is to cut the remains of the tenon away, so producing a square end on the rail. Next the broken tenon is drilled out of the mortice, and the mortice filled with a neat-fitting piece of hardwood. This must be securely glued in position and flushed off with the face of the leg.

The rail is now drilled to receive the dowels, and similar holes are drilled in the hardwood filling piece in the mortice (Fig. B115).

Another fault which develops in chair frames is loose joints. The first indication of this trouble is movement or rocking of the timbers. Dismantling the chair will be unnecessary if the trouble is given immediate attention by adding a brace to each corner (Fig. B116). The brace is simply a triangular piece of hardwood which is cut to fit around the chair leg and butt against the rails. Neat fitting is essential and when this has been achieved the brace is glued-and-screwed in place. All four corners should be braced in this manner.

Chair Backs: A breakage sometimes occurs in chair backs of the curved design (Fig. B117), and again dowels can be employed to effect a repair. In such cases it is impossible to drill through both pieces in one operation as can be done with a chair leg, so careful marking out is necessary. The drawing shows a line marked-off down the centre of the timber and another is made on the opposite side of the break. A drilling template is made up from a scrap piece of sheet metal, and it will be seen that a line is scribed down the centre of this, also. The mark on the template is lined up with the mark on the timber, and the drilling position is marked through the small hole in the template. If the template is carefully used in this manner on both pieces of timber, the two holes will line up when brought together. The hole in the template is positioned so that the hole drilled in the timber will be in the centre.

The same method of marking-off and drilling can be

Fig. B114 (*left*). How to drill a broken chair leg.

Break

Fig. B115 (*below*). Dowels used to replace a broken tenon.

Fig. B117 (*left*). Marking-off a chair back for drilling.

Guide lines

Ⓐ Cut off

Ⓑ New part

Cup castor

Fig. B118 (*above*). How to repair a leg for a cup castor.

Fig. B116. Chair frame strengthened by a brace.

Fig. B119. An angle plate fitted to a sideboard plinth.

employed for chair legs where the break is too far from the end to allow drilling.

Castors: Many of the older type arm chairs are fitted with cup castors (Fig. B118). The screws which hold these in place often come adrift and sooner or later the wood becomes split and full of nail holes as shown at A. The best plan in such circumstances is to cut off the defective timber and shape a new part as illustrated at B. This is attached to the leg by means of a dowel.

The new part can be turned up on a lathe or shaped from a piece of round material with the aid of a spokeshave

Sideboard Repairs: When the timbers of a sideboard rock, it is possible to remedy this by fixing angle plates. These are screwed in place (Fig. B119).

Another trouble sometimes experienced with sideboards and similar pieces of furniture is the hinges of the doors. In many cases the hinges have simply reached the end of their useful life, and so replacement is called for. In other cases the screws are no longer effective as the holes have become enlarged. If at all possible the screws should be replaced with larger ones which should be both greater in diameter and in length. Where this is not possible the holes should be plugged with small wood plugs.

Floorboard Repairs

There are many occasions when the home handyman needs to take up one or several floorboards, yet very little written information on the right method seems to exist. Boards that are loose, springy, creaky need not be the result of your efforts if you take just a little forethought and care.

Removal: The most important tool required is the 'electrician's (also plumber's, gas-fitter's, etc.) bolster'. This is a cold chisel with a wide flat end, normally used for cutting channels in walls for burying pipework. For this job, however, it enables you to exert leverage on the sides of floorboards with the least risk of damage. Other necessary tools include a nest of saws together with such usual items as a hammer and brace-and-bit. For very occasional jobs a pad saw might be useful and, if a great deal of flooring work is tackled, the simple saw attachment to the power drill is well worth having.

When the floor covering is lifted, check what type of floorboards you have. These instructions concern butt-edge boards; other types are dealt with later. The floorboards may already be cut in various places; if these places prove useful to you, all that is needed is the bolster placed down the side of the board (Fig. B120) which is then carefully levered up. But first check whether the board has been screwed down—this may be the case if the board was previously cut and relaid by an electrician, plumber or gasfitter. If so, remove the screws before levering up the board. Work along from the cut, lifting at the rear of the nails, and on alternate sides, so as to lift evenly. Avoid using the tool on the end of the wood, as this part is more prone to split.

When cutting is unavoidable, first locate the positions of the joists—easily done by observing the run of the nails which are normally fixed across the boards at about 14 in. apart (Fig. B121). Next, mark the exact position of the edge of the joist, using any thin feeler (Fig. B122), such as a saw blade. A start hole for the saw is drilled; ¼ in. is adequate, but the drill should be placed on the board approximately ½ in. inside the joist edge mark, i.e. above the actual joist. The drill is held at an angle of about 45 deg. so that when through, you have drilled a slanting hole which just enters the cavity beside the joist (Fig. B123). Cut with a pad-saw, keeping a straight line across the board, and the same angle of cut (Fig. B124); this is important, as only a slight divergence will cause you to saw along the joist. The completed cut should leave you with an edge-section like that in Fig. B125 where the cut board is turned edge-wise to the camera, and the end has been chalked to show it more clearly. The benefit of this work is found when re-laying the board, as the diagonal cut gives support while a vertical cut would leave one end free, and springy, unless the cut was central on a joist at each end.

Fig. B126 shows an example of the *wrong* way to cut. Here the cuts at both ends were made vertically, between the beams, and when the trap was replaced it rested on a lath of wood tacked to a beam at one end and on a gas pipe at the other!

After lifting from one sloping cut as in Fig. B125, it is usually possible either to take up the remainder of the board, or make the next cut with the board levered up, so it will fall directly on the supporting timber. The cut should be made on a line near to the nails (Fig. B127) so that the boards are safely held when put down (Fig. B128).

If the first cut has been made as described, it will be necessary to screw a wood fillet to the joist—and level with the top face of the joist—to support that end of the board when it is re-layed. Sometimes a board can be raised sufficiently to permit sawing through directly over a joist. This is ideal because the supporting fillet would not be required.

Fig. B129 shows the use of a power drill saw attachment. When this is used, it is possible to make every cut fall over a beam, working near to the floor nails, but taking care, for the sake of your saw, not to actually hit them. We must mention that a special flooring handsaw is made with the teeth arranged on the edge of a semi-circle, allowing a cut to be made while the board is down, but these are so uncommon that you are not likely to be able to get hold of one.

Re-laying: When re-laying boards, knock out all projecting nails from them. Carefully lift any nails that may have stayed in the beams. Use a hand broom to clear any dust or dirt from the joists. Make sure that you have the boards in the right places, and right way round, then re-nail securely, replacing any broken nails. If you are likely ever to want to lift the board again (to gain access to an electrical junction box, for instance) it is best to screw the board down, ensuring that the screws are countersunk. Screwing also obviates the risk of cracked ceilings below, due to over-enthusiastic hammer blows! Before replacing floor coverings, sweep up and check for projecting nail or screw heads. If left, they will ruin lino or carpets.

Types: We have only dealt with butt-edge flooring, so far, but the same principle applies with tongued-and-grooved boards, except that it is essential to remove the tongue on the board being lifted, and usually the one seated in its groove. This may be done by cutting it off with the bolster (which should be a keen-edged tool) or by sawing down the length of wood. Failure to remove the tongue will always result in the adjacent groove being ripped, damaging the floor.

Some floors are also secret-nailed. Here the nails are driven in slantwise through the lower edge of every groove and automatically hidden by the next board. The only thing to do here is to cut off a tongue, and then locate the beams as in Fig. B123.

One more type of floor board should be mentioned. This is parquet. It is usually tongued-and-grooved, secret-nailed, made from very hard wood, and splits almost before the tool touches it. Advice on this is simple, get a specialist firm to lift it, or leave it alone.

Renovation: Sometimes a slightly worn floor can be renovated by planing down any unevenness or, better still, by sanding it with an electric sander. Prior to planing or sanding a floor, any open joints can be filled by thin strips of timber or papier-mâché. The papier-mâché is made of newspapers pulped in water with a little glue size added. This mixture is pressed into the cracks and allowed to dry before sanding or planing down the floor.

Badly fitted or shrunk skirting is a constant source of draughts. This can be cured by nailing quarter-round moulding over the joint of the skirting and floor (Fig. B130). The moulding must be nailed to the floor with small oval-headed nails. Nailing the moulding to the floor ensures that any further shrinkage of the skirting is taken care of. Outside corners are mitred in the usual manner. While inside corners can also be mitred, a better way is to scribe them is shown in Fig. B130.

Here, one piece of moulding is butted right up to the skirting as in the sketch. The end of the piece to be joined to it is cut at a 45-degree angle, thus forming a quarter-round section. This is cut round the curve with a fret-saw or pared with a sharp knife, so that it fits over its neighbour.

Fitting New Floorboards: In some cases so much damage will have been done to floorboards that the only remedy is to lay some new ones. If a cramp is not available, to get a close fit, an old, fairly blunt firmer chisel is needed. Press the board firmly against the previous one, then drive the chisel well into the joist below at an angle of about 20 deg. to the vertical face of the board. The chisel is now used as a crowbar, being elevated to the perpendicular, when the board will be forced tightly against its neighbour whilst nails are inserted. Each board should be nailed at the middle first, then to alternate joists at each end, using different joists for successive boards. It is possible to carry out the job single-handed, though it is far easier if one person operates the chisel while a second hammers in the nails. The last board is trimmed to the wall and nailed in position after removing the wooden slips from the ends of the joists.

All nails are punched well below the surface and the holes filled with filler stained to match the intended colour of the finished floor. Always nail across the grain.

Secret-Nailing: The best nails to use for secret-nailing

Fig. B120 (*above left*).   Insert the bolster at the side of the board, not the end.

Fig. B121 (*above centre*).   Joists are usually about 14 in. apart.

Fig. B122 (*above right*).   Use a saw blade as a feeler to locate the joist edge.

Fig. B123 (*left*).   Drill at an angle, half an inch inside the mark.

Fig. B124 (*right*).   Saw at an angle to just miss the joist edge.

Fig. B125 (*below left*).   A sloping cut gives a neater fit.

Fig. B126 (*below centre*).   Never let a board rest on gas or waterpipes.

Fig. B127 (*below right*).   The run of the joists will be shown by the lines of nails.

Fig. B128 (*lower left*).   The board should rest on at least one inch of joist.

Fig. B129 (*lower centre*).   A power saw making a sinking cut.

Fig. B130 (*lower right*).   Quarter-round moulding stops skirting draughts.

strip tongued-and-grooved flooring are 2¼ in. 'lost' head nails. These nails are normally round in section with a very small bulbous head suitable for punching below the surface. The method adopted is to drive the nail at an angle, back through the tongue of the board, punching it below the surface so that it draws the board tight back to the previous board. It therefore follows that the tongue should face the way in which you are working (see Fig. A315 in Section A). As already suggested, drive a chisel into the edge of the joist and lever the board back. It is advisable to insert a small strip of wood between the chisel and the tongue of the board to avoid damage to the latter.

Fig. B131. Sandpaper with a cork block for flat surfaces.

TRICKS OF THE TRADE

It would be impossible to attempt to cover woodworking practice in a few hundred words, but the following main points are intended to summarise the little tricks of the trade which are in everyday use by the experienced joiner.

Basic Know-how

A clear bench with a flat surface and a vice should be fundamental equipment.

Marking requirements would be a four- or two-fold 2 ft. rule; a straight-edge; a carpenter's square with a 6 in. blade; a marking gauge; a striking or marking knife and, perhaps, a pair of wing compasses with 9 in. legs.

Marking and Sawing: Always work from one trued side of timber before marking out; mark on the trued edge with a square and knife and carry subsequent squared marks from that side; always saw on the waste side of the mark; when sawing across the grain straighten through and ease pressure on the saw to achieve a clean finish, supporting the waste piece with one hand.

If you saw in a vice, use scrap pieces of thin wood as shims, slightly above vice level and each side of the timber.

When planing, do so with the grain—not against it. If the grain offers a mixed surface set the plane iron to give a very fine cut.

Drilling in wood for dowels, etc., requires the use of an auger bit, not a centre bit. The former's parallel sides ensure that the hole is straight and true.

Dowels, made usually of birch or beech, should be cut to size and nicked with a saw completely along one side so that when the joint is under pressure from the cramp, excess glue will be forced out instead of causing a solid obstruction and consequently a bad joint.

Preparing New Timber: When using timber bought planed-to-size it is advisable to dampen the surface with hot water because the power planing cutters were under pressure; so, as well as planing the wood the operation also packed the timber fibres tight. Otherwise this pressure will be released when the job is stained, the cutter marks becoming visible.

After the cutter marks have been raised by dampening, the wood should be planed with a smoothing plane.

Following planing, slight cutter marks and tears will be visible. To remove these a scraper is employed.

Any remaining marks can be removed with sand or glasspaper, commencing with a medium grade. This is folded around a cork rubber (as seen in Fig. B131) and the job given a good rubbing over with the grain, using plenty

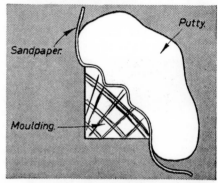

Fig. B132. Sandpaper with a putty former for mouldings.

of pressure. Finish off with a fine sand-paper and dust the surface clean.

Mouldings must also be sanded after treatment with hot water. For sanding it is a good idea to use a piece of putty in place of the cork rubber as this will shape itself to the moulding (as shown in Fig. B132).

Cutting Hardboard: The best way to cut hardboard is to lay it on the floor, placing a piece of wood approximately 18 in. × 2 in. × 2 in. beneath the part you intend to cut. Using a tenon saw, cut as far as the wood extends, then move it up and cut again, and so on. The arch provided by the piece of wood is ample for the tenon saw, and you will find that you can saw the hardboard quickly in this way, kneeling on it instead of stretching over the bench with a panel saw (Fig. B133). To prevent the outside piece from flapping up and down when sawing a long length of hardboard, fix a heavy bulldog paper clip across the sawcut after you have sawn the first few inches (Fig. B134).

By the way, always cure hardboard by damping the back surface and standing the sheet in the room where it is to be used at least overnight and preferably for 24 hours.

Fig. B133. Cutting hardboard is easier with a block underneath.

Fig. B134. A clip prevents flapping when sawing long lengths.

Fig. B136 (*above*).   One way of measuring recesses.

Fig. B137 (*below*).   A simple, but more exact method.

This will prevent warping with a convexing of the surface at some time after fixing. It is a good plan to warm all timber that is being joined with scotch glue, or similar types of hot glue, some time beforehand, to prevent chilling and loss of glue strength.

Adjustable Corner Template: Where shelving has to be fitted in the corner of a room, the corner usually proves to be either greater or less than 90 deg. so that the shelving material has to be cut to an odd angle to fit properly. One way of dealing with this problem is to trim a piece of cardboard until it fits the corner of the room exactly, then use this as a pattern for cutting the shelving material. A better method, however, is to make up the gadget shown in Fig. B135, which can then be used for all future jobs of a similar nature. If shelves are to be fitted at different heights in the same corner, the corner angle may well vary for different shelves, owing to irregularity of the walls. The gadget shown here will quickly register the different angles, and amply justify the small amount of time required to make it.

Two lengths of wood (A and B) are fixed together with a single screw at C, so that A and B can be adjusted to fit the corner of a room exactly, A being placed against one wall, and B against the adjacent wall. A third length of wood (D) runs diagonally across from A to B as shown. D is screwed to B permanently, but nailed lightly to A after A and B have been opened out to fit the room corner. A and B are thus held at the required angle when taken away from the walls, and can be used as a template or pattern for marking out hardboard or any other shelving material which is to be cut to fit the room corner. Note that B is made thicker than A, and stepped out where it meets A, so that the lower surfaces of the two lengths of wood are level. This facilitates accurate marking out of the shelving material. In order to fit the room corner properly, A and B must be screwed together so that their

ends only overlap slightly, as in the plan view, Fig. B135 inset. This gadget can, of course, be used for a variety of jobs, such as measuring the angle between floor and wall, or ceiling and wall, when fitting partitions. It is also useful for measuring the angle of a room corner at floor level when lino has to be cut to fit into the corner.

Internal Measurement of Recesses: Fig. B136 illustrates another problem which often crops up when making built-in constructions. A wall recess is shown here in plan view. Let us assume that a cupboard is to be built in the recess, and that two or three wooden framing members have to be cut to fit the width of the recess exactly. Even when a flexible steel rule is used, it is difficult to measure the exact width, since the rule is bent for about the last half inch at point A. It is important to cut the framing members exactly to length, since a gap of as little as $\frac{1}{8}$ in. between framing member and wall will show up badly.

Fig. B137 shows how two lengths of wood are held overlapping each other across the recess, their outer ends just touching the wall on each side. If held firmly at the overlap, then withdrawn carefully, they can be used to mark off the framing member to the exact length required to fit the recess.

A refinement of this idea is shown in Fig. B138, the two overlapping lengths of wood being held together by springy metal clips. The clips exercise frictional pressure

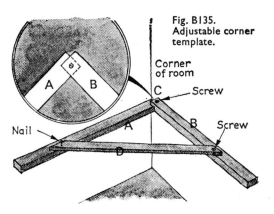

Fig. B135.
Adjustable corner template.

Corner of room

C — Screw

Screw

Nail

Fig. B138.   A refined version of Fig. B137.

Fig. B139. Fitting a wooden frame into a plaster cove.

Pencil lines

Fig. B140. How to cut away a section of a plaster cove.

Fig. B141. Frame can be cut to fit simple skirting board.

Wood framing member

Skirting board

Fig. B142. Fitting a wooden frame into a moulded skirting board.

Framing upright

on the wood, allowing the two lengths to slide against each other, but not too freely, so that the assembly is held fairly firmly when set to a required length.

As shown in Fig. B138, upper insets, one metal clip is nailed or screwed to length A, and the other to length B. For anyone who has no metal-working facilities, the clips can be made quite simply from sheet tin, cut from an empty food container with an old pair of scissors. Just file the edges smooth, bend the clip as required, then put rubber bands round the clip, strong enough for it to exert reasonable pressure on the wood. For more accurate measurement, reduce the area of the wood at each end, as shown in Fig. B138.

Profile Work: Old-fashioned plaster coves often present a difficulty when making built-in wardrobes or cupboards which reach to the ceiling. Wooden framing members (A, B and C) may be required, as indicated in Fig. B139, running across the ceiling and against the walls. Where these members meet the plaster cove, they must fit against it at all points between X and Y (Fig. B139, inset), to achieve a good appearance. Traditionally, the wood is cut to fit the profile of the cove, but in the case of the complicated moulding shown here (and this is often met with in old houses) the work would be very tedious indeed. An easier method is to cut the plaster away locally, so that the wood fits right into the cove. Plaster is comparatively soft, and can be chiselled or sawn quite easily. Provided a fine-toothed tenon saw is used, and reasonable care is taken, there will be few cases where the plaster chips away outside the required area. These parts can be filled in with cellulose filler after the woodwork is in position.

First, mark out in pencil the area of plaster to be cut away (see Fig. B140A), then make saw cuts along the two pencil lines, as in Fig. B140B. In the latter illustration, the saw is shown in the two positions necessary for cutting along pencil line Y. Line X would be cut in the same way. Make these cuts to the necessary depth, thus separating off the area which is to be cut away. Hold the saw lightly, and avoid any twisting of the blade once the cut is started, otherwise the plaster may chip off outside the required area. Finally, chisel out the waste area as at C. If preferred, the saw cuts may be made just inside the pencil lines, for safety, after which the plaster is carefully trimmed back to the lines with a chisel.

A similar problem is presented by the skirting board of a room. Where this has a simple shape, as in Fig. B141, it is easy, when fitting a wooden upright against the wall, to cut it to fit over the skirting board as shown. If the skirting board has a complicated, old-fashioned moulding as in Fig. B142, however, it is quicker to cut the skirting board away locally, and let the wooden upright into it. The skirting board need not be cut away right to the floor. It is sufficient to remove an area extending to just below the moulding. This is done by chiselling a recess at K (see Fig. B142A). Stab in first with the chisel across the grain of the skirting board. Done in any other way, the wood may split badly along its length. Two such stabs are made, fairly deep, as shown in Fig. B142A, thus establishing the width of the recess. Chiselling out of the recess can now be completed. This enables the saw to be used more easily for cutting along lines X and Y, since the tip of the saw can move freely in the recess. It now only remains to chisel out the wood from between the saw cuts, thus leaving the enlarged recess shown in Fig. B142B, into which the framing upright is fitted. Only the bottom of the framing upright need now be stepped out, to fit over the lower part of the skirting board. In the case of the complicated skirting moulding shown, this is a quicker operation than cutting the framing upright to fit all the ins-and-outs of the moulding.

If the skirting board is not very high, it may be just as easy to cut it away right down to the floor, in which case the initial recess K would be chiselled out at the bottom of the skirting board. This obviates the necessity for cutting a step at the bottom of the framing upright.

Improvised Cramping: Most people use panel pins for fixing hardboard, plywood, or other panelling materials to a wooden frame. If the finished job is to be painted, this method gives a reasonable finish, since the paint tends to hide the panel pins. Moreover, the latter can always be punched below the surface, and the holes filled with stopping prior to painting. In some cases, however, especially if paint is not to be used, it may be necessary to rely entirely on glueing the panelling material to its frame, in order to achieve a first class external appearance.

The problem here is that pressure has to be applied at frequent intervals along the edges of the job. For instance, if a fairly large sheet of plastic-faced hardboard is to be glued to a frame, pressure must be applied all round the edges. Even when an impact adhesive is used, the hardboard often tends to lift, and pressure must be maintained for some time. Most people are familiar with the method shown in Fig. B143, which obviates the use of numerous cramps. Battens are placed along the edges on top of the hardboard, and a cramp applied at either end of each batten. The snag here is that, owing to the length of batten involved, there is insufficient pressure at the centre of the batten. This is overcome by planing the lower surface of each batten to a slight curve, as in Fig. B144. Thus, when the cramps are tightened, the ends of the batten are pulled down on to the hardboard in the usual way; but the extra bulk at the centre of the batten ensures adequate pressure at this point as well.

There is, of course, a tendency for the framework to be bent slightly to the curve of the batten, resulting in a warped job. This can be prevented by using a batten which is thinner than the actual wood of the framework, and planing the lower surface of the batten to only a slight curve.

FINISHING

Many beautiful effects can be obtained by using dyes, stains and bleaches. It is necessary, however, to know something about the substances themselves, their characteristics, and the procedure to follow for the best results.

Dyeing, Staining and Bleaching

First some general remarks and facts on stains and dyes. To a great extent, the names are interchangeable; the differentiation only becoming really apparent when the stains become so pigmented that they are almost half-way between a stain and a paint. But, strictly speaking, both of them are very fluid and penetrative, the dye being especially characteristic in this respect.

For this reason they should be applied only when a permanent effect is desired, for they cannot be removed as easily as paint. Indeed, if they are properly applied, nothing short of planing the wood will eradicate them completely. But the stain can be painted on as a surface coat only, as will be shown later.

Fig. B143. A common form of improvised cramping.

Fig. B144. Curved battens provide more pressure points.

Covering Capacity: Another reason for forethought in the use of these substances is that they have very little covering capacity. They are practically transparent in that they do not hide any blemishes that may be present in the wood-knots, sap marks, etc. Therefore, care should be taken in selecting the work to be done with them. The hard woods, with their beautiful grain, are the best mediums; the stain, when it is finally rubbed up and polished, will bring it out in great prominence. If soft woods are to be tackled, they should be chosen carefully with special attention to absence of knots and other marring blemishes. Remember that the stain will exaggerate them to the detriment of the finished result.

It is commonly thought that dyes and stains are available only in limited shades, confined chiefly to browns. This is not so. A considerable variety of greens, reds and yellows can be obtained, ready-mixed; judicious blendings and thinnings can produce more. In fact it is possible to produce dyes and stains to match the room décor in much the same way as with paint, and (provided the woodwork has a good grain) the final effect can be even more artistic.

An additional recommendation in these days of high costs is that the outlay is very considerably below that of paint, and also the average practical man-about-the-house can produce excellent results in quicker time and with less experience.

Dyes and stains can be listed under five heads—chemical, spirit, oil, water and tar derivatives. Let us examine the special characteristics of each and their effects, so that the correct type may be chosen for the kind of work in prospect.

Chemical Types: The two most commonly used in this category are ammonia and permanganate of potash. Their advantage is their cheapness, and their drawback the fact that they produce poor results on soft woods. But on the better class of woods (such as oak, cedar and walnut) good results in varying shades, depending on the kind of wood used, are obtained. Of the two, permanganate of potash is preferable for the rich, warm brown it produces. Another chemical that provides a rather unusual effect is ferric chloride or muriate of iron. If a 20 per cent solution is used on well-seasoned English oak, the resultant shade will vary between a silver-grey and a blue-grey, depending upon the original shade of the bare wood.

Spirit Types: These normally consist of dyes dissolved in a spirit or a spirit varnish. If the latter, they tend to remain on the face of the wood, drying very quickly, and are therefore liable to be affected by scratches, hard knocks or wear. They are, however, more suitable for use on cheap woods where uneven absorption would result in a patchy finish. In such instances a coat of sealer should first be applied to prevent the varnish disappearing into the wood (Fig. B145).

When used as a spirit dye, they are very penetrating and are practically fadeless in sunlight. Another advantage is that they do not raise the grain of the wood, and so the work of finishing-off is made quicker and easier. They are, therefore, preferable for use on the hard woods into which they penetrate and dry dull. The rich colour is later brought up by rubbing over with a polish. One rather serious fault, however, must not be ignored. Owing to the capacity for quick drying, this type of stain is somewhat difficult to apply without the overlaps showing. The best method of avoiding this is to put it on in two thin coats instead of one normal coat, at the same time taking care that the overlaps do not occur in the same places. Also, use as wide a brush as is convenient, and work very quickly.

Oil Types: Most of the better known gloss-stains come under this heading. They are more in the nature of stains than dyes, and are more easily applied than the spirit variety because they take considerably longer to dry and harden off. But again it must be remembered that these stains penetrate very little—and in fact are better painted on wood that has been previously sealed—so that they will not stand up for very long to hard wear (as on a floor, for instance) without some kind of protection. This can easily be provided by covering them with a wax polish or an additional coat of varnish. But even so, care must be taken in moving furniture, etc., for the surface is easily scratched. This type of stain is most satisfactory for use on soft woods, but does not give a high class result on the better kinds of wood.

Water Types: These stains are the cheapest of all, but

that refers strictly to the monetary aspect; for they can be safely used by the amateur decorator to produce most excellent results. They are bought ready-ground and mixed in water, and the shades can be varied by intermixing, or by the addition of a darker or light pigment as desired.

The application of this type of dye—it is more dye than stain—is simplicity itself. In fact it can be done on large, flat surfaces with a sponge, without leaving any overlap marks at all. The addition of a little ammonia or stale beer to the mixture will aid penetration, and will also give the dye a better adhesion on the harder portions of the grain (Fig. B146).

From the point of view of a professional finish, however, there is one quite serious drawback to the use of water dyes; they tend to raise the grain of the wood. This entails the additional work of giving the surface a coat of size, waiting about 12 hours for it to harden sufficiently, then rubbing down with fine glasspaper to remove the risen fibres which have been stiffened by saturation with the size. But if this extra work is acceptable, water dyes are a very economical and easy method of achieving a satisfactory result.

Tar Derivatives: These are much better known today than they used to be. A number of firms have demonstrated that they can be decorative as well as curative of various kinds of timber diseases, and supply them in a variety of colours. They therefore serve a double purpose in preserving the wood from dry rot and wood-worm, while at the same time providing an acceptable range of colours to be incorporated into the home décor. They can be treated in much the same way as other deeply-penetrative dyes.

Before going on to deal with the preparation for, and application of, dyes and stains, a word of warning must be given. The shade of colour produced by this means is not always that shown on a card or on any other piece of wood. It must be tried out on an obscure corner of the work proposed before proceeding with the whole job. Any amendment can then be made by thinning or other adjustment without the risk of spoiling the work by a disappointing finish.

Preparatory Work: As in all other methods of decoration, the preparatory work contributes much to the finish

Fig. B146. A little ammonia added to the dye aids penetration.

Fig. B145. A coat of sealer prevents varnish disappearing into the wood.

Fig. B147. Using a glasspaper block to rub down a surface.

and must never be skimped. In fact, a clean surface is more important to successful staining than to painting, because stains will not camouflage blemishes by covering them as paint does. Therefore the work must first be cleaned down thoroughly, if necessary by scrubbing, and all grease marks should be removed with a rag dipped in turpentine or benzine.

The next step is to obtain a perfectly smooth surface. This involves the use of glasspaper and a certain amount of common sense. The latter commodity is not always employed in the use of abrasives, even by professionals. Glasspaper, as everyone knows, comes in differing grades from very fine to very coarse; and the correct grade should be carefully selected to suit the kind of surface to be treated. It is a mistake to suppose that a short cut to a quicker finish can be obtained by using a coarse-grade paper to reduce the surface roughness. While it does take off the lumps more rapidly, it will also leave deep scratches which, if not removed with fine paper, will show through the finished work, no matter how many coats are put on. Even at the cost of more time and elbow grease, use the finer grades to take off the initial roughness and finish off with the very finest. In fact, a useful dodge is to use half-worn fine grade paper to achieve a high-class finish (Fig. B147).

Type of Wood: Another consideration is the kind of wood under preparation. To use anything but the finest grades of paper on hard woods after they have been planed down will result in a sub-standard finish. Quick, light strokes, always along the grain, never across it, will give the finest results. Soft woods, since they will probably be sealed in any case before staining, will benefit from a coat preparatory to rubbing down. This process will stiffen the fibres against the glasspaper. A coat of thin size, or Polycell, will be satisfactory for this purpose. It is sometimes recommended that the glasspaper should be wrapped around a block of wood in order to present a constantly flat face to the work. This ensures even application when working on large flat areas, but you can get an improved result by using a block of rubber in place of wood. By this means any slight undulations or inequalities in the surface are compensated for by the resiliency of the rubber. Otherwise the shallow hollows from which planed surfaces are rarely free do not make contact with the glasspaper.

Filling In: The rubbing down, especially of the soft woods, will have caused holes to appear where the soft fibres have been torn out. These should be levelled up by using one of the fillers, of which there are several reliable brands on the market, both wood and plaster as well as plastic.

These fillers should be tinted slightly with a pigment such as umber, sienna, or a coloured stainer, to match the wood on which they are being used. For hard woods they are better used thinly, and can be painted on with a brush. In the case of the coarser-grained soft woods, they should be of thicker consistency, and can be applied either with a very pliable knife or a clean rag. The surplus should be wiped off with a clean linen pad against the grain in order to force the filler well into the pores. The work is then left for some time—overnight if possible —to harden thoroughly, and finally finished off by being lightly (but well) rubbed down with half-worn fine glasspaper. The filler should dry out a good match with the wood, or the finished work will not be evenly shaded.

Stopping: The advent of the new type filling agents

Fig. B148. Use as large a brush as possible, and apply stain with even strokes.

has made the use of putty obsolete for this purpose. And a very good thing too; for putty, being non-absorbent, always showed up badly in a stain finish. All large cracks or holes should be filled up with one of these materials, tinted as above to match the wood, and the surface fined-down ready for the stain.

Applying the Stain: Although a good stain finish does not require the degree of skill necessary to obtain first-class results in painting, there are several points to watch and snags to avoid. The first is to guard against dark ribs caused by overlapping. This is quite difficult, especially in the case of the quick-drying spirit stains and dyes. The best method is to avoid overbrushing from a horizontal plane on to a vertical; as, for instance, when doing rail doors. Cut off cleanly where the rails join the stiles. Apply this method wherever possible, using the joins between boards, drawers, legs, etc., as a cut-off line. Where wide flats have to be stained, unevenness can be reduced to a minimum by not overloading the brush with the stain, by using as large a brush as possible, and by working with quick, light strokes. These should be evenly but surely applied so as to avoid the need to go over the same place twice to make good any deficiency (Fig. B148).

To obtain an even finish, do not brush the stain either across or against the grain if it can be avoided, or unless its drying quality provides an opportunity for laying off with the grain. If the stain fills any roughness left through faulty preparation, remove it at once with the brush before it has a chance to dry, otherwise areas much darker than the surrounding shade will result.

Polishing: Stains which have a gloss ingredient, and which have been applied over a sealer, will need no further attention unless there is reason for a protecting coat as already mentioned. But the more-fluid stains and dyes

Fig. B149. Floorboard nails must be well punched in.

will require bringing out with a polish of some kind. There are several methods of doing this. The simplest is by the application of a coat or two of varnish. This may be quite satisfactory for a soft wood finish, or where the surface is not sufficiently smooth for polishing to be really effective, but it is by no means the best method for hard woods. In fact, it is something of a desecration to varnish such woods as oak, walnut, rosewood, etc.

The best medium for bringing out the beauty of these woods (apart, of course, from french polishing), is ordinary wax polish and plenty of hard rubbing. This method takes much longer than the easier brushing-on of liquid polishes, but is well worth it. Anyone who has seen a piece of stain-darkened English oak after a year's regular polishing with ordinary furniture polish will prefer it to any other effect, even french polish. The grain is brought out in much better relief: and this applies to the other precious woods also.

There is, of course, a range of easily-applied polishes (available from any paint-shop) which can be brushed on to imitate the high gloss of french polish quite successfully. They are designed to assist the amateur to approach this standard without going to the trouble of producing the genuine article. So that if quick results are desired they can be obtained by this pseudo-french-polishing-without-tears process. On the other hand, 'if a job is worth doing, it's worth doing well'—and french polishing is described in detail later on this page.

Floors: A separate word must be said about the preparation of floors for staining, since they are too often the least prepared of any woodwork in the house. First of all, new floors.

Careless workmen will have inevitably spilt cement, plaster, spots of distemper, paint and so forth on the floor, and will also have neglected to wipe them up before they had a chance to set. Now they must all be removed—the cement and plaster by scraping and glass-papering; the others similarly, but with the use of paint remover in stubborn cases. The boards should be well scrubbed and allowed to dry out thoroughly. All nail heads should be well driven in and the holes filled up flush with a stopping material (Fig. B149). This is in addition to the procedure already described above.

Old floors will probably need even more preparation. These are the points to observe. All nails or tacks used

for securing carpets or lino must be taken out, or (if this is impossible without further indenting the boards) should be driven in with a punch and the hole filled. Any previous stain should be removed as far as possible, or the new finish will be uneven. Paint remover, or in the case of a spirit-varnish, methylated spirit, will assist materially in this operation. Badly shrunken boards should be filled at the joints after first being planed to remove any 'curl'. Needless to say, all dirt and dust which has accumulated in the holes and corners must be cleaned out. The staining procedure can then be followed for new and old floors as already described.

French Polishing

There is undoubtedly a great mystique about this extremely decorative finish. But any handyman worth his salt should be able to master the technique. Here are all the 'secrets': all you need is practice!

Practice is essential: no important job such as the polishing of a suite of furniture should be undertaken in the early stages. Instead, preliminary trials should be carried out on scrap pieces of timber; then, when some degree of proficiency has been achieved, attention can be turned to small items of furniture such as a coffee table.

Basic Requirements: The main requirements for french polishing are as follows: polish, 'rubbers', linseed oil (or mineral oil), methylated spirit, airtight tin for storage of rubbers, canvas for applying filler, polishing mop, filling material, stain and glasspaper. It should be stressed that the above are the main items needed; others will be mentioned at appropriate stages.

Make Your Own Polish: Unless you can purchase a good-quality french polish, usually known as 'trade quality', why not make your own? This is not difficult, although it must be made several days before commencing work. It will give you a deeper satisfaction and provide a finer finish. French polish contains two items only, namely shellac and methylated spirit. There are several grades of shellac, each one producing its own particular tone or colour of polish. For example, bleached shellac gives a white polish which is used on marquetry pictures, or in cases where the colour of the timber must not be darkened.

At the other end of the scale we have garnet polish which is produced by using garnet shellac. The resulting polish is used over dark stains.

Between these two come orange and button polish. Orange polish is the product of orange shellac and is generally used for the golden shades of stain and for toning other polishes. Button polish, made from button shellac, is also used for some of the golden tones and can be mixed with other polishes to produce a particular shade.

From these remarks it will be obvious that the polish used should match the work; experiment with mixing different shades of polish to produce a desired shade for the particular job in hand.

To make the polish, add 6 oz. of any of the above shellacs to a pint of spirit. Allow to stand for a few days until the shellac has dissolved. The polish is best made in a corked bottle, and the dissolving process will be speeded up if the bottle is agitated from time to time.

When using the polish, cut a groove in the bottle cork as shown in Fig. B150: this is the best method of applying the polish to the rubber.

Staining: The ready-made stains usually sold as 'wood dyes' are quite suitable for most of the jobs the average handyman will undertake around the home. These stains can be intermixed to produce a wide variation of tones, and this is very important. Under no circumstances should the stain be applied straight from the container to the job, as the shade may be too dark. It is advisable in all cases to try out the stain on a scrap piece of the same timber and to take careful note of the results: adjustment is then possible. This is of particular importance if the job in hand is to be stained to match an existing piece of furniture.

An interesting departure from the usual types of stains is the use of bichromate of potash to colour mahogany. The crystals are steeped in water and the resulting solution, which is an orange colour, is applied to the wood. The actual colouring of the wood is the result of a chemical action between the bichromate of potash and the tannic acid in the timber. The tone of the colour can be adjusted by adding more water to the strong solution, and here again you can experiment.

The work is cleaned-up in the usual manner and sanded smooth, and it is wise to give the job a quick wash over with clean water. This will raise the grain which can be papered smooth when the work is again dry. By doing this there is no danger of the grain lifting after the staining operation.

The stain is applied with a clean rag, made fairly wet. Staining is done with the grain, commencing at one edge of the panel and working across to the opposite edge. Quick strokes of the rag are necessary to keep the edge of the stain 'alive' in order that the next stroke of the cloth will deposit a wet layer of stain which will mate up with the still-wet previous layer (Fig. B151).

While a rag is the best method of applying the stain to large flat areas, it will be found that a small brush or 'fitch' is the best tool for small mouldings and similar-shaped areas of the work (Fig. B152).

The staining of end grain presents a problem because the wood here is more porous and consequently absorbs more stain. The best method of dealing with this is to thin the stain so that it is weaker in colour. The greater quantity taken up by the end grain will then tone with the remainder of the job; but in order to get the stain at the correct tone it is necessary to try it out on the end grain of a similar piece of scrap material.

Allow the job to stand for several hours, until the stain is really dry, and then apply a sealing coat of french polish. This coat should be fairly thin; its main function is to provide a barrier between the stain and the filling which is next applied. The polish can be applied with the polishing mop; Fig. B153 shows this particular brush in action.

Filling: As the name suggests, the object of this operation is to fill the grain and so produce a perfectly level surface for the polishing operation. A good filling material is plaster of paris, which can be tinted with powder colours to match the wood in question. For example, rose pink can be used for mahogany and vandyke brown for the darker colours such as walnut. In the case of the lighter shades of timbers, the plaster can be used in its natural state.

The plaster is applied with a rag which is damped with clean water. It is best kept in a small container close to the job and into which the damped rag can be dipped. A better material for applying the filler is a piece of light

Fig. B150 (*right*). Transfer the polish to the rubbers through a grooved cork.

Fig. B151 (*below*). Applying the stain with a cloth.

Fig. B152 (*left*). A fitch brush is used for staining mouldings.

Fig. B153 (*right*). A polishing mop brush is used to apply a sealing coat.

Fig. B154. Filling the grain, using rag or canvas.

canvas, the open texture of which is easily charged with the plaster.

When applying the filler, scrub it well into the grain. Allow a few minutes for the initial set of the plaster to take place, then, with a clean piece of rag or canvas, scrub off the surplus.

The job must now be levelled off by sanding with a fine paper and the addition of a little oil at this stage will kill the whiteness of the plaster. If the plaster has been used in its natural state, use a white mineral oil; if tinted, use raw linseed oil.

Pay particular attention to the corners of the mouldings and similar places where the filler is inclined to build up. Removing the filler from such places can be best done with a small pointed stick. Fig. B154 illustrates the filling operation.

Fadding: Fadding is the name given to an extension of the sealing of the timber when the staining is complete. At this stage a further sealing coat of polish is applied over the filler; this can be done with the polishing mop.

Some workers use a 'fad', which is simply a piece of wadding dipped in polish and allowed to harden by contact with the air. The fad is then softened in spirits and dipped in the polish. However, from the beginner's point of view there is a danger of small particles of the wadding becoming embedded in the polish, so the use of the mop is recommended.

Apply a thin coat of polish over the whole job with the mop, and allow a few minutes for it to become hard. Take a piece of very fine abrasive paper, and work over the surface with it, taking care to wipe clean all traces of the dust produced by rubbing down.

Continue in this manner until the polish film is quite visible.

To complete the fadding, a 'rubber' similar to that used for the remainder of the polishing operations, is made up. A piece of wadding about 9 in. sq. is folded as shown at A in Fig. B155, and the four corners are then lifted upwards to give the pyramid shape shown at B. The wadding is now covered with a piece of clean linen rag and the sole of the rubber flattened slightly to give the finished shape shown at C.

In use, the 'tail' of the rubber is held in the palm of the hand, the thumb, first and second fingers are closed over the front of the rubber, and the remaining two fingers are curled behind it.

The rag is opened and polish is poured on to the wadding. A slight pressure on the rubber when in use causes the polish to ooze through the cloth and so provide a controlled flow of polish to the job.

The rubber is used at this stage to apply the final coat of polish in the fadding operation, and it is used without oil. Should the rubber drag up the polish, leave the work until the polish is hard. Commence with short circular strokes as shown at A in Fig. B156, then change to figures-of-eight as at B and finally finish off with long, straight strokes which run the full length of the job, C. At this stage there should be a good film of polish on the work, but not a high gloss.

Colouring: The work should now be carefully examined to determine if there are any light areas in the stain which require attention. These areas will require colouring with a tinted polish to make them match the general tone of the job.

The tinted polish will have to be made; mix equal parts of methylated spirit and polish and add a very small quantity of dry colour to give the required tint.

The polish is applied with the polishing mop or a small pencil brush, according to the size of the areas. Work at arm's length to give a good view of the job and endeavour to apply the tinted polish in one operation. It will be found that the polish will soften the surface, so if a second application is necessary some time must elapse before the next coat can be applied.

When the whole surface has been brought to a uniform tone, the tinted areas are given a light rubbing down with a flour-grade paper and sealed by a coat of polish applied with the mop.

This sealing coat will be found necessary to prevent the coloured polish working up during the later operations.

Bodying: In this operation, a little oil is applied with the finger to the sole of the charged rubber. The amount of oil should be kept as small as possible, as it must all be removed at a later date. Its sole function is to prevent dragging of the rubber.

Commence by rubbing across the grain, the object being to get the surface covered with a coat of polish. Once this has been achieved, commence working in a series of circular movements as indicated in Fig. B157.

As the rubber dries out, it is opened up and a little more polish added; when it starts to drag, a smear of oil is applied to the sole. As the body of polish is built up, the direction of the strokes of the rubber are changed to figures-of-eight as seen in Fig. B158 at A, and these in turn are reduced in size to give smaller movements as shown at B.

Do not overcharge the rubber with polish in an attempt to build up a body of polish quickly. This would cause the shellac to build up in ridges due to the rapid evapora-

Fig. B155. The three stages in making a wadding rubber.

Fig. B156. Rubber paths in fadding.

Fig. B157. Rubber paths in the first stage of bodying.

Fig. B158. Rubber paths in the second stage of bodying.

tion of the spirit. Another cause of ridges is rubbing too much in one direction, especially with straight strokes.

Try and develop a sense for the control of the flow of polish from the rubber. With a newly-charged rubber apply only a light pressure, and increase the pressure accordingly as the rubber dries out. When using the rubber, never stop its movement over the job. This would mark the film and in some cases may lift it completely. The golden rule is to glide the rubber on to the job, keep it moving and then glide it off again.

Finish off by changing from small figure-of-eight strokes to long straight strokes with the grain.

Cutting Down: When a good body of polish has been built up, the oil is removed from the surface by lightly rubbing all over with the clean rag slightly damped with spirit. Work quickly and lightly, and change the cloth as the part in contact with the work becomes stained with oil. The job is then set aside for twenty-four hours, after which the surface is examined. If it is found that the polish has sunk in places, this denotes that the filling operation has not been properly carried out. The fault can be corrected by cutting the body down with a very fine paper until a level surface is obtained, but the first body should be cut down in any case. However, the degree of cutting down will be greater where sinking of the polish has taken place.

The work is well dusted and a second body applied, and this too has the oil removed and is cut down. A third body is given to the work, but this is left with the oil in place and no cutting down should be necessary.

Pulling Over: The need for proper movement of the rubber, to avoid the danger of the polish building up in ridges, has been stressed. However carefully the rubber is used, there are bound to be some slight 'heights and hollows' in the body, and these must be flattened out if a smooth glass-like finish is to be achieved. The job is, therefore, 'pulled over'; as the term suggests, the heights are pulled over into the hollows, thus levelling the finish.

For pulling over, a solution of equal parts of polish and methylated spirits is required on a fresh rubber. The rubber is used with a fairly heavy pressure if it is to flatten the surface, but it must be kept moving smartly.

There may be enough oil on the surface to keep the rubber moving without dragging; if not, add a few drops of oil to the sole of the rubber. However, take care not to use too much oil, as it all has to be removed.

In the case of a very uneven surface, pulling over, as described above, can be a very slow process; in such cases pumice powder should be use, placed under the cloth.

The flow of polish forces it through to make contact with the work, but a light pressure should be applied as there is always the danger of tearing the surface.

Spiriting Off: This process can be described as washing the surface with spirit to remove the oil and give a good gloss. The first requirement is a rubber charged with a 50/50 mixture of polish and spirit. In the initial stage the polish film is slightly softened; to obtain this effect, a little oil is used on the rubber sole. Work in circles, but from time to time change for a short period to straight strokes. As the rubber dries out, change to small figures-of-eight. A special rubber is required for the actual spiriting operation which immediately follows the initial stage of the work. This rubber is made up from a piece of ordinary cotton wool dipped in the spirit and covered with a piece of linen. The quantity of spirit is of utmost importance. It must not be possible to squeeze spirit from the rubber; if there is too much spirit, squeeze out as much as possible and set the rubber aside to dry slightly.

Use the rubber with a sweeping motion and use light, fast strokes. At this stage the surplus oil is being lifted by the rubber, and at the same time the surface is being burnished.

The surface is now prepared to take the type of finish you require.

Acid Finish: With this finish, the action of the acid hardens the film and separates the oil from the shellac. The oil is then lifted with chalk which is rubbed over the surface of the work.

Commence with a rubber charged with a 50/50 solution of spirit and polish as described in the initial stages of spiriting off. When the polished surface has been slightly softened or 'got working', let it stand for about a quarter of an hour.

Take ten parts cold water and to this add one part sulphuric acid drop by drop, taking care to shake the bottle well to ensure proper mixing. (Always add acid to water; never add water to acid, as heat is generated and —depending upon the quantities involved—an explosion is possible. This rule is applicable whenever acid has to be diluted.) The diluted acid is spread over the job with a piece of fine cloth and worked over the surface with the palm of the hand using loops and straight strokes. This works the acid through the oil film and the next step is to mop this up with the chalk. If you have any cuts, etc., in your hands, wash them in soapy water afterwards.

The chalk used is the Vienna variety and it is applied to the work with a pounce bag which is filled with the chalk and dabbed on to the work.

The hands are cleaned and dried and again rubbed over the job until the surface feels and looks dry. A fine, dry rag is then employed to remove the chalk. The operation is illustrated in Fig. B159.

Stiffing: Again a 50/50 solution of polish and spirit is used, but without oil. The sole of the rubber must be perfectly flat and free from wrinkles, otherwise the job will be marked. The rubber is glided on at one end of the panel and off again at the opposite end, making sure that the stroke is perfectly straight. The return stroke should overlap the previous one slightly.

When all the surface has been covered in this manner, commence again (after damping the rubber, if necessary). It will be found that the smear marks of the oil will gradually reduce to a few streaks and these too will vanish as the work progresses.

As the rubber dries out, the pressure is increased and it will be found that as the last traces of oil are removed the friction grows considerably.

Glazing: This particular finish has been kept to the last because, although it is one of the accepted finishes, it is not so durable as the others. However, it can be said that a well-glazed finish is vastly superior to a badly-spirited one. It is quite suitable for a quick finish to some small piece of furniture not subject to heavy wear and much handling.

Glaze is quite simple to make, the ingredients being gum benzoin and methylated spirit. The benzoin is crushed, placed in a wide-mouth jar and just covered with the spirit. The jar should be corked and stood in the living room for a few days until the benzoin has dissolved. Shaking the bottle periodically will help speed the process. When the benzoin is dissolved, the resulting 'glaze' is strained through muslin to free it from all foreign matter. It is now in a 'neat' state and can be diluted with spirit before use.

There are several methods of applying the glaze, but perhaps the best is to use a new polishing rubber. This is

Fig. B159. Final stages in sulphuric acid finish.

Fig. B160. Obtaining an eggshell finish.

Fig. B161. Using pumice for a matt finish.

Eggshell: Many readers will be familiar with the eggshell finish common on articles of modern furniture. This can easily be produced at home, nothing more than fine steel wool and wax furniture polish being required.

The wool is dipped in the wax, which acts as a lubricant, and is worked over the job in long straight strokes with the grain as shown in Fig. B160. Care must be taken to prevent the wool cutting through the french polish along the edges, but apart from this the work is quite simple.

To finish off, clean away the surplus wax with a series of clean rags.

Matt: With this finish there is no trace of the dull waxed effect as with the eggshell finish, so the method of obtaining this result differs slightly from that already described. The finest grade of pumice powder is used instead of the steel wool, and this is applied with a felt pad. The pad is damped with clean water, dipped into the powder, and then rubbed in straight lines along the job.

When the gloss of the french polish has been cut down to the required degree, the powder is washed off with a damp wash leather. The work is allowed to dry completely, and then rubbed with clean rags. This process is shown in Fig. B161.

charged with the glaze, and should be slightly wetter than when french polish is used. Glaze is more or less painted on the wood, so the rubber is used in a long straight stroke, *with* the grain in all cases. Each stroke should overlap the previous one very slightly as the glaze may be wiped off again. Always allow the work to harden-off before passing the rubber over the same spot again. Sufficient coats should be given to attain the desired degree of gloss, but do not be tempted to overdo things, as a very thick coat is not satisfactory.

Instead of using a rubber it is possible to apply the glaze with a sponge, used in exactly the same manner as the rubber. A brush may also be employed, in which case the work becomes akin to varnishing.

The gloss of the glaze can, in some cases, be improved by giving a quick wipe over with the spirit rubber, but care is necessary here as too much rubbing or a too-wet rubber can easily wipe off the glaze. With this in mind, experiment on a scrap piece of timber before spiriting a piece of furniture.

Working Conditions: Good work cannot be produced unless the working conditions are suitable. The first requirement is a warm room or workshop, as a low temperature and damp conditions will result in a bloomed or foggy finish. Another requirement is plenty of natural daylight to enable a close observation to be kept on the build-up of the polish so that the first signs of ridges can be detected.

Freedom from dust is essential as this will settle on the soft polish film and produce 'nibs' which must be smoothed off.

Well, there you are—all the secrets revealed. All you need now is—practice!

Graining

There are ingenious little rubber graining tools available for a few shillings which can produce a realistic impression of various woods like oak and pine, and interesting designs.

Other tools needed for graining are: two or three steel graining combs of varying sizes; two or three clean paint brushes, 1½ in. and ½ in.; a 3 in. soft brush (this is to

Heartwood: To produce what is known as heart growth of wood, rock the tool back and forward where you wish the heart piece to show. This is the heartwood. Using the comb part of the graining tool, comb down the scumble adjoining the heartwood with one straight stroke (Fig. B162). Start farthest away and work towards yourself. Next, using a fine metal comb, go over this combing in a diagonal direction (Fig. B163). Apply scumble to the rest of the wood and brush out evenly; then, using a piece of rag over the chisel end of the stick, wipe in light markings (Fig. B164); move the rag frequently to make sure that you always use a clean part.

After making the larger markings place the rag over the pointed end of the stick and make the finer markings as shown. Then go on to the combing of the heartwood (Fig. B163). Finally, go lightly over the completed work with the soft brush to blend and soften.

The graining tools, being of rubber, have the advantage

Fig. B162. Combing a straight grain next to the heartwood.

Fig. B163. Following the diagonal marking round the heartwood with a fine comb.

Fig. B164. Wiping in the finer markings with rag on a stick.

soften and blend the finished work); scumble and ground colour; a stick about 8 in. long, shaped like a half-inch chisel at one end and pointed like a pencil at the other; and a supply of clean, non-fluffy, dust-free rag.

Scumble, the actual graining colour, is made in varying shades of brown, and there is a matching ground colour which forms the base for the scumble.

Oak Style: Before starting to grain in oak style, practise on a piece of wood about 2 ft.×1 ft. to represent a door panel. Paint this with the proper ground colour and, when it is dry, prepare the scumble. Part of this is thinned slightly with turps and raw linseed oil according to instructions on the tin; an old jam jar makes a good container.

Apply scumble to one edge of the piece of wood twice the width of the graining tool. When the scumble has been brushed-out evenly, hold the graining tool with both hands and draw it down the surface of the wood.

that uneven surfaces can be dealt with. Squeeze the ends towards each other to 'bow' the tool in the middle for graining hollow surfaces; squeeze the other way to make the comb low in the middle, as when graining a staircase pillar or column.

Let the work dry thoroughly before varnishing.

Finally, a few hints to remember. Do not apply scumble with the sun shining directly on to the work. Varnish should not be applied on a cold, damp day—it is best applied in a warm, dry atmosphere. Avoid dust. Keep all tools clean. And—lastly—as in most things, practice is most important.

Veneering

Some people are funny! They wouldn't dream of using odd rolls of wallpaper to decorate a room—the thought would make them shudder. They couldn't live with an eyesore like that for three minutes—let alone three years.

Yet they are perfectly content to make a piece of furniture—which they will have to live with for the rest of their lives—from ready-veneered chipboard or veneered plywood.

The surprising thing is that they do not realise, until it is pointed out, that factory-made panels of chipboard and plywood are made with fairly plain face veneers from common, freely-available woods which the factory can repeat.

And rightly so—for the mass producer of veneered panels has to try to please the customer who buys another panel the following month or year, and expects it to match! Of course, they never do, because no two trees are alike, and in fact no two veneers even from the same tree are identical either. The only way to hope to achieve a perfect match is to use consecutive matching leaves, kept in the exact sequence as cut from the tree.

There's nothing wrong with factory-made veneered chipboard or veneered plywood. Use it by all means for shelving and other utility purposes. But in the same way that you wouldn't dream of having plastic in your living room (it belongs in the kitchen and bathroom as working surfaces) the ready-veneered panel could hardly be used to build a treasured and prized piece of furniture. Most cabinets are constructed from panels of different thicknesses—you may have 6 mm ends, 9 mm top and partitions, 12 mm doors, etc.

It is impossible for any ready-veneered plywood or chipboard panels, in these different thicknesses, to match each other.

Yet it is vital that they should, if the cabinet is to be a perfectly balanced, matched whole unit.

The only way is to buy consecutive matching leaves of veneer, kept in exactly the same sequence as cut from the log, which will match each other perfectly, and to veneer your own plywood or chipboard.

There are other errors in many people's approach to making an item of furniture.

Some people believe that buying a large sheet of beautifully veneered figured plywood gets round the difficulty, especially if they are content to make the cabinet from panels all of the same thickness, cut from the same board. Very economical! But to avoid excessive waste it usually means having to have the grain directions running in the wrong direction—and none of the panels matching each other.

In an attempt to rectify the sorry-looking plight of the cabinet, they then order veneers by post, and find that these do not match the veneer of the same name used on the plywood ready-veneered panel.

Then there is the man who wrongly believes that nothing can compare with the strength and solidity of solid timber for his furniture. How mistaken this man is; the world's museums are fighting a losing battle of repair and restoration with solid furniture—almost to the point where they are forced to renew the best pieces with laminated construction. The great Masters of the 18th century realised the folly of using solid timber; Chippendale used plywood construction extensively. The reason is obvious; solid wood will shrink and warp, especially in modern centrally-heated homes, but correctly-laminated panels are shrink-proof.

Quite apart from considerations of economy, utility and durability, there are more important reasons for the practical householder who takes a pride in his home to veneer his own furniture.

Today's universal square, box-like furniture is dictated to us by the requirements of the conveyor belt assembly lines of automated factory production. By designing his own more graceful furniture, with elegant flowing lines, perfectly suited to the task and the space available, he can express his own taste and personality, and often at less than half the cost of run-of-the-mill furniture.

Groundwork: A veneered panel will only be as good as the groundwork it is laid on. It must be the right material, correctly prepared.

Solid timber does not make the best groundwork, but in some cases you may want to use it if you already have suitable board. As the greatest shrinkage takes place along the annular (*not* 'annual') rings, boards will tend to shrink across their width and to warp or wind away from the heart side.

You can easily determine which is the heart side by looking at the end grain. To counteract this natural tendency to warp, always veneer solid timber on the heart side, and in the same grain direction as the groundwork (Fig. B165). If there are any defects in the board, such as knots, nail holes or other blemishes, these must be chopped out. Replace with pellets for small holes and plugs for larger holes, and make sure the grain direction of pellets and plugs runs in the same direction as the main board (Fig. B166). Never use dowels to plug a hole.

The best way to use a solid board is to saw it into narrow widths, and alternate each strip, with the heart side up and down to equalise the warping tendency. This is the principle of all core-constructed laminated boards such as laminboard (in which the core strips are only 7 mm wide), and blockboard (in which the core strips are 1 in. wide). Fig. B167 refers.

If you make up your own laminated board from solid timber cut into strips, test the panel for 'wind'. If not perfectly level, plane across the panel from high corner to high corner diagonally. Then 'tooth' the core-slab with the teeth of a saw dragged across the surface in both directions. The purpose is twofold, firstly to form a key for the adhesive and secondly to detect any hollows missed by the plane.

The best solid timber for a groundwork is Honduras Mahogany; others are Obeche, American Whitewood or Yellow Pine. Oak does not make a good groundwork because the flat-sawn boards are prone to warp and the quarter-sawn boards tend to show a prominent ray figure which shows through the veneer.

Where possible, try to select a board which has been radially cut, quarter-sawn so that the end grain shows with almost vertical rings, in which case any future shrinkage would take place in the thickness—and this is practically eliminated if only thoroughly well-seasoned wood is used.

Having made your core-slab from alternate strips and keyed them for veneering, the core must be cross-veneered with a cheap soft veneer laid at right angles to the core strip direction. When dry, this crossband would also be keyed to receive the face veneer which would be laid in the opposite direction to the outer casing, i.e., in the same direction as the core strips (Fig. B168). The outer casing crossband would have been applied to both sides of the core-slab, so in addition to a face veneer, a backing veneer would also be applied.

Laminboard: This makes excellent groundwork for veneering, but is rather expensive. It is made as described above with the core strips only 3 mm to 7 mm wide,

Heartside   Veneer

Fig. B165.

Fig. B166.

Solid timber

Batten board

Block board

Lamin board

Fig. B167.

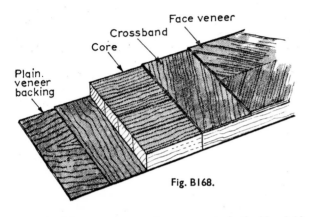

Face veneer
Crossband
Core
Plain
veneer
backing

Fig. B168.

covered with stout outer casing veneers to both sides, laid in the opposite direction, and ready to receive your face veneer and backing veneer.

Blockboard: Second only to laminboard in preference as a groundwork, blockboard is made with core strips up to 1 in. wide, with the fractionally greater tendency to warp in very large areas, but this can be ignored in most small panels.

Blockboard has outer casing veneers laid opposite to the core strip direction, ready to receive face veneers; but certain imported blockboards, instead of a stout outer casing veneer, employ two thinner veneers to each side, with the result that the first runs across the core strip direction and the outer casing runs in the same direction as the core. As you have to lay your face veneer opposite to the direction of the outer casing, it is important to watch this point.

Battenboard: The same principle of construction is used except that the core strips are up to 3 in. wide and there is a much greater tendency to warp in large dimensions.

Plywood: This is a much-abused material and contains many pitfalls for the unwary. Most plywood is made from an odd number of laminations of constructional veneer, 3-ply, 5-ply, 7-ply and 9-ply. For most practical purposes 3-ply would be used only as a core material to be built up into 5-ply for veneering. 5-ply is excellent for small panels, but for lids, tops, doors and other hard-wearing surfaces and for larger panels, the minimum recommended would be 7-ply or greater. The best plywood for veneering is Gaboon multi-ply and not the much harder Finnish Birch ply.

The act of veneering plywood unbalances it—exerting a pull which will warp the panel unless a compensating veneer is laid on the other side. The golden rule is always to veneer two sides, even on the thickest plywood.

Chipboard: This material is universally used as a groundwork and should also be veneered two sides. If the panel has been made from two different grades of chips,

lay the face veneer on the finest side and the backing on the reverse. If you have a panel of veneered chipboard, you can 'key' the veneer and veneer over it—but always in the opposite grain direction.

Hardboard: For small panels, ends, plinths and infillings, hardboard makes a satisfactory groundwork if veneered two sides; lay the face veneer on the canvas side, and key the smooth side for the compensating veneer. It also makes good core materials and can be built up to form thicker panels, with veneer outer casings.

Metal: When exposed to heat, metal tends to expand and wood to shrink. Although it is possible to bond veneer to metal using impact adhesives, this is a task best left to specialist factory production using correct adhesives and controlled pressing techniques. The best groundwork for wood veneers is a wood base.

Specification of Groundwork: It is a trade custom in Britain, when ordering laminated boards, plywoods or veneers, to state the length along the grain as the first stated dimension, even when this happens to be the shortest side of the panel. Thus a panel 12 in. × 36 in. has a 12 in. grain direction and a panel 36 in. × 12 in. has a 36 in. grain direction. This is most important when specifying groundwork.

As you must always veneer across the grain direction of the groundwork, you must first decide in which grain direction the face veneer is required to run on your finished project. Suppose this to be the 36 in. direction, then you must specify a groundwork panel of plywood 12 in. × 36 in. to enable you to lay the face veneer in the opposite direction.

As explained above, laminboards and blockboards already have their outer casing veneers laid opposite to the core strip direction (in most cases).

Where, for reasons of strength, you decide you want to use the panel with the core strips and outer casing in the same direction as that in which you intend to lay your face veneer, then you must first lay an under-veneer to both sides, across the outer casing, so that your face veneer can be laid in its proper direction, parallel with the core.

Also, if you have cut up a large panel of plywood for reasons of economy, and discover that your panels have the wrong grain direction for your face veneers, these, too, must be cross-veneered to enable you to lay the face veneer correctly.

Remember, always, to veneer across the grain of the groundwork; therefore specify groundwork to suit the project.

Edges: As it is not practicable to veneer end grain, the edges of laminboard, blockboard and plywood need to be covered—usually with a strip of solid wood, known as a lipping or facing. This may be from timber of the same species as you propose for the face veneer, but most people use Ramin or Obeche and stain it to match any veneer of their choice.

If the edge of the panel has to be shaped in any way—bevelled, chamfered, rounded, fluted, etc.—the strip should be wide enough to allow for this machining.

Lippings may be applied to the edges by straight-forward pinning and glueing (Fig. B169a) or by being tongued-and-grooved (Fig. B169b). The corners are mitred.

The edges of all panels which receive hard wear, such as the front edges of lids, closing edges of doors, etc., should be lipped to protect the veneer edge, which may chip with rough handling.

Lippings of edges may be applied before the face and backing veneers are laid, in which case they are concealed by the veneers. Great care must be taken to ensure that these lippings are planed and sanded level with the groundwork, prior to laying the final veneers.

Alternatively, lippings are often applied after the panel has been faced and backed, trimmed square. In this case the lippings will show, but are made part of the decoration and also serve to protect the veneer edges.

Shaped and Curved Groundwork: There are several methods of making shaped or curved groundwork.

Fig. B170 shows: (a) for slight curves, bandsaw the shape from the solid and save the waste pieces to use as cauls (shaped pressure pads) for laying the veneer; (b) more-rounded shapes, such as kidney-shaped tables, are usually built up from small wooden bricks, laid to a prepared template 'out of course', then bandsawed to shape; (c) more elaborate shapes may be built up from coopered blocks of wood; (d) the most common method is to laminate, or bend by steaming, and then clamp under pressure between curved bearers with a greater curvature than will finally be required.

How Veneers are Cut: No two trees are ever identical. Differences in grain, figure, markings, hue and texture may vary, even in the same log. Every angle of cut through a log will produce a different visual pattern in the veneer. It is the skilled task of the veneer cutter to decide which method of cutting will produce the most attractive figure.

There are four methods of converting a veneer log (that is the cylindrical, straight section of the tree bole above the root-butt and up the first limb): these are sawing, rotary cutting, half-rounding and slicing.

Sawing: This method has now become obsolete owing to the very high wastage and cost. It is used only to cut very small girth logs such as ebony, or for cutting limbs into oyster veneers.

Rotary Cutting: The de-barked log is first prepared for cutting by being steamed or boiled in large vats for a period of hours or days. It is then mounted in a giant lathe and revolved against a knife to produce a continuous sheet of veneer. This method of cutting around the growth rings of the tree produces the constructional veneers used for the manufacture of plywood, core stock, and the outer laminations of blockboard, etc. The veneer is 'wild grained' and impossible to match. There are notable exceptions—decorative veneers such as betula and bird's eye maple are produced in this way.

Half-Rounding: The steamed log is converted on a giant bandsaw into flitches; roughly squared-up sections with the heart and sapwood removed. The flitch is then mounted on the rotary lathe eccentrically so that the cutting commences at the sappy edge towards the heart side; sometimes it is mounted to bring the angle of cut from the heart side out towards the sap, which is known as backcutting. It gives a greater swoop through the growth rings and a more attractive figure.

Slicing: The majority of all decorative veneers used today are sliced in one of two ways. First, to produce crown-cut veneer (Fig. B171), the log is halved on the bandsaw, and mounted on a flat bed. The knife cuts across the crown, producing a pattern of sap at the edges and fancy heartwood figure in the centre.

Crown-cut veneers are those used by the traditional cabinet makers, such as figured walnut, mahogany, butts, burrs and curls. Burrs are wart-like growths, dormant buds which have the appearance of tightly-clustered knot formations and are the most highly prized of all veneers. Curls are cut from the intersection of a limb with a trunk, producing a feathered curl figure (Fig. B172).

Quarter-cut veneers are radially cut in a direction parallel with the medullary rays (Fig. B173). The log is

Fig. B169a.

Veneer

Fig. B169b.

Veneer

Short grain

(b)

Curving with bricks

Short grain

(a)

Fill saw kerfs with veneer after bending

(c)

Fig. B170.

Fig. B171 (left). The flat-cutting method produces the highly decorative veneer shown.

Fig. B172 (centre). African mahogany curl on crotch.

Fig. B173 (right). The quarter-cut method produces striped veneers.

converted into six or eight flitches and this type of cut produces the ribbon striped, straight-grained, or attractive ray-figured veneers so popular today, such as pencil-striped sapele, striped teak, figured oak, etc.

Different Types of Figure: The all-important figure in decorative veneers results from several features in the log—the scarcity of frequency of growth rings, colour tone variations, peculiarities of grain and the type of cut selected by the mill.

In addition to straight grain, there are several combinations of irregular grain (near knots or butts), diagonal grain (caused by mill conversion), spiral grain, interlocked grain, and wavy grain.

Irregular grain provides blistered or quilted figures, interlocked grain gives pencil-striped or ribbon figures, wavy grain yields fiddleback, bees-wing or crossfire figures. Other self-descriptive types of figure are: lace, silver grain, raindrop, flake, flowery, pigment, finger-roll, roe, rope, broken stripe, mottle, snail, plum pudding.

Characteristics: The variation in the size of the wood cells provides different textures. Oak is coarse-textured, mahogany is medium, sycamore is fine-textured.

Lustre depends on the ability of the cell walls to reflect light. Generally, the striped woods are the more lustrous.

Certain woods retain distinctive odour, even when polished, and this may be utilised as insect or moth repellent—or to conserve aroma, as in the case of the various cedar woods.

Handling and Storage: The effect of light and moisture on veneers is important. The steaming process will have slightly changed the colour tone of the wood from its original hue; the veneer will become slightly darker than solid timber from the same tree.

The veneers are then mechanically dried to a precise moisture content – usually about 12½ per cent. in Britain —and are then tied in bundles of 24 or 32 leaves in the exact sequence of matching consecutive leaves as cut from the log. Veneers are then stored in humidity-controlled warehouses.

It is therefore important that you store them in a well-aired, cool part of the house, away from heat which may reduce the moisture content and cause the veneers to buckle.

When your parcel of veneers arrives from the specialist veneer supplier (very few retailers can store veneers

properly) it comes to you in a roll, with the ends taped to prevent splitting. Place the veneers under a weighted board and they will flatten naturally overnight. If your veneers do tend to buckle, perhaps caused by local conditions, changing humidity, a heatwave or central heating, etc., simply sprinkle with water and leave under a weighted board for the veneers to restore their correct moisture content. Certain veneers such as burrs are often buckled. To flatten them, sprinkle with water, cover with paper, and press between two heated cauls of plywood until dry.

If you have very stubbornly buckled burrs or veneers to deal with, dip them in hot glue size (10 parts water to one of glue) and allow to drain; then gradually tighten down in the press using heated metal plates of zinc or aluminium, with polythene sheets to prevent sticking.

It is also important to store veneers away from direct strong light, which will cause certain veneers to fade and others to darken. A basement room or bedroom makes the best store.

Preparation of Veneers: Some highly-figured veneers or burrs may contain knot holes or other blemishes not considered as defects. These slight imperfections can be patched. First, cut around the hole with a sharp knife by following the irregular contour of the markings in the veneer. Then underlay part of the identical veneer, and use the newly-shaped hole as a template to cut a patch which is then fixed into the original hole with gummed paper tape. Splits along the grain, caused by handling, are unimportant, as they tend to lose themselves when the veneer is laid.

Veneer Matching: Apart from narrow panels used for shelving, plinths, etc., it is not advisable to veneer a decorative panel with one leaf of veneer, even if you have a leaf wide enough to cover the panel without making a join. A centre-jointed two-piece match is common practice; in fact, two quite ordinary plain veneers made into a two-piece match can become decorative.

By holding a mirror vertically on a leaf of veneer you will see reflected in it the effect of a two-piece match. Move the mirror about over the leaf to search for the best effect. Pencil or chalk the veneer along the mirror baseline, transfer both leaves to a flat cutting board and pin them together. Make sure both leaves exactly coincide in pattern, then cut through both leaves along the pencilled or chalked line by placing a straightedge over the veneers and making two light cuts with a sharp knife. Do not try to cut through both veneers with one cut; this may cause the veneer to tear along the grain.

Now place the pair of veneers on a shooting board, with about ⅛ in. overhanging. Hold the veneers down with the straightedge or with pins. Set the plane iron as finely as possible to prevent digging in, and then shoot the veneer edges their full length (Fig. B174). The veneers are then opened like a book, and the two edges butted together to form an exact matched pattern. Affix a few straps of extra-thin, double-gummed veneering paper tape across the join in a few places, then one strip along the entire length. This tape goes on the front, or outside, of the veneer. A good tip is to drive in two pins about 1 in. from the join, then by slanting the pins towards each other they force a tight join. Rub the veneer tape vigorously with the rounded end of a stick – the tape will stretch and further tighten the joint as it dries. Fig. B175 shows many of the favourite match patterns, and descriptions of these follow.

Four-Piece Match: Hold two mirrors together at right angles, and their reflection will show the effect of a four-piece match if marked and cut along the mirror baselines. A four-piece match is shown in Fig. B176b.

Diamond Match: Cut the veneer diagonally across the leaf and assemble to form a diamond. If cut from dead-straight striped veneer, the diamond match may be cut from one single leaf.

Reverse Diamond Match: The diagonal sections are reversed to form an X pattern instead of a Diamond.

Triangular Diamond Match: The veneer is cut to form triangles instead of rectangles as before. The triangles are equal-sided for a square panel and unequal-sided for a rectangular panel.

Herringbone Match: This is formed from two-piece diamond matching cut into strips and re-jointed.

Eight-Piece and Sixteen-Piece Match: These are possible only when the consecutive matching veneers show a pattern throughout which does not vary too much, which is not very common. See Fig. B176a.

Segmental Match: This is when matched leaves are cut to precise geometric angles to form 'sunburst' segments usually meeting at the centre of the panel.

Crossbanding: This is often used to form a decorative border surround (see Fig. B177) and may be taped together with plain butt joins, or pattern matched, or mitred to form curves or radius crossbandings. By compressing several leaves of veneer between thin plywood outers, and nailing together to form a pad, crossbanding may be cut to the required length on a circular saw.

Casual Match: A modern decorative treatment is to arrange leaves together to form a repeating rather than a matched pattern.

Slip Matching: This is another form of casual matching in which the veneers are arranged deliberately without an attempt to match or repeat a pattern, mainly for wall decoration panelling.

Irregular Match: When the veneer possesses no natural markings or figure suitable for matching, the craftsman may use a combination of 4-piece matches, crossbandings and centrepiece inserts – usually in the form of an oval, diamond or other attractive shape. The surface may be further enlivened with strips of veneer about 1/16 in. or ⅛ in. known as bandings or lines. By these means, the skilled veneer artist-craftsman can convert plain, ordinary veneers into panels of great beauty.

The Craftsman's Pallet: The veneer artist's pallet of colours are his woods—and he has a wide range to choose from. The largest wood collection in the world (housed at Yale University in the U.S.A.) contains over 52,000 specimens—and there are 70 other collections in various parts of the world. However, only about 200 of these are commercially available in Britain in decorative veneer form. These fluctuate in availability, either due to seasonal scarcity or the whim of furniture fashion and changing trends in architectural demand.

The Art Veneers Company of London has a collection of 100 commercially-available veneers in 6 in. x 4 in. size comprising all the best figured decorative woods used in Britain. The specimens are individually labelled and provide the trade and botanical names, country of origin, etc.

The following list of veneers is based upon their popularity over the past few years from their own sales records:

Ash,* Afara, Afrormosia, Bird's Eye Maple, Beech, Betula, Cedar, Elm,* Fruit Cherry, Lacewood, Mahoganies (African and Honduras), Oak, Rosewood * (Brazilian and Indian), Sycamore Teak,* Tola, Walnuts (Australian, African, European,* and American). Zebrano Satinwood, Tulipwood, and Ebony are used mainly as crossbandings.

The veneers marked* are also available crown-cut in addition to the normal quarter-cut form.

Veneers are stocked in lengths up to 8 ft. and are 9 in. average width. The crown-cut varieties are wider—up to 12 in. or 14 in.—but as these are normally cut to make matches, it is safe to calculate them as being 9 in. wide to allow for pattern-matching wastage. Always order enough from the same bundle as it would be impossible to match leaves at a later date; for this reason it is a good tip to add an extra leaf to allow for errors.

Laying Methods: There are three methods of laying veneer: 'slip-sheet', 'hammer' and 'caul'. Which method you adopt depends on several factors—the size of the panel and number of joins in the veneer match; the adhesive to be used and the equipment at hand; the ultimate use of the project.

But don't let that worry you, because nine out of ten normal domestic veneering projects can be accomplished successfully by the easiest and most straightforward method, and you can make a first-class job of veneering the very first time you try! All normal domestic cabinet work (even flush door size), is formed of simple two-piece matched veneers with one centre join—and you can lay a two-piece match with the 'slip-sheet' technique, which requires no previous experience, no pressure, heat or cramps, and uses the latest veneering impact adhesive.

More-decorative panels with four- or eight-piece matches, or crossbandings, are laid with hot Scotch glue by the traditional 'hammer' method, one piece at a time.

Intricate veneer assemblies and marquetry pictures, which have been taped together ready for laying as one whole unit, are laid in one operation, by pressure veneering by the 'caul' method, in a simple home-made press. This enables both sides of a plywood panel to be laid simultaneously to keep it in perfect balance. Heatproof and waterproof resin cold glues can be used. Alternatively, hot Scotch glue may be used in a press if the cauls are heated.

Preparation for Laying: The veneers should be flat, free

Fig. B174. Shooting the edges of a selected pair of veneers to obtain two true mating edges.

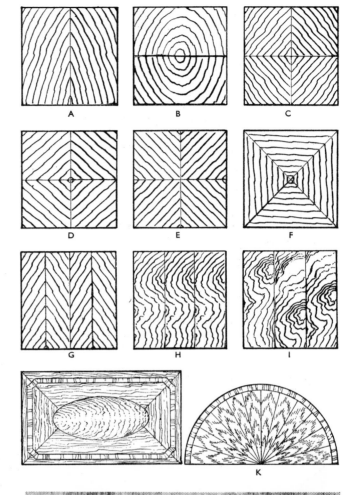

Fig. B175.

A. Two-piece match, with the grain.

B. A two-piece match across the rings.

C. The four-piece match.

D. The diamond four-piece match.

E. A variation, in the form of a reverse diamond.

F. Cut this way—a triangular diamond match.

G. Herring-bone match, based on two pieces.

H. Casual matching arranges repeat leaves.

I. Slip matching—random form of casual.

J. Irregular matching combines inlays.

K. Precise geometric angles—a sunburst.

Fig. B176a (above). Multi-matching, with eight pieces.

Fig. B176b (below). A typical matched walnut veneer.

Fig. B177 (above). A quartered walnut panel with crossbanding border.

from buckle or other defects, and matched, trimmed and jointed together with the joins securely taped on the face with gummed veneering tape. The veneers should be about ½ in. larger in both directions than the panel, to allow for a trim down to size after laying.

Groundwork should be perfectly dry, flat, and level in both directions. Test it for shallow indentations—which could have been caused by a knock—by dragging the teeth of a saw across the panel in both directions (Fig. B178).

All porous groundwork (such as plywood, blockboard, laminboard and chipboard) should be given one coat of thinned glue size to prevent it from taking more than its fair share of the adhesive when it is applied later. After sizing, lightly abrade the surface with 4/0 grade 'garnet' paper to form a keyed surface for laying.

If under-veneers have been laid to the groundwork, remove all gummed veneering tape from them before sizing, and then abrade with 4/0 garnet paper.

Slip Sheet Technique: The great advantage of impact adhesives is that they enable the amateur to make 'unbalanced' panels without the dread of warping—without pressure of cramps. Because the adhesive does not contain water the veneer does not absorb moisture and swell—with the consequent later shrinkage which is the prime cause of warped panels. Do not use ordinary 'household'

Fig. B178. 'Keying' the baseboard with a saw will reveal any indentations.

formula adhesive, which you will find will 'string' and form into lumps and does not spread easily; and do not use the special metal comb often provided for use with plastics, as this provides far too thick a coating for veneering.

The best adhesive to use is special veneering Evo-Stik formula 5309H which can be brushed on, or scraped on with the edge of a veneer.

Apply one coat of Evo-Stik 5309H to the groundwork and to the veneer assembly (not the side with the gummed paper tapes over the joins—these come off later). Keep both surfaces free from dust, and allow twenty minutes to tack. Examine both surfaces against a strong light to make sure that you have not missed a spot—the surface should have a varnished appearance. Work diagonally in both directions and for best results give two coats to the groundwork and veneers.

Now cover the groundwork with a sheet of wrapping paper or kraft paper. Evo-Stik will only adhere to itself,

not to the paper. Then place the veneers unhurriedly into position, taped side uppermost on top of the paper separator. Check to see that pencilled centre-lines on the groundwork coincide with the join in the veneers. Location pins driven in at the end of the panel will ensure perfect alignment or you could actually tap in a couple of pins through the veneer to make sure it does not move.

Fig. B179. Laying a veneer with a boxwood roller.

Withdraw the slip sheet gradually, in easy stages. Begin by easing out about 3 in. of the slip sheet, and press down the veneer with a boxwood roller (or even a rolling pin) where the two wood surfaces are in contact. Keep the other end of the veneer held up with the left hand, as you roller down the veneer with the right hand in one easy flowing motion (Fig. B179). It is a great help if you have someone to pull out the slip sheet whilst you are working the roller with firm pressure, from the centre out towards the edges, driving out all air from the bond.

Making Joins: By using two slip sheets you can actually make joins as you work one at a time. Pencil a line on the groundwork where the join will come, and cover this with a strip of kraft paper about 4 in. wide. Then place the normal width slip sheet over this and lay the first veneer as described, overlapping the centre line. Then place the slip sheet in position again and lay the second veneer overlapping the first.

Carefully using a straightedge to guide the knife, cut through both veneers and discard the upper surplus strip (about ½ in. wide). You can now easily withdraw the surplus strip which is trapped underneath the second veneer, by withdrawing the first 4 in. wide slip sheet, and then rolling down the two veneers to effect a perfect join. By this technique the amateur with no previous experience can lay veneers on flat or curved surfaces of any material without difficulty.

Hammer Veneering: A veneer 'hammer' is actually a homemade squeegee—4 in. strip of brass, rounded at the working edge, fitted into a wooden block with a dowel handle. Hold it with the handle pointing away from you and draw the squeegee towards you in zig-zag movements. An electric iron—an old fashioned iron will do—a basin of hot clean water and a sponge or swab, are all the tools you need, plus a supply of hot Scotch glue. Proprietary brands such as Cox's No. 1 Scotch, or Croid Aero Scotch, come in tins which you can heat by standing them in a saucepan of water. The ideal temperature is one you can just bear your finger in. The iron should be hot enough to evaporate a drop of water but not cause it to spit.

The groundwork should have been prepared by sizing

and abrading with 4/0 garnet and kept dust-free by brushing.

Brush on one coat of hot glue (it should run freely from the brush, not form into drops) and wait for it to chill. Now brush one coat on the veneer and lightly dampen the other surface to prevent the veneer from curling up. Wait for this to tack so that you can handle the veneer without it sticking.

Now lay the veneer in position on the groundwork and press down with the fingers. Again, lightly sponge the veneer with hot water (taking care not to soak it) to prevent the iron from sticking or scorching the veneer as you work the hot iron over the veneer to melt the glue. This closes the veneer pores and draws the glue up into the veneer.

What you are really after is absorption without penetration—if the iron is too hot the glue may come through and stain the surface of the veneer. Now apply firm pressure with the veneer hammer, working along the grain in zig-zag movements outwards from the centre of the panel towards the edges to force out surplus glue and exclude all air pockets.

As you work, the glue will chill again. Remelt by further ironing (after a preliminary daub with the sponge) and continue laying the veneer with the hammer. Repeat this simple sequence until the job is done, dampen-iron-hammer, using light strokes with the hammer at first, increasing pressure only gradually to avoid stretching the veneer. Wipe off surplus glue from the edges with a damp cloth.

The chief attraction of the hammer veneering technique is the simplicity of making joins. The first veener is laid as described, followed by the second veneer which is allowed to overlap the first by about ½ in. The join is cut with a sharp knife against a straightedge (Fig. B180), the top surplus strip is discarded and the trapped underneath strip is easily removed (Fig. B181) by dampening, ironing and peeling off. Then the join is hammered down with a touch of fresh glue, damp-iron-hammer as before.

Always affix special extra-thin, double-gummed veneering tape, across and along all joins to prevent the joins from opening as the veneers dry out. The tape goes on the face, or outside.

Crossbanding: If the panel is to be fitted with a decorative crossbanding, the veneers are laid slightly under the overall size of the panel, which is then used as a guide for the marking gauge square to the edge. The surplus veneer can then be dampened, ironed and peeled off and the crossbanding veneers can be laid with the hammer as described.

If the panel is not to be crossbanded, the veneers are laid oversize, and about ½ in. surplus veneer may then be trimmed off (Fig. B182), the panel laying face downwards on a sheet of clean strawboard. Make light tracing cuts with the knife or chisel from the outer edges towards the centre to prevent breaking out. Clean up with a forming tool. Panels laid by the hammer method must be allowed to dry out thoroughly before any attempt is made to remove the paper tapes or clean up the panel. Leave the face-side covered with newspaper; stack the panel under a light weight with a free circulation of warm, dry air around it. If several panels are veneered at one session, place wooden slats between them to allow a free circulation of air and leave for at least 24 hours. The back of a panel must be veneered right away—not the following day—or the panel may warp.

Fig. B180. Cutting through two leaves of veneer with a knife and straightedge to form a joint.

Fig. B181 (*above*). Peeling off the lower waste strip, after cutting through two leaves as shown in Fig. B180.

Fig. B182 Trimming off surplus veneer.

Defects: Test for 'blisters' by tapping over the surface with a pencil or the fingertips. If a hollow sound results, indicating the presence of an air pocket, dampen, iron and re-lay the veneer. If the blister persists because the wood is glue-starved, slit the blister and work in fresh glue; dampen, iron and re-lay.

Caul Veneering: If you have an elaborate assembly of many joins, or a marquetry picture, or you wish to lay both sides of a panel simultaneously to keep it perfectly balanced, the caul method is best. The veneers are pressed in a simple home-made press made from two panels of ¾ in. blockboard—which are known as cauls—slightly larger than the size of the panel to be pressed. Pressure is applied from four 2 in. x 1 in. crossbearers fitted above and below the cauls and tightened with bolts or G-cramps. These crossbearers are tapered towards their ends and are tightened in sequence from the centre outwards to force out the surplus glue at the edge (Fig. B183).

Cold glues may be used, either animal, fish or resin glue of the Cascomite One-shot type, which has the advantage of being gap-filling, heat- and water-proof. No heat is required and the adhesive is only applied to the groundwork and not to the veneers. Cover the taped side of the veneers with a sheet of polythene to prevent sticking. A sheet of linoleum may also be used as a pressure-pad to equalise the pressure and take up any unevenness caused by criss-crossing tapes.

Faster working is achieved by using some heat—or hot Scotch glue may be used with heat. This is achieved simply by inserting a heated sheet of aluminium or zinc into the press; or, better still, have the linoleum sheet heated in the oven. Many people prefer to heat the actual wooden cauls through both sides before a blazing fire. Heat is not essential if cold adhesives are used.

If a blister results from a cold pressing, it will be impossible to re-heat the glue to repair it. Therefore slit the blister, insert fresh glue, cover the slit with polythene and place a heated wooden block above the blister and apply pressure.

Shaped Veneering: For shaped and curved panels, a press can be made from a home-made rig-up of ½ in. square tambours, which are corded so that they will adjust to suit any shape required (Fig. B184). The tambours are supported by two cradles, one convex and the other concave—the curvature depending on the thickness of the panel. Bandsaw the cradles from ½ in. boards and dowel together about 8 in. apart.

You can fabricate the groundwork in such a press. Lay in about three layers of ⅛ in. constructional veneer, in the same grain direction to form a core, with outer casing cross-veneers of 1/16 in. Gaboon veneer on each side of the core in the opposite grain direction. Nail the complete assembly at the ends with panel pins and nip off the heads. Cover the outer veneers with newspaper, and press between two thin metal plates of aluminium or zinc—or lino would do—to prevent the veneers from cracking. Leave overnight to set and then the ends and edges may be trimmed off and solid edge lipping applied. The groundwork may then be coarse-sanded ready to receive the face and compensating back veneers may be laid in the same press.

If you have to veneer a curved shape from solid timber, accurately bandsaw the shape and save the waste piece to use as a caul for pressing the shape (Fig. B185).

Irregular-shaped curves may be veneered by using hot sand. The groundwork is bedded down in the sand-filled bag, and when the shape is determined, the veneer is laid in and the glued groundwork is pressed and clamped into position (Fig. B186). Bran, sawdust or plaster of Paris may also be used.

Veneers may be laid around a curved edge, such as a circular coffee table, by clamping battens above and below the edge. Nails are spaced along the battens, and the edge is then laced with cord to exert pressure on the veneer.

Tightly curved surfaces may be bound with webbing, which may then be dampened so that it exerts extra pressure as it dries.

All sorts of improvised presses can be rigged up, either by using heavy weights, or even by using struts from a joist or a car jack!

Finishing the Job: There are three simple decisions to make. Do you want a stained or natural finish; open or full grained; matt or high-gloss finish?

Stained Finish: The belief that stain blinds out the grain, obliterates the figure and drastically changes the colour tone of wood is quite wrong. Stain is not opaque like paint.

Stain is used to enhance the natural beauty of the wood's own colouring, to emphasise the inherent features of grain and figure. In fact, the stained finish is most beneficial to most veneered projects. If you want to match your project to existing furniture, you will need to stain it, because a match cannot be achieved simply by using veneer of the same type. Factory-produced furniture is usually provided with a colour treatment to ensure every unit sold is brought to a standardised finish. It is often described as 'mahogany-colour' or 'teak-colour', when in fact the veneer has been treated to resemble those woods.

Other reasons for staining veneered projects are when veneers are used in conjunction with solid timber of the same wood—the veneers are always a tone darker due to the steaming treatment in cutting the log. The effect of the patina (the natural ageing of the finish) on old furniture needs to be matched when a new project is being finished.

Natural Finish: If your project is not required to match existing furniture and the decorative veneer used has a pleasing natural colour tone grain and figure, there is no reason why you should not finish the work with a transparent film of polish.

This will reveal the natural beauty of the wood, protect the surface from wear or damage, and provide an easily-maintained and enduring shine.

Open or Full Grain Finish: This has to do with the 'feel' of the surface to the touch. Certain veneers (such as sycamore) are smooth to the touch, and are fine-textured, close-grained woods which do not need grainfilling. Some veneers are medium-textured (such as the mahoganies) while many others (such as teak) are coarse-textured, open-grained and porous. These woods will absorb polish according to their porosity. You can obtain a perfectly good matt finish on any veneer, without having to fill the grain; but to obtain a perfect high gloss finish the grain must be filled to provide a sound base for the polish. A paste grainfiller is used, toned to match the colour of the veneer. Exceptionally, the grainfiller may be used in deliberate contrast with the veneer colour, for example, the white filler used for the limed oak finish.

Matt or High Gloss: The answers have already been provided; the easiest and most straightforward finish for the beginner is the matt. For a beautiful 'mirror high gloss' it is necessary to select a type of polish which dries hard, and which will withstand burnishing to a gloss with progressively finer abrasives.

To illustrate the polishing sequences step by step, we will work through the procedures necessary to obtain a full-grained, stained, high gloss finish. Simply by omitting the sequences that do not apply in your case, you will achieve the result you want. It's knowing what NOT to do that counts.

Cleaning Up: We are going to raise a dust: every sequence of polishing creates dust—our greatest enemy. Have a soft brush handy and, if possible, a vacuum cleaner.

Begin by dampening the veneer tapes with a moist sponge. Wait for the humidity to soften the tape and peel them off. Wrap a sheet of 4/o polishing garnet paper around a cork rubbing block, and superficially clean off gum traces, glue spots and fingermarks. Keep the block flat on the surface and work with the grain to avoid causing grain fuzziness. The careful use of a scraper is permissible on veneer assemblies, but for all normal cabinet work, the papering is sufficient.

Stopping: If the sanded surface reveals any imperfections, open joins, poor mitres, tiny pinholes, etc., these are filled with a matching wood stopping such as Brummer Yellow Label stopping, which will not clog the garnet paper, or blind out the grain. Select a tone darker than the veneer as it tends to dry lighter. When dry, lightly paper the surface again with 6/o garnet paper. Keep the surface brushed well clear of dust and wait for it to settle.

Wash Coat: Brush on one coat of lacquer, such as Lustashine Polish, and allow one hour to dry. The object is to raise the grain and stiffen the wood fibres so that they may be block-sanded smooth with 6/o garnet paper prior to staining.

Staining: There are two golden rules:

1. Always tone down. You can progressively darken a wood tone, but you cannot lighten it (except by bleaching). It is best to select a veneer which is lighter in tone than the furniture to be matched, and then gradually darken the tone to match.

2. Always 'wet-test'. Test the shade of the stain on a scrap of veneer, allow to dry, and then wet it with the polish, to provide you with a better idea of the final tone. The polish tends to tone down the stain slightly. Never assume a close match judged by the stain colour alone—which should be a tone lighter than the desired match.

The Furniglas range of wood dyes are all intermixable water stains. Prepare the tone you require and wet-test on a scrap of veneer. Flow on the stain, in straight strokes along the grain, with a lacquer brush. Leave to dry overnight.

Fixative Coat: Brush on one coat of Lustashine Polish with the grain and allow two hours to harden. Now the stained surface may be papered with 9/o polishing garnet paper, taking care not to use too much pressure. Brush clean and wait for the dust to settle.

Grainfilling: Grainfilling comes in paste form, toned to match the veneer. It is applied with a coarse rag, with some pressure, in circular motion across the grain. Finish off by removing the surplus in straight strokes along the grain, using some pressure. Now lightly paper the surface with 9/o polishing garnet, brush off dust. It is a good tip to wipe the surface with a chamois leather.

Sanding Sealer: The purpose of a sealer is to prevent undue suction when the following coats of polish are applied and to prevent grain sinkage. It dries into a tough elastic skin over the wood, but because sanding sealer contains a white base, it is never used on woods which have not been grainfilled, otherwise the sealer might show as white specks in the open grain.

Brush on a coat of Sealcote Sanding Sealer. Do not brush it on like paint, but let it flow ahead of the brush.

Fig. B183. Sequence for tightening a veneer press.

Fig. B184. Clamping method for curved door.

Fig. B185 (*above*). Veneering a curved rail or apron for a round table.

Fig. B186 (*below*). Using a sandbag in a box for odd-shape veneering.

Allow one hour to dry, then lightly paper with 9/0 garnet paper; brush off dust and wait for it to settle.

Bodying Up: The finest polish possible to obtain for all interior veneered work is the two-pot catalyst-hardened lacquer of the Furniglas Hardset type. This is also the best polish to use for all marquetry work as it is water clear, and of such low viscosity and deep build that it makes the resulting finish impervious to heat, water, alcohol and abrasion.

Brush on one coat of Hardset and allow one hour for it to set. Lightly cut back the surface with special flour-grade pouncing paper. Apply the second coat in the opposite grain direction after brushing the surface clean of all dust and allowing it to settle. You now have a full, grain-protected finish which can be completed in either matt or high gloss finish.

For other interior work (shelving, room dividers, doors) and for all exterior veneered surfaces, use Furniglas P.U.15 polyurethane lacquer, which is a one-pot straight-from-the-tin type of varnish lacquer.

(a) Matt Finish. Dip a pad of grade 0000 wirewool into veneer wax polish, siliconised, and apply in straight strokes with the grain to remove all brushmarks from the film.

Dust off with a soft cloth and you have a stain matt sheen, impervious to all hazards, and easy to keep clean of fingermarks.

(b) High Gloss Finish. This all depends on how much time you can take over it. The longer the interval between steps, the better the final result. If you can leave the work for up to two weeks before proceeding beyond this point, you will find the surface very slightly patchy, due to grain sinkage, and slight drying out of the work generally.

Fining Down: This assumes you have waited two weeks and the surface requires fresh treatment. If you are continuing from the bodying-up stage without a two-week break, this stage is ignored; but three coats should be applied in the bodying-up stage.

Block-sand with flour-grade pouncing paper, and brush on two coats of Hardset, papering between each coat and allowing to dry.

Flatting Down: Now to get rid of those brushmarks. Use wet-and-dry silicon carbide paper grade 600, wrapped around a felt-lined wood block. Wipe dry with a chamois leather to reveal any low spots which appear shiny. Touch in with polish and repeat the process.

Now apply flatting paste with a coarse rag, in circular movements until you feel the rag begin to pull, when the strokes should even out along the grain.

Burnishing: Repeat the above hand burnishing with special Burnishing Cream applied with a soft cloth. When dry, complete the film with a lambswool buff or polishing cloth.

'Instant' Finish: If you want to complete the job in an evening, then plump for the open grain natural matt finish straight from the tin! Brush on two coats of Furniglas P.U.15, papering between each coat with 9/0 garnet paper. Complete the job in under three hours with wirewool and wax.

Teak Finish: After filling and sealing the grain as described, apply three coats of teak oil applied with a felt-covered block; allow each coat to dry, and lightly cut back with 9/0 garnet paper.

A much quicker finish, with greater protection and ease of maintenance, is achieved by brushing on two coats of P.U.15 lacquer, papering between each with flour pounc-ing paper, and finish off with special teak wax impregnated in grade 0000 wirewool.

French Polishing: This is the really superb finish for an expertly-executed veneered job. Full details are given in an earlier part of this section.

WORKING UNDER DIFFICULTIES

While the ultimate goal of every practical householder is to have a spacious and well-equipped workshop, such a place has to be regarded as an ambition only perhaps to materialise long after the more important jobs have been done. This applies especially after moving into a new house. Those who live in flats or furnished rooms may never have the chance or space to be able to work in ideal surroundings. Does this mean that the fascinating world of Do-it-Yourself is out of reach for these poor unfortunate brethren? No, of course not! Working under difficulties *is* possible.

The Bare Necessities

Having dealt at some length with the vast range of tools and equipment which are currently available, and the methods of using them, we now investigate suitable methods and principles for those with no workshop facilities, a few simple hand tools, and limited spare time. The floor of the spare room can be used as a workbench. A fixed vice would be a welcome luxury, but a small machine vice is a real necessity. Get one which can be stood on its side. An assortment of cramps will come in useful, and a good plane is worth while. The remainder of the tools will be found in any householder's normal stock, plus a few twist drills and a hand wheel brace.

One's working space will depend on what is available. The worst mess occurs at the beginning when loose fibres of chipboard will walk everywhere; therefore it is recommended that all rugs, mats, carpets, etc., are removed from the working space, and the work done on bare floor boards or lino. As most of the working is done in a crouching position, an old pair of trousers and shoes should be worn. If one can obtain the use of the kitchen table, a small measure of comfort can be enjoyed when working on the smaller parts. Otherwise, a working space can be improvised by using an upturned box or two.

What to Make: The standard method of approach can be applied to virtually any piece of furniture it is required to make. As an example, the construction of a simple bookcase and cupboard will be described—it is shown in Fig. B187.

A drawing is prepared outlining the general proportions and design (Fig. B188) and should include a cutting list of all the sizes to be used. The sliding doors are of Laconite at the bottom, and glass at the top. The back is made from 1/8 in. hardboard, covered with one of the wood-design self-adhesive plastic sheetings. The carcase and middle shelf are of chipboard 3/4 in thick. The use of chipboard offers many advantages over conventional timber. It can be glued and worked like wood, yet because there is no end grain, it can be screwed, dowelled and worked in any direction, thereby enabling simple box-like construction to be adopted, yielding joints equal in strength to very elaborate ones found in conventional woodwork. Additionally, there is no warping or shrinking, and because of its uniform thickness the basic problem of preparation of wood is avoided. Supplied in 1/2 in. and

¾ in. thick sheets 8 ft. × 4 ft., one is given four straight and square datums to begin marking out the pieces straight away.

It will be seen that the grooves for the sliding doors are made from standard ⅞ in. × ⅞ in. double-channel strips suitably planed to suit the chipboard thickness.

Construction: If the timber merchant cannot supply the pieces of chipboard cut to the finished sizes, then a full sheet of chipboard must be obtained.

When this is delivered, make sure that there is someone at home to receive it so that it can be stored indoors. Only one light shower of rain is sufficient to ruin the sheet, since the usual brands of chipboard are not waterproof. The full sheet is very heavy and unwieldly, and should be cut down to the various sizes as soon as possible. The rectangles are marked off using a tee square, rule and pencil.

Fig. B187 (*above*). This is the bookcase and cupboard chosen as an example of what can be made with a bare minimum of tools and facilities.

Fig. B188 (*left*). Working drawing and cutting list.

MATERIALS

ITEM		FINISHED SIZE	ITEM		FINISHED SIZE
1	¾″ Chipboard	9⅞″ wide × 3′ 6″ long	7	Double channel	⅞″ × ⅞″ × 14′ long approx.
2	¾″ Chipboard	9⅞″ wide × 3′ 6″ long	8	Glass ⅛″ thick	10¾″ wide × 1′ 10″ long
3	¾″ Chipboard	9⅞″ wide × 3′ 4½″ long	9	Laconite black	1′ 5½″ wide × 1′ 10″ long
4	¾″ Chipboard	10¾″ wide × 2′ 4½″ long	10	Laconite white	1′ 5½″ wide × 1′ 9″ long
5	¾″ Chipboard	4″ wide × 3′ 0″ long	11	Hardboard ⅛″	2′ 5½″ wide × 3′ 5½″ long
6	¾″ Chipboard	4″ wide × 6½″ long	12	Hardwood	¼″ × ¼″ × 8′ 6″ long

Fig. B189. A machine vice and an assortment of cramps are most useful.

A space large enough to allow the sheet to be cut must be at hand (you could use the lawn or yard, propping the work up on house bricks positioned at strategic points to avoid the pieces breaking off before they are completely sawn through).

The panels will need truing up to size, and this is done by means of a plane as in Fig. B189. The wall is the bench stop; to ensure matching edges are the same width, they are treated in pairs, and held together with a cramp. The machine vice keeps the work upright, and if necessary one foot can be used to stop the vice from moving about. Fig. B190 shows how the lengths are prepared; the greater overhang of the work requires the strip of wood to be clamped to the work to avoid any 'chatter' that would otherwise result. In the case of the work being described,

Plank resting against wall acts as stop and protects plaster

Wood strip clamped to work as shown

Good edges marked thus

Machine vice on edge may be held steady with foot if required

Plane away shaded portion

Smooth flat with chipboard

Plane away shaded portion

Plane away shaded portion

$\frac{1''}{8} \times \frac{1''}{8}$ Hardwood inserts if required

Protruding length planed flush with side

Any gaps, imperfections & screw heads filled in with plastic wood & finished flush with face

$1\frac{1}{4}$ x No 8 Csk. Hd. woodscrews. Heads sunk below surface.

Fig. B190 (*left*). Trimming the timber edges.

Fig. B191 (*below, left*). The top, middle and bottom channels. The back-to-back section is in the centre.

Fig. B192 (*above*). The plinth.

outer piece of the joint, and countersunk to a depth sufficient to allow the screwhead to lie well below the surface. By adopting this technique there is little chance of swelling of the chipboard, an important factor as far as strength of joint and appearance is concerned, particularly with the ½ in. thick chipboard. Except on exceptionally wide joints, two screws per joint are ample.

The order of assembly is to join the two end panels to the middle shelf first, thereby forming an H-assembly; then add the top and bottom pieces. At all stages of assembly it is important to keep all the front edges flat at the corners, and to ensure all corners are square. If a screw pulls the assembly out of line, then it is best to block up the offending screw hole and drill a new hole about an inch away from the first.

The sliding doors can now be cut from the Laconite, and the glass doors, if not already ordered cut to size, can be cut to size and deburred and chamfered using an oil stone as a file. You should be able to drop the doors in, and remove them, without any bending or straining of the chipboard.

Finishing Stages: The plinth (Fig. B192) is made up from chipboard and assembled complete, and all the screw heads are sunk below the chipboard surface, and filled with plastic wood. Any gaps, holes, cracks, etc., are made good and rubbed down with glass paper, and smoothed off with a finer grade ready for finishing.

The ebonised appearance of underframes used on contemporary furniture can now be achieved on the plinth in the following manner.

The smoothed surface of the chipboard is filled with a normal wood filler, and rubbed down with the fine glass paper. The surface is then sealed by applying two coats of sealer, and rubbed down using flour paper (extremely fine sand paper). Two coats of black cellulose are brushed on, and the shiny surface is removed by rubbing down with fine steel wool. A dull and effective shine is obtained by polishing the surface with furniture cream.

The finished plinth is now screwed on to the bottom panel, and the screw heads sunk below the chipboard surface as before.

Veneering: With the main assembly now complete, the order of veneering can be decided. The main consideration is to hide all the fixings so that, when complete, the work presents a clean and professional appearance. When this has been decided the carcase is dismantled ready for veneering.

This is the first step in the chain towards obtaining a perfect finish for the work, and patience and care are the main contributors to success. It is popularly believed that

the top and bottom members are best left about ⅛ in. too long; the middle shelf only should be planed to length, checking carefully to ensure squareness to the face and the edges.

The channel members are now planed to match the ¾ in. thickness of the chipboard. The back-to-back channels are dealt with as shown in Fig. B191, it being remembered that the deeper channels are on the top to allow the sliding doors to be dropped in after assembly.

The prepared channel strips are now glued and pinned to the chipboard edges, and are then sanded flush.

Trial Assembly: A trial assembly can be made at this stage. 1¼ in. × No. 8 countersunk steel screws are used; to ensure positive and reliable grip, a ⅛ in. dia. hole is drilled to a depth equal to the length of the screw. A clearance hole of ¼ in. dia. is then drilled through the unless one has elaborate clamping facilities available, veneering cannot be done at home. Thanks, however, to the arrival of contact adhesives, very satisfactory results are possible, even when working under difficulties.

Best results are obtained from straight-grained flat veneers, and the more elaborate and expensive veneers should be avoided at the beginning, until one's confidence is assured. The most suitable veneer for the inside faces is the striped mahogany veneers used by many furniture makers. This is about the cheapest available, and is very easy to work with. Its straight grain enables joins to be incorporated on large widths without trouble, and it can be cut with scissors if preferred. The simple outline of modern furniture lends itself well to the simpler straight-grained type of veneer, and interesting effects can be created by deliberately cutting the veneer to yield a design, or pattern.

A fairly-large scrap of chipboard is laid on the floor to act as a cutting board. A piece of veneer is cut so that it is about ¼ in. larger than the area to be veneered. Always cut across the grain first, then cut the width; this ensures that if the last part of the cut splits the last corner of the sheet, then it can be included in the waste area when cutting the width.

Remembering that all the inside faces have to be veneered first, the chipboard surface is prepared by sanding with medium glasspaper, and all imperfections made good. The back of the veneer is sanded smooth, and reference to Fig. B193 will show how to hold the glasspaper round a block to avoid any accidents with the fragile edges of the veneer. All traces of sawdust and loose pieces should be removed, preferably using a vacuum cleaner, and by wiping the surfaces with the hand.

The adhesive is now applied to the surfaces of chipboard and veneer. Any good synthetic adhesive can be used; the contact variety is very good and spreads well on the surface. The serrated spreader supplied with the tins is *not* suitable for this type of work, since the ridges of glue (giving a combed effect) prevent the veneer touching the chipboard, giving rise to bubbling and other defects. Two simple flat spreaders can be made up, one ¾ in. wide × ⅛ in. thick and 6 in. long is for edges and to remove the adhesive from the tin, and the other made from a piece of wood ⅛ in. thick, 2 in. wide × 6 in. long, for spreading out the adhesive over the surface.

The prepared surfaces are now given a layer of adhesive, being careful to work well to the edges, and to keep the centre evenly coated. No patchy areas should be allowed, and the two surfaces should be kept well apart until the surfaces are dry.

On bringing the two surfaces together, the joint is secured, and cannot be broken apart without spoiling the veneer. Thus it is essential that the veneer is applied correctly first time. This is done by laying out a sheet of

brown paper over the chipboard, then lowering the veneer into position on the brown paper. The paper is then moved away a little, and the two surfaces brought together. As the paper is moved outwards the work of bringing the two surfaces together continues until the whole piece is finished (Fig. B194). Strange as it may seem, the paper will not stick to the adhesive.

The veneer is then pressed hard down all over, using hand pressure or by using a roller. The overhanging veneer should be trimmed, using a razor blade, treating the cross grain first, then working with the grain to trim the width. The edges are then sanded flush with the chipboard edge using medium-grade glasspaper. To avoid the glasspaper catching the edges of the grain, the method of holding the glasspaper wrapped round a block should be adopted, since this will also ensure the veneer is finished straight and square.

The face of the veneer is now sanded down with the medium-grade glasspaper, and to be sure that the veneer is in complete contact a good pressure should be applied on to the glasspaper block. By viewing the face against a strong light, the shine on the veneer will reveal any bubbles and defaults; these should be corrected while the adhesive is still tacky.

The treatment of the faces which have the grooved sections is the same as above, but the grooves are cut clear with a razor blade (Fig. B195) and finished with glasspaper wrapped round a steel rule (Fig. B196).

As mentioned earlier, a butt joint may be necessary for the veener. If the joint is to be visible, it should be arranged that the strips of veneer should be regular, and thus form a pattern of the different grain formations. Pencil lines are drawn on the chipboard, to indicate where

Brown paper shield moved outwards as work progresses

Veneer in contact and pressed down

Veneer overhanging edge of chipboard

Edges finished flush with medium grade glass paper

Trim overhanging veneer with razor blade working with grain

Slot finished with medium glass paper wrapped round steel rule

Slot picked out with razor blade

Glass paper block with rounded edges

Glass paper

Edges of grain

Sanding motion thus

Fig. B193 (*left*). Sanding the veneer back.

Fig. B194 (*right, top*). Laying veneer.

Fig. B195 (*right, centre*). Trimming with a razor blade.

Fig. B196 (*right, bottom*). Method of finishing grooves.

Second sheet of veneer ready for fixing

Reference marks

Fig. B197 (left). Laying second veneer.

Paper shield

First sheet of veneer in position

Fig. B198 (right). Assembly of parts.

Finished corner dowels filled & edges filed flush

Screw heads sunk below surface & filled with plastic wood

Finished face

Projecting veneer

Oneway motion with glass paper—as arrow

Fig. B199 (below). Hiding the hardboard back.

Protruding ends filed flush with sides

Fig. B201 (below). Veneering the edges.

¼"x¼" Hardwood glued and nailed flush with chip board face

Veneer strip 7/8" wide cut to length

Applied veneer sanded flush

Fig. B200. External corner treatment.

the joints will come and to serve as a guide for fixing the first piece.

The butting edges of the joint are prepared, and are labelled 'AA' on the veneer. The adhesive is spread out as before on the chipboard and on the first piece of veneer. The first piece is then applied using the pencil line as a guide, and pressed down as before. The second piece is now laid alongside, and any final preparation of the edge is done. When a perfect butt seems assured, a line is struck across the joint to line up the two edges in the same position.

Adhesive is now applied to the second piece of veneer, then laid, starting at the joint, and working out away from it as in Fig. B197. Any adhesive visible on the surface of the veneer should be removed, using petrol.

Interior Finishing: When all the inside faces are veneered, rubbing down for polishing can begin. A better result can be obtained by applying the finishing process before the parts are put together, since successful rubbing down into a corner is not then satisfactory. As the inside edges are not as important as the outside edges, rubbing down with fine glasspaper, then applying two coats of shellac to act as a primer, is all that is necessary. This is then sanded with flour paper, and two finishing coats of shellac are applied. The hardboard back can be covered with wood-faced adhesive sheet, and one coat of shellac will make it match the veneered faces.

Assembly: The parts are now assembled (Fig. B198) and contact adhesive may be used on the mating faces and edges. The woodscrews are pulled home tight, and sunk well below the surface. Two holes per joint to suit ¼ in. diameter hardwood dowels are drilled, and dowels 1¼ in.

long are cut to length and coated with Aerolite 300 before being driven in. The resulting joints are stronger than those attained by conventional woodworking joints.

It is now that the projecting ends of the top and bottom panels are finished flush with a forming file or plane. To avoid splitting the tool should be worked inwards.

If the finished article is likely to be viewed from end or top, the hardboard back should be hidden by fixing ¼ in. × ¼ in. wood strips to the top and side panels as in Fig. B199; these will be covered by the final veneer covering later.

The outside faces of the carcase are now prepared for the application of the main veneer. Great care is necessary on the preparation of these faces and edges for veneering, and when prepared a vacuum cleaner should be used to remove all dust.

It is not necessary to repeat the veneering procedure since it follows that already mentioned, but reference to Fig. B200 should be made to see the treatment for external corners. It will be necessary, when veneering the last side, to rest the work on one of the veneered faces. To avoid damaging this veneered face, all the chippings of the veneer should be swept clear, and the work carried out on a protective mat.

The edges are veneered by cutting strips of veneer ⅞ in. wide and applying them to the edges of the carcase, using the contact adhesive. The corners are mitred as shown in Fig. B201, the surplus veneer cut away with a razor blade, and finished flush using medium glasspaper. Any sharp edges should be sanded down where necessary and all traces of the adhesive removed. Any of the well-tried and established methods of polishing and finishing can be applied.

ITEMS TO MAKE

ITEMS TO MAKE FOR THE:—

Using the knowledge gained from studying the two previous Sections of this book, the practical woodworker can construct many useful and decorative pieces of furniture.

In this final Section, working details and instructions are given for various articles for each particular part of the house.

BEDROOM

FITTED FURNITURE FOR A SMALL ROOM

The fitted furniture described here and shown in Fig. C1 was evolved as the answer to a problem often faced by many householders. It may be a small spare room that is required to be furnished attractively but economically, or the transformation of a child's small bedroom to a teenager's room providing a 'grown-up' atmosphere with as much space as possible. The prime object was to produce sensible but attractive furniture without heavy expenditure on material.

The cost was minimised in the first place by searching for suitable available material from market stalls and shops, which led to the selection of various off-cuts, which could readily be used in making the furniture. This resulted in the purchase of chipboard off-cuts, all 1 ft. wide × 6 ft. high × ¾ in. thick, and rigid wood-grained plastic sheets 4 ft. × 2 ft. which were considerably reduced in price because the grain ran across the sheet instead of along the length of the sheet.

The design was then evolved to accept the limitations of these materials; because of the space limitations, furniture of unit construction fitted round two sides of the room was decided upon. It was agreed that the wardrobe, being the central feature, should be placed in the corner of the room. This was to be supported on one side by a dressing table and a tall-boy, while on the other side there should be a chest. The plan and elevations are shown in Figs. C2–C4.

The colour scheme used off-white plastic tops to the dressing table and chest, with the sides and front of the furniture faced with off-white plastic having a corn-coloured grain. A few narrow panels of dark red plastic were let in to give some contrast in the colour scheme and white pearly knobs were added. All exposed edges of the wood were covered with strips of black plastic.

The outstanding feature of this piece of furniture was that no glue at all was used in any of the joints. All joints were simply butted together at right angles and dry screwed together with large countersunk screws 2 in. in length. Typical joints are shown in Fig. C5. Care had to be taken to ensure that all joints were square.

The design was based on the use of the 6 ft. chipboard planks so as to avoid waste. That is to say, the wardrobe was made from 6 ft. lengths, the double-shelved 3 ft. long dressing table was made by halving these boards, the tall-boy was made 3 ft. high, and so on. The outlines were marked on the wall and the basic structure was made single-handed in 12 hours. When the structure was complete, the parts were unscrewed at certain positions so that the bare wood could be veneered with the plastic sheet, using impact adhesive. This had the advantage of covering the large screw heads and making the joints rigid. The components were screwed up together to make a complete unit, only 14 screws being used for this purpose. The unit was steadied by two brackets held by Rawlplugs. This was necessary to square up the furniture to get accurately-fitting doors. The walls formed the back of the furniture, and there was no need to use gussets or ply backs anywhere. A plywood top integral with a ply shelf and coat hanging rail (Fig. C5) was dropped into place to rest on the top edges of the chipboard sides of the wardrobe, the whole being secured with 4 screws. The narrow wardrobe doors were made as a pair, to leave

Fig. C1. Since space was restricted, units were made to fit closely, though removable for redecorating.

Fig. C2. Plan of the complete installation.

CHEST

WARDROBE

2'-1"

2'-1"

DRESSING TABLE

TALL BOY

Fig. C4. Elevation showing chest.

HINGED FLAP

2'-6"

DOOR   DOOR

SPACE UNDER

3'-0"

SHELF

WARDROBE

Fig. C3. Elevation showing dressing table.

RAIL

6'-0"

DOOR

MIRROR

DRAWER

1'-6"

DOOR

HINGED FLAP

2'-6"

SPACE UNDER

3'-0"

Fig. C5 (right).

Fig. C7.

HEAD CUT OFF

TOP

SHELF

DOOR

Fig. C9.

Fig. C6 (below).

TOP OF WARDROBE

SIDE OF WARDROBE

SHELF

RAIL

WIRE HOOK

Fig. C8.

SIDE

DOOR

PLAN VIEW

METAL PLATE ON EACH SIDE OF FLAP

HINGE SCREW

more room when open, and used available sizes of material.

Piano hinges were used for these doors; the two hinged flaps utilised simple metal plates: the remaining doors were just pivoted top and bottom by spigots made from large screws which, when in place, had their heads removed. All these methods are shown in Figs. C6–C9.

Because chipboard was used, edges had to be veneered with ¾ in. strips of plastic to provide a neat and attractive finish.

MATERIALS

Plastic sheets, 4 ft. × 2 ft.
Plastic strips, ¾ in. wide
Weyroc, 6 ft. × 1 ft. × ¾ in.
Impact adhesive, 3 tins
Knobs, plastic, 8
Hinges
Plywood
Catches
Mirror with fixtures, 2 ft. × 1 ft.
Screws, etc., as required

The complete job, including the mirror, provides a very attractive unit and shows a considerable saving on what would have been spent if a new bedroom suite had been purchased. It is all easy to dismantle when it has to be moved for room-decorating. The total time to make the units single-handed was just under 3 weeks, working only evenings and a small part of each weekend.

SINGLE DIVAN HEADBOARD

The type of headboard described here and shown in Fig. C10, includes a reading lamp, or night light, together with a shelf and space for keeping pyjamas, etc.

The dimensions given apply to the standard single-bed base which is 3 ft. wide and which is usually provided with two headboard attachment bolts in the frame at one end.

The basic material is ⅛ in. thick hardboard which could be obtained cut to size by the supplier but will cut from two pieces of the size shown in the list of materials, below. The six hardboard pieces comprising back, side wing, and box portions are first cut to size and shape. Note that the top and bottom parts of the box portion are

Fig. C10. The completed headboard for a single divan.

identical (see Fig. C11). Frame all these parts with the 1½ in. × ½ in. material on the back side. As each member is cut, pin it to the hardboard with a couple of panel pins from the back side. By this means you can work round each panel, cutting and marking as work proceeds. All joints are simple butt joints. At the curved edges, cut as shown in Fig. C12, leave battening material projecting over the edge. This surplus material will be trimmed off later.

On the top part of the box one additional member is required for attachment of the box end (see Fig. C13). Two extra members, each 8 in. long, are also required for the bottom of the box. These last members are used to increase the batten width at the front edge of the box bottom, and are located approx. in line with the bolts in the bed end (see Fig. C14). Attach the framing members to the hardboard by ¾ in. panel pins at about 3 in. pitch, with a few additional pins at the end of each member. A stronger job is obtained by also using ordinary Scotch glue applied hot, but this is not essential. The panel pins

Fig. C13.
Detail of the
box end.

Fig. C12 (right). Wooden
reinforcement pinned to
reverse of hardboard.

Fig. C11 (left). The box
section; top and bottom are
identical.

Fig. C14. Method of securing the legs of the unit to the divan.

ADDITIONAL 8″ LONG MEMBER

6 1/2″

BASE 7″

1 1/2″

5″

2 SCREWS EACH LEG 1 1/2″ x No.8

BASE BOLT. DRILL LEG TO SUIT

SHELF 3′-4 1/2″ x 4″ x 1/2″
4″ CORNER RAD.

3 SCREWS 1 1/4″ x No. 6

6 SHELF SCREWS 1/2″ x No.6

3′-8 1/2″

10 1/2″

2′-6″

5″

12″

1/4″

1′-9 1/4″

1′-9″

7 SCREWS 1 1/4″ x No.6

2 SCREWS 1 1/2″ x No.8

Fig. C15. Screw location in back, wing and shelf.

SHEET OF SELF ADHESIVE PLASTIC TO BIND VERTICAL STRIPS

WIRE APPROX. 22 S.W.G.

Fig. C16 (below). Ball catch and stop.

DOOR

Fig. C17 (above). Construction of lampshade.

back. Fill the pin-head holes with woodfiller and sand smooth when set. After allowing time for the glue to set, plane all edges so that hardboard and frame edges coincide. Keep all edges reasonably square. Cut off the surplus material at the rounded corners, and trim to the curve with a rasp. Use medium-fine sandpaper to remove all sharp edges and roughness at the rounded edges.

Drill screw holes in back and wing, and assemble wing, back and shelf (see Fig. C15). Recess the hinges in the door edge and assemble box portion to back portion. The top hardboard lip of the end member is screwed to the edge of the additional batten mentioned earlier so that no screw heads appear on the top surface. Fit the ball catches and door stops (see Fig. C16). Next, make up the two supporting legs which attach the headboard to the bed base. Each is made from two pieces of hardboard and two short lengths of 2 in. × 1 in. Nail the parts together with 1 in. roundhead nails and screw the legs to the bottom of the box (see Fig. C14). Locate to suit the position of the bed-base bolts. The rise of 7 in. shown in Fig. C14 allows for a mattress 6 in. to 7 in. deep. Adjust the length of the legs to suit any other size. Screw the side wing to the base and check that the edge of the door does not rub on the wing. Cut and temporarily secure the two shade-form plates. One is attached to the underside of the shelf and one to the top of the box. Keep the edges in line.

The shade used was made of eleven strips of clear plastic, each 3/16 in. × 1 in. × 8 in. long, sanded on the back surface to render opaque. With a hacksaw, cut a slot approximately 1/8 in. deep down each end of each strip and insert the wire, thus threading the strips together. Seal the wires in by applying a hot iron to the strip ends, so as to close the plastic over the wire. Alternatively, drill the plastic strips with an 11/64 in. drill. Make four small holes in the headboard back to suit the location of the wire ends, and draw the shade up to the form plates (see Fig. C17). Trim the wire ends to about 1/2 in. long and bend over to secure the shade.

A simpler shade can be made from lampshade opaque plastic. In this case, cut to size and curve the heated plastic to a radius somewhat smaller than the form plate radius, so that the shade will clip into position round the form plate edges. Provide small flanges on the vertical edges of the shade. These flanges engage behind a shallow rebate cut at each end of the form plates where the plates abut the headboard back. A small hole is cut in the back adjacent to one side of the shade so that the shade can be pushed off when it is required to change a lamp.

Self-adhesive plastic sheet is used to provide the finish on the unit. This material is available in many colours and patterns under various trade names. White was chosen for the wing, back and door surfaces, and mauve-white check for all other visible surfaces in the unit shown here: both the top and bottom of the shelf were covered. Lap the material over at the edges. At the rounded edges, scallop the material so that wrinkling or double thickness is avoided on the edge. When all parts have been covered, re-assemble the complete unit and attach the two shade-form plates by means of a few panel pins.

The plastic strip can now be fixed to the edges of the shelf, side wing and back edge. A strip is also run along the top edge of the box and on the curved end of the bottom box member. A black plastic strip was used here as this colour outlines the unit very effectively. Make a mitre joint at the top edge where the back joins the side

specified will protrude through the frame and are clinched over at the back. The pin heads are then punched below the hardboard surface. Use a metal reaction block under the pin, otherwise the clinched end of the pin will be forced away from the rear surface and might present sharp points liable to catch anything brushed against the wing. Apply a coat of impact adhesive to the strip and to the edges on the unit, let them dry, and then lay the strip in position accurately. The inside of the box can be lined with spare wallpaper left over from decorating. The door tag is made by enclosing a 2 in. piece of ⅜ in. dowel in a strip of the self-adhesive plastic, and joining the adhesive surfaces together after encircling the dowel. Attach the free end of the tag to the back of the top batten on the door, using a spot of glue and a couple of drawing-pins. The rear surfaces of the back and side wings were coloured with dark woodstain.

A battery-powered light is specified, using a 3.5v bulb and a twin cycle battery. The switch for the light is located on the underside of the projecting end part of the top box member, adjacent to the light. The battery can be held in a suitably-sized pocket made from wood or hardboard strips and attached to the back of the unit near the shade so that the two wires for the battery penetrate the back inside the shade area. Use of a lamp powered from the mains is left to the constructor's discretion. If this type is used, all safety precautions should be observed, including use of a low-wattage bulb and provision of adequate ventilation.

MATERIALS

Hardboard
1 piece 4 ft. 3 in. × 4 ft.
1 piece 2 ft. 6 in. × 1 ft. 9 in.
Softwood
55 ft. of 1½ in. × ½ in. planed softwood (10 per cent for waste is included)
3 ft. of 2 in. × 1 in. planed softwood
3 ft. 4½ in. of 4 in. × ½ in. planed softwood (for shelf)
Surfacing
3¼ yds. of self-adhesive plastic sheet 18 in. wide (for back, door and wings)
1½ yds. of self-adhesive plastic sheet 18 in. wide (for other visible surfaces)
18 ft. of soft plastic edge beading, ½ in. wide (colour to suit) half-round type
Ironmongery
2 ball catches (type with combined door stop)
8 csk screws, to suit ball catches
2 hinges, 2 in. × ⅝ in.
1 dozen csk screws, to suit hinges
10 rh screws 1¼ in. × No. 6
1 dozen rh screws ½ in. × No. 6
7 rh screws ⅝ in × No. 6
6 rh screws 1½ in × No. 8
Sundries
3·5v cycle battery, bulb and switch to choice
¾ in. panel pins, 1 in. roundhead nails, impact adhesive, wire, paper

---

DESIGN FOR A BED-HEAD UNIT

A saw, hand-drill, carpenter's square, hammer, and 17 ft. of 6⅛ in. × ½ in. mahogany plus a 4 ft. × 2 ft. piece of hardboard is almost all that is needed to make the bed-head unit illustrated in Fig. C18.

Before making a start, study Fig. C19. First cut the top piece to a length of 3 ft. 11 in. and drill ⅜ in. ventilation

holes at 2 in. centres. The lower shelf piece is cut to the same length but 1⅝ in. narrower. Drill the ventilation holes as for the top piece.

A shallow channel is then cut in the middle section of the back edge to take the flex from one compartment to another. This channel can be V-shaped with a penknife or a gouge, Fig. C20. Make a notch at each end of the channel to lead the flex into the light compartments.

Saw two 2¼ in. × ⅜ in. slots to take the vertical divider —on the inside of the pencil marks for a snug fit.

Screw the two 9¼ in. × 6⅛ in. × 4½ in. end pieces to

Fig. C18. This attractive and versatile bed-head unit could be used in other rooms too.

Fig. C19. Constructional diagram.

Fig. C20. Cutting the channel to take the flex.

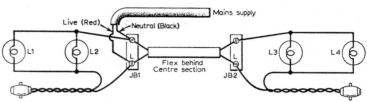

Fig. C22 (above). Wiring diagram.

Fig. C21. Fitting the lampholders.

the shelves with 1 in. No. 8 countersunk screws. Don't glue them, because they have to be removeable to replace lamps.

When the centre unit is cut to shape and sanded smooth, slide the vertical pieces into the notches on the centre shelf and apply glue to all the touching surfaces. Pin and glue the lower shelf in place and, with a carpenter's square, line up accurately before leaving to dry.

Each side of the compartment houses two batten lamp-holders and a junction box which are screwed in place (Fig. C21). It may be necessary to drill holes in the base of the lamp-holders to lead the wires through, or you may find specially-moulded thin areas to be broken away to allow for the wiring. In either case, complete the connections before screwing the holders into position.

Study the wiring diagram (Fig. C22) carefully and follow it scrupulously. The junction boxes (JB1 and JB2) may be round, but are shown rectangular in the diagram to avoid confusion with the lamps (L1 to L4). Note that the flex to the pendant switches is connected between one terminal of a junction box and one side of a lamp, in each case. Mark the juction box terminals concerned with an L or an R. These become the LIVE terminals, to which only RED wires should be connected. In JB1 we shall have three red wires: one from the mains, one from the switch flex and one from the flex which fits into the groove behind the centre section. In JB2 we shall have two red wires: one from the switch flex and one from the flex behind the centre section.

If all these are connected correctly, the rest of the wiring will be correct if the diagram is followed exactly, and the lamp-holders will be safe if the switches are in the OFF position. If the mains leads are crossed over, however (i.e. the colours are reversed), then the lamp-holders would be alive even with switches OFF. The lamps would

not light, but you could get a shock when changing lamps. This is an important point in all domestic wiring —always connect switches to the LIVE side of the circuit. The diagram assumes that the mains supply enters the left-hand compartment. If, however, it is more convenient to bring the supply to the right-hand compartment, simply read the diagram as laterally-reversed; i.e. as though viewing through the back of the unit.

After the wiring has been completed, cut and fit the back panel. Lay the unit on a 4 ft. × 2 ft. sheet of hard-board and mark round the outline with a pencil. Cut the hardboard to the line and then pin to the back of the unit at 3 in. centres. It is not wise to use glue because you may want access to the wiring at a later date. Also avoid locating any pins along the line of wire when pinning; and do not pin the two end pieces or they will be difficult to remove when replacing lamps. Cutting the glass to size can be a tricky job for the inexperienced. To make things easier, buy a good quality sand glass and have it cut to exact size; take a pattern of the compartments on a piece of cardboard (or, better still, hardboard) and allow 1/16 in. all round. Two 3/16 in. strips of mahogany, pinned to the top and centre pieces, hold the glass in place (Fig. C23).

Once satisfied that the glass fits, prepare to finish the job. After a general sanding over, apply four coats of thinned eggshell varnish. Sand lightly between coats. When this is dry put the glass in place and pin the strips of mahogany.

Either mirror plates at each end or direct 1½ in. screws through the back of the compartment can be used to fix the unit to the wall. Two 60-watt lamps inserted in each side finish the job, it is advisable not to exceed 60 watts because the ventilation would be insufficient. The assembled unit is shown in Fig. C24.

Although basically designed as a bed-head unit, it may also be used for various purposes in other rooms in the house. For example, in the lounge it could house lights or loudspeaker extensions from the radio. The radio idea could also be developed for use in the bedroom unit. A small radio could quite simply be built into one of the

Fig. C23 (left). Pinning the strips to hold the glass.

Fig. C24 (below). The completed unit ready to be fixed to the wall.

centre compartments of the bed unit. Those who read in bed could use one of the compartments for books.

When ordering the wood it would save a lot of time to have the four sides planed to a finish. It will cost a little extra but it is well worth it for the overall even appearance on the final finish.

MATERIALS
17 ft. of 6⅛ in. × ½ in. mahogany
1 sheet 4 ft. × 2 ft. hardboard
4 batten lamp-holders
2 junction boxes (two-way)
2 pendant switches
2 sheets sand glass (see text for size).
Flex, etc.

BEAUTY BAR AND STOOL

The main material, apart from the legs, used for the design shown in Fig. C25, is ¾ in. and ½ in. blockboard. This has the advantage that very little framing is required since the thickness of the material permits screwing or nailing with butt joints. It also takes very well to covering with plastic laminates. For the legs, use rectangular hollow-section steel tube (R.H.S.). The legs for both this and the stool can be cut out of one stock-size length of 1 in. × 1 in. R.H.S. Although they look neat and elegant they're really strong! Even allowing for having the brazing or welding done for you, it's not an expensive method. Of course, ordinary wooden legs can be used if preferred —either buy the ready-made screw type or make them out of 1¼ in. × 1½ in. oak, planing to a taper for elegance.

The exploded drawing in Fig. C26 shows the construction clearly. The drawers are simply butt-jointed boxes, glued-and-screwed, made from ½ in. blockboard with plywood bottoms. They are given a flat front of ½ in. blockboard which is slightly oversize compared with the drawer itself. No handles are fitted, but a semi-circular recess is made in the centre of the top of the false front to provide a grip. Alternatively, handles of suitable design could, of course, be fitted.

Cutting-out diagrams given in Figs. C27–C30 show how to lay out the components. It is best not to cut everything out at once, but to cut out only one section at a time, offering up and checking for size as work proceeds; any slight errors in dimensions can then be corrected. Blockboard or chipboard is equally suitable, though chipboard requires rather more care in working to avoid rough edges. Glue is advisable as well as screws or nails for all joints, and to develop strength pressure must be applied while the glue sets. In many cases, the screws or nails used will provide this—otherwise use clamps.

R.H.S. tubing is sold in 21 ft. standard lengths, so one standard length is just enough for the stool as well as the table. The big advantage in using R.H.S. is that the frames need only to be joined at the top, as can be seen in Fig. C31. No rungs are needed between the stool legs, although it is advisable to fit the two struts shown for the dressing table. To get the same degree of rigidity in wood construction of the same type would require very carefully-made and close-fitting joints. When completed, a wooden plug should be made to fit inside each leg, to avoid any damage to carpets from the metal edges. For the stool, which is likely to be moved about more often than the dressing table, plastic gliders can then be screwed into each leg. For the stool cushion top, a foam squab is the obvious choice, fixed to a wooden base and covered with any suitable material to suit the finish given to the dressing table.

Fig. C25. This is the elegant beauty bar and stool described here.

Fig. C26. Constructional details of the beauty bar.

Fig. C27 (left). Cutting plan, ¾ in. blockboard.

Fig. C28 (above). Cutting plan, ½ in. blockboard.

Fig. C29 (above, right). Cutting plan, white plastic sheet.

Fig. C30 (right). Cutting plan, ¼ in. plywood.

MATERIALS

21 ft. (one length) of 1 in. × 1 in. R.H.S. tube
4 ft. 6 in. of 1 in. × ⅛ in. steel strip
9 ft. of 1 in. × 1¼ in. wood batten (joinery quality)
2 ft. of 1 in. × ¾ in. wood batten
5 ft. × 4 ft. of ¾ in. blockboard
2 ft. × 2 ft. 6 in. of ½ in. blockboard
2 ft. 6 in. × 3 ft. 6 in. of ¼ in. plywood
1 ft. × 1 ft. 4 in. of ½ in. plywood

6 ft. of ¾ in. quadrant moulding
12 ft. of ½ in. × ½ in. beading
4 ft. × 2 in. plastic sheet (black, or to choice)
2 ft. 6 in. × 2 ft. plastic sheet (white, or to choice)
4 ft. × 1 ft. 6 in. plastic sheet (white, or to choice)
12 in. × 16 in. of 2 in. foam rubber
1 sq. yd. of covering material (for stool)
White enamel, glue, screws, etc.

Covering material tacked under ½" plywood seat

2" thick foam rubber (12"x16")

½" plywood seat (12"x 16")

1"x ¾"x12" seat bearers

Detail at corners, when welding square section tubing

Frame construction from 1"x 1"square section tubing

Fig. C31. Construction details of the stool.

Fig. C32. Suggested finishes.

Top edging strip all round, black plastic sheet.

White plastic sheet top.

Both sides white plastic sheet.

All drawer fronts white plastic sheet

Tops and sides of drawers and wood strips in between drawers painted with black enamel.

The mirror is fixed to the wall with the usual chrome-domed screws inserted through holes drilled at the corners. It is therefore not adjustable—but if it is of adequate size this is no disadvantage.

Readers who have had experience of covering ordinary table tops with any of the plastic laminates will find no difficulty in covering the dressing table, since the method is the same. The point is that the impact adhesives used are of the instant-grip type, so that the plastic stays put where it touches. It is necessary, therefore, to tack temporary guides to the edges of the blockboard so that the plastic is correctly placed the first time. For smaller areas, such as drawer fronts, it may be advisable to cut the plastic very slightly oversize. It can then be planed or rasped square. Suggestions for finishing are shown in Fig. C32.

DRESSING TABLE FOR A BOW WINDOW

Although this useful piece of furniture (Fig. C33) was designed for a bedroom with a bow window, the idea is easily adaptable to any size of room, with any type of window, with or without a recess.

It is not difficult to make. As Fig. C34 shows, there are seven features. There is (1) ample surface for all the usual dressing-table requirements such as triple mirror and trinket trays; (2) side-shelf for the morning tea tray; (3) small bedside shelf; (4) space to stand the soiled-linen basket; (5) ample shelved cupboard space for clothes and shoes, or for storing bed-clothes; (6) drawer for dressing-table accessories, with space under for dressing-stool when not in use; and (7), a locked medicine cupboard, on the extreme right.

First decide the height; 2 ft. 4 in. is probably convenient, but the height of the window-ledge must be taken into account. Two inches under the window-ledge can look right but only if the window is not unduly high or low from the floor level.

Then consider the depth. It may be preferable to take

the fitment straight across, this being simpler than the recessed centre in the example shown. Remember that if it is too deep it may be difficult to lean across to open and shut windows. The layout in Fig. C35 represents a total width of 10 ft. 8 in. and a maximum depth of 18 in.

Draw a plan. Mark the line of the fitment on the floor so that you can see how much space will be covered. Once the overall dimensions have been worked out a start can be made on the vertical frames, which should be 1 in. less in height than the overall height.

Although (as shown in Fig. C36) the frames are the key parts, since they are out of sight and have no wear and tear, the joints can be very simple. The cross-pieces could be joined to the uprights by angle-brackets, but half-lap joints or dowels are almost as easy. Shelves can be placed on the cross-pieces in the middle of the frames, but if these are likely to carry any weight a simple housed joint is advised. All the frames are made of 2 in. × 1 in., though the supports for the small shelves in the medicine cupboard (the two frames on the extreme right) are only 1 in. × 1 in.

Fig. C33. This dressing table provides generous storage space, including medicine chest, linen basket and bedside shelving.

Fig. C34 (right) The seven features of the fitment.

Fig. C35 (left). The suggested dimensions are 10 ft. 8 in. wide, 1 ft. 6 in. deep at centre, with the shelf extension at the left to suit the space available.

Hardboard joints

Fig. C36. The frames are the important feature; amend the overall dimensions to suit.

Check that the window-ledge is parallel to the floor. The window-ledge where this particular fitment was installed was 1 in. higher from the floor at one end and this had to be taken into account; the height of the frames was adjusted to keep the top parallel to the window-ledge, and the toe-rail was planed down to finish 1 in. less at one end. Adjustment at floor level is less noticeable.

Position frames and toe-rails carefully. Remember that if using frames in the centre of the cupboards these must come, not merely behind the toe-rails, but behind the 3 in.-wide base boards which are fitted on top of the toe-rails.

(The two centre frames each side of the dressing-stool recess are shown square at the base in Fig. C36, but if cut away so as to line up with toe-rail and baseboard, as shown in Fig. C34, a little dust-trap is avoided by getting rid of the angle between toe-rail and frame).

When properly positioned, screw frames and toe-rails into the floor. For rigidity the frames can also be screwed into skirting-board or wall, but it is wise to delay this until the top boards are in place. The position of the frame shown on the extreme left depends upon the position of the bed or other furniture.

With the frames in position the base-boards and top front boards can be fitted. The base-boards are of 3 in. × 1 in. and the top boards of 5 in. × 1 in. and are grooved to take sliding hardboard doors. Grooves are 3/16 in. wide to take ⅛ in. hardboard; they are ⅜ in. apart and set in ⅝ in. from the front. The grooves in the baseboards are ¼ in. deep; in the top boards they are a fraction over ½ in. deep. After the boards are fixed the panels forming the doors are easily inserted by pushing up into the top grooves, slipping over the front of the base-boards and then dropping into the bottom grooves.

The framework forming the rounded shelves on the extreme left is of 2 in. × 1 in. You can use a simple butt joint with small plates screwed in diagonally at corners, or the normal corner blocks, or use halved joints. The small bedside shelf should be trenched into the frame, and the further support piece fixed to the wall, on the extreme left, will make it quite firm (Fig. C36).

The interior shelves to the cupboards are of hardboard. If there is likely to be any weight it would be advisable to support the shelves on lengths of 1 in. × 1 in. timber fixed to the cross-pieces of the frames.

The drawer can be made specially and fitted on runners fixed to the frames or, as was done in this particular fitment, an odd drawer was used and hung from runners fixed to the boards above. A dummy front was added, which fills the space between the frames.

It only remains to cover the framewood with hardboard cut to shape. In this case, the joins on the top (Fig. C35) were about 20 in. each side of the centre.

MATERIALS

Timber—planed all sides:
11 ft. of 5 in. × 1 in.
7 ft. 6 in. of 3 in. × 1 in.
97 ft. of 2 in. × 1 in.
7 ft. of 1 in. × 1 in.
Hardboard:
3 sheets of 8 ft. × 4 ft.

WALL-MOUNTED DRESSING TABLE

Dimensions of this useful fitment, shown in Fig. C29, are left to choice, but a maximum depth of 18 in. is suggested, from front to wall. Working to this dimension a length of 4 ft., or slightly over, will give a symmetrical balance.

The table top is a sheet of hardboard, marked off to the semi-circular shape by the string, pencil and drawing pin method.

The original sheet was 4 ft. × 1 ft. 6 in. and to take full advantage of this the pencilled arc must touch the centre of the front edge and pass through both corners of the rear edge. This radius is large enough to be cut with an ordinary handsaw, finishing off the edge with sandpaper.

The underside is stiffened with five battens, as shown in Fig. C38, cut from 1 in. square softwood. These should be made slightly longer than finally required, to allow for

Fig. C37 (*above*). This wall-mounted dressing table is a simple week-end job.

Fig. C38 (*above*). Battens before trimming.

Fig. C39 (*left*). Battens after trimming.

Fig. C40. Side view showing brackets.

subsequent trim. Note particularly the position of the front batten before trimming.

Battens are attached by means of impact adhesive, positioned by a few deep-driven panel pins.

When securely fixed, the batten ends should be trimmed absolutely flush with a rasp or forming tool.

The two cross-members, shown in Fig. C39, are made from 2 in. × 1 in. softwood screwed to the undersides of the longitudinal battens. The cross-members receive the brackets as shown in Fig. C40.

The side panels which actually carry the drawer are made from ⅜ in. plywood, each rounded at the lower front corner (Fig. C41). Before screwing these to the cross-members, the upper and lower drawer guides should be

Fig. C41 (below). The side panels.

SIDE VIEW

DRAWER GUIDES

STIFFENING WEB

Fig. C42. Front view, showing the side panels but omitting the brackets for clarity.

Fig. C43. Drawer details.

fixed to the inside of each panel, as shown in Fig. C42. These are ½ in. square section hardwood.

Do not assemble the panels to the main structure at this stage, but wait until the table top has been fixed to the wall with the 12 in. shelf brackets, spaced according to the centres of the two cross-members.

First plug one bracket to the wall at an effective height of 30 in., then offer up the other at the same estimated height. With a straight length of wood across the two brackets, and a spirit level, adjust the free one until the two are perfectly horizontal. Mark the position on the wall, and fix the second bracket.

Next, wipe the top perfectly clean and cover it with self-adhesive plastic; a wood-grain effect gives an excellent finish.

The edging strip consists of a band of hardboard, 2 in. wide, and of the correct length to fit all the way round the circular edge. It is fitted flush with the top and held by means of a panel pin in the end of each longitudinal batten as it goes round.

Before fixing the strip, it may be covered to match the top, or it may afterwards be painted to suit the decorative scheme of the room.

Now lay the completed top on to the brackets, push it firmly up to the wall, and screw it to the brackets from underneath.

Take the plywood side panels, which have been left off, and fit each panel into position, pushing firmly up and back; attach each one to its appropriate cross-member, using three screws along the lower edge (Figs. C41 and C42).

Immediately below the lower drawer guides, join the panels together with a stiffening web of 2 × 1 in. timber, screwed from each end. Measure this carefully before cutting, to ensure that the panels are parallel from top to bottom. The stiffener is not visible underneath the drawer.

The final structural item is the drawer. This is a simple box structure consisting of a hardboard base, with ¼ in. plywood back and sides retained by strips of ½ in. square section hardwood fitted to the inside corners and glued and pinned to the base and sides (Fig. C43).

The drawer front is a double-thickness assembly, screwed together. The inside piece is exactly the same as at the rear end, but is shrouded by a larger overlapping piece to present a neater appearance to the front. This will look better in ½ in. plywood, and may be either **painted or covered to match the top.**

An ornamental knob or handle completes the drawer front, and the inside may be lined with baize.

All structural work is now completed, but as a finishing touch a length of ¼ in. quadrant or filter should be glued along the back edge. This has the effect of blending the table top to the wall.

The best type of mirror in this case is a frameless one, fitted flat to the wall. The mirror shown in the photograph was a particularly heavy one, and was therefore allowed to rest actually on the table, being retained by a strip of rebated hardwood at the lower edge and two mirror clips at the top. The hardwood retainer was left in natural grain and polished. In the centre of the table, just in front of the mirror, may be seen the ivory flush fitting switch for the two wall lights which added a luxury finish.

If desired, the dressing table can be made to fit in the corner of two walls. In this case the table top becomes a quarter segment of a circle and can be screwed to battens fixed to each wall. As a rule, a radius of 30 in. will give plenty of table-top space for a corner dressing table, without projecting too far out into the room. Naturally, the mirror cannot in this case be mounted on the wall and it may be better to have one of the familiar 3-wing mirrors standing on the table top. Alternatively, the angle of the corner can be squared off, and a mirror placed across the angle, though this restricts the size of the glass that can be accommodated.

MODERNISING DRESSING TABLES

A piece of furniture that can easily be given a new lease of life by being restyled is the dressing table. It often suffers from the cumulative effects of spilt perfume and nail lacquer, together with scratches and dents from brushes and combs, and these can soon make a relatively new piece of furniture look drab. Most dressing tables can be easily turned into the 'kidney-shaped top, and drapes' style and yet still remain part of a suite, provided that some link is made between drapes and room curtaining.

Fig. C44. Three pieces suitable for 'kidney-shaped top, and drapes' treatment.

Fig. C47 (*right*). Setting pressure can be contrived by wedging in a doorframe.

Fig. C45 (*below*). Allow enough overhang for fixing the curtain rail.

Fig. C48 (*below*). An old unit completely modernised.

Fig. C46. It may be necessary to re-position pivot-plates to allow mirrors to clear new tops.

An old corner cabinet transformed into a serviceable dressing table is shown in Fig. 44, together with other pieces suitable for easy conversion using one of the wide range of materials available.

The drawing on the right in Fig. C44 shows a typical and rather dated design, but the piece is structurally sound, and provides plenty of storage space. To start the face-lift, remove the mirrors; these can be sent for re-silvering if needed and perhaps a new set of chrome clips and screws might be worthwhile. Tape out a large sheet of wrapping paper to the top of the unit, and mark out a kidney shape; allow for the overhanging drapes, being as generous as possible without making the top too large (Fig. C45).

Having estimated the size of the top from the paper template, obtain some ready-veneered plywood, ½ in. thick; alternatively, any type of pre-veneered block/chipboard will do, provided that it is of sufficient thickness for its area to make a rigid top. Cut the shaped top from the board with a fine-toothed coping saw or even a pad or bow saw.

Cut two slots out of the back of the board to accommodate the upright supports for the mirrors. It may be necessary to raise the pivot-plates for the mirrors about 3 in. to allow the mirror to clear the new top, as in Fig. C46.

Suspend the drapes from below the top on a length of ordinary curtain rail (either the plastic or metal type is suitable), ensuring that the rail follows the gently curving outline of the top. The job of fixing the rail is easier if it is done before the top is fixed into position.

The rail and runners are hidden by a small pelmet which runs around the edge of the top; this can consist of a 3 in. strip of hardboard glued into a routed groove, about ½ in. from the edge, but routing out this groove is quite a task, and it is far easier to glue and pin the pelmet directly to the edge of the top. Prior to fixing, the pelmet strip should be sponged with warm water and carefully bent around the top; the strip should be tied into position and left to dry before fixing.

If the pelmet is fitted in a routed groove, it will be necessary to veneer the cut edge using a long length of cross-banding; such edging veneers are now available already taped together ready for fixing. Alternatively, use a strip edge beading, available in various designs and materials, to make a neat job of covering the exposed edge grain of the board.

Having secured both the pelmet and the rail, glue the new top down on to the existing surface of the table. All old polish must be removed from this surface, and it is an added advantage to roughen or key both the gluing areas. Drawing a saw blade across the surface is one method. If using a contact adhesive the job of placing the new top into position will require assistance, for it will have to be carefully done. If one of the excellent modern wood glues is used, a certain amount of shuffling time is allowed for. One way in which pressure can be provided is shown in Fig. C47.

Finish the top in the following manner: rub down the veneered surfaces with glasspaper, and finally smooth with flour paper. Then give the veneer a sealing coat with french polish applied with a brush. The brush can be cleaned with methylated spirits. When this sealing coat is dry, repeat the process of rubbing down and flooding-in (sealing). Use a good transparent wax polish and buff to a sheen; several applications of wax are necessary. If possible, it is sound policy to cover the top with

glass; a sheet of 32 oz. glass can be cut to the paper pattern, and does not prove expensive even with having the edges levelled.

Make the drapes to match, or tone in with, the room curtains, and the result should look something like Fig. C48.

There are several materials that can be used to enrich this basic idea. Plastic quilting—some of which has an adhesive backing—adds the luxury touch, but will definitely need covering with glass on top, and need a beading around the edge.

BEDHEAD RECESS WITH TWIN WARDROBES

The wardrobe units described here, and shown in Fig. C49, are ideal for building-in to any bedroom where space is rather restricted. Even in a spacious bedroom they can be installed to provide wardrobe space and an elegant surround for a modern bed headboard. These particular units were built on a 12 ft. wall.

Assuming the bed is 4 ft. wide, allow an outside width of 30 in. for each wardrobe, leaving 3 ft. to be equally divided between the spaces required for the shelves on each side of the headboard. A Formica-faced headboard can also be made to blend in with this particular wardrobe design.

The first stage is carefully to mark out the ceiling to take the top front, and top side members. At this stage it is advisable to inspect the joists in the loft which are above the proposed position of the wardrobes so that the dimensions may be adjusted slightly, in order that the top members can be screwed through the ceiling into the joists to provide a firm anchorage.

Planed softwood, 2 in. × 1 in., is ideal for the framework. All the joints are half-lapped then screwed-and-glued on assembly. Each one should be cut after carefully working out the length of each member of the framework and cutting to size.

The two vertical members which are to be in contact with a wall should be drilled to suit 2½ in. × No. 8 woodscrews at approximately 8 in. pitch. Each hole should be countersunk extra deeply so that the screw heads may be covered with filler. Similarly drill and countersink the top and bottom members. When positioning these members a smear of glue should be placed along the contact faces to add extra rigidity to the finished structure.

The next step is to position the two top members carefully. Owing to the fact that the walls of most rooms are slightly out of square, care should be taken to ensure that the corner farthest from the walls is constructed exactly square. Now hang a plumb line from this top corner to the floor so the bottom members can be positioned in line. Screw-and-glue to the floor after cutting away the skirting boards as shown in detail A in Fig. C50.

Next, place in position the vertical members which are to be in contact with the wall, and 'spot-through' the pre-drilled screw holes. Remove the members and drill and plug at the spotted positions. Now screw-and-glue the members firmly in position and also install the third vertical member.

Install the structure for the base of the top cupboard as shown in detail B. The member next to the wall should be screwed-and-glued in position in a similar way to the vertical members. Now is the time to position the hanger

Fig. C49. The wardrobe units provide an elegant surround for the modern bed headboard.

SEE DETAIL 'C'

SEE DETAIL 'B'

THESE RAILS PROVIDE END SUPPORT FOR HANGER RAIL

WARDROBE STRUCTURE

SEE DETAIL 'A'

SIMILAR TO 'A'

A Skirting board

Cut away skirting board to provide tight fit for corner joint of upright and floor members. Smear glue in cut out before inserting framework.

B ¼" ply base to cupboard to be tacked and glued in position. ⅛" hard board side panel.

C Hanger rail to be made from ⅝" dia. brass tube. Drill and countersink each end

D Radius front edge / ⅝" x ⅞" battens / ¼" plywood / ⅛"hardboard

DOOR CONSTRUCTION

Fig. C50. The wardrobe structure and details of joints and door construction.

rail and end supports (detail C) and a decision must be made as to the height required. You will probably find you have ample space for a shelf above, if desired.

Use ordinary ⅛ in. hardboard for the full length side panel. This must be glued and pinned in position, the front edge being carefully radiused and smoothed off. The back and top edges can be blended with the wall and ceiling respectively, by tacking ½ in. × ½ in. quadrant beading along the joints.

Make the doors as shown in detail D. They are basically a ⅝ in. × ⅞ in. framework with ¼ in. ply front panels and ⅛ in. hardboard or ply back panels glued and pinned in position. Care should be taken to avoid having pin

heads on the outer faces of the doors as these spoil the final finish.

Now fill in any cracks in the joints and sand the finished wardrobes. The final touch is added by a pelmet joining the two wardrobes at ceiling level and the whole unit is painted to suit the colour scheme of the room. Choose some attractive handles for the doors and the job is complete.

To finish, make the headboard and add a curved shelf on each side to fit the space available.

An added touch of elegance is given by installing a pair of reading lights on the wall above the headboard and papering this recess in a bold contrasting wallpaper.

Fig. C51 (*left*). Capacious and impressive when open, the finished wardrobe looks really solid.

(*Right*) Closed, the wardrobe presents clean and pleasing lines, suitable for most furnishing and decorating schemes.

A BOW-FRONTED WARDROBE

Oak-faced hardboard is used for the door fronts and sides of the wardrobe shown in Fig. C51. The hardboard bends easily to the required curvature without any special treatment; if a nicely-figured sheet is selected for the door fronts, a most attractive appearance can be obtained. It is best to use a hardboard which is counter-veneered on the inside (usually in striped mahogany).

For economy, ordinary hardboard can be used for the insides of the doors and for the centre partition, top, bottom, back and shelves of the wardrobes.

For simplicity, the body or carcase of the wardrobe itself is made rectangular, the whole of the bow front being contained in the doors. Since this entails quite thick doors, the space inside them is utilised for shelving which can take handkerchiefs, gloves, scarves, etc. Construction should present no difficulties, if the illustrations are followed. For example, Fig. C52 shows one completed end frame of the wardrobe, as seen from inside, rear view. Fig. C53 shows how an identical frame is used at the other end, plus a third frame mounted off-centre and serving as a partition to divide shelf accommodation (left) from the hanging accommodation (right). All three frames are connected by rails running across at front and back as shown.

Fig. C54 shows how to make the end frames, consisting of 2 in. × 1 in. timber, except for the front uprights, which are 2 in. × 1½ in. Halved joints are employed throughout, these being glued and nailed together with two or three ¾ in. panel pins to each joint. Put the pins in from the outside, so that their heads will be hidden by the hardboard covering when this goes on.

Before fixing the hardboard to the end frames, it is important to cut away the necessary parts of the frames to take cross-rails A, B, C, D, E and F (Fig. C55). These rails run the full width of the wardrobe and are all half-lapped to the end frames, as shown in the inset, the front rails A and B (3 in. × 1 in.) being glued-and-screwed in

position (with brass screws for preference) and the rear rails (2 in. × 1 in.) being glued and nailed. Note that bottom rear rail F is located slightly up from the bottom of the frame, so that its top edge comes level with the top edge of front rail B. (The hardboard bottom of the wardrobe will rest on these.) Note also that rails D and E are positioned so that their bottom edges are just ⅛ in. higher than the top edges of rails G and H respectively. This allows for hardboard shelves to rest on G, H and their equivalents on the centre partition, with the rear edges of the shelves passing below E and D to which they are screwed from below. The left-hand end frame has small areas cut away on members G and H to take the 1 in. × 1 in. shelf supports shown in Fig. C56. These areas should also be cut away before the hardboard facing is fixed to the outside of the frame.

Incidentally, the hardboard facing is best fixed before the individual frames are finally connected and assembled with cross-rails A, B, etc. Each frame can thus be laid flat on the floor (make sure the floor is reasonably level), and the hardboard glued and pinned to it with panel pins. At front and bottom of the frame the hardboard edges come level with the frame's edge, but at top and rear the hardboard projects a good full ⅛ in., so that these side hardboard panels will cover the edges of the top and back panels of the wardrobe. In any case, the best policy is to let the hardboard overlap the frame slightly, even at top and bottom, so that it can afterwards be trimmed flush with a finely-set steel smoothing plane, giving a neat finish.

Punch all panel pins slightly below the surface of the hardboard and fill the holes with hard stopping (light oak shade, assuming oak-faced hardboard is used). Slightly over-fill each hole, and leave the stopping to shrink for a few days before finally sanding down level.

The centre partition (Fig. C56) can be positioned as re-

Fig. C52 (*left*). A completed end frame, simply jointed and notched.

Fig. C53 (*below*). The other end frame and an off-centre frame have been added, plus shelf and back rails.

Fig. C54 (*above*). End-frame details and dimensions.

Fig. C55 (*below*). Rail joints and dimensions.

Fig. C56 (*below*). Position the off-centre partition to suit yourself. Project rail notching to the end frame before the cladding is mounted.

quired. In the original wardrobe it was placed 1 ft. 5 in. from the left-hand end of the wardrobe, leaving plenty of space on the right for hanging clothes. The centre partition consists of entirely 2 in. × 1 in. timber, and is put together in the same way as the end frames—but note that its width is ½ in. less, since its front edge is set back that amount from the front of the wardrobe. Again, its height is slightly less than that of the other frames, so that the top edge of its bottom is resting on all three. The intermediate horizontal members of this frame are spaced to come level with their equivalents (G and H) on the side frame shown in Fig. C55.

Fig. C57 (*above*). Plinth details and dimensions.

Fig. C58 (*below*). Framework for one bow-front door. The cross piece rails are inside-shelf bases.

The centre partition is covered on the right-hand side with plain hardboard, this being glued and pinned on as before. The only operation necessary before the hardboard is fixed is to cut away the recesses shown in inset, Fig. C56 to take the shelf supports. All the other recesses or steps to receive cross rails A, B and the rear cross rails C, D, E and F are cut after the hardboard is fixed, the latter being cut with the frame. Note that the recesses and steps at the rear of the frame are cut to full depth, so that the whole thickness of the rear rails (C, D, etc) is let into the frame. The steps at top and bottom front corners of the frame are only cut back ½ in., so that half the thickness of rails A and B are let in. At these points, A and B are glued-and-screwed to the frame with brass screws. Rear rails are glued and nailed into their recesses on the frame. The front edge of this centre partition can later be covered by a strip of hardboard, or thin oak, to mask the front of the joints which are otherwise left showing.

Plinth: This is made from 5½ in. × 1 in. unplaned timber, and is shown in Fig. C57. It is set in about 3/16 in. at the sides of the wardrobe, allowing for a covering of oak-faced hardboard on the sides of the plinth, as shown inset in Fig. C57. This enables the plinth to be fixed by screwing upwards at an angle from inside. Rear corners of the plinth can be joined by screwing through at an angle or by glueing-and-screwing corner blocks inside. The arrangement at the front of the plinth should be followed as nearly as possible, otherwise the wardrobe may not be stable. Two front lengths of the plinth are fitted at an angle, so as to form a point 4½ in. in front of the wardrobe. They join the sides of the plinth about 5½ in. rearwards from the front. Fixing is again by screws, put through at an angle from the sides of the plinth. The two front lengths of the plinth are also securely fixed by screwing downwards into them at an angle from inside bottom rail B. This makes a strong foundation, to which the oak-faced hardboard plinth front can be pinned and

Fig. C59 (*right*). Door details. Allow for the hardboard piece J in dimensions.

Squares are 1 in. × 1 in.

Fig. C61 (*above*). The bow is constructed on one-inch squares; this shape is common to the top, bottom and the inside shelves, but the joints are cut in the top and bottom only (see Figs. C58 and C62).

Fig. C60 (*right*). Hinges project slightly.

HINGE

DOOR

glued. It should assume the required curve automatically on being fixed, fillets of wood X having been screwed below rail B at intervals. The straight edge of the Y is glued and pinned down to these fillets and its curved front edge is fixed in the same way to the small blocks fixed at intervals along the inside of the oak-faced hardboard front. Where the latter joins the oak-faced panels which cover the plinth sides, it is best to fill in the front plinth corners with a thin slip of solid wood ⅛ in. square in section. This protects the exposed hardboard edges, which might otherwise have their veneer chipped off through accidental knocks.

Bow-front doors: These are simple framework for the most part, of 6 in. × ½ in. prepared timber, giving a finished size of 6 in. × ⅜ in. The only exception is the upright on the hinge side of each door, which is of 2 in. × 1½ in. timber. Fig. C58 shows one door prior to covering, and details are given in Fig. C59. The internal and external coverings help to hold the framework rigid, but they must be very securely glued and pinned to it. The height and width of the doors should be taken from the finished wardrobe itself, the doors reaching from the top of rail A, almost to the bottom of rail B, but leaving a little clearance between the door bottoms and the top (Y in Fig. C57) of the plinth. In assessing the width of the doors, allow for hardboard coverings (J, Fig. C59) to go on the meeting edges of the doors. These coverings are wide enough to hide the edges of the main internal and external hardboard door facings and show as thin strips of contrasting colour when the doors are closed. Make the doors very slightly over-size in length and width, to allow for final trimming to a good fit. Each door is fitted with three 2½ in. brass butts; Fig. C60 shows the principle of the hingeing—the knuckle, or pivot of each hinge just projecting outside the wardrobe. Hinges are recessed into the doors and into the wardrobe itself.

The shape of the top, bottom and two internal shelves of each door is identical, and is shown on a grid of 1 in. squares in Fig. C61. The shaded areas here represent the parts cut away to form the joint at the top and bottom of the doors (see Fig. C62).

The two internal shelves are not jointed in position, but simply fixed by glueing-and-screwing blocks K (Fig. C59) to the shelves and the door uprights. The comb joint shown at top and bottom of the door's thick edge is not essential, but gives a stronger construction. With a comb-jointing attachment to an electric drill this can be machined quickly. If it has to be cut by hand, fewer tenons can

Fig. C62 (*left*). The top and bottom door joints. Note the bevel planed for the hardboard cladding, and how the bow shape runs into it.

Fig. C63 (*right*). Outer-edge bevel for cladding.

OAK-FACED HARDBOARD

OUTER CORNER BEVELLED OFF

be employed, to save time. Alternatively, these corners of the door could be held together internally by blocks similar to K. Also add blocks internally where handles and catches are to be fixed.

Before final assembly of the door frames, plane a bevel on the outer corner of the thinner door uprights, as in Fig. C63. This bevel should be a continuation of the general curve of the bow-fronted door. When glueing up the frames, make sure they rest on a flat surface and are not warped. It is important that their internal flat surfaces should close flush against the wardrobe at all points.

Cut the two openings in the inside plain hardboard door covering (Fig. C59), then glue and pin the hardboard to the frame at frequent intervals round the edges and along the shelves. The hardboard should overlap the frame slightly all round, and is afterwards trimmed flush by planing. Before it sets, wipe off any surplus glue inside with a damp rag. This internal door covering will help to prevent the framework distorting as the oak-faced covering is bent round and fixed on the outside.

This operation starts along the outer door edge, the oak-faced hardboard being glued and pinned firmly down along this edge only. The hardboard is not bent at this stage, but left flat, so that there is no strain until the glue has thoroughly set. Later, the other edges are glued and pinned down, so that the hardboard follows the curved shape of the door frame. Do not pin the oak-faced hardboard to the door shelves; glueing is sufficient here. Again, the hardboard sheet should be large enough to slightly overlap the frame all round, thus allowing for final trimming to a neat finish.

Punch all panel pins just below the surface, but pay particular attention here, otherwise the appearance of the veneered surface will suffer. The same procedure applies as for the side panels of the wardrobe itself for filling the pin holes with stopping. After smoothing the whole surface with glasspaper, polish the door fronts and side panels of the wardrobe with one or two coats of clear french polish. When hard, smooth down lightly with finest glasspaper (flour paper) then finish off with a clear wax polish. Polish the plinth in the same way.

When fitting the hardboard back, top, bottom and shelves of the wardrobe, glue and pin these securely to the framework which will greatly increase the strength of the general construction. The hardboard bottom is finished in two pieces, one either side of the centre partition, resting on the bottom members of the wardrobe framework. Where the existing framework does not provide support for the hardboard, wood fillet or packing is added. A block of wood should also be fixed between the rear

member of the plinth and the bottom edge of the centre partition towards its rear.

A brass rod is fitted in the right-hand section of the wardrobe—to take coat-hangers—between the centre partition and the right-hand end of the wardrobe.

WARDROBE WITH FITTED DOORS

This is an ideal fitment for a bed-sitting room. Built floor to ceiling height it allows plenty of storage space with shelves in each door, hanging space and drawers. and extra stowage space above for light bulky articles. In fact, with a mirror fitted into one of the inside door panels, the unit can also serve as a dressing table.

The wardrobe has virtually no framework and the joints are either lap joints or simple rebates. To achieve this means using mainly self-supporting material of substantial thickness, ¾ in. Douglas fir plywood, blockwood or chipwood. Naturally, lighter stuff can be used for the door panels and back panel (¼ in. ply or ⅛ in. hardboard) and ½ in. and ⅜ in. thick for drawers and shelving.

It is advisable to make the top unit separately and adjust the dimensions of this to suit the ceiling height. The wardrobe itself must not be less than 6 ft. 6 in. in height (unless you omit the drawers at base) to provide full-length hanging space.

Full constructional details are given in Fig. C64.

BEDSIDE CABINET

The cabinet described here and shown in Fig. C65 was designed so that it would be convenient with a contemporary divan, and yet would not look unsightly if used in any other room—for example, as a telephone table.

Basically it consists of polished wood sides, back and front, with two open shelves, one being covered with plastic upholstery fabric. The main body is mounted on ready-made splayed legs. The cabinet is built around a platform chassis, so there are no joints to make, the whole assembly being glued and screwed together.

It is recommended that a template of the side piece should be cut from thick cardboard before starting the cabinet. To produce this template the shape should be marked on the cardboard with angular corners. The curves are easily added afterwards; those marked P in Fig. C66 are drawn around a penny, while that marked C is drawn around a 16 oz. baked-bean tin. If the template is given to the timber merchant when buying the wood, he will be able to cut out the shape on a fine band saw, saving time and labour.

Shaping The Sides

To obtain the best effect for the sides the grain should run at right angles to the base. The curves should be smoothed down with a file or spokeshave, while the longer edges can be planed (Note: The back should be planed only from top to bottom).

The next operation is made considerably easier if you have a power saw with a swivelling base plate. The forward ends of chassis members C, the leading edge of base board B, and the upper edges of front pieces D and E all need bevelling off to an angle of 80 degrees.

The rear ends of chassis members C and F, the rear edges of base boards B and K, and the top edge of the back piece J also need bevelling, to an angle of 82 degrees.

However, if a power saw is not available all the above

MATERIALS

Prepared (i.e. planed) timber unless otherwise stated. Add a little to lengths to allow for cutting.

Two End Frames
2 off 5 ft. 6 in. × 2 in. × 1 in.
2 off 5 ft. 6 in. × 2 in. × 1½ in.
8 off 1 ft. 8 in. × 2 in. × 1 in.

Centre Frame
2 off 5 ft. 5 in. × 2 in. × 1 in.
4 off 1 ft. 7½ in. × 2 in. × 1 in.

Rear Cross-Rails
4 off 3 ft. 10 in. × 2 in. × 1 in.

Support for Shelf Fronts
2 off 1 ft. 8 in. × 1 in. × 1 in.

Top and Bottom Front Rails
2 off 3 ft. 10 in. × 3 in. × 1 in.

Plinth (Unplaned Timber)
2 off 1 ft. 8 in. × 6 in. × 1 in.
2 off 2 ft. 1 in. × 6 in. × 1 in.
1 off 3 ft. 8 in. × 6 in. × 1 in.

Doors
2 off 5 ft. 6in. × 2 in. × 1½ in.
2 off 5 ft. 6 in. × 6 in. × ½ in.
8 off 1 ft. 11 in. × 6 in. × ½ in.

Oak-Faced Hardboard
2 off 6 ft. × 4 ft.

Plain Hardboard
1 off 6 ft. × 4 ft. for inner door linings.
1 off 6 ft. × 4 ft. for back panel of wardrobe.
1 off 6 ft. × 4 ft. for top, bottom, and shelves of wardrobe, also for plinth top.

Additional pieces for centre partition and linings for meeting edges of doors.

MATERIALS

Timber
12 ft. of 5 in. × 1¼ in.
20 ft. of 5 in. × 1 in.
4 ft. of 4 in. × 1 in.
18 ft. of 3 in. × 1 in.
42 ft. of 2 in. × 1 in.

4 ft. of 1⅜ in. dia. dowel
6 ft. of ½ in. dia. dowel
Panels
3 off 8 ft. × 4 ft. × ¾ in. Plywood
1 off 8 ft. × 4 ft. × ½ in. „
2 off 8 ft. × 4 ft. × ¼ in. „
1 off 8 ft. × 4 ft. × ⅛ in. Reeded hardboard

Fig. C64. Wardrobe with fitted doors—all the details and dimensions.

Fig. C65. This jointless bedside cabinet was designed for use with a low modern bed or divan.

can be done quite easily with the aid of a sliding bevel gauge, a tenon saw, and a sharp plane. The actual size of each member will be found in the cutting list.

As with the side pieces, it is advisable to make a template for the curved chassis members G (See Fig. C66 for details of this). The actual curve was drawn around a 29 oz. fruit tin. When cutting these sections it is advisable to have the grain running parallel to the longest straight edge.

The curve is produced by cutting off small tangential bits with a tenon saw and then smoothing it down with a file, working outwards from the centre towards each end. These pieces should be cut from a hardwood such as mahogany, into which one can screw easily without any risk of splitting.

Once all the components have been cut to shape it is advisable to rub them down until smooth with o, oo and flour-grade glasspapers in that order.

Just two more major parts are needed before assembly can commence. For the curved front of the top shelf a strip of 22 gauge aluminium 18 in. × 4 in. is required. This should be bent longitudinally around the same size tin as the curve on the formers G.

Both shelves are covered with plastic, leather cloth, or upholstery fabric which can be obtained from an upholsterer or coach trimmer. The colour is entirely a matter of personal choice; but dark blue has been found to be most effective, contrasting with the light-coloured wood. Half a square yard of plastic fabric is needed from which a piece 20 in. × 13 in. should be cut, and the remainder carefully saved.

Assembly

Assembling the cabinet is quite straightforward, but the following order has been found to be most practical. As well as screwing or pinning the various sections together, it is advisable to glue them with one of the proprietary brands of household adhesive.

At this stage in the proceedings the diagonals should be clearly marked on the underside of the base board B; this will facilitate the fitting of the legs later on.

The two chassis members C are joined together by the front piece D, which is screwed into position. The upper edges should be kept level with each other so that the base board B can be screwed to the chassis members; care must be taken to ensure that the bevel is carried through from one piece to the other. As there is little strength in end grain, B should be secured to D with 1¼ in. panel pins. Throughout, all screw and pin heads must be left below the surface level, or they will show through the covering material.

The upper surface and outside edges of the chassis should be covered with a thin, but even, film of impact adhesive. Allowing for a ½ in. overlap at the edges, slowly unroll 20 in. × 13 in. of fabric across the base board, removing any creases and pressing it down with clean rag. The overlaps should be folded sharply over two opposite sides, then over the others, and the resulting little bits at the corners cut off.

To save the risk of marking the material later on, the hardwood sections should be given whatever finish is desired before being added to the chassis.

The front-facing piece E should be fixed in place with screws, from the inside of D—the bevelled upper edge being flush with the shelf.

The positioning of the supports F for the upper shelf K is very important; they must be exactly ⅜ in. in from the back and 1 in. down from the top. These sections should be screwed to the inside faces of the end pieces, but great care must be taken not to put the screws right through the sides.

From this stage onward the bedside cabinet really begins to assume its final shape, for now the sides are added to the main chassis. Here again the positioning must be exact, the rear edge should be ⅜ in. in from the back and the fabric surface 2⅝ in. from the bottom edge of the side member. While screwing into the side pieces it is advisable to protect the outside faces with cardboard.

In order to give the structure a little more strength, the upper shelf K should be fixed in place with either 1 in. panel pins or screws; the heads must be left below the surface level. The rear edge of K should be flush with the back of the side members, i.e., overhanging its supports by ⅜ in.—this recess is designed to receive the back H.

Once again the body should be turned on its side, so that the curved formers G can be screwed into position, just the thickness of the aluminium below the surface of the upper shelf K. With the third former G attached in the centre, the curved aluminium should be screwed to the outside members with ⅜ in. brass screws, the heads of which should be filed down to follow the curve.

From the remnant of material, a piece of 18 in. × 12 in. should be cut to cover the upper shelf, using the same process as before, except that there is nothing to fold down the sides.

The back is pinned in place with 1 in. panel pins driven into the ends of members F and C and the rear edge of the base board B. To eliminate any possible flexing of the back panel, the strip H may be screwed to the back J just below the upper shelf.

Now only the legs remain to be fitted to the underside of the base board. To ensure that they are all equidistant from the corners, put a mark on each of the diagonals 6½ in. from their point of intersection. The rear edges of the base plates should be placed on these points with the

Figs. C66 and C67.
Construction is not
difficult, but accurate
positioning of the upper
shelf supports is
important.

Designation	No.	Size in ins.			Type
		MATERIALS			
A	2	16 × 15	× ⅝		Hardwood
B	1	18 × 11¼ × ¾			Plywood
C	2	10 × 1½ × 1½			Softwood
D	1	18 × 2¼ × ½			Softwood
E	1	18 × 2¼ × ½			Hardwood
F	2	5⅝ × 1	× 1		Softwood
G	2	4 × 1¼ × 1			Hardwood
H	1	16 × 1	× 1		Softwood
J	1	18 × 13	× ⅜		Veneered Plywood
K	1	18 × 6⅝ × ⅜			Plywood

Where a side is bevelled the longest dimension is
given. Allow for a little extra over the above measurements for cutting.

All timber should be planed.

Also needed

4 off 15 in. splayed legs and fitting attachments
1 piece 22-gauge aluminium 18 in. × 4 in.
1 piece upholstery fabric or leather cloth 36 in.
× 18 in.

Screws, panel pins, and impact adhesive.

through the angle of each corner.

It would be perfectly possible to make legs from any
suitable lengths of reasonably straight-grained wood,
planed to say 1½ in. × 1 in. section at the tip. However,
firm anchorage will be needed to make a sound job of
attaching the legs without departing from the idea of
jointless construction. If the recommended dimensions
are followed, the two sides of the cabinet project 2 in.
below the battens C and this allows reasonable depth for
screwing-on the legs, which will naturally be at an angle.
The side being ⅝ in. thick and the legs 1 in., No. 6 screws
1½ in. long could be used (as well as glue) to secure the
legs, putting three in the top of each leg, two from the
legs into the side, and one from the side into the legs.
This screw should be countersunk sufficiently for the hole
to be concealed by filling with stopping.

Once completed, the woodwork should be given a thin
coat of wax furniture polish, which should be left for
about 48 hours before attempting to bring up the lustre.
If that bedtime drink is accidentally spilt on the fabric,
then just a little warm water and non-caustic soap will
remove the stain. However, household bleaches, cleaners
and methylated spirits, etc., must not be used.

FOLDING BED-TABLE

A meal in bed may be a week-end luxury, or a necessity
for someone who is convalescing. In either case, a folding
bed-table which also serves as a tray on which to carry
the meal is a most useful article to have about the house.

The design here (Fig. C68) is an old one with which
many people will be familiar, and it serves the purpose
admirably.

It is easily portable, the dimensions permit it to be used
comfortably on a single bed and, when not in demand in
the sickroom, it will make quite a useful and attractive
low table in the living room.

sloping haunches facing the corners; then each unit is
screwed down and the legs inserted.

The ready-made legs of the type which screw into base
plates are adequate for the job, especially since they need
only be about 15 in. in length. One point to watch is not
to fix the legs so that they project outside the base, where
they would be an obstruction and generally get in the
way. The base plates should therefore be screwed on to
the cabinet bottom some distance in from the corners
settling the precise position by trial. For good appearance
the tip of each leg should coincide with a vertical line

Fig. C68. This folding bed-table can also be used as a tray.

Fig. C69. Leg frames open.

Fig. C70. Legs folded.

MITRED AT CORNERS

6" x 2¼" x ¾"

13" x 1½" x ⅛"

1'-2"

2'-3"

2" x ⅜"

Fig. C71. Details of the top.

1'-1"

2"

1½"

5½"

9"

1"

RAIL 10" x 2" x ¾"

LEG 9" x 1½" x ¾"

LEG FRAME

2 BRASS BUTT HINGES

Fig. C72 (above). Leg frame details.

Fig. C73 (left). Hinges must allow legs to lean outwards.

MATERIALS
All dimensions are finished sizes
Top: One piece hardboard or ply board 2 ft. 3 in. × 1 ft. 2 in.
Cross Battens: Two pieces 1 ft. 1 in. × 1½ in. × ⅜ in.
Edge Fillets: Two pieces 1 ft. 3 in. × 2 in. × ⅜ in. One piece 2 ft. 5 in. × 2 in. × ⅜ in.
Legs: Four pieces 10 in. × 1½ in. × ¾ in.
Leg Rails: Two pieces 10 in. × 2 in. × ¾ in.
Centre Block: One piece 6 in. × 2¼ in. × ¾ in.
Spring Board: One piece 2 ft. × 2½ in. × ¼ in.
Two pairs 2 in. brass butt hinges, screws and polish.

Materials

It is best to make the table in good wood such as oak or mahogany or in one of the tropical hardwoods now available. A good 5- or 6-ply board, either veneered or faced with plastic, would provide a good substitute for the top—although there is a tendency for the plastic surfaces to be a little too smooth and slippery to make the ideal surface for a bed tray.

The main constructional features are shown clearly in the photographs. In Fig. C69 you can see a view of the table turned upside down, showing how the two leg frames are hinged to the underside of the top in such a way that they lean slightly outwards from the vertical, and how they are retained in this position by the pressure of a thin, springy board screwed to a block in the centre. Fig. C70 shows the legs folded, again being retained by the springy board; in this position the table becomes an easily-portable tray.

Construction

The main top is 2 ft. 3 in. long by 1 ft. 2 in. wide and cut from ⅜ in. plywood or planed hardwood.

Fig. C71 shows that at each end of this top piece are screwed two cross battens each 1 ft. 1 in. × 1½ in. wide × ⅜ in thick. These will prevent any twisting or warping of the top, and will also provide an extra thickness to which may be screwed the three fillets which go round the two ends and the back of the tray. These should be about 2 in. × ⅜ in., well rounded on the top edges and mitred together at the corners as shown. When fitted they should be screwed to the top with brass screws, or, neater still, with raised-head, chromium-plated screws.

To complete the tray portion, a central block of hardwood is prepared—6 in. × 2¼ in.—and is screwed to the centre of the underside.

The two leg frames should now be prepared; the sizes of these are shown in Fig. C72. The legs are prepared from 1½ in. × ¾ in. wood with a slight taper planed on the inner edges as shown. The simplest (yet adequate) joint between the rail and the legs is to dowel them together with ⅜ in. or 5/16 in. dowels, as indicated. They should be well glued and, if possible, cramped together until the frames are set. When dry, the two leg units should be carefully cleaned up and the sharp edges of the legs well rounded by means of plane, file and glasspaper. They are now ready for hingeing in position. The most suitable hinges for this purpose are 2 in. brass butts.

It will be seen from Fig. C73 that these hinges are screwed to the underside of the top in such a fashion that the legs lean slightly outwards. This is easily done. First screw the hinges to the underside of the top (making sure that they are in the correct position and in alignment). Then put the leg frame in position against the hinges, but raised slightly by inserting a slip of wood about ¼ in. or 3/16 in. thick between it and the top. Screw on the hinges and it will be found that on removing the slip of wood the leg frame will lean over at a suitable angle.

It now remains to choose a suitable fairly springy strip of hardwood 2 ft. long × 2½ in. wide × ¼ in. thick, and to screw it securely to the central block. This completes the main construction of the table.

Finishing

Take the various components apart again and clean up all the surfaces, using, if necessary, a sharp finely-set steel smoothing plane, followed by various grades of fine glasspaper. Clean off all sharp edges, especially the front edge of the table top, which should be well rounded.

The actual finish depends upon personal taste and ability—the table shown was first given a couple of coats of button polish put on with a soft brush and rubbed down between each application with worn, fine glasspaper.

NURSERY AND CHILDRENS' ROOMS

INFANT'S COT

This is an easily-made cot which will serve admirably for the first six or eight months of baby's life.

It consists of a base cut from ¾ in. chipboard, with hardboard sides and ½ in. plywood ends, the whole standing on 15 in. contemporary legs.

Following the construction details shown in Fig. C74, cut the base 2 ft. 8 in. × 1 ft. 3 in. from ¾ in. chipboard and slightly chamfer the underside of the top end, to take the sloping plywood top piece; then fix the leg fittings to the base. Shape the sides from 2 ft. 10½ in. × 11 in. hardboard pieces and then nail and glue them to the edge of the base, leaving ½ in. at either end to take the plywood ends, which are fixed in the same way.

The next step is the lining. The base is made to take the standard-size pram mattress; the sides and ends are covered with ½ in. plastic foam, and finally covered with plastic material.

MATERIALS
1 off 2 ft. 8in. × 1 ft. 3in. × ¾ in. chipboard
1 off 1 ft. 3 in. × 1 ft. 2in. × ½ in. plywood
1 off 1 ft. 3 in. × 11 in. × ½ in. plywood
2 off 2 ft. 10½ in. × 11 in. hardboard
4 off 1 ft. 3 in. contemporary legs and mounts
Aluminium corner cope, padding, plastic, mattress, braid, screws, nails, glue, paint, nursery transfers.

Fig. C74. Constructional details.

Fig. C75. The completed cot.

After painting, aluminum corner cope is fitted, with chrome screws to all four corners and along the base of the sides. This strengthens the corners and adds much to the final appearance of the cot. The aluminium should be polished with wadding.

Fix four nursery transfers to the sides, and glue upholsterer's braid along the top edges. The completed cot is shown in Fig. C75.

BABY'S BATHROOM

The unit shown in Fig. C76 is designed to fit over an ordinary bath and consists of a single panel of waterproof plywood, coated and shaped to take a polythene bath and with a compartment for toilet accessories built alongside.

The top is divided into two, so that either section of the base can be covered or uncovered as needed. For instance, the bath compartment can be covered to provide a space on which to put the baby while he or she is being dried.

MATERIALS

One off ½ in. thick waterproof plywood
  24 in. × 24 in.
Two off ½ in. thick waterproof plywood
  24 in. × 12 in.
Two off ¼ in. thick waterproof plywood
  18 in. × 4½ in.
Three off ¼ in. thick waterproof plywood
  9 in. × 4½ in.
Two off ½ in. thick foam plastic 24 in. × 12 in. for
  top of flaps, together with waterproof upholstery
  fabric
Two pairs brass butt hinges with screws
2 oz. of ¾ in. galvanised panel pins.

Fig. C76. Compact and easy to fit, this unit provides baby with his own bath without wasting valuable space.

Padded hinged tops
Foam plastic fixed on back
Toilet Accessories
Polethene bath
Brass hinges
Assembly set over bath
Finger holes to lift out bath

To make it, lay the bath over the panel and mark the shape for cutting. Cut out the 18 in. × 9 in. toilet compartment space. Fix padding to the flaps and cover with a waterproof upholstery material. Make up box for toilet accessories and fix with glue and panel pins. Hinge flaps to the baseboard. The underside of the unit should be sealed and given two coats of good quality oil paint.

TABLE SEAT-CUM-TOYBOX

The problem of junior wanting to discard the highchair and sit at table can be solved by making the seat seen in Fig. C77. The top of the seat is actually a hinged lid hiding a roomy toybox (Fig. C78).

There are many other uses for which the box could be used, such as an occasional table, a foot-rest, an invalid bed table, a stool for children to stand on to give them additional height at the bathroom washbasin, or—with a padded top—a more comfortable stool seat. The toybox part could be used as a receptacle for knitting, cards, sewing, etc.

The size of the box is determined by the height of the dining chair and table. The dimension inside the legs should be sufficient to clear the side rails of the chair bottom. If the chair has a loose padded seat this should be removed when the box is in use.

The wood used for the box was 13/16 in. thick finished and, for the bottom of the box, 3/16 in. thick plywood.

Method

Cut the four sides of the box and make the corner joints as shown in Fig. C79. Cut the rebate on the bottom to take the 3/16 in. plywood bottom (Figs. C80 and C81). On the rear piece cut the recesses for a pair of 2½ in. hinges (Fig. C82). Glue, cramp and nail the four corners (not forgetting to square up the job) and punch home the nails.

An alternative method is to use butt joints on the corners, glue, cramp and nail, and, in addition, use four quadrant mouldings glued and nailed to the inside corners (see Fig. C83). Do not cut a rebate for the plywood if using butt joints.

Assembly

While the glue is drying, cut four legs to the shape shown in Fig. C84. Cut timber for lid of the appropriate size if using solid stock, and glue up, using joints like those in Fig. C85. Also cut two 3/16 in. × 13/16 in. facing strips to cover the end grain; glue and pin these in position as in Fig. C86. As an alternative, the lid can be made of 13/16 in.-thick blockboard. In that case, four facing strips should be cut and, when fixing to the blockboard, the corners should be mitred. Finally cut the 3/16 in. plywood bottom. If the rebate has been cut, make the bottom a neat fit in the recess; otherwise cut the plywood ¼ in. smaller than the outside dimensions of the box (Fig. C81).

When the glue has dried on the box, dress up with the plane and sand smooth. Mark out the position for the legs; glue, nail or screw them in position. The plywood bottom should then be glued and nailed in place, using flat head nails for preference (see Figs. C80 and C81). The best face of the plywood should be to the inside of the box.

Fit the hinges to the lid and box, ensuring that the lid will open more than 90 deg. and the lid overlap is a minimum of ⅛ in. all round.

Fig. C77 (*left*).   This seat allows junior to sit at table.

Fig. C78 (*above*).   The hinged top hides a roomy playbox.

Fig. C79.   Detail of corner joint.

Figs. C80 and C81.   The plywood bottom is recessed as shown.

Fig. C82. The hinges are recessed on the rear piece.

Fig. C83.   An alternative corner joint.

Fig. C84.   Front and end elevations and dimensions.

Fig. C85 (*left*).   Joints to obtain the width for the seat.

Fig. C86 (*right*).   Glued and pinned strips conceal the seat end-grain.

Fig. C87. A simple construction your child will be proud of.

Fig. C88. The template for the sides.

Fig. C89. Details of the padded seat and back.

PLASTIC COVERING

PADDING

SEAT

HARDBOARD

It is wise to fix a stay in the appropriate position, to prevent the lid going too far back and straining the hinges and screws.

Lightly punch home all the nails and give the lid and legs a final dressing up and sanding. After the undercoat is applied, stop up all nail holes with a suitable filler and, when dry, sand off flush. Finish painting with two top coats of a good gloss paint.

A CHILD'S CHAIR

This chair shown in Fig. C87 is made almost entirely of half-inch plywood, which gives ample strength and will stand up to hard wear.

The first step is the cutting of the two sides and this is most simply done by using a jigsaw or fretsaw. To make the design accurately, draw a pattern on a piece of cardboard by means of 1-in. squares (Fig. C88). Then cut out a template. Place the template on the plywood and pencil round. Then cut out with jigsaw.

The next step is to make the seat and back support. The seat consists of 2 pieces of half-inch plywood; cut the top piece 12 in. × 9 in., and the bottom 11 in. × 9 in. Screw them both together leaving ½ in. recess at either end for the seat supports (Fig. C89). These are screwed-and-glued to the sides of the chair 8½ in. from the base and in position as shown in Fig. C88. The seat is then glued in position on the supports and the top piece of the seat is also secured by screws through the sides of the chair, the heads being slightly recessed and the holes filled before painting.

The back support, 12 in. × 6 in., is then screwed-and-glued in position as in Fig. C88. Cut the plastic foam or padding and place in position on the seat and back support as shown in Fig. C89. Both are then covered with plastic material. The material is glued or taped to the underside of the seat. A piece of hardboard 12 in. × 9 in. is then nailed underneath (use upholstery nails) to make a neat finish and hold the plastic firmly in place. The same is done to the back support; the hardboard in this case can be covered with a piece of plastic too, but it is advisable to cover the hardboard first with a piece of white paper or paint it, as some plastic material is semi-transparent. The foam or padding of seat and back should also be white, or covered with white material first. Now for the arm rests; roll two pieces or plastic material about 11 in. long and nail these to the arms with upholstery nails, folding in each end before nailing.

The plastic material is waterproof and so can be washed easily, but, of course, other types of material can be used if preferred.

CHILD'S FIRESIDE CHAIR

The back and seat of this scaled-down fireside chair are based on 1 in. timber, 12 in. wide. It will be covered, so there is no need to spend much on new wood, which in these dimensions could be expensive.

Cut the rear end of the seat portion at a slight angle to give the back of the chair a rake and then glue-and-screw the two parts together, adding for extra strength a couple of angle brackets opened out slightly to fit the angle of the joint (Fig. C90). Cut the rear legs from 3 in. × 1 in. timber according to the pattern (Fig. C91) and glue-and-screw them into position. Then attach to the seat strips of 1 in. square wood (Fig. C92). Their purpose is to strengthen and deepen the seat, and also to provide a more secure anchorage for the front legs. Don't forget that this chair will have to stand up to rough treatment; it needs to be strongly constructed.

When preparing the strip for the back of the seat (A in Fig. C92), cut recesses to take the depth of the angle brackets. Cover the strips with a square of plywood or hardboard, and add a strip of 1 in.-square wood at the back. This will be needed to anchor the covering.

Legs and Arms

The front legs, in 1 in.-square hardwood, are cut at the top at an angle, to give the arms a downward slope. Attach them to the sides of the seat by glue and dowels (or screws countersunk and plugged, if preferred). Remember that the legs should make a right angle with the floor—not with the sloping seat. When attaching the arms, make sure that they line up with each other.

A strip of wood screwed across the top of the chair back, for extra strength, completes the woodwork. Before covering, finish off the arms and legs with a thorough sandpapering, and then either paint them or use stain and polish.

Covering

Cover foam rubber pads with an undercover of a fairly stout, closely-woven material. It should be long enough to extend over seat and back and have a border sufficiently wide to reach the frame. Place the material in position and first anchor it with a line of gimp pins along the edge of the wooden strip at the rear of the seat. Pull the lower section of the cloth taut across the seat and take it, with the overhanging rubber, over the edge, nailing it to the underside of the seat. Fasten the sides and then deal with the section for the back in the same way. Cut recesses in the material where the arms and front legs are fixed.

Use any stout furnishing material for the final covering, which is applied to the seat and back in two sections. Cut the seat section to size, allowing sufficient length to reach the rear of the chair back. Then cut out a section the width of the chair back, fit the material in place and run a line of gimp pins into the wooden strip which is anchoring the undercover. This leaves a couple of 'ears' of material at the back of the seat, after the rest of the fabric has been stretched and attached to the underside of the frame; flatten the 'ears' against the sides of the seat frame and nail them.

The cover for the back is dealt with in the same way, except that the 'ears' left when the material is pinned into position are folded diagonally and then nailed. This makes a neat mitred joint. The gimp pins at this joint, and in the joint between the seat and back, are concealed by a length of upholstery cord fastened beneath the frame.

Cover the rear of the chair back with the same material, or possibly something in a contrasting shade; turn in the edge before attaching. Cover the underside of the seat in the same way. Fig. C93 shows covering details.

PLAYTABLE AND CUPBOARD

This arrangement is useful for those hobbies which require plenty of horizontal space (model railways, race-tracks, etc.) but where room is at a premium. A smaller variation will serve as a desk and games repository for the younger girl and boy.

Fig. C91. Pattern for the rear legs.

Fig. C90. The back and seat assembled.

Fig. C92. Square wood strips strengthen the seat.

Fig. C93. Details of covering.

The unit is easily made from inexpensive materials; there are no complicated joints; it is easily fixed to a wall and, if suitably decorated, can enhance an otherwise bare wall. The dimensions given here can readily be altered to suit particular requirements. Figs. C94 and C95 show the table in operation and closed, respectively.

The assembly basically consists of a frame fixed to the wall and a hinged table supported, when brought down to the horizontal, by two swing-down legs. The space between the folded table top and the wall, within the frame, is storage space.

Fig. C94 (*left*). The playtable in use.

Fig. C95 (*above*). The unit in the stowed position.

Fig. C96 (*below*). Details of the assembly with main dimensions.

Turn Button

Shelf Unit

Wall

Hinge

Leg

Fig. C97 (*left*). Bottom brackets made from ½ in. plywood.

Fig. C98 (*right*). Top brackets let into back of frame.

Fig. C99 (*left*). Arrangements for electric wiring.

Fig. C100 (*above*). Section through the whole assembly (stowed).

Table Top (Ply)

Spacer

Outer Skin (Ply)

The Frame

Details of the frame are given in Fig. C96. It is supported on the wall by two brackets underneath (Fig. C97) and by two or three brackets along the top, these being let in flush with the back edge of the frame (Fig. C98).

The Table

This consists of a simple butt-jointed frame on which a plywood or hardboard top is fixed. The legs, which hang down flush inside the outer table timbers, each require only a bolt, washer and nut for fixing.

For a hobby which requires electrical wiring to pass under the table top, a second skin of ply or hardboard can be fixed in three panels on the outside (or underside, when the table is down) of the table frame. This is spaced out to allow the wires to pass up and down through the table top. Fixed with a screw at each corner (capped chrome mirror screws look best), the skin can be removed easily whenever wiring has to be done (Fig. C99). The inner vertical timbers of the table frame should be drilled across close to the inner face (*before assembly*) to allow for the passage of wires across.

Brackets

Scrap pieces of ½ in. plywood can be used for the four main brackets—or suitable brackets can, of course, be bought.

The dimensions of the table and frame should be adjusted to allow for the storage space required, i.e. the space between the wall and the face of the table (when folded up), and should allow for any projections on the table top. The dimensions shown were found to be ample for an oo-gauge railway. Shelf units, to suit the internal dimensions, should be made up separately and fixed with screws.

Construction

The drawings show the simple construction of each part. All the joints are plain butts, glued and nailed or screwed (for the backets). Remember to cut away the portions in the frame to take the thickness of the top brackets *before assembly* (Fig. C98). Fix the hinges to the rear face of the table frame directly over the bottom wall brackets. Do not cut the table legs to final length before the table is fixed to the frame. Paint, stain or varnish the frame before fitting to the wall. Brown paper or other protection may be slipped down behind the shelf units to protect the wallpaper.

Fix bottom brackets to the wall, making sure they are horizontal and level with each other. Offer up the frame and mark the bottom members of the frame for screws into bottom brackets (one in each is enough). Drill and countersink these holes. Put up frame and screw loosely into bottom brackets.

Make sure the frame sits squarely then mark and drill the top bracket holes into the wall. Plug holes, and screw up all screws tightly. An additional bracket should be fixed in the middle of the back of the frame if the top is to be used as a shelf.

Now support the table horizontally in front of the frame and screw the hinges into the wall frame. Screw turn-buttons into the top of the frame to secure the table when raised. The table should now fold up snugly into the frame.

Lower the table again and support it horizontally in front of the frame. Offer up one leg and mark it for the hole into the table end member. Repeat with the other leg (do not drill and cut both legs the same unless you are sure the floor and table are quite parallel). Place the drilled leg again in proper position and drill right through the table member. Counterdrill the other side of the table member to allow the bolt head to fit flush. Now radius the bolt-end of the legs and fit to the inside of the end table members. Make and fit the shelf units.

Fig. C100 shows a section through the fitment in the closed position.

A CHILD'S DESK

Most children like to have a desk of their own—it gives a sense of importance and when homework has to be done, there is something to be said for giving them a proper place to work on.

Beech is the wood usually used for children's desks, and other straight-grained woods such as pine are equally suitable. If making it up from deal, order 50 per cent in excess of requirements in order to be able to avoid lengths with unsightly knots.

Timber should be purchased 'finished', i.e., planed; the amounts required are given in the list of materials.

Constructional details are given in Figs. C101 and C102. First prepare the legs by marking off the depth of the rails, say 4 in., and with the try-square draw a line on two sides. Saw down with the tenon saw to a depth of ¼ in. With a gauge, mark off ¼ in. on two running sides and across the top, and with a sharp saw cut down to the cross cut on both sides. This will leave a 'horn' on the top of the leg to receive the rails.

Fix the leg in the vice and with a gauge mark a line ⅜ in. from both sides of the corner, starting 1 in. from the rails. Take a spokeshave or chisel and work a stop chamfer preparatory to forming a round. With a cabinetmaker's scraper, held in finger and thumb of the right hand and the palm of the left hand, gently stroke off the angles of the chamfer and form a round corner.

Finish off with a medium sandpaper. Take a sheet of paper, divide into three equal pieces, place them together and wrap them round a strip of wood about 12 in. × 1½ in. and tack down the back. Use this sanding block for finishing with a hand on either end as one would do a file. Complete the other legs in the same way. Cut off the four lengths for the rails—two at 21 in. and two at 15½ in. Select the sides for the face and mark them. Select edges for top and mark them.

Assemble the two sides first. Place the horn left on one of the legs on the inside end of a 15½ in. rail, mark and saw down ¼ in. as shown in the sketch. Mark a line with a gauge on each edge and saw. Clean up and leave true and square.

With a ½ in. bit, sink three holes 3/16 in. deep, as shown, to receive the screw heads; in the centre of each, drill through with a 3/16 in. drill. Prepare the other end similarly, and then prepare the opposite side. When preparing the front and back pieces, note that the piece taken out will be ¾ in. longer. See C102.

Assembly

Place a side rail in position, holding it with a G-cramp and protecting the face with a piece of wood. Square up the leg and rail with the try-square. Pass a ⅛ in. drill

Fig. C101. The two front faces of each leg are rebated to receive the front and side rails.

Fig. C102. Leg assembly details.

MATERIALS
10 ft. of 4 in. × 1 in., finished
4 ft. of 7 in. × 1 in., finished
9 ft. of 2 in. × 2 in., finished
2ft. × 1 ft. 6 ins. of 10 mm plywood
2 ft. of ¼ in. dowelling
2 ft. of ⅜ in. dowelling
1 ft. of ½ in. dowelling
Hinges, nails, screws and varnish as required.

through one hole and put in a 1½ in. × No. 10 screw. Remove the cramp, again check with the square and put in the other two screws. Do this with all the rail-leg joints in turn. Take the sanding block already made for the legs and clean up the end grain of all ends.

On the inside, number the ends of the rails 1 to 8 with a corresponding number on the horns of the legs. Unscrew all rails; glue all edges and re-assemble. Cut ¼ in. thick discs from a ½ in. dowel, glue and place in the holes to cover the screw heads. Wipe off surplus glue with a rag dipped into hot water, touch with a plane and sand down.

Prepare the square of 10 mm. plywood for the base by chamfering the edge all round to an angle of 45 deg. Drill a ¼ in. hole in the front centre of the base, drilling from both sides, to facilitate the desk being cleaned out of dust, pins, pieces of pencil, etc. Carefully mark the four corners for the small squares to be taken out at the legs, and saw them out. Tack on the base with four pins leaving ¼ in. all round between the edge and the front of the rails. Bore and countersink for ¾ in. × No. 6 screws and put in four in the front and back, and three in the sides.

Cut off a 22 in. length of 4 in. × 1 in. and true-up both ends to form the back board. Fix a lip, made from a piece of 3/16 in. dowelling, on the back edge to prevent pencils and pens rolling off. Place the dowelling between two pieces of wood tacked to the bench and a piece across the top to act as a stop and plane off ⅓ in. of its diameter. This produces a more-or-less half round mould. Glue and pin on the back edge of the back board with 1 in. panel pins. Do not knock the pins right in but nip off the heads and file flat. Sand off flush with the back edge and round the ends.

Desk Top

For this take two 22 in. lengths of 7 in. × 1 in. Since the boards have been purchased 'finished', it is reasonable to expect that the edges are good, but check them with a steel rule or other straight-edge. Place one length in the vice with the other length on top—any bumps may be easily felt or the joint may be 'sighted through'. Should there be anything to come off, use a plane with a very fine cut as the smallest shaving makes a big difference. Glue both edges and cramp up. If sash cramps are not available then two wooden ones must be made. Cramps are indispensable. Make the necessary wedges neatly and the cramps will be easy to use. When the joint is quite set (i.e. after about 12 hours) mark off with a square about 1 in. from either end, leaving the centre 20 in. which should be cut off true with a tenon saw.

Cut out two 16 in.-lengths of 1 in. × 1 in. for the flap ends. True up and glue to the flap. Hold in position with two 2 in. thin wire nails, but do not knock them right in. Alter the position of the blocks on the cramp already made and cramp up. When set, remove the nails and trim the ends. Bore four ¾ in. holes 2 in. deep through each end piece to receive dowels. Roughen ¾ in. dowelling to give a 'bite' for the glue—glue, knock in, and cut off. Touch all dowels with a plane and sand off flush. Round the front edge of the flap, leave the sides square, and round the four corners.

Manufactured desks usually have large iron side-hinges but alternatively a piano hinge is suitable; otherwise three 2 in. brass butts could be used. Sink in on the back board edge only, marking width and depth with a gauge. Take out the waste and leave neat and in alignment. Fix the hinges to the back board with the centre screw only, using ¾ in. × No. 6 brass screws. Get all three in line with a straight-edge and then put in the remaining screws. Don't forget that a brass screw in hardwood can easily be broken off, so it is necessary to bore a suitable hole.

Fix the hinges to the flap side, marking off with a gauge to match the opposite side.

Fix the back board to the body of the desk in the same way as the legs were fixed—with concealed screws. Put two 1½ in. × No. 10 on the back and one on each side.

RIGHT-ANGLED BUNK BEDS

These bunk beds (Fig. C103), are one answer to the problem of fitting two beds into a smallish bedroom. It's actually an adaptation of an American design which has

several advantages. Since the bunks are at right angles to each other, the lower bunk is easily accessible and gets plenty of light and air. Also, it doesn't matter if either occupant is a restless sleeper because each unit is independent of the other.

Constructional details are shown in Fig. C104. The upper bunk is fixed to the wall through one long side with about six No. 8 or No. 10 screws, at least 2 in. in the wall —that is, two full inches in the brick below the plaster. It is best to arrange the screws in three groups of two; one pair in the centre, and a pair about 6 in. from each end of the long side, should be adequate. However, it is important to note that these six screws depend upon a lot of support being given to the upper bunk by a long cleat underneath (also firmly screwed to the wall) and by the ladder, which must not be omitted—otherwise the upper bunk won't stay upper for long!

The ladder is made of two lengths of ordinary 4 in. × 2 in. timber, with well-planed and sandpapered edges. Leave the upper ends of the ladder sides above the level of the bunk frame; they help to prevent a child from falling out if he has a tendency to roll in his sleep.

The front side of the upper bunk is well anchored in the notches in the ladder posts. The bottom ends of the ladder should be screwed direct to the floor, or secured with L-shaped iron brackets. The ladder can be replaced by a short flight of steps if preferred, but any amended design must provide support for the upper bunk.

The lower bunk is really a single bed, which is not fastened down at all but is left free for easy cleaning.

The beds can be painted in bright, gay colours, painted to harmonise with the decorative theme, or stained to bring out the full beauty of the wood grain.

Fig. C103 (above). Two bunk beds to economise on space—yet they are quite independent of each other.

Fig. C104 (right). Constructional details and dimensions.

BATHROOM

BATHROOM CABINET

The whole of this cabinet (shown in Fig. C105) is made from ⅜ in. and ½ in. plywood.

Make up the box part first, using corner housing joints. Easy-to-follow construction details are given in Fig. C106. Before glueing and nailing together, bore ¼ in. holes to take the shelf dowels if a shelf is to be included. Clean up the inside of the box and assemble, using a good glue and 1 in. oval nails. Check for squareness before punching in the nails. When dry, level off the front and back edges and fasten the back in place, again using glue and 1 in. nails.

The shelf is to be fixed next. Four ⅞ in. × No. 6 screws through the back and into the edge of the shelf are reinforced by the two dowel pillars, which have the ends shouldered to ⅜ in. diameter for a distance of ½ in. from each end. Saw cuts are made into the ends of the dowels and wedges are sawn to drive in after assembly. When cutting wedges, make sure that the grain lies along the length for maximum strength.

If laminated plastic is to be used, this lower shelf and

cabinet will hold more, whereas with the latter type door the inside cabinet shelf must obviously be narrower. Probably ½ in. plywood is strong enough for these doors, the main essential being that the ply be perfectly flat; doors which are twisted complicate the fitting of catches and handles.

Sliding doors can be fitted. It is better to groove some softwood and then glue this in place rather than attempt to groove the plywood, which tends to split away on the cross-grain layer. Alternatively, ready-grooved track is not at all expensive. The shelf here is narrower still.

The provision of an internal shelf (or shelves) is entirely optional: the width will depend on the choice of doors. Square or triangular supporting pieces should be glued and nailed as required.

All parts of the cabinet not faced with mirrors or plastic should be painted after a final clean up and removal of sharp corners.

For fixing to the wall, simply bore two 3/16 in. holes straight through the back; plywood is very stout stuff and no wall-plates are needed.

Fig. C105 (*above*). This is the cabinet, easily made with plywood.

Fig. C106 (*right*). Constructional details and dimensions.

lower back should be covered before fitting the dowels. The ends of the shelf look better if they are slightly shaped.

After a trial assembly, glue the ends of the dowel and the holes in the shelf and carcase bottom. Insert the dowels, then the four screws and finally tap home the glued wedges after making sure the dowels are correctly in place with no gaps at the shoulders. A bench cramp will pull these up tightly and then they may be wedged, cleaning off the surplus when the glue is dry.

Three types of door are possible and these in turn may be painted, faced with plastic or even have mirrors affixed. A hinged door can cover the whole carcase or can fit within the carcase. With the former, the edges of the carcase do not show, no door stop is necessary and the

MATERIALS
2 off 17½ in. × 6 in. × ½ in. ply (Box)
2 off 12 in. × 6 in. × ½ in. ply (Box)
1 off 18 in. × 5 in. × ½ in. ply (Shelf)
1 off 19 in. × 18 in. × ⅜ in. ply (Back)
1 off 17 in. × 6 in. × ⅛ in. ply (Internal shelf)
2 off 7½ in. × ½ in. dowels
2 off 12 in. × 9 in. × ½ in. (Doors)—or as required
Nails, screws, glue, doorknobs, catches, door track, shelf supports, laminated plastic, etc., as required.

LINEN BOX WITH REMOVABLE BAG

This bin is designed to hold the week's soiled linen of a family of three or four.

To avoid carrying the whole bin to the washing machine, an easily-removable bag is incorporated. This is held open by two dowel rods which rest in holes and notches at each end of the container—see Fig. C107.

Cut the legs and rails of the bin frame first. These must be to exact sizes as shown in the materials list—and the ends must be square. They are best cut in fours, taped together to ensure that their lengths do not vary. Before untaping the legs scribe a line 3 in. from one end right round the bundle. This marks the bottom limit of the panels (Fig. C108).

Assemble the front and back frames by butt-jointing the rails to the legs with impact adhesive and securing in

round the legs, and drill six ⅜ in. holes in a line along the back of the panel, about 2 in. inside the edge. These are for ventilation in conjunction with a similar line of holes in the top of the back panel. Glue the floor in place and sand-off any slightly projecting edges flush with the outside of the legs.

When all is set, rub down the inside surfaces of the legs and rails quite smooth with medium-grade sandpaper, paying particular attention to the sharp edges of the squared wood. The outside surfaces need no smoothing as they are all covered with hardboard.

Using a ⅜ in. drill, bore a hole ⅝ in. deep in the inner face of the top back rail 2 in. from each end as shown at X, Fig. C110. Repeat on the inner face of the front top rail, but in this case form the holes into slots or notches by chopping down from the top of the rail with a ⅜ in. chisel (Y, Fig. C110).

Fig. C107 (*above*). The completed linen bin, open.

Fig. C108 (*right*). Constructional details and dimensions.

place with two 1½ in. oval brads driven through previously-drilled holes in the legs. Note that the top rails are flush with the top ends of the legs, and the lower edges of the bottom rails are in line with the marks scribed 3 in. from the feet of the legs. Square up each frame to an accurate rectangle before connecting them by the end rails.

These are fixed in exactly the same way with adhesive and brads. Cut and fit the floor joist similarly in the middle of the front and back lower rails (Fig. C108). Square up the whole frame, making sure that it will stand on its four feet without wobble.

Now cut a 20 in. × 14 in. hardboard panel for the floor (C, Fig. C108). Notch out the corners ⅞ in. square to fit

These holes accommodate the dowel rods which support the removable bag.

The frame is now ready for the hardboard cladding.

Cut the two end panels first (B, Fig. C108). They are best cut slightly oversize in width and planed off flush with the legs after fitting. Cut two pieces of scrap soft wood about 6 in. by ¾ in. and glue them one to each panel at the positions shown in Fig. C108. These go inside and are to form attachments for the handle screws later on. In applying the impact adhesive to the panels and legs make sure that the glue is spread right up to the edges of the panel all round. In this way you will avoid gaps which will have to be closed by panel pins and subsequent filling.

The front and back panels (A, Fig. C108) are next fitted

Fig. C110 (*left*). Fitting arrangements for the bag.

Fig. C109 (*centre*). Details of the removable bag.

Fig. C111 (*above*). The completed linen bin, closed.

in a similar manner. Note that the back panel has a row of ⅜ in. holes drilled in it about 2 in. below the top edge. If these two panels are also cut slightly oversize, a much better fit will be obtained at the sides after they have been planed and sanded flush with the ends. Check the finished bin for gaps at the edges, and close any up with a panel pin driven just below the surface. Smooth off the sharp edges of the vertical corners and proceed to make the lid.

As the frame for the lid has to fit flush with the top of the bin it is easier to mark off the wood for the front, back and ends against the actual bin top. In assembling, butt joints can again be used, but as the outside surfaces of the frame will not be covered, mitred joints will make a far neater and more professional job. For extra rigidity fit the middle bar as shown in Fig. C108. For lifting the lid, fit a small piece of wood (about 4 in. long and ½ in. thick and rounded in an arc 1 in. deep) to the middle of the front rail by gluing-and-screwing from the back.

Finally, cut the hardboard panel D, Fig. C108, and glue it to the lid frame. When set, trim the edges flush with the frame all round. Note that the two holes are not required unless the foam plastic top is to be fitted, as described later.

Position the lid on the bin and carefully mark off the positions of the hinges on bin and lid. Cut the recesses in both lid and bin with great care for it is important that the lid must not bind but should close down flat and evenly all round. The hinges should be positioned 4 in. in from each end.

If no further embellishment is desired the bin is now ready for painting—after any nail holes and small gaps have been filled with a cellulose filler and rubbed smooth with fine sandpaper. In this case a better appearance will be gained by working a bevel or chamfer all round the top edge of the lid.

The addition of an upholstered top to the lid converts a utility article into a presentable piece of furniture (Fig. C111). To make this top, cut an additional hardboard panel the exact size of the lid (which should not be bevelled at the edges, of course) and drill two 1 in. holes in it as shown in Fig. C108. Mark off these two holes on the lid and bore them in the lid to match. They are air

holes to prevent the foam-filled upholstery covering from bursting when pressed. Decide on a pattern for the buttons and drill 1/16 in. holes in the appropriate positions in the panel. The one shown has six buttons.

With a few dabs of glue, lightly attach a sheet of ½ in. foam plastic to the rough side of the panel and trim to exact size. Cover the whole with a sheet of thin plastic material evenly drawn over the edges and glued to the underside. Trim off all surplus plastic material. Take care not to bunch the corners; they require to be neatly pleated to give a smooth appearance.

The buttons are ½ in. button moulds covered with self material and are attached by passing a needle threaded with button-twist up through the small hole in the hardboard and out through the cover. The button is threaded on the needle which is returned through the same hole. The ends of the thread are pulled until the button has sunk about halfway into the padding and are then secured to the panel with sticky tape and the ends are cut off. Make sure that all the buttons are evenly sunk in the padding. The top is now ready for attachment to the lid.

Before doing this apply two undercoats of paint all over both inside and outside of the bin and lid (except the lid top if it is to be upholstered), and finish with a coat of hard gloss enamel on the outside only. Let the enamel dry quite hard, then attach the upholstered panel to the lid by gluing all round the edges. Finally screw on the plastic handles at each end of the bin as shown.

If there is a danger of the lid opening back too far, fit a couple of chromium-plated chandelier check chains with chrome screws.

The removable bag can be made of any material such as sheeting. unbleached calico, etc., to the shape and size shown in Fig. C109. It is supported in the bin by two ½ in. dowel rods passed through the large hems at the top of each end of the bag. These rods are 13 in. long and have their diameter reduced to ¼ in. for half-an-inch at each end. They should be an easy fit in the holes and slots in the frame. Figs. C109 and C110 show how the arrangement works.

Some self-decorated (plastic-covered) hardboards are available which make painting unnecessary, and another possibility is the use of the self-adhesive decorative plastics which can be bought in a very wide range of colours and patterns.

An advantage of this material is that the joints between the hardboard at the corners can be covered, thus giving a more 'solid' appearance. If this method is chosen, lay the bin flat on its back and apply the plastic first to one of the sides and wrap round the front, smoothing out any wrinkles. It may be more convenient to apply in three separate panels—the two sides and the front. In this case, the plastic should be put on the front last of all and cut about ¾ in. over width, so that it laps over the corners accordingly.

Fig. C112 (right). Closed, it is a towel rack.

Fig. C113 (left). Open, it is a drying rack.

Fig. C114 (top). Box details.
Fig. C115 (centre). Rack details.
Fig. C116 (left). A bottom bracket.
Fig. C117 (below). A top bracket.

MATERIALS

⅞ in. sq. Ramin
  4 off 24 in. bin legs
  4 off 18¼ in. bin rails
  4 off 12¼ in. bin rails
  1 off 12¼ in. floor joist
  2 off 20¼ in. lid rails
  2 off 14¼ in. lid rails
  1 off 12½ in. middle bar
⅛ in. Hardboard
  2 off 21 in. × 20¼ in. panels (A)
  2 off 21 in. × 14 in. panels (B)
  1 off 20 in. × 14 in. floor (C)
  1 off 20¼ in. × 14¼ in. top (D)
Hardware
  2 off 2 in. brass butt hinges and screws
  2 off 4 in. plastic handles and screws
  Approx. 18 in. of chrome chandelier chain
  ¾ in. panel pins
  1½ in. oval brads
  Impact adhesive
  Plastic, foam and sheet—as required

TOWEL AND DRYING RACK

Drip-dry shirts may be a great boon, but they still need somewhere to drip. Here is one solution for this domestic problem—a combined towel and drip-dry rack which can be screwed to the wall over the bath. Figs. C112 and C113 show the finished unit. As shown, it is extremely simple. When used as a towel rack (Fig. C112) it is held vertically by two spring clips. When it is required to hold drip-dry garments over the bath, the rack is lowered as shown (Fig. C113).

Construction

Make the box first. Fig. C114 gives the dimensions. It is very simply made, the end-pieces being pinned and glued to the shelves. Now for the rack itself. This consists of two lengths of white wood (see Fig. C115 for dimensions) supporting four rails of ⅜ in. dowel. Note that the lower rail is longer than the rest as it acts as the pivot rail.

Supporting brackets (Figs. C116 and C117) are made from ¾ in. wood or chipboard. Drill the holes in the positions given and glue the 1½ in. stud in place.

The back-board consists of a 2 ft. × 2 ft. 7½ in. sheet of hardboard. It should be decided at this stage if the back-board is to be painted or covered with a plastic film. If the latter method is desired, the film should be applied after cutting the board to size, and before assembling the rest of the unit. The box unit is screwed-and-glued in place, as are the lower brackets. Next screw-and-glue the clip blocks.

Finishing Touches

The rack is now ready for painting. Use reliable class undercoats and paint, bearing in mind that the finished

job will be subjected to steam and condensation.

When the paint is dry, screw the spring clips in place on the blocks and fit the rack in place by sliding the lower pivot rail through the brackets. Pins hold this rail in place.

The rack may be fitted direct to the wall, or it may be mounted on two 2 ft. 7½ in. battens screwed to the wall.

In either case, a masonry drill should be used to make the holes, especially if the walls are tiled. Non-rusting screws are desirable throughout—brass or stainless steel.

HALL, LANDING AND LOFT

TELEPHONE CUPBOARD

As with most well-balanced construction jobs of simple design, the overall appearance of the finished article depends on the quality of the finish. The attractive hall unit, shown in Fig. C118, is an excellent example.

Material requirements are simple, as is the method of construction: ⅝ in. ply in a standard width of 15 in.; some ⅝ in.-square hardwood (planed size); hardboard for the back; ½ in. dowel for the rack; and self-adhesive plastics to give the finish. The fabric chosen for this was a Fablon woodgrain to give an authentic texture, and for contrast, one of the terrazzo effects was used for shelving, giving a clean and durable surface.

Construction is simply a matter of sawing clean and perfectly square edges to the ply, to accurate dimensions. Jointing is non-existent as the pieces butt on to each other and are secured by impact glue. They are pinned first as a guide, carefully drawn apart again, mating sides are coated with impact adhesive and they are finally pinned and cramped until the glue sets hard.

The ⅝ in. square material is used as rails, shown in Fig. C119, to add strength and solidity where required. These rails must be cut accurately and squarely, as they reinforce the jointing method.

When the completed structure is dry, a sanding and preferably a gloss sealing should be given to all surfaces before the plastic is applied. This is run from lower and outside surfaces to inside and higher ones, overlapping being confined to positions less likely to wear. The top for the telephone should be cut to pattern before the paper backing is removed; after firm application, working from centre to edges with a soft clean pressure pad of cloth, the edges can be sealed and enhanced with successive coats of black enamel.

BLANKET BOX

The blanket box, illustrated in Fig. C120, with its richly-grained wood and gleaming brass fittings, looks like a family heirloom. Since it is 42 in. long by 18 in. high, it

Fig. C118 (*below*). This telephone cupboard has space for shoes as well as directories.

Fig. C119 (*right*). Constructional details. A bottom rail and doors to hide the shoes could easily be added.

Fig. C120. This chest has an air of quality far above its modest cost and simple construction.

Flush brass handles

These edges reveneered after lid is sawn off

Brass hinges sunk into back of chest

Sides set in 1/16" to front and back of chest

Fig. C122. Constructional details.

Top set down 1/4"

42"

7" 7"

Flush brass handles

Solid brass butt hinges

Stay suitable length of fawn webbing

3 1/2"

18"

Front view

Side view

Box made up complete with concealed dowel joints

17 7/8"

Plan

Sides set in 1/16"

Position of dowels 2 5/8"

Bottom fitted any suitable way

2 1/2"
1/2"
1/2"
7/8"

Fig. C121. Plan sheet with dimensions.

will hold plenty of linen or blankets; alternatively it can be used as a telephone seat.

It is made from veneered chipboard, one panel of 3 ft. × 18 in. and four of 3 ft. 6 in. × 18 in.

Following the plan sheet in Fig. C121, begin by selecting two of the 3 ft. 6 in. × 18 in. boards for use as the back and front. Cut the 3 ft. × 18 in. board into two equal pieces for use as the ends, and make sure they *are* equal and square. Reduce the widths of the remaining 3 ft. 6 in. × 18 in. boards, which will form the top and bottom, to exactly the length of the end pieces, which will be about 17⅞ in. Also reduce the length of these top and bottom boards to 3 ft. 4½ in.

Assemble the chest by fixing the end pieces, with the un-veneered edge to the back, to the top and bottom boards, using concealed dowels as shown in Fig. C122. An easier method is to use countersunk brass screws with screw sockets. Make sure that the edges of all four pieces are flush at the front and back. Add the front and back boards in the same way. Note that they overlap the ends by about 1/16 in. The top and bottom (of the front and back boards) are set ¼ in. from the respective top and bottom edges of the ends.

You now have a completely closed box. Draw a line round this, 3½ in. from the top, and cut through with a tenon saw or other saw with fine teeth. Clean up the sawn edges and make sure the lid is a close fit on the lower part. Re-veneer all the cut edges with strip veneer, applied with an impact adhesive.

Fix the lid, using three 2½ in. brass butt hinges completely recessed into the lower part. A length of canvas webbing is fixed with screws and large washers to act as a stay. Two cabin locker catches in brass are fitted to the front of the lid.

Any of the usual methods of polishing can be used.

SAFETY GATE FOR THE STAIRS

The rails of the gate (Fig. C123) are made from 1 in. × 1¾ in. hardwood and the bars are cut from ⅝ in. dowel. The gate slides up and down and also pivots on a length of ⅝ in. dowel, the bottom end of which is fixed into a block screwed to the tread of the first stair, and the top end into a bracket screwed to the wall. When not required, the gate is raised and pushed back against the wall out of the way. Having the gate arranged to slide up and down on the pivot enables it to be secured in the closed position by dropping it so that it engages with wood strips attached to the newel post.

Dowel Bars and Cross Rails

To make the gate, cut the rails and bars to length, shaping one end of the rails as shown in Fig. C124. The length of the rails and the pivot will depend, of course, on where the gate is fitted; the bars should be cut 2 ft. long. Mark a centre line along the length of each rail and mark off the position of each bar. The rails can now be drilled to take the ends of the dowels; a centre-bit can conveniently be used for this. When drilling the top rail, care should be taken that the point of the bit does not break through and spoil what is to be the top surface of the rail. The

Fig. C123 (*left*). This safety gate is suitable for the top or the bottom of the stairs.

Figs. C124 and C125 (*below*). Details of the gate and bracket.

Fig. C126. The slip-down loft ladder is shown in the lowered position, ready for use.

holes in the bottom rail should be drilled as deeply as possible, but the cutters of the centre-bit must not break through. This allows for small differences in the length of the bars. Drill the end holes (farthest from the shaped end) right through and enlarge them slightly with the aid of a piece of sandpaper to give a sliding fit over the $\frac{5}{8}$ in. dowel.

After sandpapering to give a smooth finish, glue the bars to the top rail and then glue on the bottom rail. Pin here and there for extra strength. Lay the gate flat and let the glue dry.

Bracket Details

Arrangements should now be made to fix into position the dowel on which the gate slides. Drill a $\frac{5}{8}$ in. hole in the centre of a block about 3 in. × 1 $\frac{1}{4}$ in. × $\frac{5}{8}$ in. and screw the block down to receive the bottom end of the bar. Make a bracket similar to the one shown in Fig. C125 to secure the top end of the dowel and fix the bracket to the wall.

The free end of the gate drops between strips of $\frac{3}{4}$ in. × $\frac{1}{2}$ in. wood screwed to the newel post.

Although the gate described in this article was fitted at the bottom of the stairs, in many cases a similar gate could be fitted at the top. However, it would be advisable to replace the dowel on which the gate slides and pivots by something stronger—a length of conduit, for instance.

SLIP-DOWN LOFT LADDER

Access to the loft may present awkward problems, which the cleverly-designed ladder described here may solve. It is shown operational in Fig. C126.

The first thing to decide is size and position of the trap door. This may not arise if the existing trap is big enough. Otherwise work to multiples of the joist centres and enlarge the present trap. Remember that the ladder swings over when the trap is closed and that clearance is needed above as well as behind the trap door, as shown in Fig. C127.

The principle of this sliding ladder is that the two ladders together are first brought down by pulling a cord hanging from the trap door. At this point the ladders are vertical and can be reached. A bolt is slid back and both ladders (one over the other) slide downwards until a stop prevents further movement. Then one ladder slides over the other until a second stop comes into play when the ladder is 9 ft. long (or longer if required). This is about the right length for a modern house with a storey height of 8 ft. or thereabouts.

To return the ladder, reverse the actions and the ladder (being counter-balanced) will return to position by the lightest swing on the trap door. The sides of both ladders are of 3 in. × 1 in. softwood. The rungs are of similar section so long as the ladder is not made too wide. The sliding is achieved as shown in Fig. C128. Two or three hardwood strips are fixed across the trap door frame and a built-up timber angle is fixed for the length of the trap door.

The top ladder now slides under this angle, bearing on the hardwood strips. Notch the treads as shown to clear this angle arrangement and groove the side members to let the treads into the sides by $\frac{1}{4}$ in. each side. Nail through from the outside and punch down the heads. When setting out the ladder allow about 8 in. between treads. The lower ladder is wider than the upper and

Fig. C127. To lower the ladder, pull back the bolt (*left*), then both ladders will slide down until the lower one reaches the floor.

Fig. C128. Constructional details and dimensions.

MAKE ABOUT 3'-6" TO GIVE HEADROOM

BOLT OR SCREW HERE AS STOP ON TOP OF LADDER

METAL STRAP

TIMBER ANGLE ON TRAP DOOR

HARDWOOD RUNNERS

5'-3"

COUNTER BALANCE WEIGHT HERE

METAL STRAP
WEIGHT
BRACKET
HARDWOOD STRIPS
LADDERS STOP
6"×1"

1'-6" OVERLAP

8'-0"

UPPER LADDER (fixed to trapdoor)

RUNGS AND SIDES 3"×1"

2"×1" FRAMING
HINGE
CEILING JOIST
¼" PLYWOOD
TRIMMED JOIST QUADRANT

5'-3"

METAL BRACKET

1'-3¾"
TREAD 3"×1" 1'-0½" LONG

BOLT FIXED TO TRAP DOOR SHOOTS THROUGH BOTH LADDERS FIXING THEM IN THE UP POSITION

HARDWOOD STRIPS

SECTION A-A

ENLARGED DETAIL

WEIGHT

STRAP

METAL BRACKET ONE EACH SIDE OF LOWER LADDER

METAL STRAP

TREADS, THIS SECTION

2⅞"
LOWER LADDER
1'-2"

1'-0"
UPPER LADDER
3"×1"
2"×1"

NOTCH FOR RUNNERS

2"×1"

HARDWOOD STRIP

SCREW OR BOLT, METAL BRACKET STOPS AGAINST THIS

LOWER LADDER

straddles it. The rungs therefore have to be vertical to allow the sliding actions.

Make the lower ladder ¼ in. wider than the upper to allow for any swelling of timber later. Let the ladder overlap about 1 ft. 6 in. when extended. Two metal brackets are needed. These are fixed to the lower ladder at the point where the upper ladder ends. The brackets are angle-shaped as shown and should be of ⅛ in. steel at least. It is wise to strap each ladder under the top and bottom rungs with 1/16 in. × 1 in. steel flat to prevent the sides coming apart. Use bolts or screws for stops, two at the top of the top ladder and two at the bottom of the top ladder, on which the metal brackets engage. These stops must be good long screws, well driven and left projecting. They are best fixed when the ladder is in position when it is easier to see how it works and how far it should extend. The weight itself can only be determined by trial and error. The correct counter-balance should mean that when the ladders have been slid up and bolted, a light swing of the trap door should suffice to close it. Stop the trap from slamming by holding the cord. The bolt has to take quite a bit of load so do fix this securely. Drill a hole in the side of both ladders and ensure that the bolt-shoot is long enough to secure both ladders. Ensure that stout hinges are used as they take the entire load, of course.

Nothing can be stored behind the ladder as when the trap is swung up the ladder goes through 90° and lies flat, its weight then keeping the trap closed. Much of this job has to be done when the ladder is being fixed by adjustment and trial and error. To avoid any possibility of the trap opening suddenly, fit a small spring catch on the side of the frame. For the counterweight use the heaviest material available (lead or copper is ideal) otherwise so much will be needed as to be impractical. Also fix the weight as high as possible on the lower ladder. This increases the lever arm and gives a more advantageous result. A piece of copper 1 ft. long × 2 in. wide × ½ in. thick is about the weight needed. The cord should be left just long enough to be reached and can be put at one side so as not to obstruct the landing. Waxing the timber helps the sliding action; if the timber is to be painted or varnished, do this before you put the pieces together.

STAIRHEAD CUPBOARD

Here is an easy idea for a landing cupboard particularly suitable where the landing is too narrow for the built-in type. This cupboard is shown in Fig. C129.

The space over the stair well is usually wasted and if the stairway is at all dark it is possible to combine the cupboard with a light installation in one unit.

Reeded Hardboard.

Blockboard Door.

Pegboard Shelf.

2' Tubular Heater, and switch.

Frosted Glass.

40 w Lamp.

Reeded Hardboard.

Shelf on 1" dowels.

Existing Bannister.

Fig. C129. This stairhead cupboard utilises space which is usually wasted. It can supply a useful light, too.

The framing is made of 2 in. × 1 in., and 1 in. × 1 in. timber is screwed to the ceiling joists and plugged and screwed to the walls. The existing banister rail provides a support for the front and side members.

Reeded hardboard is panel-pinned to the outside cupboard wall, and shelves are fitted inside.

A 40-watt lamp is coupled to the existing 2-way switched hall light and concealed behind a frosted glass panel. This satisfactorily lights the stairs and landing.

As a means of adding interest to the wall which faces the stairs below the cupboard, it is a good idea to cover it with reeded hardboard, and add a small shelf supported on 1 in. dowel rods.

The cupboard illustrated has been adapted to an airing cupboard by means of fixing a 2 ft. tubular heater behind the lamp compartment. This is fed from the junction box in the loft via a cable simply dropped through the ceiling. Of course, in this case the shelves have to be made of slats or pegboard to allow the heat to rise, and suitable ventilation holes provided at the top of the cupboard.

LIVING ROOM

COMBINED POUFFE AND WORKBOX

This modern pouffe (Fig. C130) provides a handy additional seat for the fireside or TV viewing and at the same time serves as a workbox. The interior is fully lined and padded, and the top is upholstered with foam rubber.

A general idea of the construction is shown in the end elevation in Fig. C131. The carcase consists of two sets of main frames, which are joined by an upright at each corner, all angles being braced with triangular blocks of hardwood. The blocks which house the turned legs are glued and screwed to the underside of the lower main frame. Construction commences by making up the two main frames, one of which is shown in the plan view, Fig. C132. Material required is 2 in. wide and ¾ in. thick hardwood; the front and sides are slightly rounded to remove the square look from the finished job, while the rear rail is kept straight. Begin the work by making the halved joints at each corner, but do not secure at this stage.

Select one of the rails and mark a line in the centre at each end, the marking gauge being set at 1 in. for this operation. This gives the 1 in. measurement shown at the bottom of the left hand corner of the drawing. Mark the centre of the length with the try-square, this dimension being 7½ in. Bend a piece of springy lath to mate up with the two ends and the centre, and hold in place while the curved line is marked off. The surplus material, shown shaded in the drawing, is then cut away and the curved edge must be sanded smooth. This one rail can act as a template for all the others.

Halved Joints

The halved joints are glued-and-screwed, but the screws must be kept away from the centre, as a dowel hole has to be drilled in this position through each joint. When the joints are made, there will be an overhang of timber at each corner which must now be trimmed away (Fig. C132).

The same drawing also shows the bracing of the corners, for which ¾ in. square timber is required. The exact size of the braces is unimportant, provided each one is wide enough to provide a ground to which the 3 in. long leg blocks can be fitted. No braces are needed for the upper main frame. The two completed main frames are joined by four 1¼ in. square uprights. When positioning these uprights, let the two front faces overhang the corners in each case; these two faces must be planed away to

mate up with the curve of the rails. The uprights are dowelled in position, each dowel being ½ in. in diameter, and, in addition, corner blocks are glued-and-screwed in place (Figs. C131 and C133). The rounding of the corner faces of the uprights to mate with the curve of the rails is carried out after the two frames have been joined and the glue has set.

At this point, cut a piece of ¾ in. chipboard to the shape of the top main frame, and cut recesses for hinges in the straight rail of this frame only. Do not actually fit

Fig. C130. This pouffe is also a useful workbox.

this lid until it has been padded and covered, as described later.

The legs can be purchased, but if a small lathe is available they can be made quite easily (Fig. C134). Start by making the blocks into which the legs fit. Material for each is ⅞ in. thick hardwood, 1¾ in. wide × 3½ in. long. Mark across the width of each block, 1¾ in. from the end.

Figs. C131, C132 and C133.

Chamfer the front section, reducing the end thickness to ⅝ in., so providing an angle. In the centre of the cut-away section, drill a 1 in.-diameter hole square with the chamfered face, and then round off the outer end of the block as shown in the plan view. The leg is turned from 1¼ in. round material, the top being reduced to 1 in. to fit the hole in the block. From this shoulder the leg tapers off to give a final diameter at the bottom of 1 in. Cut a wedge-shaped saw-cut in the top reduced part and make a wedge to fit this. Glue the leg into the hole in the block and drive the glued wedge into place. When the glue has set, cut away and sand smooth the section of the leg projection above the block. The leg fixing blocks are screwed diagonally to the corner braces of the lower main frame after the covering and lining have been completed.

Covering and Lining

Cover the frames with thin plywood. On the outside it is glued and pinned to the frames using cramps. Ply should therefore be cut to be a neat fit between the frame rails and uprights, and it should be remembered, when fitting the braces, that they must be set back to form rebates at these points.

Cut the lining material to size, allowing about an extra 1½ in. in width for tacking. Drop the material through the bottom opening and secure along the lower frame rails with a line of tacks. Spread a thin layer of wadding over the ply lining and bring the material up over this. The bottom edge of the material is thus doubled over and the tack heads hidden (Fig. C135). The free edge of the lining is strained over the top of the upper main frame where it is tacked in place. Fig. C135 also shows how to fit the outer cover. Again the material is allowed to hang down through the bottom opening while the top edge is secured.

To give a firm edge here, a strip of 1 in. wide cardboard is used; the material edge is placed behind this and the tacking is done through the cardboard and material into the top member of the main frame. Place a thick layer of wadding over the outer ply skin and pull the cover over it. Strain at the centre first of all and tack off to the under face of the lower main frame. Continue tacking from the centre towards each end. When the end is reached, double the cover over and tack. Finish the edges by stitching as shown in Fig. C136.

Base and Top

When the lining and covering are complete, measure off and cut the base. This is ⅜ in. thick plywood, and should be a neat fit between the lined faces. It is not practical to give exact measurements, as much will depend on the amount of wadding used and the thickness of the lining material. It should be a push-in fit, resting on the four corner braces and fixed in place by screws from the underside.

The base for the foam rubber top is the piece of ¾ in. chipboard which has already been cut to the shape of the top main frame. To the upper face of the chipboard, a shaped piece of 1 in.-thick rubber is secured by an adhesive after all four edges of the rubber have been chamfered as illustrated at A in Fig. C137. The covering material is tacked to the front edges of the chipboard and, because of the curved shape, tacking should be commenced in the centre of each side. At each corner the material is folded round and tacked down, and a pleat formed in the surplus as shown at B in Fig. C137. The lid can now be hinged to the main frame.

Finally, fit an automatic stay (if required), fit and stain the legs, and the job is complete.

Figs. C134–C137.

KNITTING AND SEWING CABINET

The construction of the cabinet shown in Fig. C138 is extremely simple—there are no joints to cut, and tools required are kept to a minimum.

The body of the cabinet is made from well-seasoned material, the cutting following the pattern set in Fig. C139. These pieces, if not already from planed wood, are finished and marked for position of the compartments, and ½ in. holes are drilled to take the back rods.

For the partitions and drop front, use ½ in. ply. Fig. C140 shows how the 24 in. square sheet is cut, making allowance for wastage and smoothing down.

The front leg assembly shown in Fig. C141 is made from two pieces of 1 in. × 1 in., the 9 in. length allowing for trimming upon assembly, joined by the front rod for which ½ in. holes are drilled at about 3½ in. from the rounded-off ends.

To assemble, nail and glue the top and bottom to the sides, not forgetting to include the back rod. Similarly, nail and glue the vertical divider, shelves and horizontal divider, and pin and glue the hardboard in place to form the back.

Then the front legs are marked in position, holes drilled and countersunk (two to each leg) through the cabinet sides, and the legs fitted. If necessary, trim the legs at this stage to make the cabinet stable.

After ensuring that nails and screws are below the surface, fill and rub down when dry. Then fit the drop front with two 1½ in. brass hinges and a ball-catch as shown in Fig. C142.

The surfaces inside and out can be finished to personal taste—painted, varnished, covered with adhesive plastic, etc.

Finally, pierce holes for the reel pegs and glue them in.

Drop leaf stays, or brass chain, may be fitted. A small handle near the centre top of the drop front completes the job.

Fig. C138. This useful cabinet is deceptively easy to make; no joints are required.

MATERIALS

Timber (preferably finished sizes) A, B, and C in Fig. C139, all ⅝ in. cut from one 7 ft. length. A, 22¾ in. × 8 in. (top); B, 22¾ in. × 7½ in. (base); C, two, 19 in. × 8 in. overall (ends)

Plywood: from one ½ in. sheet, 24 in. square. G, D, E, and F as marked off in Fig. C140. G, 22¾ in. × 10 in. (drop front); D, 10 in. × 7 in. (vertical divider); E, two, 8 in. × 7 in. (shelves); F, 14½ in. × 2½ in. (horizontal divider)

Legs and Rods: H, two pieces of 1 in. × 1 in. × 9 in. long (legs); I, two ½ in. diameter dowel, 22¾ in. long (rods); one piece of ¼ in. diameter dowel for reel pegs (about 12 in.)

Hardboard: J, 24 in. × 12 in. × ⅛ in. (back)

Also panel pins, nails, screws, glue, cabinet handle, hinges and brass chain

Fig. C139.

Fig. C140.

Fig. C141.

Fig. C142.

Fig. C143. Combined book-trough and magazine rack.

BOOKTROUGH AND MAGAZINE RACK

A combined booktrough and magazine rack is useful especially when it is fitted with swivel castors to enable it to be moved readily into the most convenient position at any time. Fig. C143 shows the completed rack and Fig. C144 gives details of its general construction. All the dowels are ½ in. diameter and 18 in. long; the sides are cut from 9 in. × 1 in. cleaned whitewood and the bottom from 5 in. × 1 in. cleaned whitewood. The two sides are cut to length and clamped together, the face of one side is marked out for drilling as shown in Fig. C145 and both sides are left clamped together during drilling. To avoid jagged holes, drill from one side and when the spur of the drill just comes through the wood, turn over and complete the drilling from the other side. Mark out and cut out the rebate in the inside edges of the lower ends, as shown in the drawing. Drill holes centrally in the bottom edge, 1 in. in, to take the castor sockets. Radius corners and sand all surfaces with fine glasspaper. Cut the bottom piece to size and radius bottom edges. Coat ends and bottom all over, except the rebate and the end of the bottom piece, with two coats of wood dye (mahogany). The wood dye is best applied with a soft cloth.

Assembly

Spread some glue in the holes in one side and push all dowels into place with their ends projecting ¼ in. Next glue holes in the other side and push corresponding dowel ends into position, also projecting. Glue ends of bottom piece and nail to bottom of sides. Remove any surplus glue from around the dowels. Hammer-in castor sockets and push castors into place. Leave until the glue has hardened, then coat all over with two coats of shellac varnish to give the two-tone finish. Prepare suitable varnish by putting a few ounces of lemon flake shellac into a container and pouring-in methylated spirit just to cover the shellac. The varnish is ready for use after a few hours when the shellac has completely dissolved.

½" DIA. × 12" LONG BIRCH DOWELS

1" DIA. SWIVEL CASTORS

BOTTOM GLUED AND NAILED TO SIDES

DOWELS PROJECT ¼" AT EACH END

Figs. C144 and C145.   Constructional details.

MATERIALS
2 off 18 in. × 9 in. × 1 in. cleaned whitewood
1 off 17 in. × 5 in. × 1 in. cleaned whitewood
15 off 18 in. × ½ in. diam. birch dowels
4 off 1 in. diam. swivel castors
Wood dye, glue, shellac varnish and nails

PAPER AND MAGAZINE RACK

This rack (Fig. C146) is light and easy to handle. The materials required are very few, and, as most of the plywood can be picked up as offcuts from any timber merchants, the cost is kept to a minimum. Even if veneered plywood is used the cost is quite reasonable, and the rack itself can easily be polished.

Cutting to size

The first thing to do is to cut all the pieces of plywood to the required size and shape, and sandpaper all edges smooth. Details are given in Fig. C147. The centrepiece has a grip space cut in it; this is easily done with a fret or coping saw. Finish off by filing the inside of the aperture smooth and rounding off the two top corners.

½" RAD. CORNER

2¼"

9"×1" CLEANED WHITEWOOD

5"×1" CLEANED WHITEWOOD

BOTTOM

17"

RADIUS BOTTOM EDGES

SIDES

½" DIA. HOLES 2" BETWEEN CENTRES

DRILL TO SUIT CASTOR 1" FROM EDGE

18"

12"

2½"

2"

REBATE INSIDE EDGE ¾"×½"

Dowelling

Once the ends, base and centre have been cut, the dowels for the sides should be prepared. The top dowel is ⅝ in. diam. and this is drilled in seven places to take the ¼ in. diam. dowels that form the uprights. Care should be taken when drilling the ⅝ in. dowel; it is easy to split or drill right through, especially if you are using an electric drill. Also, ensure that the holes are centred and in a straight line. Failure to do this makes the sides rather difficult to fit. Assemble the dowels with a touch of glue in each joint and lay to one side to set in position.

Drilling and Dowel Holes

The next operation is to drill the base to take the ¼ in. dowels. Theoretically, as the sides are sloping, the holes for the dowels should correspond to the angle of the slope. However, in this case the angle is so shallow that the holes may be drilled vertically and the sides bent downwards. This actually tightens the dowels in the base, and the strain put on them is only slight.

Legs

Whether the legs are fitted or not is a matter for personal choice. If they are used they are simply fitted with one screw each and glued to the side. Secured in this way, any weight in the rack forces the base down causing the screws to act as pivots, in which case the tops of the legs are pressed even more tightly together.

Polish or Paint

Before finally assembling the parts, decide whether to polish the rack or to paint it. In either case it must be done at this stage, as it is impossible to make a good job of it when the rack is assembled.

One method of polishing is to give the parts several coats of shellac, rubbing down well with fine glasspaper after each application. Finish off by rubbing polish in with a piece of steel wool, working in the direction of the grain. This brings up the grain even more and gives the wood a wax lustre. If the rack is to be painted, prime all parts and paint in the selected colours.

Assembly of the Parts

Finally, assemble all parts, using panel pins and glue for the sides and centre piece, and a screw each for the legs.

Fit the ⅝ in. dowels to the side by drilling into the ends

Fig. C146. This magazine and paper rack is a neat-looking project for the beginner to make in inexpensive plain or veneered plywood.

and fitting in a short length of ¼ in. dowel. This dowel fits tightly into a hole drilled in the plywood end and is glued into place. When the dowel is firmly set in place, cut flush with the end and polish over.

Elegant Variations

Using the same basic principles, various other articles can be made. For instance a small book rack; or even a flower-pot stand, the base of which could be made to take a layer of earth for direct growing (Fig. C148).

Together with the paper rack, and all polished or painted similarly, they would make an attractive and useful trio.

MATERIALS
¼ in. Plywood 2 off 7 in. × 10½ in.
            1 off 13 in. × 18 in.
½ in. Plywood 1 off 18 in. × 6 in.
⅜ in. Hardwood 4 off 1 ft. × 1½ in.
⅝ in. Dowel 1 off 3 ft.
¼ in. Dowel 4 off 3 ft.

Fig. C147. Constructional details.

Fig. C148. A flower-pot stand and a book rack based on the same original design.

A SMALL TABLE

Made out of blockboard, the table in Fig. C149 is very simple to make.

Method

Decide from an examination of the blockboard which of the two sides is best for the top. Mark out the other side (underside) as shown in Fig. C150.

Draw four pencil lines, 7 in. in length, bisecting each of the four corners at an angle of 45 deg. At the end of each line strike off another line at right angles to provide a guide for fixing the baseplates supplied with each set of legs. The baseplate has holes through which the fixing screws will pass, and in the centre is a built-in nut to receive the built-in bolt with which each leg is provided. The plate is so designed that the leg will protrude at an angle; hence the need for setting them well back from the edges of the table (Fig. C151).

Fix the plates into position, using sturdy ⅝ in. screws that will really grip the blockboard firmly; then fit the legs. Turn the whole lot over; from now on the table is its own work-bench.

Preparing the Blockboard

The plastic covering material is available in wood grain effect and, although extremely tough, is quite thin; thus the surface of the table must be absolutely smooth and free from scratches or other cavities. Fill in as needed, allow to dry thoroughly, and then rub down with fine sandpaper wrapped round a wooden block.

Laying the Surface

Very easy indeed, if done the right way. Lay the material across the table and make sure that there is a generous overlap all round. Now, starting at one of the 2 ft. 3 in. ends, peel off about 1 ft. of the paper backing and lay the material lightly in position. With the aid of a duster, smooth the material down, working from the centre and making sure that no air-bubbles form.

Trimming the Edges

The material is now smoothed firmly right to the edges of the table and cut at the four corners as shown in the directions printed on the backing paper. Using the palm of the hand, it is worked over the sides of the blockboard and pressed into position. The surplus is trimmed off with a razor blade or trimming knife.

Fixing the Lipping

The hardwood lipping, which has previously been carefully rubbed down with sandpaper, is now mitred at the corners with the aid of a mitre block and fixed into position with panel pins; these are punched well home and made good with plastic wood, tinted to the colour of the wood used (Fig. C152).

MATERIALS

Blockboard, 4 ft. × 2 ft. 3 in. × ¾ in.
Adhesive material, 1½ yd.
Hardwood lipping, 13 ft. × ¾ in. × ¾ in.
Set of 4 legs, 38 in. length, with fixing plates.

Fig. C149. Sturdy, easily cleaned, will withstand heat up to boiling point, and it is easily dismantled.

Fig. C150. How to mark out the underside for the baseplate.

Underside of table marked out   45°

7"

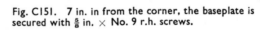

Fig. C151. 7 in. in from the corner, the baseplate is secured with ⅝ in. × No. 9 r.h. screws.

Fig. C152. Fixing the lipping.

Fig. C153. This extending table will accommodate six people when both leaves are out.

Fig. C154 (left). How it is done.

FIG. 2

EXTENDING LEAF

Fig. C155 (below). Pin details.

PINS TO PROTRUDE 1in. AND 6in. FROM EDGE

1in.   1in.

MORTISE AND TENON JOINTS

16in.

Fig. C157 (left and below). Legs and rails details.

⅝in. ⅜in. ⅝in.   1in.

END RAIL

Fig. C156. Tongue and groove details.

LEG

GROOVED SIDE RAIL   FIG.4

23½in.

30½in.

AN EXTENDING TABLE

The extending dining-room table seen in Fig. C153 is large enough for six persons when both leaves are out. The size of the table is 3 ft. 2 in. × 2 ft. 9 in. extending to 4 ft. 4 in. It is 30 in. high. Perhaps the most difficult part of making an extending table is knowing how the leaves extend, so that they do not lift when carrying any weight. This is how it is done; on the underside of the leaves there are screwed two L-shaped lengths of wood; the tongues of each length fit into a groove enabling the leaves to open and close, Fig. C154. When the leaves are in the closed position, two pins in the edge of one leaf fit into corresponding holes in the other leaf, Fig. C155. Similarly there are pins and holes in the extension piece.

With a reasonably well-equipped workshop it is quite easy to make the tongues and grooves by routing, planing, or sawing from solid. But if the correct tools are not available the best thing is to ask the timber merchant or handyman's supplier to make the tongued pieces and cut the grooves. They will usually do this work for a few shillings extra. The measurements are given in Fig. C156.

Start by tapering the legs to about 1½ in. at the bottom. Join the two short rails to the legs by glued mortise-and-tenon joints. When the glue has hardened, screw the long rails to the legs (Fig. C157), and countersink the screws sufficiently to enable them to be covered with filler. Place the two leaves upside down on the floor with their inner edges together. Place the rest of the table also upside

MATERIALS

4 Legs 31 in. × 2 in.
2 Rails 19 in. × 4 in. × 1 in.
2 Mahogany leaves 33 in. × 19 in. × ¾ in.
1 Mahogany extension piece 33 in. × 14 in. × ¾ in.
2 Rails with grooves (see Fig. C156) 36 in × 5 in. × 1 in.
4 Tongued lengths of hardwood 14 in. long (see Fig. C156 for other measurements).
2 Centre buffers 3 in. × 1 in. × 1 in.
4 Wood screws 2 in. × ¼ in. approx.
Sundries, nails, screws, etc.

down on top of the leaves. Get all square and straight and fit the four L-shaped lengths into position with the tongues in the grooves and with a space of 3 in. between the lengths on each side. Screw these to the leaves.

Turn the table on to its correct side and try the leaves for sliding easily. A little wax polish applied to the tongues and grooves will help. Next screw the two wood screws into the inner edge of one leaf about 6 in. from each side. Leave the screws protruding an inch and cut off the heads. Drill corresponding holes into the other leaf (Fig. C155). Do the same with the extension piece, so that there are pins in one edge and holes in the other to correspond with those in the leaves. The holes must be just slightly larger than the pins to allow the pins to enter easily.

Screw small pieces of wood on to the underside of the leaves to stop them coming right out. Close the two leaves and, with the joint in the centre, screw a 3 in. strip to the inner side of the two grooved rails, to act as buffers to the tongued lengths. These will ensure the leaves always close with the joint in the centre.

Smooth all edges and round off the outer corners of the leaves. Finish the legs and rails with black enamel, and stain the leaves and extension piece; finish off with a polyurethane glaze. When not in use, the extension piece lies underneath the leaves with its end resting on the two short sides.

A DINING SUITE

The complete suite, illustrated in Fig. C158, consists of a set of eight upholstered chairs, and a full-length matching table.

Dining Chairs

The set consists of six plain chairs and two carvers which are identical apart from the arms. Except for the top back rail, everything is cut from the straight. The com-

ponent parts are shown in Fig. C159 and the constructional details given in Fig. C160. Glued and dowelled joints are employed and a dowelling jig, such as that shown, is a great help.

The method of making is clearly shown in Figs. C161–C168. The chairs can be upholstered in any of the usual ways. The seats can be fixed or lift-out squab type; both have the usual webbing underneath with padding or foam. In the chairs illustrated here foam was used. This is available in a wide variety of thickness—cavity sheets (that is the kind that has lots of holes on the wrong side) from 1½ in. upwards, and plain foam (same both sides) from ½ in. upwards. The thicker material is really needed only on the seat. It is, of course, possible to get seat squabs ready moulded to shape, but they are more expensive.

If making up seat squabs, it's a good idea to stick a small square (about 9 in.) of plain ½ in. foam in the centre of the underside of the squab. This gives a slightly domed effect to the seat. You can also taper the thickness of the seat to give it a slight backward slope. Do all the cutting with really sharp scissors or knife. It is a good idea to stick on 2 in. tape or calico strips to the sides of the squabs to give a way of tacking them to the chair bases. Fix the back squab in place first, tacking down the tape. Then

Fig. C159 (below). The completed parts of a chair ready for assembly:

1   Seat panel
2   Front legs
3   Front seat member
4   Leg braces
5   Side seat member
6   Seat corner blocks
7   Rear seat member
8   Back legs
9   Backrest panels
10   Top backrest member

Fig. C158 (above). The 6 ft. 6 in. of length provides room for three people on each side and one at each end.

SIDE ELEVATION

FRONT

BACK PANELS
FROM ⅛ in. HARDBOARD

SEE
DETAIL
BELOW

CUT BOTH
ARM MEMBERS
FROM ¾ in.

2 in.

2 in.

BACK

BACK SUPPORT
¾ in. SQUARE

1 in.

14½ in.

SEAT PANEL FROM
¼ in. HARDBOARD

CORNER BLOCKS
⅝ in. THICK

SEAT SUPPORTS
⅝ in. × ¾ in.

12⅝ in.

10½ in.
9 in.
7 in.
1¼ in.
13 in.
32 in.
3¾ in.
1 in.
1⅛ in.

13 in.
2 in. × ⅞ in.

14½ in.

2 in. × ⅞ in.

2 in. × ⅞ in.

1 in.

15¼ in.

5/16 in. DIA.
DOWELS

1 in. × ½ in.

14 in.

14⅛ in.

17⅜
in.

1 in. × ½ in.

5/16 in. DIA.
DOWELS

FRONT LEGS
1¼ in. SQ. AT TOP
TAPERING TO 1 in. SQ.
AT BOTTOM

3/16 in. DIA.
DOWELS

BACKREST MEMBERS
ROUNDED OFF TO
CONFORM WITH
SHAPE OF BACK

1 in.

1¼
in.

1 in.

1 in.

THIS MEMBER MAY BE CUT FROM A BLOCK
2 in. × 2 in. OR MADE UP FROM THREE PIECES
OF PLYWOOD ⅓ in. THICK AND GLUED
OVER A FORMER

Fig. C160 (above).   Chair details.

1 in.   14⅛ in.   2 in.

18½ in.

15 in.

2 in.

17⅜
in.

3¾ in.

1 in.

FRONT ELEVATION

Fig. C161.   A dowelling jig
ensures accurate location of
holes.

Fig. C162.   Drill through each
bush in turn.

Fig. C163.   Bushes are available for
¼ in., 5/16 in. and ⅜ in.

Fig. C166
(left).
Corner blocks
strengthen
frame.

Fig. C164.   Use good high-strength
glue.

Fig. C165 (left).   Tap the seat rail
into place.

Fig. C167. A dowel draws the tenon firmly into its mortice.

Fig. C168. Use hardboard or plywood for back and seat.

Fig. C171. Tack the corners with gimp pins and braid.

Fig. C172. Table details.

Fig. C169. Foam rubber is the simplest upholstery. Use thick on seat, thin on back.

HOLES FOR ⅜in.DIA. DOWELS

OAK VENEERED FLUSH DOOR. THREE EDGES WILL NEED FACING

6ft.6in.

2in.
4in.
1¼in.
¼in.
2in.
4½in.
3¾in.
1½in.

7in.
2ft.6in.
6¾in.

12in.

1⅜in.

THESE MEMBERS ARE SHAPED FROM 4in.x2in., USE OFFCUTS TO FORM INWARD FACING SUPPORTS

LEG SUPPORTS ARE SCREWED AND GLUED TO TABLE TOP

ALL LEG JOINTS SHOULD BE GLUED AND DOWELLED FOR MAXIMUM STRENGTH

27¾in.

10in.
1in.
1¼in.DIA.
4ft.9in.

6½in.

10¼in.

USE SELECTED TIMBER FOR LEG PARTS. THIS IS SELECTED OAK

2in.
1⅜in.
3¾in.
3in.
1½in.

HOLES FOR ⅜in.DIA. DOWELS

HOLES FOR ⅜in.DIA.DOWELS

TAPER LEG FROM 4½in. AT TOP TO 3in. AT BOTTOM

FEET CUT FROM 1⅜in.THICK PLY AND EBONIZED

1¼in.
½in.
1½in.
2½in.
1⅜in.

⅜in.DIA.DOWEL 2in. LONG

Fig. C170. Mitre the covers at the corners.

Fig. C173 (right). Foot dimensions.

2in.
2¼in.
1in.
6in.
2½in.

FOOT DIMENSIONS

2¾in.
21½in.
2¾in.

Fig. C174. One bearer, one leg, one foot, and the stretcher.

Fig. C175. The bearer should be a close hand fit.

Fig. C176. Good glue and two dowels are required.

fix the seat squab, and tack the tape to the seat rails.

The cover material is simply cut to shape and tacked in place with gimp pins and braid.

Figs. C169 to C171 show various stages in the covering.

Dining Table

The table is a family affair, a full eight-seater. The top is bought ready-made in the form of a good quality flush-panelled door, obtainable from any good timber merchant. Oak veneered is fairly easy to get; mahogany and similar veneers are a little more expensive, but can be obtained to order.

The recommended size, 6 ft. 6 in. by 2ft. 6 in., is a stock one, and since this size is just right and attractively proportioned for a refectory table top, there is no alteration or cutting of any sort involved.

The rest of the construction is not complicated, but it does call for careful marking out, cutting on the waste side of your marking out lines, and patient fitting. The drawings in Figs. C172 and C173 show how the base is constructed. A slot in the top of each upright engages in a housing at the centre of the cross pieces. It's better to cut the slot first and then make the housing to fit, offering up frequently, making on the tight side to begin with and easing gradually to a firm press fit. The same applies to the bottom slot through which the feet pass, but the fit is not so precise here, since dowels are also used.

The illustrations in Figs. C172 to C178 give the inside story of the dining table and show clearly how it's made. The top is bought ready made as a flush door. All that is necessary is to make two-off of the other parts, except the single stretcher which braces the legs.

Glue and dowels hold the table together, but use a good high-strength glue and keep the parts under moderate pressure while the glue is setting. Most flush doors have several internal cross pieces, and one of these should be found near each end so that the bearers to which the legs are joined can be given a few screws as well as glue. Chamfer dowel tips, and cut a glue nick in each.

CONTEMPORARY TABLES

Though it is not possible to include all the various types of contemporary design, details are given for a few of the simplest and most attractive styles.

Rectangular and Square

The rectangular table is easily made, and blends well with both conventional and contemporary furniture.

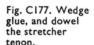

Fig. C177. Wedge glue, and dowel the stretcher tenon.

Fig. C178. Glue-and-screw bracket to inside top of each leg.

The first step is to decide upon the size, bearing in mind that larger rooms demand large tables. A practical size is about 30 in. × 18 in. with 15 in. legs—ideal for use as a coffee table. The thickness should not be greater than $\frac{3}{8}$ in. if the table is to be square-edged; or greater than $\frac{5}{8}$ in. if the edge is to be bevelled.

Having determined the size, obtain a piece of ply from the local wood merchant, allowing an inch on all measurements for trimming. While it is not difficult to make round, tapered legs if a lathe is available, smart sand-finished legs together with mounting plates, sold in sets of four, are quite inexpensive.

Check the sides of the ply to see if one is square. If not, draw a straight line parallel to, and approximately $\frac{1}{2}$ in. from, the longest side, and cut this edge off with a panel saw. Measure 30 in. along this side, leaving about $\frac{1}{2}$ in.

Fig. C179. Locating leg plates in a square or rectangular table.

Fig. C180. Marking-out plan for a boomerang table top. It is essential that the dimensions be geometrically balanced. Locate the leg plates last.

Fig. C181. An elementary but practical pencil-holder for bevelling.

Fig. C182. Assembling the rails and surface bearers of the long low table.

Quadrant

1½" block

Fig. C183. Side elevation of the long low table, showing the distinctive design—two-tone finish and brass legs, set vertically.

spare at each end. Using a square, draw lines at right angles at each end of the 30 in. length. Measure 18 in. along these lines and join the two points to produce a rectangle. Measure this last line and check the angles at

each end. If it is not exactly 30 in. and all the angles exactly 90°, then one or more of the angles or measurements is incorrect.

When they are correct, trim off one of the sides and again check the measurements.

When satisfied with the angles, cut off the two remaining sides.

Look at the grain on each side, and decide which will make the more attractive top. On the underside mark four lines 3 in. from the sides and join the intersections with the nearest corners. Each leg plate usually has five holes, three at one end and two at the other. Place the centre hole of the three on the diagonal so that one hole from the pair at the opposite end lies on each of the remaining lines, as shown in Fig. C179.

Holding the plate in position, use a sharp point to make a small impression on the wood through each hole. Run five round-headed screws into the wood leaving ⅓ protruding from the plate, and then remove the screws and plates. (When selecting screws make sure that they are not too long, but, in view of the thickness of the plate, a screw of the same thickness as the wood can be used, i.e. ⅜ in. screw for ⅜ in. ply.)

If the sides are to be square, take the sharpness off the corners and edges with a piece of sandpaper wrapped round a block of wood. Finish by staining and polishing.

To make a nest of tables, use legs 18 in., 15 in. and 12 in. in length and ensure that, while the width remains the same, the length is adjusted so that there is about half an inch between the end of one table and the legs of the table above.

Square tables should always be higher than rectangular ones.

If the edge is to be bevelled, draw lines on the underside which are separated from the edge by margins equal in width to the thickness of the wood, e.g. on ⅝ in. wood draw lines ⅝ in. from the sides. Trim these 45° triangular pieces of wood off the sides, but do not cut too near the remaining edge as plywood has a tendency to tear and splinter when cut like this. The corners can be curved top and bottom by using a coin. Sand, using a coarse grade paper and a block; finish with fine paper.

While the sharpness of the bottom edge is smoothed away the top is usually left sharp and, if this is desired, care should be taken to ensure that the edge is absolutely straight, as slight imperfections are conspicuous.

Finish by staining and polishing.

Boomerang-shaped Tables

Boomerang-shaped tables are extremely useful because they fit snugly against the sides of armchairs and are consequently less likely to be knocked over.

There is an infinite variety of shapes for these tables but one of the simplest and most practical is as follows.

Take a 3 ft.× 2 ft. piece of ½ in. ply, which allows ample wood for two table tops, and, using a compass, construct a circle of 8 in. radius (1 ft. 4 in. diam.) in one of the corners (the largest circle shown in Fig. C180). Draw lines approximately parallel to the sides of the board which form a right angle at the centre of the circle. Measure off 2 in. (b) and 6 in. (c) along the line parallel to the shorter side of the wood. Draw a line (e) at right angles to the 6 in. mark (c), measure off 3 in. along this line. This point becomes the centre of a circle of 3 in. radius (6 in. diam.), the circumference of this and the larger circle should be connected by a common tangent.

From the 2 in. mark (b) construct a line parallel to the other side of the right angle, and measure off 15 in. along this line (d). From the 15 in. mark (d) construct a circle of 2½ in. radius (5 in. diam.) (g), noting that (d) is on the circumference and is not the centre point. Connect this second circumference with that of the larger circle by means of the common tangent (h).

Construct a square of 4 in. sides, based on points (b) and (c). Draw diagonals and use the intersection (i) as the centre of a circle of 2 in. radius. Connect this circumference to the two small circles by tangents to (c) and (d) as shown. The shape to be cut out (using a fretsaw or key-hole saw for the curves) is now clear; but, before cutting, mark the positions for the leg plates.

Using the two radii at right angles in the centre of the larger circle, draw a square and produce a diagonal (j). Place one leg plate 3 in. in along this line measured from the circumference of the circle. The other two leg plates are located 4 in. from each end of the table, as shown.

It is normal to bevel the edge of this type of table; a simple pencil-holder (Fig. C181) is an invaluable aid. Using a 4 in. length of ½ in. dowelling, connect two pieces of wood, approx. 1½ in. × 1 in., one about 6 in. long and the other about 3 in. long. In the shorter piece, ⅝ in. from the dowelling, drill a vertical hole wide enough to accept a pencil. Place the 6 in. side under the table top and, keeping the pencil holder at right angles to the side, trace a ⅝ in. margin round the outside. This should be trimmed off in sections, and the edge should be sanded as for the previous table. Note that the bevel can be on top or underneath, to choice, the pencil-holder being used on the one side or the other as appropriate.

Long Low Tables

Long low rectangular tables are becoming increasingly popular in contemporary furnishing. They make ideal stands for tape and record players, indoor plants, and the miscellany of household objects which have no permanent home of their own.

While the top is made in the same general way as those for other tables, the edges are usually more rounded. Assuming that the table is to be six feet in length, then the height would be about a foot. In order to give the table a more solid appearance, a heavier support is required for the legs.

On a 6 ft. table, 18 in. in width and ¾ in. thick, 23 ft. of 2 in. × 1 in. wood is required, with one foot of 1½ in. × 1½ in. wood and one foot of 1 in. quadrant.

First of all make a rectangular frame using two five-foot lengths, two one-foot lengths, and four blocks of wood 1½ in. × 1½ in. × 2 in.

Use two 2½ in. screws through the corner blocks into the sides, and one screw between the other two into the end. (Softwood is usually sold in widths which allow a comfortable margin, so 1 in. thickness plus the 1½ in. block should measure about 2¾ in. Check this, however; if there is any doubt, use a 2 in. screw.) Ensure that the end faces are screwed flush with those of the block, so that a piece of 1 in. quadrant can be inserted in each corner. All joints should be glued before fixing. Assembly of the frame is shown in Fig. C182.

Next take two 4 ft. lengths of the 2 in. × 1 in. wood and, using a compass, draw an arc at each end with a radius equal to the width of the wood. Cut out these sections with a fretsaw and smooth the curved face with

sandpaper, leaving the edges sharp, as shown at (a) in Fig. C182. Nine inches in from each end, chisel out slots which should be 1 in. deep, 2 in. long, and go to within ½ in. of the outside (b). Next place the longer edge of the shaped piece of wood along, and in the centre of, the upper edge of the frame; using 3 in. screws every 12 in., glue and screw the two together.

Still using the 1 in. × 2 in. wood, construct two riders to slot into the joints made at the top of the frame. Use one 2 in. screw to secure each end. Finally fasten the frame to the table top, using three 1½ in. screws in each rider. All joints should be glued. The leg plates must be screwed on to the base of the 1½ in. blocks, so that the edges of the plate are level with the inside edges of the block.

A slightly neater finish can be made by countersinking the plates about ¼ in. in the blocks, but care must be taken to ensure that the feet remain in the same plane, or the table will not be steady.

This table looks most attractive when the framework is stained black (dark oak or ebony) and the top dark brown (walnut). The legs should be mounted vertically and have brass feet (see the side view in Fig. C183).

If this two-tone finish is required it is important to stain and polish the two parts separately.

FLOWER TROUGH COFFEE TABLE

The simply-made table in Fig. C184 has a useful plant trough which offers ample scope for flower arrangement.

For a table with dimensions of 4 ft. × 18 in. × 15 in. high the following materials are required:

2 in. × 2 in. softwood slatting:
2 pieces 44 in., frame sides
2 pieces 18 in., frame ends
1 piece 14½ in., centre strut
4 pieces 15 in., legs

Fig. C184. The trough offers ample scope for flower arrange-ments.

Fig. C185. Constructional details.

¼ in. thick chipboard or plywood (trough):
2 pieces 14¼ in. × 4½ in.
2 pieces 10 in. × 4½ in.
Melameer veneered chipboard:
1 piece 4 ft. × 18 in.
Hardware:
2 doz. wood screws, 2½ in. × No. 12
2 doz. wood screws, 1 in. × No. 7
Impact adhesive.

Cut the pieces to size and make up frame as shown in Fig. C185. Glue and screw on legs. Cut out top board as shown. Use the cut-out piece for the base of the flower-trough. Screw flower-trough box to inner edges of frame. Trim board to top of frame and fix with impact adhesive.

A SIMPLE BOOKCASE

Many bookcases are too small to take large size books; and if they are large enough, but of the same width all the way up, they are none-too-steady on their feet.

The design shown in Fig. C186 avoids these two faults —the bottom shelf is of ample size and yet, since the book-

Fig. C186. The bookcase shelves decrease with height, giving stability.

case decreases in depth at each shelf, it should be perfectly stable.

The wood used was kiln-dried Japanese oak, finished thickness 11/16 in. However, most firms can now offer quite a wide range of new tropical woods, such as Meranti, Irolo, Obeche, Agba, Ramin, Sapele and many more. Parana pine is by no means a new wood, but it is about the least expensive; Nigerian pearwood, Nigerian walnut and Agba come next.

Shaping the Sides

First, examine the wood and decide on the best surfaces (the most-beautifully grained) which are to be the outside of the finished bookcase; these surfaces should be marked with a soft pencil. Next, the wood is marked out according to the dimensions given in Fig. C187. Saw off the ends, after squaring up, with a tenon saw. Place both sides or ends in the vice with the insides together and the edges in line. With a sharp smoothing plane, trim up the edges, working from each end to the centre. This brings up grain on the ends and imparts a high polish. With a handsaw, cut down the vertical lines which give the taper effect and hence a better balance when full of books. Saw down almost to where the curves begin, and continue the curves with a coping saw.

Having cut all the shaping cuts, we now have the two ends roughly in the required shape. Clamp them in the vice with the insides together and the base and rear vertical edge in line. Now, with a medium wood rasp or rough sandpaper block, rub down any difference in contour between the two. This should ensure that both sides are identical in shape, which is very important when assembling and will enable the shelves to line up with the sides exactly the same at each end.

Stopped Housing Joints

Having completed the outline of the two sides, the stopped housing joints for the shelves have to be cut. This is likely to be the most difficult job, but can be made considerably easier by clamping 1 in. × ½ in. wood saw guides to each side of the housing before cutting.

In order to mark out correctly, lay the sides out on a flat table with the insides placed upwards and the rear edges butting together. The housings are then marked across both at one scribe of the pencil. This will ensure that the shelves, when fitted, will be level.

After marking out the portions to be cut out, chop out the end nearest the front, taking care that the housing joint is stopped the required distance from the front edge. The end of the housing is chopped out for a distance of about 2 in. and at the required depth by vertical and horizontal paring with a chisel and mallet. Next, use the tenon saw to cut the lines to the required depth, the saw being kept pressed against the wooden guides while sawing. The cut is made first with the tip of the saw pointing downwards and, as the cut progresses, the handle of the saw is gradually brought downwards until sufficient depth has been reached.

The housing is then completed, beginning at the rear edge with the bevel of the chisel facing downwards and taking an upward cut; the ideal chisel to use is ½ in. firmer or mortice. When the rough has been removed the bottom should be cleaned up by turning the chisel over and using it flat on the bottom of the joint, so that any

Fig. C187. Dimensions and constructional details.

Rear of side and shelves showing stopped housing and rebate.

Foot.

high spots are removed. The completed joint is now cleaned up with sandpaper wrapped around a suitable size square piece of wood, care being taken not to increase the width of the joint by rubbing the edges. The shelves should then be a tight push fit when correctly finished.

Shelves, Top and Bottom

The remainder of the wood should be carefully examined and the best pieces selected for the top, since this will always be on show whether the case is full of books or not. The edges should be squared-up as before. When all the shelves have been cut to the correct length, they should be placed on top of each other and all the ends should be in line, i.e., being exactly the same length. Before assembly, the underside of the top shelf at the rear should be rebated, together with the rear top side of the bottom shelf—this is to take the plywood or hardboard backing.

Assembly

First of all make a trial assembly—fit the shelves into the housings with the side placed on the bench; lightly tap the shelves into position. Do not force; if they are too tight, ease off the end of the shelf with a finely-adjusted plane.

When assembled, the case should stand up quite firmly and the space between shelves should be checked with a square.

Very lightly scribe a pencil mark on the sides at a centre point of the housing; this is to ensure that the nails or pins are driven into the centre of the thickness of the shelf and not to one side.

Next, the case is taken apart and glued together, the parts being nailed together with 1¼ in. panel pins. When nailing, remember that if the hammer leaves marks they will be very difficult to cover up, so drive the pins in to about a ¼ in. and then use a punch.

Having nailed up and glued, apply twisted ropes or tourniquets, one at the top, one at the bottom. Take the strain evenly, checking with the square before the glue

dries. After the glue has set, the top rail can be screwed and glued into position, as shown in Fig. C187. The front base is finished by screwing the strip below the bottom shelf into the shelf, and then screwing-and-glueing the two radiused feet at each end of the front. When completed, the whole front face can be lightly skimmed over with a plane, being careful to work with the grain.

Finish

The whole bookcase should now be sanded down with medium, fine, very fine, and flour paper in succession. The more labour and patience put into this operation the better will be the final polish. Special care must be taken on curved surfaces, and it is often better to use the thumb than a block, because pressure can be applied where it is required, such as in a recess where a block could not reach.

Perhaps the easiest and most pleasing finish is to stain the wood to the desired shade with spirit stain, since this does not bring up the grain. Try out for effect on a piece of scrap. After staining, the best finish is french polish.

BOOK AND MUSIC LIBRARY

Fig. C188 is an up-to-the-minute design which makes use of the modern trend to unit furniture and can provide planned storage space for everything—books, radio, record player and record library. Fig. C189 shows one unit adapted to take a radio receiver; Figs. C190 and C191 show another designed to house a record player, with sliding doors fitted so that when the record player is not in use, it can be slid back and hidden behind closed doors. Any number of these units can be built according to requirements, each one separate and to the same overall dimensions; it would be perfectly easy, for example, to build three instead of two, and give the third a fold-down writing flap to convert it into a writing desk or bureau. This is the great advantage of unit furniture—it can grow and be re-arranged as needed.

There are no joints in the usual carpentry sense of the word, except for a few half laps. That is why ¾ in. plywood is a suitable material for the amateur woodworker. It has tremendous strength, is available in large sheets, takes nails and screws easily right up to the edge, and reduces the amount of skill necessary.

The shelving shown in the units is adjustable, which is always a good feature. There are various types of adjustable shelving supports—the rack and clip pattern, as illustrated, or a similar type in which iron pegs with heads about as round as a sixpence fit into holes drilled at about 1 in. intervals into wooden fillets screwed to the sides. The advantage of metal racks is that the holes are ready made and accurately spaced.

Mark out the components in outline on the sheets of ply so that there is the minimum waste—the offcuts will come in useful for other odd jobs. Do not saw them all out at once. Cut out one piece first, sawing on the waste side of the marking-out lines. Then cut the piece it is to join and 'offer up' the two. If they fit satisfactorily, cut out the next piece—the other side or bottom, for example, and try for fit again. Working this way, it is easier to correct any error of marking out or cutting than if all the components are cut out at once.

When all the components for one unit are ready, make a trial assembly of the whole thing, tacking in place with light oval nails or panel pins. If it fits, take it to pieces,

Fig. C188. Unit furniture in the modern trend.

Figs. C190 and C191. (*below*). A unit designed to house a record player.

Fig. C189. Details of a unit to take a radio receiver.

sand lightly all over and make a permanent assembly using nails, screws and a good adhesive. Once plywood has been screwed-and-glued, it will never come apart again. All screw holes should be drilled and countersunk, all nail heads punched lightly below the surface. When assembly is complete, wipe off any surplus glue, fill over nail and screwheads with stopping and sand lightly when dry.

When it comes to finishing, personal ideas can be given full range. The only thing to remember is that if a clear natural finish is wanted, it may pay to get one of the special decorative plywoods which have a textured veneer on one side.

Painted plywood usually requires three coats for a really good result. First give it a thin coat of primer. Next, an undercoat suitably tinted to match the final colour. Then the final gloss or eggshell finishing coat. Interesting textured surfaces may be obtained by priming as above, followed by a heavy coat of stippling paint. Use brush roller or sponge to texture. When using water-thinned emulsion paint, first seal plywood with clear sealer, shellac or flat white oil paint. Then paint according to maker's directions.

For an easy inexpensive natural finish, first apply a coat of interior white undercoat thinned so that the grain pattern shows through (tint if colour is desired). Second, apply clear shellac, flat varnish or lacquer. Using a four-step system you can get a luxurious light stain glaze. First apply white undercoat thinned with equal parts of turpentine or painter's thinners. Wipe or dry-brush for more grain to show through. Second, apply a coat of thinned white shellac or clear sealer. Third, to provide colour, apply interior undercoat or enamel thinned as in step one. Choose any colour you want for this coat. Wipe or dry-brush to proper colour tone. Fourth, one coat of flat varnish. Rub with steel wool for added lustre.

MATERIALS

Radio Unit
1 Panel 3 ft. 10½ in. × 18¾ in. × ¾ in.
3 Panels 4 ft. × 18¾ in. × ¾ in.
1 Panel 3 ft. 10⅛ in. × 12 in. × ¾ in.
1 Panel 3 ft. 11¼ in. × 16 in. × ¾ in.
1 Panel 16⅞ in. × 13½ in. × ½ in.
1 Panel 16 in. × 25¾ in. × ½ in.
1 Panel 3 ft. 10½ in. × 8 in. × ¾ in.
1 Panel 3 ft. 10½ in. × 3 ft. 11¼ in. × ½ in.
4 Pieces dowelling 17½ in. × ¾ in.
1 Piece timber 3 ft. 10½ in. × 2 in. × 1 in.
1 Piece timber 27 in. × 1 in. × 1 in.
1 Pair 2 in. × 2 in. Butt hinges
1 Pair Spring catches
4 Thumbscrews
2 Spring clips
4 Shelf Standards
Record Player
2 Panels 4 ft. × 16¾ in. × ¾ in.
2 Panels 4 ft. × 18¾ in. × ¾ in.
1 Panel 3 ft. 10⅛ in. × 12 in. × ¾ in.
1 Panel 3 ft. 10⅛ in. × 16 in. × ¾ in.
1 Panel 3 ft. 10½ in. × 3 ft. 11¼ in. × ½ in.
2 panels 29⅛ in. × 13 in. × ½ in.
2 Panels 13 in. × 13 in. × ½ in.
3 Panels 13 in. × 12¼ in. × ¼ in.
2 Panels 24 in. × 25½ in. × ¼ in.
For Sliding Doors
Runners for above—top and bottom
2 Pieces 4 ft. × 2 in. × 3 in.
1 Piece 4 ft. × 2 in. × 1 in.
1 Piece 16¼ in. × 4 in. × ¾ in.
2 Pieces 16 in. × 1 in. × ½ in. Hardwood
4 Shelf Standards

RECESS SHELVING

The unit in Fig. C192 was designed to fit the recess between chimney-breast and wall, although it could be fitted to any suitable wall. Sizes given can be varied to suit individual requirements, but an increase of 6 in. on the overall length should be regarded as the maximum. Some sagging of the main shelves will occur if this length is exceeded.

Choice of timber depends on the type of finish required. Main parts could be of Japanese oak, stained and polished in the usual manner, with the dowels of birch left a natural colour by the application of two coats of white polish. Alternatively, a selected softwood can be used if an enamelled finish is preferred. Here Obeje was used for

the construction and the whole prepared in the usual way to receive a finishing coat of good quality white enamel. This method proved to be very pleasing to the eye and blended well with the general decoration of the room.

Method of Construction

Begin by preparing the two ends A and B. These are identical and can be set out together (end B is simply turned upside-down in assembly). Fig. C193 shows all the dimensions required. Housings are cut in these ends 5/16 in. deep for the centre shelves (F, C, D and E, Fig. C194); half-lap joints are used for the top and bottom shelves (G and H). In the diagram it is suggested that these cuts are stopped ⅞ in. from the front. In the prototype (Fig. C192) they were cut right through. Take your pick! The half-lap joint illustrated shows the type of cut required irrespective of length.

Fig. C192. An attractive unit to transform a bare wall.

All six shelves should be set out together as shown in Fig. C195. This ensures that the holes to receive the dowels are exactly in line, which is most important during assembly. Cramp all the shelves together as shown in Fig. C195 when setting out, and square all setting out lines across the front edges. Uncramp the shelves and square all the lines across on the face side of each one. Mark out the position of the dowel holes as shown, taking care to be accurate and working from the rear edge for each shelf for every measurement. Dowel holes can now be bored, but first check that the dowels are a push fit in the holes by boring a trial hole in a scrap piece of timber. Wood bits and dowels do sometimes vary in size, but if good quality beech or birch dowels are used no difficulty should be experienced. Holes for dowels which are not required to pass right through a shelf should be stop-bored, i.e. to depth of only ½ in. Shelves E, F, G and H can now be rounded off (Fig. C196)—and the small cut-out sawn from the end of each one, if you decided to stop the joint cuts short of the front edges of sides A and B.

Fig. C193. (below). Details of the ends.

Fig. C194 (right, centre). Constructional details.

Fig. C195 (right, top). The shelves assembled for drilling.

Fig. C196. Radius for rounding-off the shelves.

Fig. C197 (far right). Dowel details.

Shelves E, F, G, H.

A and B

Dowels

As can be seen from Fig. C197, the dowels are in two sets of five, three of these being full length and two are shorter ones. These lengths are given in the drawings and accurate marking and cutting is essential. Should timber of a different thickness be used for the shelves, then an allowance must be made accordingly on the dowel lengths.

All parts can now be cleaned up and sanded, taking care to transfer any marks on to the back edge of the shelves.

Assembly

It will be found an advantage if the whole unit is first assembled dry, thus ensuring that the dowels are a sliding fit in the holes and the shelves fit in their respective housings. Any adjustment can now be carried out to dowel lengths if this is necessary. After checking that all joints and measurements are correct, it can all be dismantled ready for the final assembly.

Although the original unit was glued up with Scotch glue, cold water powdered glue may be used; this provides a much more prolonged assembly time before the glue begins to set.

Begin by glueing-and-pinning the main shelves C and D into the ends A and B, at the same time inserting the two short lengths of dowels after having applied glue to the ends. Next insert the remaining dowels, but do not glue these until they are nearly in position.

The remaining shelves, E, F, G and H, can now be glued-and-pinned in position, and the dowels can be glued and inserted.

Check all measurements between shelves carefully and,

if necessary, apply a sash cramp to adjust until the whole unit is square. Panel pins can now be driven in obliquely through the shelves and into the dowels, and should be punched in just below the surface.

When the glue has completely set, the unit can be finally cleaned up and glasspapered, rounding off slightly all corners. Stop up all pin holes using an appropriate filler depending upon the finish desired.

Fixing is best done by using four brass mirror plates plugged back to the wall.

MATERIALS

A & B 2 off 2 ft. 5½ in. × 9 in. × ¾ in.
C & D 2 off 4 ft. × 8¼ in. × ¾ in.
E & F 2 off 1 ft. 6 in. × 7 in. × ¾ in.
G & H 2 off 1 ft. 4 in. × 5½ in. × ¾ in.
J 2 off 1 ft. of ½ in. diam.
K 2 off 1 ft. 10 in. of ½ in. diam.
L 6 off 2 ft. 5 in. of ½ in. diam.
Allowance has been made on lengths
Widths and thicknesses are net

A VERSATILE ROOM DIVIDER

Naturally, all room dividers are intended to make two rooms out of one, but this divider was designed with three additional main points in mind—adaptability, simplicity and adjustability. It is adaptable since it can be used to divide a lounge from a dining room, a kitchen from a dinette, a bedroom from a sitting room, or to divide a bedroom for teen-age sitters.

It is simple, because the units are designed as simple boxes made from standard sizes of veneered chipboard. Doors, divisions and shelves can be added and the arrangement changed as desired.

If necessary, it can be made 'solid' to give a greater degree of privacy.

The four uprights, spaced 3 feet apart, are the only fixed dimensions. Width can be changed in multiples of 3 feet to suit larger or smaller rooms. The three-feet module was chosen for economy in material, since it suits most standard sizes of veneered boards now available.

One arrangement, suitable for a dining/living room

GLASS FRONT DISPLAY UNIT

BOOKCASE UNIT

SHELF

2 ft. 10 ⅝ in.

7 ft. 10 in.

DRAWER UNIT

RECORD STORAGE UNIT

WRITING DESK UNIT

9 ft. 3 ½ in.

STORAGE UNIT

COCKTAIL UNIT

STORAGE UNIT

4 in.

4 in.

BASE PLATE

WOODSCREW

¾ in.

6½ in.

¾ in. DIA. CONDUIT

2½ in. DEEP HOLE TO TAKE SHAFT

HOLES AT 3 1/10 in. CENTRES

FILLETS

⅞ in. DOWEL

4 in. x 2 in. SUPPORT MEMBER

3 in. DEEP HOLE TO TAKE FOOT SHAFT

WASHER

3 in.

NUT

¾ in. DIA. CONDUIT

3 in.

WOODSCREW

¾ in.

BASE PLATE

Fig. C198 (*above*). A typical arrangement; in this case, a dining/living room divider.

The bold letters A to J identify units which are shown in detail in Figs. C202 to C210.

Fig. C199 (*above*). The living-room side, and (*below*) the dining-room side of the same unit.

Fig. C200 (*above*). The kitchen side, and (*below*) the dining-room side of another unit.

Fig. C201 (*above*). The living-room side, and (*right*) the bedroom side of a further unit.

RECORD
DIVISIONS
¼in. HARDBOARD
PEGBOARD

5 OFF

¼in. HARDBOARD
OR PLYWOOD

VENEERED
CHIPBOARD

ALUMINIUM
CHANNEL

7 OFF

Fig. C202. Record
cabinet and shelf unit.

A

Fig. C204. Bureau and
storage unit.

C

SLIDING DOORS
¼in. HARDBOARD

¼in. PLYWOOD

DRAWERS MADE
FROM ½in. THICK
TIMBER

DRAWER RUNNERS
½in. SQUARE

BALL CATCH

PIANO HINGE

B

Fig. C203. Double-sided drawer unit.

PEGBOARD

D

Fig. C205. Bookcase
shelf unit.

½in. SQ.
TIMBER

Fig. C206. Double-
sided cocktail cabinet.

PIANO
HINGE

BALL
CATCH

E

division, is shown in Fig. C198; this gives details of the
uprights. Other arrangements are possible; some suggestions are given in Figs. C199–C201. These show front and
back views of three varying dividers built from nine different types of unit, drawings or plans of which are shown
in Figs. C202–C210. These can be combined in any way.

Naturally, the back view of a divider is mainly dependent on the front, so to obtain an attractive appearance
for both sides calls for a little thought in arrangement. For
the larger components, such as wardrobes or cupboards
which must go right through, use some decorative material
for the rear panel. Display shelves will be 18 inches deep
and you can take advantage of this to break up the storage
areas and improve the appearance, since anything on the
display shelves, such as a bowl of flowers, can be seen
from either side. Cupboards which do not need to be the
full 18 inches deep can be divided in the centre and made

to open from both sides. If radio and TV sets are to be incorporated, extra support may be needed for the shelving
and ample space must be left for air circulation to avoid
overheating.

Sliding doors can be faced with decorative laminates.

To take advantage of standard sizes of materials the
units should all be 3 feet wide and 18 inches deep. The
height between shelves should be 18 inches, plus two
thicknesses of material—remember this when you drill
the dowel holes in the uprights.

The holes in the wooden 4 in. × 2 in. upright members
are bored at 3 1/16 in. centres to take the ⅞ in. dowels
which support the shelves and units. The spacing of the
holes may seem odd, but it is determined by the height of
the uprights (7 feet 10 inches), the 18-inch vertical spacing
between shelves etc., the thickness of the veneered boards
(11/16 inch) and the number of shelf positions. The unit

Fig. C207. Cupboard, shelf unit.

18in.

DINING   END VIEW   LIVING   PLAN VIEW

Fig. C208. Storage unit.

27¼in.

DINING   END VIEW   KITCHEN   PLAN VIEW

Fig. C209. Bureau, dressing table unit.

18in.

LIVING   END VIEW   BEDROOM   PLAN VIEW

Fig. C210. Wardrobe, display panel unit.

58½in.

BEDROOM   END VIEW   LIVING   PLAN VIEW

Figs. C211-C214 (*below*). 4 stages of unit assembly. A few screws temporarily hold parts for dowelling.

here is intended for a floor-to-ceiling height of 8 feet 6 inches which is normal. The adjustable mounting cups at top and bottom of the uprights add 8 inches to the height. The cups used are from heavy electrical conduit junction-box covers with a short length of threaded conduit. The method of making a basic unit is shown in Figs. C211–C214.

The quantities of materials required will depend on how the unit is planned. The main materials are veneered chipboard, adhesive plastic sheeting, plastic laminate and hardboard, both perforated and solid.

A PUT-UP JOB

As a sofa, this piece of furniture adds comfortable luxury to any lounge; converted to a bed, it offers ample room for a six-footer to sleep, with the end cupboards doing duty as head and foot boards. Fig. C215 shows the unit in normal position. The base is simply a standard flush door, size 6 ft. 6 in. × 2 ft. 6 in. These can be readily obtained from timber merchants. However, some of them have very little framework inside, and it would be difficult to find a place to screw on the legs! It is therefore advisable to tell the merchant what the door is going to be used for, so that he can supply one with a good solid internal construction. If you feel at all uncertain about it, it is best to glue on squares of ½ in. ply to the underside of the door, where the legs are to go. If a good resin glue is used and pressure is applied with a clamp while the joint sets, there'll never be any risk of a leg coming unstuck. The cupboards at each end of the sofa improve its appearance as a piece of furniture, but they are also severely practical in that they will hold the bedding. The mattress forms the upholstery and stays in

ably the best answer, since it gives useful extra space when the unit is in use as a settee.

2 The first step is to screw four 6 in. legs to the underside of the door. Whitewood can be used and afterwards stained to match the boxes; or ready-made legs fixed to metal plates as in Fig. C218. The positioning is not critical; approximately 1 ft. 6 in. from the ends of the door, and 6 in. from the sides would be suitable.

3 Next bind the front edge of the door with PVC imitation leather. Cut a strip of leather cloth 15 in. wide and 2½ yd. long, also a similar strip of felt, and place them together. Using upholstery tacks, secure the strip 6 in. from the front edge of the door. Pull the materials taut and secure underneath in the same way (Fig. C218). The materials can be taken round the ends of the door and the corners mitred.

4 Using 2 in. × 1 in. hardwood, construct the back support as shown in Fig. C219 then glue-and-screw to the door. Stain to match boxes.

5 Make a fitted cover for the mattress from 4½ yd. of 48 in. material. The method of covering is the same as for a fitted cushion. The pieces for the cover should be cut

Fig. C215. Impressive and luxurious as a sofa, removal of the backrest cushion makes a bed with ample room for a six-footer, the end cupboards becoming head and foot boards.

place all the time. For real luxury, go for a 6-inch foam one—it makes all the difference. The small cushions for the back rest can be a couple of latex or foam pillows. The back is not adjustable, but it doesn't get in the way when in use as a bed.

Construction

The following fifteen stage-by-stage instructions, together with the exploded drawing and plan in Figs. C216 and C217, show how simply this unit can be made.

1 The door which, as already explained, forms the basis of the unit, is 6 ft. 6 in. long. This is the standard size; and the standard mattress size is 6 ft. 3 in., which leaves 3 in. of base to be disposed of. There are several possible answers to this: (a) an inch can be cut off each end of the door (but ask the suppliers first if they recommend this); (b) a larger mattress can be used; (c) the design can be altered so that the end cupboards actually overlap the door, thus reducing the length by the required amount; (d) a fillet of sizeable quadrant moulding can be fitted at the base of each end cupboard. A larger mattress is prob-

to allow ½ in. turnings. Cut the top and bottom pieces and four boxing strips the depth of the mattress. Join the four boxing strips into a ring. Stitch the boxing strip to the top cover piece, taking up a little over ½ in. to ensure a tight fit. Tack the bottom piece to the other side of the boxing strip, then machine together around three sides, leaving a short side open. This side can be fastened with a zip so that the cover can easily be removed for cleaning.

6 For the backrest, use a piece of foam rubber 2 in. thick measuring 2 ft. 2 in. × 6 ft. 6 in. This foam rubber can easily be stuck with impact adhesive, so two pieces can be joined end-to-end to get the correct length. Place a strip of 2 in.-thick wadding or foam rubber 8 in. wide, 4 in. from the top of the foam, see Fig. C220. (Instead of wadding or a foam rubber strip, an old blanket folded up or any roll of thick material can be used as the padding.) Fold the piece of foam in half lengthwise to make a long roll, and so that two 4 in. strips of foam come in contact and may be glued together. The back rest is now ready to be covered; 2½ yd. of material are needed and the cover is easily sewn by hand. Just place the material over the

All back rest framework
2"x 1" hardwood

All back rest joints
are screwed and glued

⁵⁄₈" veneered blockboard

1"sq.
1' 3¾" long

¼" plywood

2"x1"

1" sq.

⅛" hardboard
P.V.C covered

6'6"x 2'6"x 2" flush door

Edge of door
P.V.C. covered
overlap top
and bottom by 6"

Battens 2"x1"x 8'7"
chamfer ends
as shown

⁵⁄₈"x 2"x 1'6"
P.V.C.covered

6" ready
made legs
screw to
underside
of door

Door Handle

Door ⁵⁄₈" veneered
blockboard

Base ⅝" blockboard 1'3¾" wide
2"x 1"x 1'3¾"

Hinges
½"x 2"

SIDE VIEW

2'6"
2"
1'0"
6"
1'6"

Upholstery indicated by white outline

9' 3"

6"
6"

1'2"

6"

FRONT VIEW

Base fits in
this position

Figs. C216 and C217. Plan, elevation
and exploded view.

1'6" 3" 3½" 2" 1'6" 2" 1'6" 2" 1'6" 2" 3½" 3" 1'6"

4"
1'4"
8'7"
6"
2'6"
6"
5"
1'4"
4"
6'3"

PLAN VIEW

Fig. C218. Leg and leather cloth fixings.

Fig. C219. The back support.

Fig. C220.   Construction of backrest cushion.

Fig. C221.   The underside, showing battens.

top of the back rest and pull taut. Secure underneath using a slip stitch. The ends can be turned under and also secured with a slip stitch. Tapes can be sewn to the back of the back rest, to be tied to the back supports to keep it in position.

7 Construct the side frames for the boxes as shown in Fig. C217. The front edges should be stained to match the top.

8 The sides are made of hardboard covered with leather cloth. A layer of felt goes between them as a padding to give a more luxurious appearance. Having cut the hardboard to the exact size, two strips of 1 in-sq. timber are nailed and glued to it. These fit inside the top and bottom members of the side frames and eventually will be nailed in this position. Using a hardboard side as a template, cut out the leather and felt, allowing $1\frac{1}{2}$ in. turnings on the leather cloth. Put the leather and felt together, and place the hardboard in position; mitre the corners and stick down the $1\frac{1}{2}$ in. turnings with impact adhesive.

9 Using panel pins, nail and glue the bottom and back in position, also the 2 in.×1 in. member, which fits under the door.

10 Nail the hardboard sides in position through the 1 in.-sq. members mentioned in stage 8.

11 Glue a strip of leather cloth, backed with felt, to a piece of timber 1 ft. 6 in.×2 in.×$\frac{5}{8}$ in.; then attach to the 2 in.×1 in. stub beneath the door, by screws from behind.

12 Before nailing the veneered top in place, attach a 1 in.-sq. strip as shown. This forms a nailing point for the back. Nail the top. Make sure that all edges are veneered and that the panel pins are pushed below the surface of the wood. Level off the holes with filler.

13 Offer the door of $\frac{5}{8}$ in. veneered blockboard into position so that it is flush with the hardboard sides and fits neatly under the top. Attach with hinges. Stain the top and the door and fit a door catch and handle.

14 Fit two legs to each box and screw firmly into the $\frac{5}{8}$ in. thick base; stain to match boxes. They should be about 6 in. from the front and back and 4 in. from the ends.

15 Fix the boxes to the sofa by means of battens running the whole length of the unit, about 8 in. or 9 in. from the sides of the door, as shown in Fig. C221

MATERIALS

Tops 2 off 2 ft. 6 in.×1 ft. 6in.×$\frac{5}{8}$ in. veneered blockboard

Doors 2 off 1 ft. 6 in.×$11\frac{3}{8}$ in.×$\frac{5}{8}$ in. veneered blockboard

Bottoms 2 off 2 ft. $4\frac{1}{8}$ in.×1 ft. $3\frac{3}{4}$ in.×$\frac{5}{8}$ in. blockboard

Backs 2 off 1 ft. $5\frac{3}{4}$ in.×1 ft. $1\frac{3}{8}$ in.×$\frac{1}{4}$ in. plywood

Sides 4 off 2 ft. $5\frac{3}{8}$ in.×1 ft. $1\frac{3}{8}$ in.×$\frac{1}{8}$ in. hardboard

Framing 8 off 2 ft. $5\frac{1}{8}$ in.×2 in.×1 in. timber
8 off 1 ft. $1\frac{3}{8}$ in.×2 in.×1 in. timber
2 off 1 ft. $3\frac{3}{4}$ in.×2 in.×1 in. timber
2 off 1 ft. 6 in.×2 in.×$\frac{5}{8}$ in. timber

Back Rest 1 off 5 ft. 9 in.×2 in.×1 in. hardwood
4 off 1 ft.×2 in.×1 in. hardwood
4 off 6 in.×2 in.×1 in. hardwood

Battens 2 off 8 ft. 7in.×2 in.×1 in. hardwood
2 off 1 ft. 4 in.×2 in.×1 in. hardwood

Flush Door 6 ft. 6 in.×2 ft. 6in.×2 in. hardwood
8 off 6 in. whitewood legs
1 off 2 ft. 6 in.×6 ft. 6 in. mattress
7 yd. upholstery material 48 in. wide
$2\frac{1}{2}$ yd. P.V.C. leathercloth 48 in. wide
$2\frac{1}{2}$ yd. felt 48 in. wide
2 door catches, 2 door knobs
4 hinges, screws, stain, impact adhesive
Upholstery tacks, panel pins
Foam rubber, wadding—as required

A CONTINENTAL CONVERTIBLE

In Denmark, as in most European countries, space in modern houses is usually at a premium. Today the 'guest room' is a rarity, and as a consequence most houses pos-

Fig. C222. A fold-down divan designed for compact simplicity.

sess a fold-down divan with which they can accommodate friends or family overnight. There are several types of these divans, of course, but the design covered here is exceptional for its compactness and for that simplicity of line which has become the Scandinavian trade mark.

The divan as seen in Fig. C222 is low and stable without being bulky and without a mass of mechanical connections. The overall visual effect, created by the lowness of the divan and the two loose-covered foam-rubber cushions, is of two long solid slabs of colour. The frame is deliberately designed to be inconspicuous, and only a suggestion of it is visible.

Choice of colour for the cushions depends largely on the overall decor of the room and the position the divan will occupy : contrasting pastel shades may cause the divan to blend into the room naturally. A single bold splash of colour, perhaps counterbalanced in another part of the room, can create an effect of spacious modern luxury.

Basic Design

The basic design of the divan is shown in Fig. C223. The unit hinges around one single point. To become a bed it is simply a matter of pushing the back of the divan downwards, the back support then rolls under the hinge on a small castor. An extra leg concealed within the back support must then be adjusted to give a firm structure.

The unit is stable at all times : as a divan, the seat support bears downwards, under the weight of a person, on a shoulder within the back support; as a bed, the back support provides a continuous bearing surface to brace

Fig. C223. Details of the basic design.

Back 20"
Seat 23"
Round off corners
Binding board
74"
Frame
2" wide rubber strips

Binding details
Rubber
Assembly detail (Frame to support)
$\frac{5}{8}$" x $\frac{5}{8}$" notch
Binding board
2"
1"

Fig. C224. Frame design and fixing o rubber strips.

4"
1$\frac{1}{4}$
1$\frac{1}{2}$"   27$\frac{3}{4}$" $\frac{3}{4}$"
5"
$\frac{3}{4}$"
$\frac{3}{4}$"
$\frac{7}{16}$" Bolt hole for leg axle

Fig. C225. Seat support.

30"
25"
$\frac{1}{2}$"
7" 3" Leg
2"
Back support
1"

Fig. C226. Method of cutting out back supports and legs.

the hinge and disperse the load over three points at each end.

Because of the simplicity of movement and the cleanliness of line, dimensions are critical. It is necessary to use a good close-grained wood that can be worked within close limits. A recommended combination is teak for the main frames and oak for the legs and supports.

The main frames can be made first, completed and set on one side while completing the more difficult shaping of the back supports. The design of the frames is shown in Fig. C224. Both are precisely the same except that the back frame is only 20 in. wide as against 23 in. for the seat frame.

The frames themselves are made from 1 in × 2 in. stock; in all a length of 31 ft. 10 in. is needed. Corners are made with a simple lap joint, remembering to make the shorter lengths (i.e., the ends) lap over the longer lengths (the sides) so that they bear down on a surface which is itself supported by the seat support. In this way there is no danger of the ends breaking off by anybody standing on them. The connection can be made by gluing, plus a single 1$\frac{5}{8}$ in. × No. 12 csk wood screw. Drill and countersink the top half.

To avoid splitting the wood and to ease the passage of the screw the bottom half should also be drilled to a depth of $\frac{3}{8}$ in. to give a $\frac{1}{8}$ in. hole. All drilling for the four corners of the frame should be completed before applying the glue, the screwing then being completed while the glue is still plastic.

The modern trend is to include any connections as part of the aesthetic effect, accepting them as having a functional value. So leave the screws visible but let them be of brass so that they have an attractive matching colour. Otherwise, countersink and fill the heads with plastic wood and sand off.

Back and Seat Bracing

Evenly-spaced 2 in.-wide rubber strips are recommended for the cushion bracing, or 'spring'. The same number is used for both frames, a total length of 91 ft. being required. Hessian-woven or other textile webbing could also be used for this purpose. Rubber, however, gives a much more comfortable area over which to relax the weight, and exerts less tensile stress on the frame because of its elasticity.

When purchasing such rubber strips it is advisable to obtain the kind with a rough blotchy (in fact, unpressed) surface, which ensures greater friction between rubber and the cushion-covering material and so helps the cushions to stay more firmly in place. Anchor each strip as shown in Fig. C224, with one full turn around the wooden binding board, the strip then being tacked firmly down at both corners.

Thread or weave the strips alternately under and over each other, beginning at a different end each time, to create a surface that presents an integrated whole as far as load distribution is concerned. Stretch the rubber strips slightly when fitting so that they are under slight tension.

Screw the binding board into the frame at about every 8 in. This board, of which a total length of 30 ft. 6 in. is necessary, can be of $\frac{1}{2}$ in. × 1$\frac{1}{2}$ in. good-quality deal. The boards should be fixed so that their upper surface is on the same level as that of the frame.

In order to facilitate attaching the complete frames to their supports, the binding boards must be notched in both side pieces, as shown in Fig. C224, to allow angle clips to be fitted. These notches should be ⅝ in. × ⅝ in. They are located at 8 in. from the outside end of the seat frame and the top of the back frame; for the bottom side of the back frame the notch must be located off-centre, i.e., 7 in. from the outside and edge, because of the recess for the seat support, in the back support. This is shown in Fig. C230, and explained later.

Before fitting together, the whole frame should be well sanded and rubbed down, taking all sharp corners and edges off in the process. Link together (the two completely assembled frames) with five 3 in. hinges (3 hole, 1¼ in. wide leaves), 12¾ in. apart, starting 4 in. from one end. The hinges should be recessed into the frames as necessary so that the two sections fit flush together and present a continuous flat surface when the bed is open.

Both supports are 2 ft. 3¾ in. × 1½ in. × 1¼ in. and shaped to dimensions given in Fig. C225. The end to enter the back support is rounded-off on the underside for ¾ in. (half the depth of the support.) The other end is shaped back for 4 in. from the front of the seat frame, to make it less conspicuous. The support is finally sanded off before being attached to the seat frame by means of 1 in. angle clips and ½ in. screws.

Supports and Legs

The back supports and the two front legs are all cut from one piece of timber 2 ft. 6 in. × 7 in. × 3 in. (Fig. C226). Each support must then be recessed accurately, Fig. C227. The critical dimension is the ⅜ in. of BC to ensure that the seat support beds firmly along FG when the unit is used as a divan. It is best, therefore, to begin by measuring out the distance BD accurately, and to start cutting vertically downwards to remove the wood from the volume ABFE.

The distance A to B and the depths to E and F are not critical, those shown being the minimum for free movement when lowering the divan into the bed position. When the recess is complete, cut away the material of CGHD, ensuring that GH is parallel with CD.

Fitting the Concealed Legs

The recess for the concealed leg is quite simple. Drill a hole 5/16 in., to take a ¼ in. brass (or other) carriage bolt, 2 in. long. Cut the recess for the castor to suit the exact dimensions of the wheel available. That shown is for a castor of 1 in. outside diameter; the wheel itself need not protrude more than about ¼ in. The corner of the support must be rounded off to allow the support to roll forward freely. A hole for a brass carriage bolt of the appropriate size is again drilled.

The two front legs are cut from the same stock as the back supports and are shaped as shown in Fig. C228. The top corners are rounded off over ½ in. and a 7/16 in. hole is drilled for a ⅜ in. diameter carriage bolt, 3½ in. long. Finally, the groove for the support is cut out and the whole is vigorously sanded smooth.

The two legs concealed within the back support are cut from 1 in. by 1½ in. stock, 5⅝ in. long, Fig. C229. One end is fully rounded, the carriage bolt hole is drilled and the pieces sanded off.

Assembly Procedure

The divan is now in the following state: frames complete and hinged together, seat supports screwed in place,

Fig. C227. Back and seat support details.

Fig. C228. Front leg design.

Fig. C229. Legs concealed in back support.

Fig. C230. Details of seat support and recess.

legs, castor and back supports loose. The first task is to position the legs and castor, inserting the carriage bolts and tapping them firmly home. The head of the bolt should, for appearance sake, be on the outside. Each bolt should be fitted with a washer under the nut and, after tightening, the thread should be centre-punched at the point where it leaves the nut to create a sufficient burr to prevent movement.

Get a Snug Fit

During fabrication and assembly of the legs it is best to proceed slowly, with frequent checks to fit. The idea is to obtain a snug fit at all points to avoid slack movements; careful cutting and controlled sanding will allow this. These remarks also apply to the fit of the seat support within the back support.

With the legs in place, the seat supports can be inserted within their recesses in the back supports, and the back frames tightened to the back supports. This is again done by means of 1 in. angle clips. At the top these are simply screwed with a ½ in. screw into the inside of the frame and the inside face of the back support; the same applies to the bottom of the frame except that the clip is attached on the outer side of the back support recess, as shown in Fig. C230.

Final Touches

It is a good idea to glue ⅛ in. thick rubber strips or pads to the base of the legs and back supports. These can be of the same material as the springs of the unit, but a better material is the compressible microcellular synthetic rubber now available. The pads can perform several important functions: they give a better grip with the floor, avoid scratching, and take up any minor irregularities either in the floor level or in the dimensioning of the divan itself. With such pads in place the unit is now complete and can be raised and lowered into the two positions by one single movement. The final step is to oil the wood to bring out its natural texture.

Two slabs of foam rubber are required, 73 in. long, 20 in. wide, and 2 or 2½ in. thick. Alternatively, several (two or three) separate cushions can be made for both the back and seat. A rough coarse-weave material is recommended for covering the cushions, not only because it will wear better but also because it gives greater stability from its higher friction with the rubber springs.

A BAR FOR A CORNER

The remarkable point about this rather ambitious-looking installation is that it is so easy to build—the basic structure is simple, knocked-up joinery, clad with hard-

Fig. C231. One advantage with a private bar is that opening time is any time—when friends call unexpectedly; when you're sitting up to see New Year in or just 'having a ball'. There's no doubt that a gay and professional-looking built-in job like this guarantees a happy atmosphere. The bar stools, for the occasion, can be borrowed from the kitchen. Don't forget the useful properties on the bar—dishes of peanuts, olives and, of course, an icetub. Stocking up we leave to individual tastes!

Fig. C232. Exploded view. The plan view is common to bar and canopy.

Fascia from ⅛ in. hardboard

12 in.

¾ in. blockboard

Canopy frame from 2 in. × 1 in. timber

9 in.

Make from ¾ in. scrap blockboard

Canopy ceiling from ⅛ in. hardboard recess to take light fittings

Bar flap from two pieces of ¾ in. blockboard

Shelf backing ⅛ in. hardboard

Shelves from ¾ in. blockboard 1 in. wide

Batten-pine arris rail may be used

Arch facing from ⅛ in. hardboard 1 in. wide

2 in. × 1 in. timber

Framework from 2 in. × 1 in. timber

Bar framework from ¾ in. blockboard

¾ in. × 12 in. × 37¾ in. blockboard

Counter lip make from 2 in. × 1 in. scrap

18½ in.

3 ft. 3¾ in.

Hinges

6 ft. 6 in.

Bar door frames from ¾ in. blockboard

Bar flap stop from 2 in. × 1 in.

18½ in.

12 in.

⅛ in. Hardboard 2¾ in. deep

⅛ in. thick hardboard 3 ft. 3¾ ins. deep

4 in. × 2 in. blocks to take bar rail

2¾ in.

2 in. sq. blocks

Plinth former from scrap ¾ in. blockboard set back 2¾ in. from edge of shelf

1 ft. 3 in.

2 ft. 3 in.

1 ft.

4 ft. 6 in. 1 ft. 8 in.

Fig. C233. The archway fascia is cut from two pieces of block-board, jointed at the top centre with a plate made from scrap. Use the cut-out a for template later.

Fig. C234. Further stage showing how the 2 in. × 1 in. supports are placed and how the alcove is lined with lengths of ⅛ in. hardboard—shiny side out.

Fig. 235C (right). Locating assembled alcove on batten fillets screwed to wall with plugs. The outline for the battens can be made by using the fascia or cut-out as a template.

Fig. C236. The bottom of the bar, showing blocks fixed in alignment with ends. Blocks give additional support and act as formers for plinth.

Fig. C237 (left). Tacking on the bar front. The hardboard for this should have been well damped down 24 hours previously.

Fig. C238 (right). Simple construction of the counter—with screwed butt joints. Material used is ¾ in. block-board; countersink the screws for the hardboard cladding.

Fig. C239 (*left*). The projecting counter top projects over 2in. × 1in. blocks.

Fig. 240. The door, of block-board formers and hardboard, follows the curve of the front. It should open outwards.

Fig. C241. The canopy is made of blockboard formers, 2in. × 1in. framework and hardboard.

Fig. C242. Lining for the canopy is carried into the lighting holes.

Fig. C243. The offcuts from the alcove fascia make templates for cutting the decorative glass panels.

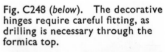

Fig. C244 (*above*). When lining the arch, start at top centre and work down each side.

Fig. C246 (*above*). When drilling holes for the aluminium edging strip, make sure they coincide with blocks beneath.

Fig. C247 (*below*). Immerse the plastic insert in hot water before easing it into the channel of the edging strip with a screwdriver.

Fig. C248 (*below*). The decorative hinges require careful fitting, as drilling is necessary through the formica top.

Fig. C245. Cut the self-adhesive quilted plastic before removing the protective backing sheet.

Fig. C249. 1¼ in. dia. aluminium tube forms the footrail, supported on standard baluster-type brackets or towel rail brackets.

Fig. C250. Two wall-lights may be fitted, but you may find the three top lights are fully adequate.

board and blockboard, forming a built-in unit anchored to the wall. The secret is in glamorizing the whole thing by using glued-on surfacing in one form or another. There is a fairly wide range and choice of materials which can be used to vary the presentation, and although the bar shown in Fig. C231 was designed for a medium-large house the whole thing can be scaled down to suit the smallest living room. The bar door may be on either side.

The lighting, which is composed of standard Rotaflex inset spotlights, should present no wiring problem other than finding a suitable point from which to take the supply.

The design incorporates only the simplest construction principles: materials are pre-finished; joints are simply butted and screwed.

Large load-bearing surfaces are made of blockboard. The advantage of this material is that, apart from its strength and trueness, it is easy to work, gives a good clean edge and it takes screws very well, most important with this type of construction. It also has a passably good ready-sanded surface which can be used for stained structural members, as shown in the exploded drawing in Fig. C232. Support, where required, is given with standard planed timber.

Cladding and lining is carried out with ⅛ in. hardboard. This material is very easy to work, particularly on bends, and the rigidity of the carcase is assured if the board is pinned at about 3 in. intervals with copper hardboard pins. The method of construction is explained photographically in Figs. C233 to C250.

When fixing hardboard for this job ensure that the shiny surface is always on the face side, as the lining materials require a good smooth surface.

No doubt the bar owes a great deal of its glamour to the finishing-materials chosen. The Anaglypta Sea-washed Pebble, for instance, gives an off-beat rugged look which directly contrasts with the rest of the decor; Anaglypta panels are just stuck to the wall.

Another decorative feature is the Flexaglas surface in

the alcove. These sheets of pre-cut glass can follow contours and are very simple to stick to any surface. They are available in tints. Apart from the novelty, they do add considerable dimension to the setting.

The lining to the alcove and canopy is a hessian weave in the Canotex series; again a rather unusual texture which adds a pleasant softness.

The counter top and alcove fascia are strikingly clad with a laminate chosen from the Formica architectural range; we chose a bold pattern called Morse, which was very easy to match up. This range is specially designed for decorative purposes and adds that touch of colour and distinction for which the project calls.

The luxury-look quilted fabric on the bar front, canopy fascia and the bar door, is from the Kapok standard Weldecor range. It is self-adhesive.

A FREE-STANDING BAR

This modest and intimate little bar can be constructed quite simply and cheaply (Fig. C251). The dimensions given can, of course, be adapted to suit the area available.

The project grew from a bookcase (a free-standing unit at floor level) previously built to fit an alcove in the lounge.

The first stage, after removing the supporting plinth, is to raise the bookcase by some 3 ft., secure it to the wall with mirror plates and re-paint it as required. This is the unit for storing glasses, collection of miniatures and various knick-knacks associated with a bar. Strip lights fitted vertically on either side of the alcove complete this phase.

Fig. C251. This bar and shelf unit was an old bookcase.

PLASTIC
BEADING

FORMICA TOP ON
BLOCKBOARD BASE

Fig. C252. Constructional
details.

Fig. C253. (below). Details of
shelf corners.

REEDED
HARDBOARD

CROSS BATTEN

METAL
BRACKET

2"x ¾"
TIMBER FRAMES

3"x 2" TIMBER
FEET

NOTE:- OVERALL MEASUREMENTS
TO SUIT REQUIREMENTS

However, should a ready-made bookcase not be available, it can be easily replaced in the scheme by small separate shelves. These can be of almost any size, and positioned according to the size and number of glasses you wish to display.

For the bar itself, simplicity of construction is the keynote as is clearly indicated in the diagram in Fig. C252. Two identical frames are made from 2 in. × ¾ in. softwood, and then formed into a skeleton unit by the addition of six cross battens. The four battens on the vertical members also serve the purpose of carrying the two shelves. No elaborate joints are employed, the corners being simply screwed together and strengthened with steel angle brackets.

The top surface of the bar and two shelves were made from single pieces of blockboard—an eminently suitable, rigid and cheap material. The shelf corners were cut as shown in Fig. C253 and secured to four stiffening battens added at appropriate points. The bar top surface, which projects in front and on both sides, is screwed to the horizontal frame members and two further stiffening battens.

A Formica panel completes the top surface; the edges being trimmed with plastic beading, while matching pieces of Formica add refinement to the front of the feet. The feet—simply-shaped pieces of 3 in. × 2 in. softwood—are added at this stage, and reeded hardboard is fixed to the front and sides.

A final touch of authenticity is provided by gin and whiskey optics mounted on a wooden fitting attached to the wall. This, positioned conveniently for service, is made from block-board, with a length of 2 in. × 2 in. (screwed from the back) across the bottom end. Two open slots are cut in one face of the 2 in. × 2 in. to the size of the square part of the optic fitting, then closed with a

narrow strip of metal—thereby forming two square holes into which the optics fit snugly. The clips for supporting the upper parts of the bottles can be fashioned from a pair of trouser clips drilled and screwed to the back-board.

SERVICE TROLLEY

The design explained here gives that professional look to a beginner's job. Without joints, it is a simple cut-out from resin-bonded plywood.

This service or tea trolley (Fig. C254) is a cunning piece of design. It is all cut out on the flat from a sheet of ¾ in. ply and the cutting plan is given in Fig. C255. It is a jigsaw job, or quicker still, a bandsaw job. If neither are available, any local timber works will cut the two sides out, after they have been marked out in outline on the ply-

Fig. C254. The
completed service
trolley; smart and
practical.

Fig. C255. Cutting plan.

Fig. C256. Exploded view.

HANDLES FORMED FROM ⅜×⅜" ANGLE AS SECTION

SHELF
16"
1¼"
1¼"
29"
14½"
26"
½"

11" 4½" 4½" 4"
10½"
12½"
13¾"
29"

SAWCUT ¾" ALL ROUND

COVER TOP SHELF WITH SELF ADHESIVE PLASTIC

ATTACH HANDLES WITH IMPACT ADHESIVE

ALL TIMBER ¾" THICK PLY

CORNERS & FLOWERS TRAY NOTCHED FOR LEGS

¾" DEEP SAW CUTS

DRAWER INTERIOR MAY BE COVERED

¾"

4¼"

10¾"

27"

DRAWER DIVISION FIXED IN PLACE WITH IMPACT ADHESIVE

MAKE DRAWER RUNNERS FROM ¾"×¾"×¹⁄₁₆" ALUMINIUM ANGLE

BEND DRAWER FROM 18 GAUGE ALUMINIUM SHEET 27"× 21⅞"

ATTACH HANDLES WITH IMPACT ADHESIVE

LEGS ARE GLUED TO SHELVES WITH WATER-PROOF GLUE BEFORE PEGGING

¼" DIA. ALUM. ROD 1½" LONG DRILL FOR DRIVE FIT

8"

2"

DRILL LEG TO TAKE CASTOR INSERTS

CASTOR

GAITERS FROM 18 GAUGE ALUMINIUM

SHELF

ALUMINIUM CHANNEL SCREWED TO LOWER SHELF

DRAWER

Fig. C257 (above). Castor fitting.

Fig. C258 (left). Drawer suspension.

Fig. C259. Lay out pattern on plywood. Pencil outlines. Cut on waste side of lines.

Fig. C260. Make a 'dry assembly' check before gluing-and-screwing.

Fig. C261. Large wheel castors are best. Metal gaiters minimise splitting of legs.

Fig. C262. The baize-lined aluminium drawer could be all-wooden if preferred.

Fig. C263. A central partition is useful, but not essential.

Fig. C264. ¾ in. × ¾ in. aluminium angle makes grooves in which drawer slides.

Fig. C265 (*left*). Underside view of trolley with drawer in place.

Fig. C266 (*right*). Metal handles (one each end) should match the metal trim. Stain wooden ones.

Fig. C267 (*above right*). Plastic laminate or self-adhesive plastic sheet make suitable non-absorbent top surface.

Fig. C268 (*left*). Leave ends open for easy cleaning. Aluminium moulding conceals plywood edges.

Fig. C269 (*right*). Drill pilot holes for screws, countersinking for heads to be filled over with stopping.

wood panel. The trolley top and the shelf below come from the remains of the sheet of ply.

It is obvious that there is no need to follow the basic design exactly, either for dimensions or shape, and the accessories and trim can be varied. A drawer below the lower shelf is useful. This can be made with some of the spare plywood for the ends, and sheet aluminium. Similarly make some aluminium spats or gaiters for the ends of the legs. These are quite useful as well as ornamental, for there is a slight risk of splitting when fitting castors and also some risk that the plywood might get chipped on the leading edges when being wheeled through doorways, etc. The drawer handle is also aluminium, ¾ in. section, one angle being dressed down to form a curve and the same again at the ends of the trolley top. The top and shelf are easier to keep clean if not fitted with an edge or moulding on all four sides—crumbs, etc., can then be whisked off.

Plastic laminate or self-adhesive sheeting is an obvious choice for the top, but you could use decorative veneered ply here and give it a good heatproof polish

Good castors are necessary, and the larger the better. Small castors will bring the trolley to a bumping stop at every irregularity in the floor.

As a guide, the exploded drawing shown in Fig. C256

MATERIALS
Plywood, ¾ in., 61½ in. × 29 in.
Aluminium sheet, 18 gauge, 27 in. × 21⅞ in. (Drawer)
Aluminium sheet, 18 gauge, 7 in. × 4 in. (Gaiters)
Aluminium angle, ¾ in. × ¾ in., 37 in. (Handles)
Aluminium angle, ¾ in. × ¾ in., 56 in. (Runners)
Aluminium rod, ¼ in., 18 in. (Pegs)
Plastic, laminate or self-adhesive, 30 in. × 14½ in.
Castors, 4 off, 4 in. dia.
Baize, glue, varnish, screws, etc.

can be followed and Figs. C259 to C269 show the method of construction. When working with plywood, make a trial dry assembly first. Then when everything fits, glue and screw together. Give a final light sanding with extra fine glasspaper before finishing, having first filled-in all nail or screw holes or small blemishes. Drill pilot holes for all screws, and use high-strength glue, keeping joints under pressure while they set.

CANADIAN-STYLE LEISURE CHAIR

The chair in Fig. C270, which was designed by Canadian architect Robert G. Calvert especially for home construction, can be made almost entirely from a single sheet of ¾ in. plywood, 4 ft. × 2 ft. The recommended quality to ask for is exterior grade Douglas Fir, 'good-both-sides' and waterproof. You will also require three pieces of hardwood (beech or mahogany), as detailed in the Materials list, for the struts and rails.

Cutting Out

The squared diagram (Fig. C271) shows the cutting plan for the plywood, each square representing 2 in. × 2 in. This has to be enlarged to full size and transferred to the 4 ft. × 2 ft. sheet of plywood. If you have access to a pantograph, there is no problem. Otherwise, mark out the plywood in 2 in. squares and copy the shapes out to the best of your ability (Fig. C272). If you cut one of a pair in cardboard, it can be used to draw round to mark its companion (Fig. C273).

Resist any temptation to re-arrange the shapes in a tighter assembly in order to save plywood; the grain direction will be affected and so will the strength of the finished chair.

Since your shapes, when cut, may not be absolutely exact replicas of the originals, the screw-hole positions in Fig. C280 must be regarded as approximate guides only: mark them, but leave the drilling until later.

Fig. C270 (*left*). One sheet of plywood, a few pieces of hardwood and some webbing make this leisure chair.

Fig. C271 (*right*). Cutting plan for the plywood.

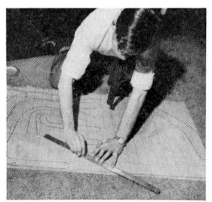

Fig. C272. Enlarge the cutting plan and transfer it to the plywood.

Fig. C273. One of a pair can be used to mark out its companion.

Fig. C274. Cutting out; bandsaw, jigsaw and power drill, or a local firm.

Fig. C275. Cut on the waste side of the lines. True-up later.

Fig. C276 (*below*). The complete set of plywood components.
Fig. C277 (*right*). Sand in pairs where possible to ensure good match.

Fig. C278 (left). Cut curved struts from one piece.

Fig. C279 (right). Cutting plan for curved struts.

1'-8¼"

5"

¼" divisions

Cutting plan for curved struts Q from 2" thick beech or mahogany

Tapes #8 and #13

Tapes #3 and 11

Tapes #2, 4, 6, 10, 12, 14

Tapes #1, 5, 7, and 9

Tapes B and D

Tapes A, C and E

Arm rest (N) from ¾" ply either side of legs (M)

¾" in from sides

6¼"

5⅝"

¾"

3¾" Upholstery jute webbing

Q

P

½"

1¼"

N

R

Q

Chair shown partly exploded

In from edge..¾"

Sides from ¾" ply

P

M1

M2

3¾"

1¼"

6¼"

8½"

Rails ¾"×2¼"×21¾" long beech or mahogany

Fig. C280. Exploded view of complete chair.

The actual cutting out (Figs. C274–276) is a job for a bandsaw, but a power drill and jigsaw could be used. If all else fails, your local joinery works would probably do the job at a moderate cost.

Fig. C277 illustrates the principle of sanding two similar shapes together to secure a good match. The three curved struts are cut from one piece (Fig. C278) to the cutting plan in Fig. C279. These struts should be well smoothed off; the ideal section is shown in the exploded view of the chair in Fig. C280.

Assembly

Take an M1 and an M2 and butt them together (making sure that they are both the right way round). Fasten two arm rests (N) by glueing and nailing one either side to provide a sturdy butt-joint. All three top edges should be aligned as much as possible, but it might be necessary to apply a finishing touch with a sander afterwards.

Now join the other M1 and M2 with the remaining arm rests (N) in the same way. This completes the two leg-and-arm units.

Next, lie one of the sides (R) on the floor or bench and place one of the leg-and-arm units on top, positioning it carefully to form the side elevation of the finished chair. Check the screw positions (ignoring the ones for the rails, at this stage) and adjust if necessary. Drill ⅛ in. holes through the leg-and-arm unit and into the side (R); then drill 3/16 in. holes in the leg-and-arm unit only. The two can now be screwed together, with 1½ in. × 10 csk screws and cup washers, to complete one side of the chair frame.

Lie this down, with the side R on top, and assemble the other side of the chair frame to match exactly, drilling and screwing as before.

Place the three curved struts (Q) in the appropriate positions. Note that the position for the centre one should be estimated by reference to the illustrations; the precise location is not critical—about three inches above the centre of the lower curve and flush with the outside edge should be about right. As before, drill ⅛ in. holes through the sides into the struts, followed by 3/16 in. holes in the sides only. It is important to see that these holes do not go in straight, but are slanted into the struts to make the fullest use of the holding power of the screws. Use 2½ in. × 10 csk screws and cup washers.

Next, position the two straight rails (P); it is possible that their precise length may need slight adjustment, so check carefully. Drill and screw as before, using 2½ in. × 10 csk screws and cup washers.

Sand, and fill nail holes preparatory for finishing; stain and/or varnish as desired. Note that it is only necessary to finish the ends of the plywood sides (R) as the webbing covers most of them.

Weaving

We used two colours of webbing, 3¼ in. wide, and woven as shown in Fig. C280; 2¾ in. webbing could be used but a greater number of rows would be necessary.

Of course, for a real luxury job, you could always use leather.

MATERIALS

1 piece 4 ft. × 2 ft. × ¾ in. Douglas Fir exterior quality plywood, 'good-both-sides'
2 pieces beech or mahogany 21¾ in. × 2¼ in. × ¾ in. for the rails (P)
1 piece beech or mahogany 20¼ in. × 5 in. × 2 in. for the three curved struts (Q)
1 dozen 1½ in. × 10 csk screws, and cup washers
1½ dozen 2½ in. × 10 csk screws and cup washers
¼ lb. of ¾ in. upholstery tacks
Webbing; a total of 31 yds. of 3¾ in. or 40 yds. of 2¾ in.
Nails, stain, varnish, etc.

VERSATILE DRAWER UNITS

These easily-made drawer units have the advantages of utility and versatility. As single pieces, the units offer storage in spaces too narrow for normal furniture; as bedside units, they are decorative and practical; in combinations of two or three, they offer remarkable drawer capacity; as extreme end bases with a well-finished flat top, they present a most elegant desk or writing table. A few of the adaptations are shown in Figs. C281 to C283—but the imaginative handyman can think up some really good ideas for using these, partly or entirely, for furniture construction. An advantage, of course, is that when the bases have outlived a particular function, or have been replaced with other furniture, they can be combined on any of the lines mentioned to begin a new life.

The carcase is a simple box-like structure with sound but easy joints. Any type of well-selected wood will do— some of the attractively-veneered plywoods available to-day will make a first-class job.

Sticking to the basic design is important as a rather orange-box-look will be the result if the recessed plinth and overlapping top are altered in any way.

First make the carcase, which is really a box with top, bottom, sides and back; joint as shown in Fig. C284, fixing the drawer runners before assembly. Always use a square for this job, marking the sides in pairs on the

Fig. C281. Two drawer units plus a writing surface; suitable for drawing room, study or office.

Figs. C282 and C283. Two bases offer functional service in lounge or bedroom; single pieces make ideal bedside cabinets.

Fig. C284. Constructional details.

inside. Now make the plinth, paying particular attention to the front mitres—but note that the rear corners are carried right back. The overall presentation is thus a jointless one as far as the plinth is concerned.

The drawers are again simple but very stout, for the

Fig. C285. Simple but effective drawer construction.

STACKED CABINETS

Fig. C286 shows what looks like a single piece of elegant furniture; but apart from the pleasantly symmetrical presentation shown, the tiers are, in fact, individual pieces of furniture which can be used as window lockers, hall chests or bedroom ottoman pieces for soiled or clean linen storage.

Similarly it requires very little imagination to be able to plan a number of these cabinets to form an attractive and functional room divider for a through-lounge or kitchen-dinette. Constructional details are given in Fig. C287.

Joints are made by generous glue application and pinning—wipe off all surplus glue squeezed from the joints —but remember that for perfect joints careful marking out and finishing are essential.

Finish depends entirely on the location of the piece or group of cabinets—or whether they are to be adapted for different rooms from time to time. Where a group of cabinets form a unit such as a divider, contrasting finishes and bright plastic surfaces can be used for effect and utility—but they can be equally pleasing in traditional finishes. Variations within the actual carcase can also be accommodated according to requirements. In a living-room divider for instance, an interior lining of smart self-adhesive plastic, or mirror surfacing plus a change to sliding glass doors will immediately convert a section to a display or cocktail cabinet.

rather heavy usage they are likely to receive. Note that the bottom drawer is deeper than the others for bulky storage items. Constructional details are given in Fig. C285. Detailed attention to finishing will be well rewarded with this particular item.

Glue and pin all joints—and where the edging strip gives the overhang to the top, a contrasting wood such as birch, glued with an impact adhesive, gives a pleasing effect. Finish, overall, can be as desired. Veneer can be used to advantage—particularly on the plinth; also a veneer on the top within the edging strip gives a striking contrast effect. With oak surfaces a wax finish looks nice.

Fig. C287. Constructional details.

Fig. C286. Individual cabinets make up this attractive unit.

WALL UNIT AND CABINET

Both these pieces, shown in Fig. C288, are basically box units with plain lap joints.

The material used is plywood of ample thickness, preferably Douglas fir plywood, ¾ in. thick, of the grade known as 'good-one-side'. Plywood has remarkable strength for its weight, and non-warping characteristics. Its main value from the viewpoint of this design, though, is that satisfactory end-grain fastenings can be made, which is something that cannot be done with ordinary wood. So the joints in these items are simply end-glued and nailed, and there is no carcassing or frame work.

These neat little units (of Transatlantic design) are specially suited to the modern home where space is at a premium. The dining cabinet is really two cabinets joined together in the middle and so one only need be made if big enough to suit requirements. Shelves or drawers can be fitted as needed. For an exciting appearance it is suggested the fronts of both wall cabinets and the dining cabinet should be given a contrasting finish. This could be a plastic laminate, or (as was done to those shown here) simply make shallow grooves (parallel saw cuts not more than 1/16 in. deep) to outline 2 in. squares. The wood was then painted with an egg-shell gloss finish. Naturally, there can be many variations.

The units are designed to be cut without waste from standard-size plywood panels. Cut and sand all parts to the exact sizes as given in the exploded view in Fig. C289.

All joints except those in the legs are glued and nailed. Following Figs. C290–C294, assemble the dining-cabinet by nailing the bottom to the back panel, the sides to the bottom and back, and the tops to the sides and back. Make

Fig. C288 (above). Box units with plain lap joints: useful together or separately.

Fig. C289 (below). Constructional details.

Fig. C290 (right). One of the two boxes comprising the dining cabinet being glued-and-nailed.

Fig. C291 (above). Fixing a side edge piece.

Fig. C292. Outline legs in pencil, then drill screw holes.

Fig. C293. Clamp legs in position; countersink screw holes from inside.

Fig. C294. Sliding or hinged doors? Piano hinges are being fixed here.

sure the front edges are flush.

Attach the sides to the edges of the top panel. The rear edges of the side pieces should be set ¾ in. forward of the rear edges of the cabinet, to allow for the back edge strip. Lay the legs in place and outline them with a pencil, placing the tapered edges toward the centre of the cabinet and lining up the straight edges with the ends of the side or edge pieces. Within each outlined area, drill the sides for three No. 9 csk screws. Countersink the holes on the inside of the cabinet.

Secure the legs with glue and 1¼ in. × 9 csk screws. When a pair of cabinets is used as one unit, as shown here, only six legs and three edges are required. Clamp the cabinets in alignment and attach them to the middle pair of legs. Fasten a single back edge measuring 50¼ in. × 2½ in. × ¾ in., to the ends of the three side pieces. On a base cabinet used singly, the back board measures 25½ in. × 2½ in. × ¾ in., Use plywood for this, too. Next, offer up the doors for fit and then fix with piano hinges.

Assemble the wall cabinet by fastening the top and bottom to the back, then secure the ends to the top, back, and bottom. Next fit and hang the doors. If the wall cabinets are to be paired to match the double dining cabinets, insert a 14 in. × 12 in. × ¾ in. plywood spacer between the two wall units. Install furniture glides on the cabinet legs, and friction catches and handles on all doors.

A professional-looking finish is easy on fir plywood if you use top-quality materials and follow a few simple rules. Clean all surfaces perfectly—do not paint over dust or spots of oil or glue. Fill all nail holes and blemishes in the exposed plywood edges with plastic wood or stopping. Since plywood is already sanded smooth, it is not hard to produce perfect surfaces by sanding with the grain.

Where surfaces must be cleaned frequently, and for durability, a high-gloss finish is recommended. After final sanding, dust off and put on a coat of primer. When this is dry, fill any surface blemishes, sand lightly and dust clean. Apply one coat of undercoat. If a high-gloss finish is desired, this coat could consist of equal parts of flat undercoat and high-gloss enamel. Sand lightly when dry and dust clean. Apply the final coat. Follow paint maker's instructions carefully, especially as to the use of thinners. Wood stains are an alternative, using polyurethane clear lacquer for a high-gloss finish.

MATERIALS

Dining Cabinet
(These quantities are for a single unit only. Modify if two are to be made)
Douglas Fir Plywood
Top : 1 piece, 24 in. × 16 in. × ¾ in.
Back : 1 piece, 22½ in. × 22½ in. × ¾ in.
Ends : 2 pieces, 23¼ in. × 16 in. × ¾ in.
Bottom : 1 piece, 22½ in. × 16 in. × ¾ in.
Doors : 2 pieces, 22¼ in. × 11 in. × ¾ in.
Fir, Pine or Hardwood
Legs : 1 piece, 14 ft. × 4 in. × ¾ in.
Side Edges : 2 pieces, 14 in. × 3¼ in. × ¾ in.
Back Edge : 1 piece, 25½ in. × 2½ in. × ¾ in.
OR (if cabinets are built as a pair)
1 piece, 50¼ in. × 2½ in. × ¾ in.
Miscellaneous
2 piano hinges, 22 in. long, with screws
2 friction catches
4 or 6 furniture glides, ½ in. size
1 dozen countersunk wood screws, 1¼ in. × No. 9
Nails
Glue
Sandpaper
Finishing materials

Wall Cabinet (one only)
Fir Plywood
Top : 1 piece, 24 in. × 12 in. × ¾ in.
Back : 1 piece, 24 in. × 12½ in. × ¾ in.
Bottom : 1 piece, 24 in. × 12 in. × ¾ in.
Ends : 2 pieces, 14 in. × 12 in. × ¾ in.
Doors : 2 pieces, 12¼ in. × 11¾ in. × ¾ in.
Spacer : 1 piece, 14 in. × 12 in. × ¾ in.
(Required only if cabinets are built in pairs)
Miscellaneous
2 piano hinges, 12 in. long, with screws
2 friction catches
Nails
Glue
Sandpaper
Finishing materials

RADIOGRAMS

It is not necessary to be an electronics engineer to build good-looking radio and gramophone housings. The 'works' can be bought in tested chassis form ready to fit into cabinets made to suit furnishing, space and convenience more exactly than the conventional one-piece radiogram. A single chassis carrying everything except the auto-change and loudspeakers is very easy to install, while separate units—radio tuner, tone control and main amplifier—need little more than plug-and-socket connection but permit the flexibility of separate housings and the freedom to assemble your own choice of equipment.

Radiogram

The cabinets shown in Fig. C295 can be used in a variety of arrangements. On the left is a low cabinet suitable either as a one-piece radiogram or as a housing for main monaural or stereo equipment using external loud-speakers. Measuring 41 in. long, 18½ in. deep and only 24 in. high, this modern piece has no opening or grille to mar the frontal appearance even when a loudspeaker is built in, for the sound is directed downwards through the bottom since the consequent air-loading improves repro-duction. Of the five items to be described this will receive the greatest attention because much of its form of con-struction is common to others. It comprises eight rectangu-lar panels in ½ in. plywood with screwed-and-glued joints augmented by ¾ in.-square fillets, as shown by exploded view in Fig. C296. The visible panel edges are turned into a decorative feature at the veneering stage.

Panel Sizes

The panels should be finished to the following dimen-sions:

End panels (two required) 18½ in. × 14 in.
Front 40 in. × 9½ in.
Back 40 in. × 13½ in.
Bottom 40 in. × 17½ in.
Deck (top panel under lid) 40 in. × 17½ in.

Lid top 39¾ in. × 18 in. (but see text)
Lid front 39¾ in × 4½ in. (but see text)

To the inside of each end panel (Fig. C296) fit fillets in a rectangle having outside dimensions of 17½ in. × 7½ in. and positioned ½ in. from the bottom edge and both vertical edges, the lower fillet ½ in. clear of the botttom front, back and bottom panels. Fit two parallel fillets 39 in. long to the back panel with ends ½ in. short of the vertical edges, the lower fillet ½ in. clear of the bottom edge and the other one spaced 5½ in. from the top edge. These will match the spacing of the end-panel fillets. The two on the front panel are identical with those on the back, and have exactly corresponding positions with respect to the bottom horizontal edge.

Built-in Speaker

For a built-in loudspeaker cut a central hole of suitable diameter in the centre of the bottom panel. The loud-speaker is screwed directly over this; no additional baffle is required. A generous pattern of vent holes must be bored in the bottom panel to air-cool the electronic units; more are necessary in the back panel, immediately below the upper fillet, for the escape of heated air. The impor-tance of adequate ventilation cannot be too highly stressed, but the holes, and others made for cable entry, must not give access to electrical parts for children's fingers.

When all fillets are fitted, screw-and-glue the ends, back, front and bottom together to form a rigid box, countersinking deeply on visible surfaces for filling prior to veneering. The removable deck panel is fitted later by screwing only. Although round tapered contemporary legs suit the cabinet well, flat ones add interest to the design as shown in Fig. C295. On planed timber 2⅝ in. × 1 in., plot the outline shown in Fig. C296; cut away the waste indicated by shading and clean up the edges. Screw-and-glue each one between tailor-made blocks as shown in the sketch and fit to the cabinet by screwing through the blocks. They can be stained and polished, or painted.

Fig. C295. Excellent radio and hi-fi equipment can be bought in chassis form ready for fitting into your own cabinets. Here are five attractive items, with full instructions and advice on ensuring quality of reproduction.

The auto-change manufacturers supply a paper template for the odd-shaped hole to be cut in the deck, to which it is fitted from above with sufficient slack wire to enable connections to be made before it is lowered into position. Further cut-outs and holes are needed for the radio and tone control. These, whether separate or united on one chassis, are generally fitted to the underside and the escutcheons and knobs added afterwards. The main amplifier, if separate as in many high-fidelity installations, should be screwed to the bottom panel in a well-ventilated position.

Unlike the conventional radiogram, this cabinet can be kept for a long succession of chassis replacements and for this reason the use of melamine laminate, available in several attractive wood-grains, is advised. Dark contrast strips enhance the visible panel edges and white is effective for the under-lid surfaces. Impact adhesive bonding is familiar enough, but it is worth while to pass on an effective treatment for edges and corners where veneers meet at right angles. Allow one to lap over the other, then trim it back with a chamfered edge to expose a dark thin line that smartens the appearance considerably. One advantage is that in trimming to a chamfer the tool is necessarily applied at an angle and cannot mark the decorative surface. The panel dimensions quoted allow for the 1/16 in. thickness of the veneer; some adjustment will be necessary if ordinary wood veneer is used.

The Lid

The lid, not shown in the drawing, comprises two panels at right-angles with a small fillet inside the angle. As a precaution against an effect of cumulative small errors in the cabinet construction, the lid should be checked, in the white, with the fully veneered cabinet to verify that it will fit correctly after veneering. The lid is held open by a conventional strut (not shown in the photograph). The finger-lift is a piece of hardwood tapered to a thin skittle shape and screwed on from inside.

Veneer the deck after it has been holed, then cut the plastic back to the edges. Fit the deck, with its attached radio gear, by means of domed-head screws for good appearance. While connections are being made (to the maker's instructions) the deck will necessarily be raised from its normal position and perhaps turned over, therefore some wires will have a little excess length which can be allowed to lie inside as the panel is lowered into place. The mains cord entering through the back panel should be anchored with a plastic clip to prevent tugs from wrenching its connections in the apparatus.

External Speakers

If external loudspeakers are to be used, as for stereo reproduction, the unused centre of the cabinet could be partitioned to provide record storage. Alternatively, a tape deck could be fitted, although most tape enthusiasts prefer to keep the recorder separate and portable.

Chair-Side Model

An idea likely to gain popularity is the chair-side cabinet, of which an example is included in Fig. C295. If a loudspeaker is crammed into this little housing the tonal quality will be comparable with an ordinary record player, but with external loudspeakers it can be used with equipment of the highest grade. As a control

unit it houses the tuner, tone-control and small amplifier (possibly all on one chassis) plus the auto-change. A powerful high-fidelity amplifier, likely to run somewhat hot, would preferably be housed elsewhere and connected by cable.

Fig. C297 shows the simple box structure of ¼ in. plywood—thinner than the photograph indicates, but adequate. The outside dimensions are 25½ in. × 15 in. × 4½ in. A partition forms compartments measuring 15½ in. and 9¼ in. inside, and ½ in. square fillets form rims on which the bottom and deck panels fit flush with the edges of the sides. The control deck panel which fits over the front compartment is 14½ in. × 9¼ in. and is holed to suit the escutcheon on washers to create an air space, but the greater heat of an all-in-one chassis demands adequate ports which can be holes or slots trimmed with decorative metal gauze not too small in mesh.

Gram-Deck

The gram-deck panel is 15½ in. × 14½ in. with a cut-out to suit the auto-change. Check the height of the mechanism before making the lid, which is a plain box 16 in. × 15 in. outside and (subject to check) 4½ in. deep, hinged to the back edge of the gram compartment. A narrow wood finger-lift is fitted. Use standard tapered legs to stand the bottom 6 in. from the floor (making the total height 15 in.) or make flat legs to fit to the sides as shown in the photograph. These can be cut from 2⅞ in. × 1 in. planed wood to the details given in Fig. C297. The upper part, above the 133 deg. line, should be cut away on one side to half thickness to provide a kind of half-joint with the cabinet, which rests on the step so formed. On two legs this must be on the side opposite to that shown in the drawing. Screw the legs to the cabinet from inside, fit a triangular filler piece ½ in. thick in the angle between each pair, fill the gaps, smooth and paint.

Decorative Angles

Contrast decoration is effective and plastic veneer with chamfered corner treatment is again recommended. The horizontal plywood edges visible after veneering should be lacquered.

External loudspeakers are convenient in many cases and practically essential for convincing stereophonic reproduction. Neat small enclosures can give reasonable tone quality; some increase of size is unavoidable for genuine high fidelity but not to the monumental proportions of some older installations. The photographed group includes a cabinet of up-to-date slim proportions—25 in. high, 13½ in. wide and only 7 in. deep—in which a modern hi-fi loudspeaker of low resonant frequency will give full bass response. Slight variations in size, and in the methods of acoustic damping and loading, are specified by different makers, whose information is readily available to purchasers, but the construction shown in Fig. C298 can be taken as basic. Constructors using the cheaper standard type of 8 in. loudspeaker can build exactly as described and will obtain very agreeable reproduction.

As rigidity is essential, all panels are of ½ in. plywood, finished to the following sizes:
Sides: 23 in. × 7 in.
Front and back: 23 in. × 12½ in.
Top and bottom: 13½ in. × 7 in.
Baffle: 11 in. × 11 in.
Fig. C298 is a scrap view of the top end; the bottom

Fig. C296 (*left*). Constructional details of gram-cabinet and legs.

Fig. C297 (*below*). Chair-side cabinet and legs.

Fig. C299 (*left*). Small loudspeaker; fabric on hardboard is held by decorative edge-strips.

Fig. C300 (*right*). Corner loudspeaker, from above.

Fig. C298.   Rear scrap view of slim loudspeaker cabinet.

is identical. Fillets on the side panels (screwed-and-glued ½ in. from the vertical edges) are ¾ in. × 23 in. and are cut to make halved joints with the 12½ in. horizontal fillets that link these two panels. Assembled to this stage, the fillets form frames on which the front and back panels will be fitted. Further short fillets fit level with the top and bottom edges of the side panels; these are unjointed.

The front panel opening measures 8½ in. vertically and 9 in. across, set 2 in. below the top ledge. The ½ in. difference from truly square seems to influence the appearance considerably. This panel, and the top and bottom, can now be screwed-and-glued in place; but the back, which must be removable, is fitted by screwing only. One part not illustrated—the loudspeaker baffle—has a 7 in. diameter hole over which the loudspeaker is screwed, and the front face is covered with decorative fabric glued at the edges. This sub-assembly is not fitted until the cabinet is ready for use.

Modifications

Certain modifications have been left until now to avoid complicating the main assembly details. A fully-enclosed loudspeaker sounds boxy, and this is overcome either by controlled leakage through the resistive path of an array of small holes or slits in one of the panels (conveniently the back) or by the reflex system employing a front vent below the main opening. For high-fidelity speakers the details are issued by the makers, but for the ordinary type a vent 9 in. × 3 in. should give good results. Line the inside of the cabinet with carpet felt or fibreglass. Mounting it on 1 in. feet brings its height to the 25 in. already indicated. Modified for all-fabric front by the method described in the next paragraph, it can be stood horizontally on table or shelf, or on tapered legs.

The small enclosure shown in Fig. C299 can be made of ¼ in. plywood without fillets and the size (12 in. × 9 in. × 5 in.) suits loudspeakers up to 8 in. diameter fitted directly to the front panel. This panel is set back slightly to accommodate the hardboard on which the decorative fabric is glued. The retaining strips can be continued over the top for decorative effect and underneath to serve as feet. Generous holes in the back will avoid a boxy tone.

Corner Speakers

An interesting little loudspeaker is achieved by corner wall mounting, as in the photograph and Fig. C300. The panel is 12 in. across the top, 6 in. on the bottom edge and 10 in. top to bottom. The small round or elliptical loudspeaker is mounted to play upwards through a triangular baffle fitted to the panel at 70 deg. so that it is actually horizontal when the assembly is in its tilted position on the wall. Technically, the performance is improved by the air loading presented to the loudspeaker by the solid wall angle, and reproduction is surprisingly good.

RECORD CABINET
WITH TIPPING COMPARTMENTS

This design (Fig. C301) is an improvement on the conventional method of storing gramophone records. It enables the records to be placed in the best position for selection and at the same time presents them at the most convenient height for handling without risk of damage. It therefore has the advantage that there is no need for the person selecting the record to crouch down and peer into the dark inner recesses of a storage cabinet of conventional design.

The whole unit consists of a cabinet with two suitably balanced compartments or hods which hold the records. On raising the lid, these are tipped by means of a simple link into the delivery position (Fig. C302); the lid in turn is hinged to the back of the cabinet. The hods are returned to their original position by raising the lid once more in the same way as in the initial movement.

Two compartments are incorporated in the design, one

Fig. C301. Safe record storage is essential. This cabinet holds discs securely, yet accessibly.

for 12 in. records and the other for small and medium sized records.

The outer casing or cabinet comprises a base, sidewalls and back, with a dividing wall to separate the record hods. Two lids are provided which are secured to the back with piano hinges. The front of the cabinet is completed by the front face of each hod. Legs 9 in. long are secured to the base (Fig. C303).

The mechanism which operates the hod is basically a slotted link retained freely to the side of the hod and screwed to a right-angle bracket fixed to the lid. When the lid is raised, the bottom of the slot engages with a peg which is screwed into a reinforcing block on the side of the hod. The hod, operated by the link, then pivots, and because of the weight which is purposely concentrated in

Fig. C302. Left-hand lid lifted, hod tilted forward for discs to be removed or replaced.

Fig. C303. Hods removed, showing operating link detached. Spring compensation allows for various weights.

Fig. C304. Constructional details.

MATERIALS

Chipboard ¾ in. thick :
  2 off 14½ in. × 16 in. for Lids
  1 off 28 in. × 16 in. for Bottom
  2 off 13½ in. × 16 in. for Sides
  1 off 13½ in. × 15¼ in. for Centre
  2 off 13½ in. × 12¾ in. for Hods
  1 off 11½ in. × 26½ in. for Back
  2 off 2 in. × 13¼ in. for Back of Lid
  12 ft. of 1 in.-sq. batten
  3 ft. of ½ in.-sq. batten
  12 sq. ft. approx. of ⅛ in. ply or hardboard
  8 sq. ft. of resinated wood veneer
  1 tin of impact adhesive
  ⅜ in. dia. metal tube, total 6 in. long for pivot dowels
  2 piano hinges, 1 ft. long each
  4 off 9 in.-long legs with end gliders
  2 right-angle brackets made from brass mirror-fixing plates
  2 upholstery springs, 5/16 in. or ⅜ in. diameter
  5 ft. of brass edging strip
  A quantity of screws
  Off-cuts for spacing blocks between partitions and to provide the necessary balance to the hods

the forward position, the hod tilts forward over the dead-centre position and is restrained from further movement by a simple stop which engages the link. The lid can be retained if necessary by a notch on the link to keep the lid from resting on the records. Two standard coil upholstery springs (which are normally used in the backs of chairs)

are anchored diagonally inside the cabinet and attached to the bottom of the hods, to compensate for the varying weight of records which are stored at any one period : the space left underneath the small record compartment can be conveniently used for a drawer if so desired.

A study of the diagrams in Fig. C304 will help to explain the construction details.

The basic material used in the construction of the complete unit is ¾ in. thick chipboard. This is cut squarely to the correct length, butted together and fixed with large wood screws.

The retaining part and the partitions of the hods are made either from ply or hardboad glued and bradded into position

All outside faces are faced with resinated wood veneer and the edges finished with ¾ in. strips of rigid plastic veneer.

Two upholstery springs are cut to length. Brass edging strips can be used to finish off the lower and top edges of the cabinet.

LONG AND ELEGANT

For a long room in which a long, low sideboard would be 'just the job', here's a design any reasonably capable woodworker can make and be proud of.

In this instance a sideboard was required which would be the major item in a layout occupying a large living room. In addition to general storage space it was planned to provide cutlery storage, a cocktail cabinet and accommodation for a record player. The design and construction chosen (and shown in Fig. C305) is sufficiently flexible to allow various permutations of the above to be made or added to with little trouble.

The length of the unit is almost 8 ft., made up of five

Fig. C305. Cutlery storage, cocktail cabinet, record player: this sideboard could be subdivided to suit a variety of requirements.

Fig. C306. An 18 in. module ensures economical use of standard panels. If you change the layout, keep to the sizes.

sections based on a 1 ft. 6 in. module. This was adopted to make full use of veneered chipboard which is obtainable in this width. The layout, with measurements, is given in Fig. C306. Selected veneered board was used for cladding to top and ends and for all doors, and very few cuts were needed, thus proving economical in use and doing away with the need to veneer many cut edges. The framing is a mixture of mahogany and ramin, and mahogany-faced plywood was used for the bottom and back.

Construction details are given in Figs. C307 to C309. The first stage of construction is to build up the subframe from 1 in. × 1 in. ramin framing, glued-and-screwed together. Great care must be taken in setting out the frame

Fig. C307 (right). Components required.

Fig. C308 (centre). End-on view; straight, not splayed, legs are required.

Fig. C309 (bottom). This plan minimises edge veneering.

¾" veneered board

1¼"×¾" mahogany planted on front of divisions

1"×1" ramin framing to divisions and ends, size 1' 4½"×1' 5⅝", division framing having ¼" ply grooved in

Door position

¼"×2" mahogany nosing

¼" ply bottom and back

1"×2¼" mahogany splayed at ends as shown on elevation

1"×1" ramin subframe

9" vertical leg screwed to 6"×6"×1" ply pad fixed to subframe

1"×2¼" ramin splayed at ends as front rail

as this forms the foundation on which the unit is built.

Next the 1 in. × 2½ in. rails can be splayed at the ends as shown, and glued-and-screwed in position through the back of the subframe, using mahogany at the front and ramin at the back.

The 2 in. × ½ in. mahogany nosing is now pinned and glued in position to the front edge, followed by the plywood bottom, leaving ¼ in. rebate at the back edge to receive the back cladding.

To complete the base, four 6 in. × 6 in. × 1 in. plywood pads are needed, glued-and-screwed in position to receive the legs. Vertical legs were chosen with both structural design and appearance in mind. The necessity for using these, as opposed to the splayed variety, will become apparent when the unit is completed. The weight is quite formidable.

The base is now ready to receive the remainder of the unit but it is wise at this stage to clean and rub down the

LID 16⅞"x 16" ONE VENEERED EDGE (BOTH EX 3' 6" x 1' 6') TOP 1' 7⅜"x 1' 6" ONE VENEERED EDGE

TOP 4' 9⅛"x1' 6" (EX 5' 0"x 1' 6') ONE VENEERED EDGE

DOOR 1' 6'x1' 5⅝" VENEER BOTTOM EDGE

DOOR 1' 6"x 1' 5⅝" VENEER BOTTOM EDGE

DOOR 1' 6'x 1' 5⅝" VENEER BOTTOM EDGE

FRONT PANEL 1' 6'x 5" VENEER BOTTOM EDGE

DOOR 1' 6'x1' 0¼" VENEER BOTTOM EDGE AND TOP EDGE

DOOR 1' 6"x 1' 5⅝" VENEER BOTTOM EDGE

ENDS 1' 6"x 1' 6" (TWO EX 3' 0"x 1' 6')

EX 3' 0"x 1' 6" USE REMAINDER FOR SHELVING AND EXTRA BOARD AS REQUIRED

TWO EX 3' 0"x 1' 6"

TWO EX 3' 0"x 1' 6"

plywood bottom as this is more easily done before the superstructure is in position.

The division and end framing is now cut and put together. Six identical frames are needed, cut from 1 in. × 1 in. ramin with angles mitred, pinned and glued.

The four division frames are filled-in with ¼ in. plywood grooved-in as shown. The two end frames are left open. These frames can now be offered up to the subframe and glued-and-screwed in position. Care is needed here to see that the distance between divisions is exactly 1 ft. 5⅞ in., except between outer divisions and end framing where 1 ft. 5 in. is required. The divisions can temporarily be held in position by a diagonal batten pinned along the back until the glue has set.

Next cut 1½ in. × ¾ in. mahogany facing strips which are glued in position to the front of the divisions. The back is now cut from ¼ in. plywood, sanded on the inner face and pinned and glued in position.

The frame is now ready to receive the top and end panels, which are cut from veneered chipboard.

End panels are fixed first, cutting two from one 3 ft. × 1 ft. 6 in. sheet. The cut edges are placed at the top; fixing is by glue and lost-head panel pins punched in. The top is made up from two sheets, using one 5 ft. × 1 ft. 6 in. and one 3 ft. 6 in. × 1 ft. 6 in. With some care, two sheets can be found which give a reasonably good continuity of veneer pattern. The smaller sheet should be cut and one section set aside to form the cutlery box lid at a later stage. The larger sheet will need trimming to length and two cut edges will be visible; these are veneered before the top panels are fixed.

Shelves are cut from chipboard and pinned and glued in position placing the cut edges at the back. Individual taste will dictate how many compartments are given shelving. In the original, three bays of shelving were fitted.

The base to the cutlery box is of ¼ in. plywood supported on two 1 in. × 1 in. ramin bearers.

The divisions are cut from plywood and glued in position.

Doors may now be fitted. The cutlery lid is cut from the piece of veneered board previously set aside, which will need to be cut to length and veneered on one edge. The doors are again cut from 1 ft. 6in.-wide board using 3 ft.-long sheets.

The fascia to the cutlery compartment is produced by cutting a 5 in. width from the cocktail cabinet door panel and pinning and glueing this in position to line up with the door under it.

Holes are now drilled for the cupboard handles, but they are not fitted until after the finish has been applied.

All doors are hung on brass piano hinges, and stays are fitted where needed. Nylon cupboard catches were used on the original.

The unit can now be cleaned up and prepared for finishing, applying stopping where necessary and finishing with a fine grade of rubbing-down paper. The original was finished with a teak colouring and five coats of matt cellulose varnish.

The cellulose is easily applied by brush, and it dries sufficiently quickly to enable all coats to be applied in one evening. Light rubbing down is needed between coats; wax polish will maintain the finish in excellent condition.

The cutlery box is lined with green baize fixed with latex adhesive, and a panel of white plastic is fitted to the inner face of the bar door to form a table top when open.

A record-player unit was installed in the original scheme, feeding two small speakers slung under either end of the unit. There is scope here for installation of tape deck, radio, etc., according to taste.

MATERIALS

60 ft. of 1 in. × 1 in. ramin
8 ft. of 2½ in. × 1 in. ramin
8 ft. of 2 in. × ½ in. mahogany
6 ft. of 1½ in. × ¾ in. mahogany
8 ft. of 2½ in. × 1 in. mahogany
1 ft. × 1 ft. of 1 in. plywood
8 ft. × 3 ft. of ¼ in. plywood
7 ft. 6 in. × 1 ft. 6 in. of ¼ in. plywood
One 5 ft. × 1 ft. 6 in. veneered board
One 3 ft. 6 in. × 1 ft. 6 in. veneered board
Four 3 ft. × 1 ft. 6 in. veneered board
Extra veneered board for shelving
4 off 9 in. legs and fixing plates
9 ft. brass piano hinge
5 brass cupboard handles
3 brass desk stays
5 cupboard catches
4 sq. ft. green baize
1 ft. 3 in. × 1 ft. plastic laminate
15 ft. board edge veneer
2 pints varnish
½ pint matching colour
Panel pins, screws and glue

PLANT TROUGH

The trough shown in Fig. C310 is a rectangular shape which is supported by four legs—two at each end. Use a softwood and cut the pieces to the dimensions given in Fig. C311. Add the side stiffeners only if the side panels tend to warp after painting.

Assemble the box, stick with impact adhesive, and then make secure with panel pins. Before painting the trough, first seal the hardboard panel with a thin undercoat.

Of course, the position of the shelf will vary according

Fig. C310. An attractive flower trough for indoor display.

Fig. C311. Details and dimensions.

to the size of pot plants. It is advisable to make several depths of side fillet with an adjustable shelf which can be positioned according to pot depth.

Finishing the legs in a different colour and lacquering looks very effective. Fix the legs to the box with 1 in. × No. 6 woodscrews, two per leg. Then use check dimensions given to avoid marking the end pieces with the leg fixing angles.

KITCHEN

SINK UNIT WITH DOUBLE DRAINERS

Kitchen furniture should both please the eye and do an efficient job for many years. The quest for originality should therefore not be allowed to produce 'gimmicks' likely to have only a brief life. The sink unit shown in Fig. C312 is basically conventional but interest is gained by setting the front in several planes to break the blankness of large surfaces, and also by two-tone decorative treatment. Although the shape of the drawer fronts adds interest the purpose is really functional, for the extended lower edges form finger-grips for opening and eliminate the need for projecting handles. With long service in mind the structure is sturdier than usual and attention has been given to moisture-resistance. A sandwich door construction prevents the warping to which thin panels on edge are prone.

Construction of the carcase, Fig. C313, is simplified by building it as the three sub-assemblies illustrated in Figs. C314 and C315. There may be variations in the dimensions of different makes of sink tops; they should be checked so that suitable allowance can be made. The topmost edges of the cabinet are shown square in the drawings but will have to be planed or chiselled to suit the contour of the flange of the pressing. To guard against kitchen dampness, use good quality timber and make the joints with synthetic resin glue. The front sub-assembly, of which Fig. C314 gives a rear view for clarity, comprises four 31⅜ in. × 2¾ in. × ⅝ in. uprights made of wood, with several horizontal members. The two outer ones are cut at one end for halved joints 2 in. wide, while the other two are plain at the ends but are cut away 1½ in. wide for a distance of 22⅛ in. to clear the sliding doors that will move in front of them. All four have a small cut-out into which the ½ in. square shelf support is jointed at a later stage.

A 62 in. length of 2¾ in. × ⅝ in. forms the bottom hori- zontal. As it is a bearer component, this piece should be of tough hardwood or multi-ply. The position of the bottom sliding door channel on this member can be seen from the drawing. The deeper upper channel is mounted on a strip of 1½ in. × ¼ in. material (preferably plywood) screwed-and-glued to the upright as shown in Fig. C314, with fillets as necessary.

As described so far, the frame will seem to lack rigidity, but this will not be so when the drawer aperture frame—shown 'exploded' away from the sub-assembly in the drawing—is added, and erection is done in the order suggested in the next paragraph. Simple nailed-and-glued joints are good enough for this rectangle of 1⅜ in. × ¾ in. wood because it both gives and receives strength when united with the front frame. Its two 2¾ in.-wide inter- mediate uprights can be fitted later, to ensure that they register correctly with the main uprights and clear the drawers.

Erection of the front sub-assembly begins by screwing-and-glueing the drawer aperture frame to the four up- rights in a position that will be obvious from Fig. C313. This squares the uprights accurately and imparts con- siderable rigidity even at this stage. Next, fit the bottom horizontal, remembering that as the four glue joints present end-grain, nails will secure them more firmly than screws. Further horizontal ties are provided by the ½ in. square shelf supports, by the 1½ in. top channel support and, to a slight extent, by the two channels. As the simple joints are arranged to be mutually aiding, the sub- assembly will be found to be perfectly rigid when the glue has hardened.

Fig. C315 gives details of the rear sub-assembly, again seen from the rear. Four 1½ in. square uprights have cut-outs to suit the horizontal parts, and some are cut on two sides to joint in two directions at right-angles as shown clearly in the drawing. As the contour of most sink pressings rises towards the rear, the width of the top

Fig. C312. Designed on robust lines for long service, this sink unit will be worthy in any kitchen.

horizontal must be chosen to suit. The ½ in. square strips are shelf supports and their positions must line up with their partners on the front frame. Assemble all rear parts first and then add the side horizontals, of which all details are given in Fig. C315. The absence of a lower horizontal means that absolute rigidity is not attained with this frame until it is united with the plinth.

This, the third sub-assembly is shown in part in both Figs. C314 and C315. It is merely a rectangle measuring 62 in. × 17¾ in. on the outside, strengthened by fillets in the front corners, by the cut-away ends of the rear outer uprights which (when eventually fitted) have the same

Fig. C313. The frame consists of three separate assemblies.

effect as fillets, and by two cross-members which support floor and side panels. The latter are flat strips of any convenient width over 1½ in. recessed into the front board. During final assembly of the carcase these two strips will also be supported on fillets fitted to the two rear inner uprights as indicated in Fig. C315. The front board of the plinth should be 1 in. thick so that ¾ in. of its edge can support the front frame, leaving ¼ in. margin to which the floor hardboard can be pinned and glued.

A plinth is a better way of providing essential toe-room than short feet or side supports, which leave a dirt-trapping space too shallow for easy cleaning. Because of the stepped arrangement of the front surfaces of the unit, the rim of the sink overhangs the plinth by about 3 in., giving adequate toe-room even when the user stands very close.

When the glued joints have hardened, the three sub-assemblies can be united with the carcase. Mount the rear frame on the plinth with the cut-away portions up the uprights fitting snugly in place to form glued joints augmented with screws. Fix the two floor-support cross-members to fillets on the rear uprights, then attach to these the ½ in. square strips—making sure their front ends do not cover the surface to which the front frame has to be secured.

At this point we have the plinth and rear frame erected complete with the side horizontals that are to joint with the front. It would be wise to have some assistance in fitting the front frame, for it must be kept upright while the first few screws are fitted, to tighten the glue joint between the bottom horizontal and the edge of the plinth. Then secure the halved joints with the top side horizontals. After this you can continue unaided, fitting the remainder of the screws through the bottom horizontal and adding the shelf supports.

Hardboard is flexible along its length and width but is extremely rigid to force applied in the edge-to-edge direc-

Fig. C314. The front assembly, from the rear.

tions; even narrow strips refuse to bend edge-ways. This edge stiffness can be employed to augment the strength of the structure by glueing it firmly, especially where it spans joints. This effect, similar to that of the familiar repair plate, can be used in the sink unit by attaching the side panels with resin glue and panel pins. Cut the hardboard to suitable shape but leave 1 in. clearance—at the top for the flange of the pressings, at the bottom to avoid floor dampness, and at the front to prevent it from being seen. If the floor and shelf panels are shaped for exact fit there will be further contributions to overall strength when they are glued in place. Fit back panels to both outer cupboards; the middle one has neither back nor shelf because there must be clearance for the plumbing.

You may prefer to delay panelling until after the the drawer runners have been fitted so that you can have elbow room for adjustment. The drawer action is easy to make smooth in operation, and imposes no wear on the cabinet structure. As Fig. C316 shows, it comprises a ½ in.-square rail on each side of the drawer and built-up hardwood channels in which the rails slide. Each channel is a screwed-and-glued assembly of two ½ in.-square hardwood strips set fully ½ in. apart and parallel on a 19¾ in. strip of 1 in.× ¼ in., the whole being fitted to the cabinet uprights with packing pieces as required to set them correctly to engage the rails of the drawer. This should be determined by trial.

Fig. C316 also shows the construction of the drawers, with dimensions, in an inverted view for clarity. Use ply-

wood ⅝ in. or ¾ in. thick for the front as a guarantee of permanent flatness. The lower edge of this panel (uppermost in Fig. C316) has a 1¼ in. extension of width to form the finger-grip. The exact shape is not critical provided it is symmetrical and all three fronts match exactly. To avoid dovetailing, the remainder of the drawer is made of ¼ in. plywood glued and pinned in an arrangement that employs edge stiffness to make the panels strengthen each other. Fillets are used to joint these panels with the thick front one. For economy, the bottom panel could perhaps be of hardboard. Only two drawers can be fitted because the bowl occupies the middle space, but the usual dummy front is included to maintain the design theme.

Hard plastic laminate is the recommended treatment for the front surfaces of the unit. In the two-tone scheme shown in Fig. C312, a pale yellow linen pattern was used for the carcase, with light mottled grey for the drawers and doors. The easiest way of cutting the material is to score both sides (deeply enough on the decorative side to reveal the dark base material) and break. Allow a little excess width in case of slight location error in glueing and to allow the completed work to be cleaned up level. Use impact glue for this part of the job. The top horizontal strip should be wide enough to be covered by the pressing but clear of the edge that has to be rounded to fit the flange.

For the drawer fronts, cut the plastic slightly oversize all round, using a fretsaw for the curves or drilling close small holes and breaking. Fix with impact glue or, if you

Fig. C315 (*right*).   The back of the unit, from the rear.

Fig. C316 (*left*).   Detail of drawer construction, showing hardwood sides.

can arrange pressure for a few hours, cheaper casein adhesive. Trim the veneer back to the plywood edges and paint these edges white to seal them against moisture and to smarten their appearance. Veneer and paint the dummy front before fitting; screw it from inside the carcase. Veneer the front of the plinth with white laminate, as in the prototype, Fig. C312.

With the exception of the door runners, all surfaces not veneered should be protected with a good brand of waterproof paint. To guard against the ravages of moisture it is worthwhile painting the underside of the plinth, particularly the edges that will be in contact with the floor and vulnerable to the effects of mopping operations. This could well be done before veneering, when the carcase can be turned over without risk of damage.

A problem encountered with sliding doors is the tendency for thin panels on edge to warp, especially in the damp atmosphere prevailing in the kitchen. Veneering one side sets up unbalanced stress conditions that can make matters worse even when the veneer is a stable material like laminated plastic. Balance can be achieved by veneering both sides, and this costs very little more if you use cheap brown 'balancer' veneer on the unseen side. This laminate, 1/16 in. thick, can be obtained by your plastic stockist. With this treatment, thin hardboard panels attain surprising rigidity and stay permanently flat.

Cut the doors from good flat hardboard and check that

they are of correct size and move freely in the channels. Check the width of the channel grooves because it is likely that veneer both sides will make the panels too thick for them—in which case a margin of bare hardboard must be left at top and bottom on one or both sides as necessary.

Perfect flatness is obtained by keeping the veneered panels under pressure, and the glue must yield while the sandwich adjusts to the flat state. This rules out impact glue because of its instant bond. As casein and synthetic resin leaves plenty of time for adjustment, the veneer can be cut exact without the error margin needed for impact glue, and both sides can be treated at once. As soon as the sandwiches are glued, stack them on a flat surface, interleaved with paper to prevent exuded glue from sticking them together. Cover the stack with flat boards and weight them with bricks, buckets of water or anything that can be arranged to apply even pressure. (You can, of course, buy 'balanced' hardboard).

You may prefer plain doors and if so the two-tone doors of Fig. C312 are a neat way of using available veneer that is not wide enough to cover the entire surface in a single sheet, for, while a simple joint would be obvious, the colour divisions makes a feature of it. The panels can be cut for flush door pulls by close drilling and chiselling, after veneering. Finally, give three edges a coat of white paint, leaving the bottom edge bare.

A SIMPLE KITCHEN CUPBOARD

The cabinet shown in Fig. C317 is suitable for use in the kitchen or pantry as a food container or a general storage unit for baking tins, etc. It is made entirely from ¾ in. chipboard and ⅛ in. hardboard with a small quantity of softwood from which the sliding door track is made. For this type of unit, chipboard is very suitable and far better than solid wood. It is obtainable in the correct width (thus obviating the need for rub-jointing, the joining of pieces side-by-side) and the surfaces do not need planing. Overall dimensions of this cabinet are 4 ft. 8 in. high, 18 in. deep at base and 2 ft. wide, but size can be varied to requirements.

Following the details given in Fig. C318, cut out the two sides adjoining each other—this method avoids any waste. All four fixed shelves are exactly 2 ft. long so that economical cutting from a 4 ft.-wide board is possible. The adjustable shelf and the lower front apron piece can be cut from the remainder of the sheet and a useful area will still be left for future use as shelves, etc. Converting one's own sheet of chipboard proves much cheaper than having this cutting list made up at a builder's yard or handyman's shop. There will also be some useful spare hardboard.

Plane up all the sawn edges and make sure that the corners and edges are perfectly square. Place the two sides in the vice with their back edges uppermost and across these two edges square the joints. Housing joints which run straight across from edge to edge are acceptable and easier to do, but stopped housing joints look better. In both cases, the joints are 5/16 in. deep. Needless to say, the shelves should be a tight fit so the housings should be accurately squared across, using a sharp knife, and the measurement checked before cutting.

Since it is important for all the housings to be of uniform depth, it is well worth buying a small router plane. Although the cutter is only ¼ in. wide, this little plane will repay its cost on this job alone.

All the housing, with the exception of the top, should be stopped approximately ½ in. from the front edge. Using a ¾ in. firmer chisel, chop a square mortise at the front end of the housing to a depth of 5/16 in., i.e., the finished depth of the groove. Cramp a piece of wood alongside the knife cut and, using this as a guide for the tenon saw, saw down to the required depth. Chisel out roughly and not quite to the finished depth. Do all three housings on each side piece and then using the router plane finish off to final depth.

The inside back edge is rebated to a depth of ⅛ in. to take the hardboard back. This rebating should be done at this stage. The shelves may now be fitted. The back edges of all shelves and the top will come level with the ends of their respective grooves, thus enabling the hardboard back to go up behind every one. The hardboard will not be visible from the sides, only from the top. The front of shelves 2, 3 and 4 will have to be notched out. They should also project beyond the sides, thus making it possible to plane them down to the correct level and angle to come flush with the sides.

Drill ⅜ in. holes ½ in. deep for the adjustable shelf and chisel the two housings under the lower shelf to take the front apron piece which forms a combined plinth and toe recess. These grooves should be 2 in. back from the front edge. This apron piece will have its long edges angled to meet up with the shelf and to stand level on the floor.

Fig. C317. Chipboard and hardboard: no rub-jointing or planing. Yet it makes an elegant and useful unit for the kitchen.

¾" THICK CHIPBOARD

⅛" DEEP REBATE

3/8" DIA HOLES ½" DEEP

HOUSING 5/16" DEEP

TRACK WITH TWO 3/16" WIDE GROOVES

⅛" THICK HARDBOARD

Fig. C318. Constructional details.

The whole unit can now be assembled. Glue all joints and secure with 1½ in. oval nails. It is a good plan to use sash clamps to hold the unit square while the nails are inserted. Be careful to get the back edges of the shelves level with the rebate. Cut out and fit the hardboard back. Nail in place with ¾ in. special hardboard nails, the shiny side of the hardboard to the inside. Nail well into the back edges of the shelves as well as the rebate. This back will give great rigidity to the whole structure. Glue in and nail the apron piece; plane off all protruding shelf edges; cut and fit the adjustable shelf on four lengths of ⅜ in. dowel and finally remove all the sharp edges with glasspaper.

The cabinet is now ready for the doors. The track is made as shown. Take a 2 ft. board, ¾ in. thick, and along the edge plough two 3/16 in. grooves. For the lower tracks, they must be of ⅛ in. depth; the upper tracks need the same spaced grooves 5/16 in. deep. The tracks can be bought ready-made, if you prefer, at very moderate cost. Bevel the underside of each track length to allow it to tilt over at the angle corresponding to the side.

These tracks should be glued in place, 1/16 in. back from the front edge of the shelves, with impact adhesive. Coat both surfaces, let the glue dry and then put the track in place (accurately, first time!) and cramp for a few seconds with a G-cramp. Cut out and fit the hardboard doors, allowing ⅛ in. top and bottom for the grooves and an overlap of 1 in. in the centre. Any sort of handle can be used, although the circular recessed type is recommended. These can be bought in different colours and it is only necessary to bore a 1½ in. hole; they simply snap into position. Two or three coats of paint complete the job.

MATERIALS
1 sheet 8 ft. × 4 ft. × ¾ in. chipboard
1 sheet 6 ft. × 4 ft. × ⅛ in. hardboard
4 lengths 2 ft. track for sliding doors
Dowels, nails, impact adhesive

CUPBOARD AND DROP TABLE

In a house with a small kitchen, a drop table and cupboard fixed to the wall can be very useful, with the space beneath used for the stools. A false bottom in the cupboard takes two main supports to rest the table on; these spars swivel round on pieces of ½ in. dowelling located through the bottom shelf and the bottom of the cabinet. The dowels should be 5¼ in. from the sides of the cabinet so that when both spars are swung out 5¼ in. of the spar is between the bottom shelf and bottom of cupboard giving sufficient support to the table to take the weight of articles it is carrying.

The details of construction and dimensions given in Fig. C319 can, of course, be altered to suit requirements.

The first stage is to make the framework for the cupboard from six pieces of wood 34 in. × 10 in. × 1 in. Two of these are grooved to take the middle and bottom shelves. If sliding doors are required for the top of the cupboard, the top piece and middle shelf should be grooved at the same time.

Next the bottom shelf and bottom of the cupboard should be laid on top of each other and a ½ in. hole drilled through 5¼ in. from each end, the centre of the holes being ½ in. in from the front edge of the cupboard. Ensure that the depth of the hole is ½ in. in the bottom of the cupboard. The next stage is to fit the main parts together. Next, two pieces of wood 18 in. × 2 in. × 1 in. are each drilled exactly 5¼ in. from one end. Care must be taken when drilling, as the drop table must rest level on both these pieces, the ends of which are cut diagonally so that when they are fitted into the cupboard they are flush with the front.

The drop table is made from 3 pieces of wood grooved and glued together to make 1 piece 34 in. × 16 in. × 1 in., or

Fig. C319. Constructional details for this multi-purpose space-saver.

alternatively from a sheet of thick plywood. The sliding doors are made from hardboard, 2 pieces each 18 in. × 13 in.

It is best at this stage to paint the woodwork as required. When dry, the two struts are fitted under the bottom shelf with ½ in. dowelling, which are cut flush after fitting. The table is hung with two hinges set into the bottom shelf and table. The sliding doors are fitted by bending the hardboard slightly and placing in the grooves. Fit a catch to hold the table in the 'up' position.

Cover the table and bottom shelf with self-adhesive covering; fit two handles to the sliding doors and two smaller handles to the table supports.

The whole fitment is secured to the wall by two strips of iron fixed to the back of the cabinet and the wall and firmly plugged. Make sure it is positioned so that the table when down is the same height as the cooker or other working surface.

The fitment has a clean appearance and all that has to be done to lower it is to swing out the table supports and drop the table. Extra shelves can be fitted if required.

STORAGE SPACE ON A DOOR

Why not use the space behind the cupboard door for storage? It can be used for tools, cleaning equipment or, as shown in Fig. C320, for food storage. The extra storage is made by mounting shelves of 8 in. × 1 in. to a ½ in. plywood panel. The diagonal of the shelves must be about 1½ in. shorter than the width of the door opening to allow the door to be opened. Cut the plywood to fit the door opening, allowing a clearance of 1/16 in. on each side of the four sides. Cut slots in the side pieces for the top and bottom, and also for the shelves. The bottom shelf should be set far enough up from the floor level to allow for a castor, which helps the hinges to support the weight of the door when it is loaded. The castor should be attached on the under part of the shelf on the latch side (Fig. C321). Next, assemble the sides, top and bottom pieces of the shelves, using a glue and flat-headed wood screws. After the shelves have been assembled and before the glue has dried, glue-and-screw the plywood backing panel in place (Fig. C322).

It should fit flush on the hinge side and extend

Fig. C322. Exploded view.

Exploded view

View showing how and where caster is fitted

Fig. C321. Caster saves hinge strain.

Fig. C320. Shelving behind door.

several inches along the latching side to compensate for the fact that the shelves are slightly narrower than the door opening. The door is hung with three butt hinges to provide support.

DRAWER UNIT

The overall width of this cabinet will be determined by the room plan, but the height and depth should match other base cabinets. The drawer arrangement can suit your individual needs, but the top drawer should line up with the top drawers in any existing base cabinets. The cutting board may be placed at the top, or, as shown in Fig. C323 under the first drawer, to make it more convenient for jobs that can be done seated. It pulls right out so that one side can be used for cutting, slicing, etc., and the other, lined with a plastic surface, for pastry work.

Build the cabinet first and tack the ¾ in. × ¾ in. runners into place so that they can be adjusted, if necessary, before being glued-and-nailed.

Make the body of the drawers about ⅛ in. slack in height and width for easy fitting, and ¼ in. less in depth than the cabinet itself. Drawer faces should be the full width of the cabinet. If ⅛ in. slack has been allowed the lip will measure 13/16 in. each side. For double units with a ¾ in. plywood partition between two banks of drawers the inner lip will be about ⅜ in.

After cutting all the drawer parts to size, begin assembly by fixing a cleat to one end of the bottom. Assemble the back and two sides, then fasten the bottom in position. Finally, position the front and fix to the sides and cleat. All connections must be glued-and-nailed. If drawers have been made ⅛ in. scant, a thumbtack fastened each side of the opening will provide a snug slide.

Fig. C323. Constructional details of the drawer unit.

IRONING CUPBOARD FITMENT

The ironing cupboard fitment described here was built in a corner of the kitchen of a new house. In this case the section of the kitchen where the cupboard is situated has a dropped ceiling. So the total height of the fitment is only 7 ft. In higher rooms the top portion can easily be made up with reeded hardboard or similar material.

The fitment (shown in Fig. C324) is 4 ft. 7 in. wide. It is shown when not in use, and also with one laundry bin tilted outwards, and the ironing board pivoted out.

The ironing cupboard consists of three parts, as shown in the working drawings in Fig. C325. At the top is a storage cupboard with two sliding doors; this part contains three shelves, made of 1 in.-thick tongued-and-grooved boarding. The shelves are put up in conjunction with the main framework, consisting of 4 in. × 1 in. upright pieces at each side and four 2 in. × 2 in. horizontals—one at the top, two over the laundry bin recess, and one at the base.

The sliding doors are made from ½ in.-thick veneered plywood; they slide on a strip of laminated plastic in grooves formed with ½ in. × ½ in. hardwood strips. The strips are nailed to the upper 2 in. × 2 in. horizontal of the framework, and on to the lower of the three shelves.

Two horizontal 3 in. × 1 in. rails form the front to the sliding channels. These front rails are let into the 4 in. × 1 in. uprights at each side to come flush with the front surface. All three shelves rest on bearers plugged to the wall at the right and screwed to the upright framework at the left hand side. Bearers for the top two shelves are 2 in. × 1 in. and 1 in. × 1 in. to the third shelf.

The centre portion of the fitment has a small cupboard for the iron at one side. This is formed with a 1 in.-thick vertical division of tongued-and-grooved boarding. A ½ in.-thick veneered plywood door on small hinges is fixed to the front and secured by a press button type cupboard catch. The cupboard for the iron can be lined out with asbestos sheets, so that the iron may be put away while still hot. The rest of the central space is left open.

In this space the electric power point is situated; when putting the iron away it is necessary to pull out the plug from the electric socket.

Below the central space with the cupboard for the iron, another shelf is formed of 1 in.-thick tongued-and-grooved boarding. This shelf has a rounded front edge and rests on 1 in. × 1 in. bearers at each side.

Underneath this shelf, and above the two 2 in. × 2 in. bearers (the back one plugged to the wall), the ironing board is fitted. This is a solid piece of deal, 4 ft. 3 in. long by 11 in. wide and 1¼ in. thick, cut to shape as shown in the plan at (C). It is secured by a ½ in. dia. bolt, 6 in. long, which allows the board to be pivoted in and out.

A 6 in. × 1 in. cross piece is fitted below the ironing board, between the two 2 in. × 2 in. bearers, to contain the bolt below the ironing board.

Two 9 in.-diameter laminated plastic plates are placed between the bottom of the ironing board and the top of the 6 in. × 1 in. cross piece to act as washers, easing the action of the ironing board. Another cross piece, 3 in. × 1 in. in section, is fitted in between the two 2 in. × 2 in. horizontal bearers. This is to take the weight of the ironing board when not in use and stowed inside the fitment.

Observe that when the ironing board is pivoted out and is ready to be used for ironing it is supported by the 2 in. × 2 in. horizontal bearer at the front. At the back, the top of the ironing board wedges under a 12 in. long 1 in. × 1 in. strip which is fixed under the shelf over the ironing board. This strip is secured to another 12 in. long, 3 in. × 1 in. bearer which in turn is plugged to the wall. This is to ensure that the 1 in. shelf will not be levered upwards by the ironing board.

Fig. C324. The fitment closed (*left*) and in use (*centre*).

2in.×2in.

10½in.

3in.×1in.

SHELF

11in.

SHELF

11in.

SHELF

3in.×1in.

1ft.3½in.

IRONING BOARD

11in.×1¾in.

SHELF

2in.×2in.

3ft.0in.

LAUNDRY BINS

3in.×1in.

2in.×2in.

SECTION

1ft. 1in.

4in.×1in.

1ft.5in. — 1ft.5in. — 1ft.5in.

1in. 1in. 1in. 1in.

4ft.1½in.

PLAN

Fig. C325. Plan (*left*), section (*right*), and elevation (*below*).

SLIDING DOORS

2ft.10½in.

7ft.

OPEN SPACE

SOCKET

IRON CUPBOARD

1ft. 1in.

1in.

IRONING BOARD

3in.

6in.×1in.

3in.×1in.

2in.

LAUNDRY BINS

2ft. 3in.

3in.

4ft.7in.

ELEVATION OF FRONT

The lower part of the fitment is just a framework which contains three laundry bins. Two 4 in.×1 in. uprights between the bins form the only division. These uprights are notched behind the horizontal bearers and are screwed to them. A 3 in.×1 in. skirting board is fixed along the base.

The laundry bins can be made in hardboard or plywood. Allowance has been made for 1 in.-thick boarded sides and hardboard fronts and back in the material list. The laundry bins shown have pegboard fronts. To allow them to be tilted forwards the sides must be sloped down towards the back, from 2 ft. 3 ins. to 2 ft., so the backs are lower than the fronts. When a bin is tilted forwards, the back should touch the underside of the 2 in.×2 in. horizontal bearer at the front above the bins.

Round dowels (1 in. diameter broom handle) are fixed on top of the 2 in.×2 in. behind the skirting board. It is necessary to pack up the dowels, using a nut to form a space between the underside and the top of the 2 in.× 2 in. timber. Secure each dowel with two screws, countersink tops, at the same time keeping them away from the rear surface of the skirting board, as in the section at (b). This is to leave a gap into which the lower end of the front panel of the laundry bins will fit.

MATERIALS

1 ironing board, 4 ft. 3 in. × 11 in. × 1¾ in.
3 uprights, 7 ft. × 4 in. × 1 in.
2 uprights, 2 ft. 9 in. × 4 in. × 1 in.
1 skirting board, 4 ft. 7 in. × 3 in. × 1 in.
4 horizontals, 4 ft. 7 in. × 2 in. × 2 in.
2 horizontals, 4 ft. 7 in. × 3 in. × 1 in.
4 hardwood strips, 4 ft. 7 in. × ½ in. × ½ in.
4 bearers, 10 in. × 2 in. × 1 in.
4 bearers, 1 ft. × 1 in. × 1 in.
1 length shelving, 4 ft. 7 in. × 1 ft. 1 in. × 1 in.
1 length shelving, 4 ft. 7 in. × 1 ft. × 1 in.
2 lengths shelving, 4 ft. 7 in. × 10 in. × 1 in.
1 vertical side, 1 ft. 3 in. × 1 ft. 1 in. × 1 in.
1 hardboard side, 7 ft. × 1 ft. 1 in.
1 bearer, 1 ft. × 6 in. × 1 in.
2 bearers, 1 ft. × 3 in. × 1 in.
1 bearer, 1 ft. × 1 in. × 1 in.
3 round dowels, 1 ft. 5 in. × 1 in. diameter
2 laminated plastic plates, 9 in. diameter
1 laminated plastic plate, 4 ft. 7 in. × 2 in.
2 pieces ½ in. veneered plywood, 2 ft. 7 in. ×
  2 ft. 3 in.
1 piece ½ in. veneered plywood, 1 ft. 1 in. × 10 in.
5 D-handles
1 cupboard catch
2 hinges (2 in. butts)
3 bottoms to bins, 1 ft. 5 in. × 1 ft. × 1 in.
6 sides, 2 ft. 3 in. × 1 ft. × 1 in. (or plywood)
3 backs, 2 ft. × 1 ft. 5 in. hardboard
3 fronts, 2 ft. 3 in. × 1 ft. 5 in. hardboard
1 bolt, 6 in. × ½ in. diameter
Screws, nails, paint, etc.

The front panels of the laundry bins are kept ½ in. lower than the base of the bins. Each bin, when placed in position, will pivot on the dowel.

The best way to make and fit the bins correctly is to fix the dowels first, then cut one side of the first bin, and try it out for tilt.

D-handles are fixed to the sliding doors and to the front of each bin. The sliding doors can be stained and polished with the rest of the woodwork.

A strip of hardboard is fixed to the side of the cupboard, and the ironing board is covered with the usual padding.

The pegboard should be painted with a roller.

DROP-LEAF WALL TABLE

With a projection of less than 3 in. from the wall when folded down, the table described is an attractive piece of furniture with obvious advantages for the kitchen where floor space is limited (Fig. C326).

Quite a simple construction job, the general arrangement of the component parts is shown in Fig. C327; the sizes given can, of course, be adjusted to meet individual requirements.

Apart from the leg, where the joint is a simple lap, there is virtually no joinery to be done.

To locate the wall plate and secure it, the best procedure is to drill the plate with four 7/32 in. diameter holes, countersinking with 7/16 in. drill to ¼ in. The spacing of the holes should be according to the length of plate used.

Next, draw a horizontal line 2 ft. 5 in. above floor level and, using the drilled wall plate as a template, drill the wall with a ¼ in. masonry drill to a depth of 2½ in. Before fixing the plate, chisel the recesses for the hinges, and transfer the hinge marks to the corresponding edge of the blockboard. Now screw the plate to the wall.

The plywood rail and hardwood leg are then shaped and jointed according to the dimensions shown in Figs. C328 (a) and (b) respectively. Assembly is by glue and two 1¼ in. × 10 brass screws. The foot of the leg is fitted with a locating dowel to prevent accidental folding. This

Fig. C326. The table in position; a practical proposition for the smaller kitchen.

Fig. C327. Component parts and details
of assembly.

4'-0"x 1'-10" plastic
sheet glued to B/Board

4'-0"x1'-10" sheet of
7/8" thick Block
Board

1" wide plastic edging

5/8" rad 1/4 round

2"x1¼" hardwood rail
fixed to wall with 3"x No12
screws

1'-5"

4"

2"

5/8" thick ply rail

recess 5/8" deep

1¾"

1¼"

4"

2'-4"

1¼"

½"

1"

Fig. C328. Details of rail and leg.

MATERIALS

4 ft. × 1 ft. 10 in. blockboard (grain of core to run
lengthways)
4 ft. × 1 ft. 10 in. plastic laminate sheet
8 ft. plastic edging strip
4 ft. 0½ in. × 2 in. × 1¼ in. hardwood
4 ft. 0½ in. × ⅝ in. radius quarter-round hardwood
mouldings
2 ft. 4 in. × 1¾ in. × 1½ in. hardwood
3 in. × 2 in. brass hinges
1¼ in. and ⅝ in. screws to fit
Four 3 in. × 12 wood screws
Four 2 in. × 12 wall plugs

dowel is a 1¼ in. × 10 brass woodscrew, set in a ⅛ in.
hole, screwed proud in the hole and cut off to leave ¼ in.
of shank projecting.

When the leg joint is set, fix the brass hinges to the
plywood rail with the knuckles in line with the edge—
see Fig. C328 (c); then recess the blockboard in the
marks previously made for the hinges, but check alignment with wall plate first.

Now attach the leg rail to the underside of the blockboard, fold the leg flat and attach the top to the plate
hinges with 1¼ in. brass screws.

Raising the table and dropping the leg plumb, mark the
floor, and drill to receive a ¾ in. length of ¼ in. internal
diameter non-ferrous (brass or aluminium) tube to receive
the dowel.

The main construction is now completed; finishing
touches are laying the plastic laminate according to the
adhesive manufacturers' instructions.

When the adhesive has set properly, round the two
outer corners of the top, working downwards from the
laminate surface with a forming tool, using a fine cut
blade; then glue-on the plastic edging.

If you are using a matching strip of laminate, it can
easily be pre-formed by immersing in hot water; otherwise the flexible strip is simple to apply.

Final stages are to fix the quarter-round moulding along
the back of the wall plate, clean up, and polish or paint
the exposed woodwork according to requirements.

BREAKFAST BAR

The simply-built bar shown in Fig. C329 is ideal for
dividing a small kitchen-dinette. The materials used are
chipboard and plastic-covered hardboard. A piece for the
top is cut 60 in. × 18 in.; the size can be varied slightly but
should not be less than 48 in. or more than 72 in. without
additional support. Three pieces 18 in. × 12 in. are cut for
end shelves. One piece 30 in. × 18 in. for the upright
support; one piece 47¼ in. × 12 in.; one piece 46¼ in. ×
5 in. and finally one piece 18 in. × 5 in.

First round off the shelves. Lay the 60 in. × 18 in. piece
on the bench and mark off the centre of the material,
end to end with pencil.

Measure back 9 in. from one end, and either with a
pair of compasses or a piece of string and a pencil mark
a radius to give the shape required. Cut out to this shape
with a pad saw or with a tenon saw and shape with a
forming tool. Keep the edge square. Each of the three
18 in. × 12 in. pieces are laid under the shaped piece in
turn, marked with the radius and cut. Then take the
46¼ in. × 5 in. piece and plane up both edges. Ensure that
these edges are both square and straight. Next the 47¼ in.
× 12 in. piece is planed up in the same way and marked
with a centre line from end to end. At 2 in. from each
end and equal distance apart, say 9 in., mark off this piece
and the top piece, 60 in. × 18 in., and drill with a 5/32 in.
drill and countersink.

Now take the 47¼ in. × 12 in. and 46¼ in. × 5 in.,
keeping the 5 in. wide in 1 in. from one end of the 12 in.
wide piece. Glue-and-screw the two together with 2 in. ×

Fig. C329. This attractive, functional and easily-built unit saves space and saves half the cost of a modern set of tables and chairs. It will seat four adults in comfort.

Fig. C331

½in. HOLE

Fig. C333

2in.×8 COUNTER SUNK SCREWS

3in.×2in. PACKING

1½in. HARDBOARD OVERLAP

SCREWS

2in. FROM EDGE

Fig. C330

Fig. C332

8 csk screws forming a 'T'-section, again keeping the 5 in. piece in 1 in. from the squared end. Glue-and-screw the 60 in. × 18 in. piece to the 'T'-section. This 'T'-section has two uses. Most important, the 5 in. piece supports the top and secondly gives added shelf space for odds and ends, i.e., newspapers, etc.

Next take the 18 in. × 5 in.; mark the centre (i.e. 9 in.), measure 6 in. either side of the centre line, mark from these marks to the end corners of 18 in. edge, and cut off. Glue-and-screw this piece into the end of the shelf and top section (Fig. C330).

Next take the three rounded shelves and clamp to the bench ensuring exact line of all three pieces on straight edges, then, on the centre line of the top piece and 2½ in. in from the edge of the radius, drill a ½ in. hole to take ½ in. rod (or ⅝ in. if ½ in. copper tube is used for shelf support). Drill this hole through the two shelves and partly through the base shelf.

Take one of the rounded 18 in. × 12 in. pieces and mark a line 2 in. from the edge of the radius (Fig. C331).

Now you will need some 3 in. × 2 in. Cut this to fit to the radius line. Next cut a piece of hardboard 3 in. wide. Screw the pieces of 3 in. × 2 in. to the shelf, and glue-and-pin the hardboard to these pieces (Fig. C332), leaving 1½ in. overlap on the ends.

Take the 30 in. × 18 in. piece and on one end at opposite corners cut out a piece 3 in. × 2 in. to line up and take the overlaps of hardboard to the base shelf. Now shape and fix the plastic to the round shelves with impact adhesive. When dry, with light pressure, drill through the holes drilled in the shelves through the plastic. Now place one of these shelves on top of the base and drill through the hole, again lightly, to drill through the plastic of the base. Screw the base to the 30 in. × 18 in. piece and trim off the hardboard overlaps and screw to the edges of the upright (Fig. C333).

Then measure from the top 8⅝ in. and 17¼ in., mark a line square across from each of these marks, and drill four 5/32 in. holes at equal distance on each line and countersink on the back. Insert the brass rod or tube, 23 in. long, in the holes in the shelves; position and screw the shelves to the support leg.

Now, with a square, position the shelves on the rod. Drill a 5/32 in. hole through the edge of the two shelves and the rod or the tube.

Cut the heads off two 3 in. round wire nails and hammer into these holes to hold shelves in position. Punch these home, slightly countersunk.

Cut and fix the plastic to the top and two under shelves and trim and file in the normal way. The whole unit is now ready for assembly and fixing.

Use a 12 in. piece of 2 in. angle-iron; drill two holes in each flange, to support and hold the top and shelf unit to the wall. Some assistance will be needed to position the units and angle-iron support.

Stand the end shelf unit roughly in its position. Now offer up the top unit and level up and mark the wall for fixing the 12 in. piece of angle-iron. Take off the top and screw the angle-iron to the wall. Now replace the top and check the other end of the 12 in. shelf for position. This may need some trimming to fit, also the rod or tube of the end shelf unit may need trimming. Having done this, put the end shelf unit in position and mark around the base with a pencil to show the position on floor. Take away the units, lie the end shelf unit on its side and knock in three 3 in r.h. nails and cut off the heads to leave about 1 in. protruding. File these ends to a point. Stand the complete unit upright and take great care to place it in the exact position required. Now mark the position of the protruding nails in contact with the floor. If a solid floor, drill with masonry drill and insert plugs. If a wood floor, drill the three holes ⅛ in. diameter. Position the unit and push down on it, to push the nails into the floor.

Now drop the top unit into position, drill up through the angle-iron support two ¼ in. holes, and insert 1½ in. dome head coach bolts. Drill three 5/32 in. holes through the upright shelf support into the 12 in. undershelf, and, using 2 in. round-head screws, fix the top to the end unit and tighten up the nuts of the ¼ in. bolts.

Obtain some soft plastic edging; stick this with impact adhesive to all exposed edges. You will have to dress the edges of the board with adhesive and allow it to dry to seal the wood before adding more adhesive to stick the edging on. The rest of the exposed board can be decorated as preferred, either with paint, self-adhesive covering or laminated plastic off-cuts.

FOLDAWAY BREAKFAST BAR

For most people, these days, it is a convenience to be able to have some meals in the kitchen. The difficulty is to make one room do two jobs.

In the small kitchen—anything with a floor area of less than about 120-150 sq. feet—there simply isn't enough room for a real dining table. This breakfast bar or dinette unit provides a place where the family can have breakfast,

Fig. C334. The breakfast bar extended for use. The seats can be folded away to leave the table as a useful working surface. When not required, the table, too, can be folded back.

Fig. C335 (below). Detail drawings.

FRONT ELEVATION

SIDE ELEVATION

LEG DETAIL

TABLE DETAIL

PLAN VIEW

Ball catch

2 in. hinges

$\frac{5}{8}$ in. blockboard

2 in x 1 in.

7

6

Hole for light fitting

3 in. x 1 in.
Broom cupboard
door $\frac{5}{8}$ in. blockboard

2 in. x 1 in.

$\frac{5}{8}$ in blockboard

Drawer box
from $\frac{5}{8}$ in.
blockboard

$\frac{1}{8}$ in. hardboard

4

5

3 All shelves
from $\frac{5}{8}$ in.
blockboard

LEG TO SEAT DETAIL

$\frac{5}{8}$ in blockboard

$\frac{1}{2}$ in. x 8 in. timber

Table
top $\frac{5}{8}$ in blockboard

$2\frac{1}{2}$ in. x 1 in. timber

2

$\frac{5}{8}$ in.
block-
board

Ball catch

Table leg
$\frac{3}{4}$ in. block-
board

Two 3 in. hinges

$\frac{5}{8}$ in. blockboard

All battens
$\frac{5}{8}$ in. sq.
timber

$\frac{1}{8}$ in. hardboard

Legs $\frac{3}{4}$ in. timber
Seat top $\frac{5}{8}$ in. blockboard

Plinth assembly
constructed
from 2 in. x 1 in.

DRAWER DETAIL

1

1 in. thick
foam rubber

Ball catch

Cupboard
door $\frac{5}{8}$ in.
block-
board

$\frac{5}{8}$ in.block⌐
board

Drawer
runners
$\frac{1}{2}$ in. sq.

$\frac{5}{8}$ in. blockboard

Ball
catch

Seat legs
from
$\frac{3}{4}$ in. timber

SEAT TO UNIT DETAIL

Drawer fronts
sides and
backs $\frac{3}{8}$ in.
timber

Drawer
bottom $\frac{1}{8}$ in.
hardboard

$\frac{3}{4}$ in. sq.

Fig. C336. Exploded view.

Fig. C337. Fix back and base firmly to wall and floor.

Fig. C338. Rigid framework is essential. A floor-to-ceiling fit is best.

Fig. C339. Side panels and shelves act as stiffeners.

Fig. C340. Slot this shelf to take a cutlery cabinet.

Fig. C341. Housing slots in cabinet. It is an optional extra.

Fig. C342. House inner uprights flush. Cut back middle shelves to take seats.

Fig. C343. Panel-in seat recesses.

Fig. C344. Table top has frame construction, allowing leg to fold inside.

Fig. C345. Hinge legs on steel pins tapped in from each side.

Fig. C346. Buss butt table hinges avoid rust.

Fig. C347. Dowels close holes after steel pins are tapped in.

Fig. C348. Upholstery must not be too plump to permit folding of seats.

Fig. C349 (*far left*).   Fix stout butts to seats. Drill pilot screw holes.

Fig. C350.   Light fittings, if required, are 'to choice'.

1

20in.

LOWER DOORS 5/8in. BLOCK-BOARD

PLINTH FROM 2in. x 1in.

2in. x 1in.

1/8in. HARD BOARD

7/8in. SQ.

3in. x 1in.

2 1/2in. x 1in.

4ft. 2in.

2

BACK AND DOOR OF BROOM CUPBOARD 5/8in. BLOCKBOARD

BOTTOM CUPBOARD DOOR 5/8in. BLOCKBOARD

5/8in. BLOCKBOARD

ALLOW 1/4in. OVERLAP FOR SEAT SUPPORT

8in.

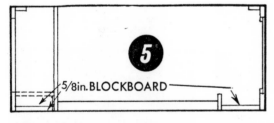

3

1/8in. HARDBOARD

1/2in. x 8in.

ALLOW 1/8in. OVERLAP FOR TABLE SUPPORT

2 1/2in. RECESS TO TAKE SEAT WHEN FOLDED 2 1/2in.

4

SLOTS CUT FOR FIXING OF DRAWER BOX

3/8in. x 2 1/2in. STRIP

1 3/8in. RECESS TO TAKE TABLE WHEN FOLDED

5

5/8in. BLOCKBOARD

6

1/8in. HARDBOARD

7/8in. SQ.

ATTACH 2in. x 1in. BATTENS TO WALL WITH SCREWS

7

TOP CUPBOARD DOORS FROM 5/8in. BLOCKBOARD

5/8in. RECESS TO TAKE CUPBOARD DOORS

Figs. C351 to C353.   Shelf plan views. The shelf numbers correspond with those given in Fig. C336.

or a snack, quietly and comfortably. When the meal is over, clear away the things, fold away the seats and table, leaving the kitchen clear; or fold away the seats and leave the table down for use as a working surface.

The finished unit, which will seat four, is shown in **Fig. C334.**

Dimensions can be Altered to Fit

From the detail drawings shown in Fig. C335 it can be seen that the only dimensions that are more-or-less fixed are the table height, which should be about 30 inches for comfort, and the seat heights, which need to be about 18 inches. Obviously, enough room must be allowed for the table and seats to fold upwards, which means that clear spaces equal to their length plus working clearance, must be allowed for in the cabinet.

The cabinet occupies a floor space 20 in. deep by 50 in. wide. With seats and table lowered, the unit projects a further 3 ft. 6 in., or a total of 5 ft. 2 in. If the kitchen is very narrow, in order to save an inch or two, it would probably be better to cut the depths of the cabinet rather than reduce the length of the table and seats, which at present provide reasonable elbow room for four. Of course, if only a two-seater dinette is needed then cut the table down to, say, 24 in. long. At this size it would still provide a useful amount of working surface when not in use for meals. After completion, sand the woodwork down lightly in the direction of the grain, and fill over all nail and screw heads. Use good quality gloss enamel as a final finish over at least one undercoat.

By studying the exploded view of the unit in Fig. C336 and by following the explanatory details shown in Figs. C337 to C350, it can be seen how simple this unit is to construct. The shelf details in Figs. C351 to C353 should be used in conjunction with Fig. C336.

KITCHEN STOOL

Any long-grained timber can be used for the legs and cross rails of this simple kitchen stool, and plywood is

Fig. C354 (*lower right*).   The completed stool, a comfort for the housewife or her visitor.

Fig. C355 (*upper left*).   Constructional details.

Fig. C356 (*upper right*).   Exploded view of leg and rail assembly.

Fig. C357 (*lower left*).   Method of covering seat.

suitable for the top (Fig. C354). Haunched mortise-and-tenon joints are used to attach the two top rails, and ordinary mortise-and-tenons for the lower ones.

Legs

The legs are 1¼ in. square and 25¼ in. long, and are made up in two pairs, each pair being connected by the top cross rail (Fig. C355). Material for all rails is 2 in. wide by 1¼ in. thick. The width is cut away to 1½ in. at the centre.

Fig. C356 shows a part-exploded view of the leg assembly and a clear indication of the rail positions is given. One top rail can be seen in place, and the other cut to shape and ready for fitting.

When the two pairs of legs have been assembled in this manner they are in turn joined by the two lower rails to form the complete leg unit. These rails are also seen in Fig. C356, and again one is shown fitted and the other cut to shape and ready for assembly. For clarity, only three legs are shown.

The positions of the lower rails are given in Fig. C355, and also details of the stool taper.

Top

The top is a piece of ¾ in.-thick plywood, 12 in. dia. This can be cut to shape with a bow saw and trimmed up with the spokeshave. The top is centred on top of the leg assembly, and glued-and-screwed to the top cross rails. The top rails and leg ends will require to be lightly chamfered to provide a flat landing for the top. Drive the screws through the top and into the rails.

Seat

For the seat, a disc of ¼ in.-thick plywood, 11 in. dia., is required. On top of this a piece of foam rubber is fixed with a rubber adhesive. When the adhesive has set, the rubber is trimmed to the shape of the disc. The rubber is covered with the chosen material, turned over and closely tacked to the underside of the plywood.

The seat is centred on the top, and held in place with woodscrews driven from the underside of the top. Six screws will be enough, but see that they do not project through the plywood disc and into the foam rubber. A section of the seat secured to the top can be seen in Fig. C357.

TOWEL RAIL FITMENT

This fitment (Fig. C358) is just the thing to fill up any odd gap between kitchen fitments providing that at least 4 in. is available.

The basic principle is a pair of dowels on which the towels hang, which pivots away from the wall (see Fig. C359). If the dowels are too long, the pivoting action will be too great, the dowel will extend too far into the room and the towel will drag. Try the idea out with a length of dowel before making a start.

Construction is simple. Two lengths of dowel are cut to size. Two blocks of wood, into which the dowel rails are fitted, are drilled and hinged to the two pieces of board back and front of the fitment. The rear board is also hinged to a piece of wood which is fitted to the floor.

A length of chain, clothes line or rubber cord is attached to the wall to act as a stop. The exact length of this depends on how far the fitment comes out when it is open. Next, the front panel is hinged to the floor and to the rail block. Make certain that the hinges are fitted correctly.

Fit a handle to the front board, and fix a cupboard catch so that the fitment will fit easily into the closed position.

No exact measurements have been given here; merely the broad principle on which the fitment works.

Fig. C359 (above). Constructional details.

Fig. C358 (left). The towel rack, which stows away.

SHOE SHINE CORNER

Shoe cleaning is a messy job and the ideal place for it is the back porch. The fitment shown in Fig. C360 comprises a slatted seat with brush drawer and a box with flap-up lid to contain a selection of polish tins. As all the timber is small-sectioned stuff, it can be made up from all those odd scraps that might otherwise become firewood. The only cost involved is the ironwork brackets which were bent up at home and then taken to be welded. Even this could be avoided if the butt joint were arranged to centre under the seat cross support.

Fig. C360 (*left*). The finished job.

Fig. C361 (*right*). Constructional details.

Fig. C362 (*a, left*).   The fitment in use;   (*b, right*).   Underseat details.

Sizes for the unit are given in Fig. C361. These can be varied to suit; but if the length is increased much, additional brackets will be required. Construction is simple. After the seat slats have been planed, place them face downwards in position on the bench. Glue-and-screw on the cross battens. Now fix and glue the hardboard sheet in between the battens; this is to prevent the contents of the drawer being visible. The drawer runner fillets should next be added. Make certain they are positioned parallel to the hardboard sheet.

The drawer and box are both made up by simple gluing-and-pinning; no joints are used at all and should not be necessary if resin glue is used.

As the shoe-cleaning equipment sheds dirt, line the interior of the box and drawer with plastic to give a readily-wipable interior. The drawer handle is made from an off-cut of $1\frac{1}{4}$ in. alloy angle and is retained in position simply by the use of contact glue.

Final touch, two coats of good exterior varnish. Fig. C362 shows the fitment in use.

GARDEN AND OUTDOORS

TAKE IT EASY IN YOUR GARDEN

The three essential requirements for garden constructions are attractiveness, practicability and simplicity. The latter two are not always so easy to combine with the first.

Practicability means that the furniture is suitable for its location and that it can be easily dissembled or folded for winter storage; simplicity means retaining as much of the structural strength of the material as possible in the design and that joints are stout and weatherproof.

Materials

For the armchair (Fig. C363) good straight-grained hardwood is necessary, perhaps well-seasoned beech or a close-grained oak. Whatever hardwood is chosen, select timber with a straight grain running along the cut, and it can be ordered ready-planed if desired.

The constructional details are given in Fig. C364.

The dining unit is also a simple construction with the load well-distributed over the four legs—so it can be made of a good quality joinery deal, free from knots and 'shakes' in the grain. This is shown in Fig. C365 and the constructional details are given in Fig. C366.

The sectional tables (Fig. 367 and C368) are quite the simplest items—use a marine ply to make the job easy and durable—and the hairpin legs can be bought at most handyman stores.

Finishes

for the hardwood chair it is best to retain the natural beauty of the timber. Advisedly, however, it must be protected, either with a clear yacht-grade copal varnish or one of the modern catalyst plastic coatings; doing this job well is essential to prolong the life of the chair.

Fig. C363 (*above*). The chair is well-balanced and comfortable. The folding action is a simple forward one which extends the length of the chair for storage.

Fig. C364 (*right*). Constructional details.

2"x 1" BATTENS

ARM REST FROM 3"x 1"x 25"

METAL BRACKETS 1/16" THICK

2"x 1"x 21"

FRONT LEGS FROM 19"x 3"x 1"

9"

SIDE VIEW

22½"x 1½"x 1"

CUT FROM 4½"x 1"x 3¼"

FRONT LEG DETAIL

BACK REST FROM 2"x 1"

16"

3/16" DIA COACH BOLT

14"

21"

18¾"

12"

23"

FRONT VIEW

Fig. C365 (*above*). Simplicity is the keynote in both the design and construction of the dining unit. What would otherwise appear to be a rather plain trestle job is offset by the way in which the seats are extended on the spider beams from the centrally-located splayed legs. Stability is good.

SEATS FROM 12"x 1"

TABLE TOP FROM 6"x 1" T AND G BOARDING

BATTENS FROM 2"x 2" x 3"x 3" ANGLE ENDS

PLAN

CENTRE SUPPORT 12" x 12" x 1" 2 OFF

6"

12"   12"   12"

Fig. C366.   Constructional details.

ELEVATION

36"

12"

12"

37"

18"

60"

4 LEGS REQUIRED 37"x 4"x 1" SCREW TO CROSS RAILS AND BATTENS

CROSS RAILS FROM 4"x 2" ONLY ONE IS FULL LENGTH

Fig. C367. Contemporary in design, these units are versatile and will be found equally at home in the lounge, dining-room, hall or bedroom.

Fig. C368 (below). Constructional details.

PLAN

ELEVATION

7"x7" PLYWOOD PADS FASTENED TO UNDERSIDE

HAIRPIN LEGS 3/8" DIA. WROUGHT IRON

TWO TABLES AND PADS CUT FROM 48"x 48" SHEET OF 3/4 MARINE PLY

Fig. C369. For real garden comfort, you will find this suite hard to beat.

The dining unit, being of deal, will look well and is best preserved with a coat of white or bright paint. It is important that any knots are treated first; then primer should be applied (two coats, preferably) and follow with undercoat and gloss. The latter should be a good exterior grade —but try to select one free of lead. The marine ply used for the sectional tables offers a little scope for imaginative decoration. Usually the outside plies of this material are of good hard veneer and will take a similar decorative finish to hardwood; another section can be painted to match the dining unit, and the edges of the ply should be bound with undercoat and a contrasting gloss.

SUMMERTIME GARDEN FURNITURE

Here is a three-piece suite for the garden! Anyone who can use a saw and a screwdriver can make it. It has no chains or springs to go rusty and spoil the removable cushions, and can in fact be left out all winter and take

no real harm. It's there ready for use on those odd warm days of spring and autumn. That is the advantage of its all-wooden construction. The suite is shown in Fig. C369.

The cord laced through the frame takes the place of springs or webbing—it is stout braided nylon and very long-lasting and weatherproof. It is normally stretchy and sags a little under weight but recovers as soon as the weight is removed. For this reason it should

Fig. C370. Joints here are a through-mortice (back top rail) and simple housings (seat frame).

Fig. C371. Seat back; a plain butt joint held by angled screws.

Fig. C372. The legs and arms stiffen the whole structure, so must be screwed.

Fig. C373. Drill heads can be filled over with stopping.

Fig. C374. Wheel axles; stout, well-threaded bolts with two or three washers each side.

Fig. C375. Lacing. Two-and-a-half or three-inch spacing; holes no bigger than the cord.

be set up fairly taut to begin with. It is best to do the whole of the bench seat with one length—you can get the cord in 100 ft. hanks—and then to inch it in to remove as much of the slack as you can. In the chairs the nylon cord is laced in one length, back and seat together, as can be seen from Figs. C370–C375, giving construction details. This is quite satisfactory for the chairs but not so good for the bench seat. It puts the whole weight on the top rail of the seat back, and with a couple of hefty adults on the seat it is better to spread the load. So the bench seat is laced separately, spacing the cords rather more closely together, between the front and back rails. The cord for the bench back can be spaced more widely since it is carrying very little weight. If you get tired of drilling holes, the cord on the bench back can be laced through brass cup hooks screwed in, but we don't recommend this method for the seat unless you get really strong screw-eyes.

All the framing is made up from ready-planed 2¾ in. × 1½ in. and 1¾ in. × 1½ in. stock. The table top and table seats are from 1 in. tongued-and-grooved boards, 7¾ in. wide; enough 8 in. × 1¾ in. wood will be needed to make the wheels, each wheel being cut from an 8 in. square.

A number of bolt holes have to be made, and since the general fixing is by 2½ in. × 12 csk screws, there'll be a fair number of holes to be drilled. You can get special

drills which make the pilot hole, shank hole and counter-sink for the head, all in one go, and these are worth having.

It pays to drill holes for screws, since it not only saves time and effort in driving the screw home but eliminates the risk of splitting the wood and wasting it.

The quantities have been given separately so that if you only want to make the table, or table and settee, or table and chairs, it is easy to see what is needed.

As far as chairs and settee are concerned, the seat frames are the things to make first since they are really the foundation; the backs, arms and legs are screwed to the seat frame as shown in Fig. C376. It is consequently worthwhile making the seat frames really rigid. The type of housing joint shown at the corners is the simplest way of getting a sound joint. With a reasonable fit at the joint and the use of a good waterproof glue and a couple of screws, it should be sound enough—but corner blocks can be put in for extra strength.

The seat arms and the settee arms help to tie things together. Square-headed coach screws (2½ in. × ¼ in.) are best to use here since they can be pulled up tight with a spanner. Naturally, the heads will not be left standing proud as shown—after drilling the pilot hole, put a centre bit in your brace and sink the top of the pilot hole sufficiently to bring the head of the screw below the

Fig. C376. Constructional details.

Brass screw eyes

Method of attaching
back rail to upright

$59\frac{1}{2}$" x $1\frac{3}{4}$" x $1\frac{1}{2}$"

25"x $2\frac{3}{4}$" x $1\frac{1}{2}$"

28" x $2\frac{3}{4}$" x $1\frac{1}{2}$"

24" x $2\frac{3}{4}$" x $1\frac{1}{2}$"

58"x $2\frac{3}{4}$" x $1\frac{1}{2}$"

26"x $2\frac{3}{4}$"x $1\frac{1}{2}$"

24"x $2\frac{3}{4}$"x $1\frac{1}{2}$"

$23\frac{3}{4}$" x $1\frac{3}{4}$" x $1\frac{1}{2}$"

28"x $2\frac{3}{4}$"x $1\frac{1}{2}$"

25"x $2\frac{3}{4}$"x $1\frac{1}{2}$"

24"x $2\frac{3}{4}$"x $1\frac{1}{2}$"

Nuts

Washers

$4\frac{1}{2}$" x $\frac{1}{2}$" dia. bolt

Wheel 8" dia. x $1\frac{3}{4}$"

26"x $2\frac{3}{4}$"x $1\frac{1}{2}$"

$22\frac{1}{4}$" x $2\frac{3}{4}$" x $1\frac{1}{2}$"

Corner
arrangement

269

Fig. C377.   The table with its seats is a quick and simple job. You can see almost everything in this photograph.

3 pieces of T and G
1" x 7¾" x 48"

23¼"

23" x 2¾" x 1½"

48"

48" x 7¾" x 1"

Fig. C378.   Constructional details.

29" x 2¾" x 1½"

23" x 2¾" x 1½"

30" x 2¾" x 1½"

45½" x 2¾" x 1½"

Fig. C379.   Here you see how the top goes on. Only a few screws to put in, and the job is done.

MATERIALS

The Chair
Back
25 in. × 2¾ in. × 1½ in., 2 off
23¾ in. × 1¾ in. × 1½ in., 1 off
Seat
26 in. × 2¾ in. × 1½ in., 2 off
22¼ in. × 2¾ in. × 1½ in., 2 off
Legs
24 in. × 2¾ in. × 1½ in., 4 off
Armrests
28 in. × 2¾ in. × 1½ in., 2 off
Wheels
Shaped from square 8 in. × 1¾ in.

The Table
Top
48 in. × 7¾ in. × 1 in. T-and-G, 3 off
23 in. × 2¾ in. × 1½ in., 3 off
23 in. × 1¼ in. × 1 in., 2 off
Seats
48 in. × 7¾ in. × 1 in., 2 off
45½ in. × 2¾ in. × 1½ in., 2 off
Legs
30 in. × 2¾ in. × 1½ in., 2 off
29 in. × 2¾ in. × 1½ in., 2 off
Wheels
Shaped from square 8 in. × 1¾ in.

The Settee
Back
25 in. × 2¾ in. × 1½ in., 2 off
59½ in. × 1¾ in. × 1½ in., 1 off
Seat
26 in. × 2¾ in. × 1½ in., 2 off
58 in. × 2¾ in. × 1½ in., 2 off
Legs
24 in. × 2¾ in. × 1½ in., 4 off
Armrests
28 in. × 2¾ in. × 1½ in., 2 off
Wheels
Shaped from square 8 in. × 1¾ in.

surface of the wood. You can putty in the hole and paint over, afterwards.

The table is, if anything, simpler to make than the chairs and settee. Start by making the two end trestles from 2¾ in. x 1½ in. and screwing on the cross pieces which carry the bench seats. Then make the table top from three pieces of 1 in. tongued-and-grooved, 48 in. long. The table boards need cramping firmly together, which can be done by wedging between improvised cramps, using some of the 2¾ in. × 1½ in. stuff temporarily for this purpose.

The table has a cross batten of 2¾ in. × 1½ in. in the centre, and two end battens of 1¼ in. × 1 in., which are screwed on at each end. Fasten the table by screwing through the top to the cross-pieces of the trestle legs. A sheet of plastic laminate fixed by contact adhesive to the table top is an optional improvement. Details of the table are given in Figs. C377–C379.

All the furniture should be well sanded after completion, to remove splinters and round off corners and edges. The leg ends should also be sanded and very slightly chamfered so that they will not be so inclined

to chip by contact with the ground. Good painting is obviously desirable for preservation as well as appearance, particularly since the suite is intended to be left out in all weathers.

The wheel mounting is clearly shown in the sketch in Fig. C376. Cutting out the wheels from 1¾ in. stock is quite easy in the sense that it does not require much more than a fair amount of effort and several sharp keyhole saw blades. However, any timber yard will cut them on their band saw, and it's worth the small charge. The wooden wheels are not intended for lengthy journeys, but they make it much easier to move the furniture about on the lawn. It also pays to sand round the wheel edges, leaving a small chamfer to reduce the risk of chipping.

GARDEN SUN-HOUSE

The small garden building will be found extremely serviceable. Besides providing a shelter in which you can sit or enjoy a meal out of doors it also includes a number of cupboards which provide accommodation for tables and chairs, garden tools and other items that are usually left lying about. The completed shelter is shown in Fig. C380.

The drawings in Fig. C381 show the details of the walls and roof of the structure.

To prepare the foundations, form a rectangle 9 ft. 1 in. long × 7 ft. 6 in. wide with boards held in position by pegs driven into the ground. With these as a guide, strip the vegetable soil to a depth of 4 in. within the area and lay a 4 in. bed of hardcore. On top of this lay 3 in. of concrete composed of 4 parts broken brick or stone to pass a 2 in. ring, 2 parts sand and 1 part cement. To fix the side and back bottom rails to the concrete two methods can be employed as shown in the sketches. Hardwood plugs can be inserted in the concrete and the rails spiked to them or, alternatively, ⅜ in. diameter rag or hook bolts about 6 in. long may be used. The concrete can either be well trowelled or a finishing coat ¾ in. thick composed of 3 parts sand and 1 part cement applied.

The main structure consists of 3 in. × 3 in. corner posts stub-tenoned into the 5 in. × 3 in. beam along the front, the 3 in. × 3 in. rail along the back and the 3 in. × 2 in. bottom rails. The drawing at bottom left shows the stub-tenon joints of the corner posts. The back and side bottom rails are half-lapped at the corners. The intermediate framing is 3 in. × 2 in., all housed together and nailed. Note the 2 in. × ¾ in. fillets at the corners which provide a neat finish to the matching. These are shown in Fig. C381. When the framework is complete the partitions and outside are cladded.

The roof is built up of 4 in. × 1½ in. rafters spaced equally and birds-mouthed over the front beam and back rail. They are covered with ⅝ in. matching on which is laid a good quality roofing felt. The rafters project 12 in. at the front and 6 in. at the back, the eaves being closed in with ½ in. matching. A 4½ in. × ¾ in. fascia plate is nailed to the ends of the joists at back and front and carried round the sides. A detail of the eaves is given at top right.

The three doors to the storage cupboards are of the ledged-and-battened type with 4½ in. × 1 in. top rails, 6 in. × 1 in. mid and bottom rails, and 4½ in. × 1 in. braces, the framework being covered with ⅝ in. matching. Fix 1⅜ in. × ½ in. door stops to the door posts. The doors

Fig. C380. This solid but simple design offers plenty of space combined with rugged, long-lasting construction.

Fig. C381. Constructional details.

can be hung on either 5 in. butt hinges or cross garnet hinges.

Provide shelves in the cupboards to suit requirements and paint the structure with one or two coats of under-coat and one coat of gloss paint. It is advisable to treat the bottom runner and the wooden plugs (if used) in the concrete with creosote or other wood preservative. All timber should be bought planed.

Fig. C382. This is the patio. Paint it in a gay colour scheme. Plant quick-growing climbers alongside.

MAKE YOUR OWN PATIO

There are plenty of days when it is quite pleasant to sit out, even in a none-too-brilliant summer. In fact, what does keep people indoors is more often a cool wind rather than rain.

The side wing of this patio design breaks the wind and gives you a little privacy: you could easily add another windbreak if desired. The roof can be left unglazed as shown here, but the woodwork is quite strong enough to be glazed with translucent glass fibre sheets. A practical alternative is a canvas awning which can be rolled-up or let-down as needed. The tinted Perspex sheets at the side provide a splash of colour. If more privacy is needed replace them with opaque plastic.

The design shown in Fig. C382 was built to a size 10 ft. × 16 ft., but the dimensions can be varied easily to suit the area available. At 160 square feet it is probably quite big enough, though it is not too much to manhandle into position, with a little help, since there are really three basic units—roof, windbreak and supports—which can be assembled separately. It is best to make a sketch plan first. This will help when measuring up the amount of wood required and will ensure that everything will fit when the final stage is reached. At the sketch stage, too, changes can be made in the design.

The side windbreak was built first, then the roof and finally the front supports. The roof beams are notched into each other, so this is a good time to apply the old carpenters' advice 'measure twice, cut once'. A certain amount of adjustment can be made at the assembly stage and it helps to put the roof together on a fairly level surface,

Fig. C383. (a) Build end windbreak first, from 6 in. x 1 in. This is different from that used for roof members but uses the same joint.

(b) The joint is simple enough – two saw cuts and a chisel are all it takes to make each one. But the notches must meet in each member.

(c) Assembly is best done on a level surface – your lawn will do. Do not glue until complete frame is ready for assembly.

Fig. C384. (a) Use a packing piece to avoid bruising the wood when assembling. Ease a tight joint.

(b) The end ready for the frame. The pieces here are three 6 in. x 1 in. by 6 ft. and two 7 ft. 6 in. lengths. The frame takes another four pieces.

(c) Fillets are screwed to the bottom panels of the windbreak to receive tongued-and-grooved boarding. Alternatively, asbestos could be used.

(d) Here the windbreak frame is ready to have the four sides screwed in place, but check for squareness by ensuring that diagonals are equal.

(e) Drill pilot holes for screws. A spiral screwdriver or power drill screwdriver attachment saves time.

(f) The windbreak well on the way to completion. The Perspex panels are not added until the patio has been erected.

(g) Vertical matchboarding looks better than horizontal. Knock it up tightly before you nail it in place with oval wire nails.

(h) Stand the end frame up and see what sort of job you've made of it. Try it in position, to see how it fits.

(i) The patio roof is made in the same way as the end frame, but using 5 in. x 1 in. Our roof is 10 ft. x 16 ft.

Fig. C384. (*j*) Estimate a suitable size by laying out the wood before you start cutting. Two-foot spacing is recommended for the joints.

(*k*) Notches take very little time. Mark out each notch with a straight edge and saw inside your lines.

(*l*) Some minor easing of a few joints is bound to be needed. You can then glue, check for squareness and screw-nail.

(*m*) The back and front boards are simply nailed on with butt joints.

(*n*) This shows the front edge member, 2 in. x 1 in. x 16 ft., being nailed on. The tapering is only to improve appearance.

(*o*) Screw a T-bracket where each cross member joins the front and back boards, and corner brackets.

(*p*) Application of a coat of good timber preservative (if you don't intend to paint) could be conveniently done before you put the roof on.

(*q*) Three $\frac{1}{4}$ in. coach screws well-plugged into the wall are needed. Use roofing felt strips to make a damp-course.

(*r*) Give the windbreak a temporary strut and then lift one end of the roof in place. Then lift and prop the other end.

Fig. C385. (a) Screw through backboard to the wall, using stout coach screws. Put one screw through the roof to the windbreak, to permit adjustment.

(b) The supports are made from one piece of 4 in. x 2 in., one of 2 in. x 2 in. at the base.

(c) The flower trough is an optional extra, but you can see here how it is slung between two uprights by stout dowels.

(d) Rest uprights in waterpipe tack-welded to plates. Screw plates to wood plugs in concrete.

(e) Close up of the flower trough and supports. You can vary the style of these, but do not omit drainage holes.

(f) This shows how the upper end of the supports is attached. Tighten up progressively as you get things in line by packing where needed.

such as a smooth lawn or concrete drive.

Following the design, it will be seen from Fig. C382 that the roof consists of nine 10 ft. × 5 in. × 1 in. members; one 16 ft. 2 in. × 1 in. (for the front edge); and five 16 ft. × 5 in. × 1 in. The joints are marked at two foot centres and cut, as were the tapered ends of the crossmembers.

The roof was then assembled, all joints were glued and skew-nailed, the edging pieces (which were just butt-jointed) being put on last. Before the glue has set, a check must be made for squareness. This is done by measuring diagonally from corner to corner, the two measurements being equal. Having completed this check satisfactorily, the corner and T-irons should be screwed into place and the whole thing put aside to set. There may be some difficulty in tapping the joints home; it is best achieved by working progressively along the members easing each joint a little at a time. It goes without saying that the job

is made much simpler if a perfectly flat area is found on which to assemble it.

First position the roof on the terrace, then raise the windbreak end and rest the roof on top of it. Temporarily brace the windbreak because the outward thrust of the roof in this position might possibly strain its joints. Raise the other end of the roof until correctly positioned and temporarily propped. Holes already drilled in the back member of the roof are continued into the house wall, plugged and screwbolted—inserting roofing felt between roof and wall before bolting. Now screw the roof permanently to the windbreak. Without removing the temporary prop, roughly position the roof supports and drive one screw through the 4 in. × 2 in. member, leaving them free to pivot and be adjusted for true vertical before bolting to the terrace.

Construction details are shown step by step in Figs. C383–C385.

FENCES

A garden fence need not be a matter of just erecting a screen for privacy, or for ensuring that the dog doesn't escape. The boundary fence can provide a 'setting' for your garden.

The attractively-designed screen described here has also many practical features and can be erected for quite a reasonable figure. From Figs. C386 and C387 it can be seen that the fence is pleasing to look at, besides having functional value, the main advantages being:

1. At 6 ft. high it ensures some seclusion.
2. It affords protection for small plants.
3. It prevents incursion of weeds from adjoining ground.
4. It is too high for dogs to leap over.
5. It does not cast too much shade.
6. High winds do not throw as much strain on its supports as they would on a solid fence of the same dimensions.

For the main structure, shown in Fig. C388, second-hand timber can be used, providing it is sound and free of old nails and other defects.

The wood used is 4 in. × 3 in. and 3 in. × 2 in.

The materials being used for the in-filling dictate the distance between the main supports. The laths for the trellis-top are 4 ft. in length, and the asbestos sheet offcuts (used for the bottom section) are 4 ft. × 2 ft. Making the bottom section of asbestos ensures a really effective barrier against weeds, the sheet being sunk into the earth to prevent surface-creeping weeds from advancing. Wood used in such a way would have a very limited life—unless it was expensive oak.

The sheet asbestos used is of the flexible ¼ in.-thick type; and it can be creosoted to tone-in with the rest of the timber of the fence. The sheet asbestos is fixed to the timber supports with large-headed glavanised nails.

The laths are bought in bundles and two of these bundles should contain sufficient material for all the square-pattern trellis top in a 50 ft. run.

The fixing posts

The problem of making the upright posts sufficiently strong and well-rooted to withstand the stresses imposed by the fence's own weight and the wind pressure can be tackled in many ways. The most important thing to note is that it is a complete waste of time to put timber posts into the soil, with the possible exception of cedar or oak posts. Even then, timber posts always have a tendency to lean out of true due to the fact that moisture gathers around the post and softens the soil.

Therefore, when wooden posts are being used, it is

Fig. C386. These arches are not strictly part of the fences, but are built in the same way.

Fig. C387. Close-up view.

wise to attach them to a more durable material that will withstand contact with damp soil more happily than will timber. Concrete spurs, or short posts to which timber uprights can be bolted, are excellent; in Fig. C389 it can be seen that they make a very substantial job. Of course, a hole has either to be dug out or drilled before inserting and concreting the spur in position.

This method, though very effective, is expensive. A far easier and only slightly less effective method is to employ relatively inexpensive metal stakes or angle-iron; these will rust in time, but if some old sump-oil is allowed to trickle down the side of the stakes before the wet season, rusting can be minimised. The majority of such angle-iron has holes ready drilled, otherwise a local garage will probably do the job quite cheaply. Use two irons for each post and drive them straight into the soil for half their length, about 3 ft. Make a constant check to see that they are 'true'; drive one iron first and use a scrap of 3 in. × 4 in. (the post size) to slide between this and the second stake to ensure that they are parallel and to allow fitting of the actual posts without planing (see Fig. C389).

As a further precaution, give every alternate post a triangular strut to stiffen the whole assembly (Fig. C390).

Cut all posts to length and soak in creosote by utilising a 6 in. sewer pipe as a can (this must be sealed at one end or embedded in the ground); it is not necessary to fill the pipe full of the liquid, as the timber causes displacement sufficient to fill the pipe to the brim, and only occasional topping-up is necessary (Fig. C390). Large galvanised 2 in. × 14-gauge screws are used to attach the

wooden posts to the irons. This job can be carried out single-handed if a clamp is used to hold the post in position while drilling and screwing. The end posts having been fixed, the height level for the intermediate posts is ascertained by using a string-line pinned to the tops of the end posts; a similar method having been employed to ensure that all the stakes were in line when driving them into the ground.

Capping pieces for the posts are cut from 1 in. wood.

Fixing the rails

Use 3 in. × 2 in. wood with a cant sawn along the top edge; this is to allow the rain to drip off. Make a simple halving joint at the ends of the rails so as just to lock in place on the posts. This jointing is not really necessary, but it does allow the use of shorter coach screws and the shoulder of the joint makes for greater rigidity, as can be gathered from Fig. C391. It will be noted that the screws are put in at an angle so as to lock the joint still further.

Sink the asbestos panels into the ground for about 4 in. The tops of the panels then decide the position of the centre rails. All rails were tested for level to make sure that they were truly horizontal. On being fixed to the supports the asbestos is given a coat of creosote to which a little tar is added; this in no way preserves the material, but it does stop moulds forming and tones in with the rest of the work.

The trellis top is easy, but tiresome, to make. The laths are nailed together on a flat part of the lawn, the 1 in. galvanised wire nails going right through the thin laths.

Fig. C388.

Fig. C389.

Fig. C390.

Fig. C388 (*top, left*). The main structure uses 4 in. × 3 in. posts, spaced 8 ft. apart, and 3 in. × 2 in. rails as shown.

Fig. C389 (*top, right*). Timber posts will rot in the soil. Concrete spurs or posts are the ideal way to make a really substantial job. Alternatively, angle-iron stakes could be used; use a scrap piece of post to ensure a good fit.

Fig. C390 (*centre, left*). Whatever the method of fixing the posts, a strut should be fixed to each alternate post. A length of drainpipe makes an ideal bath for soaking timbers in creosote.

Fig. C391 (*bottom, left*). A simple halving joint; the shoulders help to lock the rail in place on the post.

Fig. C392 (*below*). The top beam of the arch is cogged into the upright, and a corner strut can be used to add stiffness. Long narrow panels of trellis are fixed to provide a flat surface on which to train suitable plants.

Fig. C391.

Fig. C392.

When a section has been nailed in this manner, it is reversed on to a flat piece of concrete and the protruding points of the nails clenched over. Care must be taken to see that the laths are parallel to each other, by using short distance-pieces during the nailing. The two layers of laths must be at right angles to each other and this must be tested occasionally with the square. Putting two nails at a few of the intersections will help to stop the trellis panel moving out of square. Creosoting the trellis is made a little easier by stacking the panels and painting the top one, the drips of creosote falling to the panels below. The panels are fixed in place by nailing the vertical laths to the top and the centre rails. To finish, give the iron stakes a coat of brown gloss over aluminium priming.

Arches

Arches for climbing roses etc. can be designed on the same lines. Again, secondhand timber can be used in conjunction with the iron stakes. A simple but strong support is all that is needed, and visible woodwork should be kept to a minimum. Cut two 6 ft. 6 in. uprights of 4 in. × 3 in. timber; the top beam is one bar of 3 in. × 2½ in. Cog-out the uprights to take the beam, as in Fig. C392, and nail the beam into place with 4 in. spikes. Cut the ends of the beam to a traditional shape, to make them a little more artistically pleasing; and a tri-angulated strut placed in the corners keeps the beam at right angles to the uprights. Make long, narrow panels of trellis (the same square pattern to match the fencing) and fix to the arches, to provide a flat surface on which to train the roses. Again, iron stakes are used at an angle to prevent the uprights from moving out of vertical.

GARDEN SWING

A garden swing such as the one shown in Fig. C393 can bring many hours of happiness to children and is well worth considering for any garden or area of ground to

Fig. C393. The swing framework.

which children have access. Weather conditions and wear-and-tear demand the use of strong timber, which can then be maintained in good condition by regular repainting.

Uprights are made of two pieces of 6 in. × 3 in. seasoned timber, free from knots and flaws, each 8 ft. in length, planed smooth, with each corner chamfered. Mark the top ends to allow a 6 in. deep × 2 in. wide slot to be cut. A series of saw cuts after the main cuts have been made helps in removing the waste pieces; smooth off with a wood chisel.

Mark the ends representing the base to give a tongue 6 in. × 2½ in. and cut off the side panels; smooth off with wood chisel and sandpaper.

Make the head from 6 in. × 3 in. timber 4 ft. 6 in. long. Mark each end for cutting grooves so that when the waste has been cut away, the head piece will fit tightly into the slots of the upright.

The base is best made from 5 ft. lengths of 7 in. × 3 in. timber, although 6 in. × 3 in. will do. Mark off the centre of each piece, check the dimensions of the tongue on the uprights, and transfer these measurements on to the base. Cut out each of these small areas with a wood chisel. To assist in easy cutting, drill a series of holes within the area by means of a brace-and-bit or electric drill, enabling the remaining part to be cleaned out more speedily.

As a swing has to withstand considerable strain, it is important to use suitable stays; 4 ft. 6 in. lengths of 4 in. × 3 in. jointed to the base and uprights should be adequate. The top of each stay should be marked and cut. Mark off a 3 in. margin from the end of each base timber. Using this as the outside limit, mark off areas 4 in. × 2 in. and cut out. Cut the end of each stay to form a tongue that will fit into each of these holes. Insert the stays into the base holes and find the position on the uprights at which the stays will have to be secured. Mark each upright on each side, mark the top end of each stay, and cut both away neatly for a firm joint.

A capping piece, 5 ft. × 6 in. × 2 in. planed, is required to shed rainwater away from the headpiece and protect the wood.

Details of the headpiece and all joints are given in Fig. C394.

When all the timber has been prepared, examine each part that has been cut and make certain that it is clean. Assemble all parts dry and be sure that they fit properly. Paint the base joints in the uprights and in the base pieces and insert; paint the ends of each stay and the holes in the base pieces. Place these in position and drive in a number of oval nails to secure stays, base and upright, painting over the nail heads.

Place the headpiece on the ground where the swing is to be erected. The previously-cut grooves will give the position of the two holes to be dug. Allow a width of 12 in. for each hole and a length of 5 ft. 3 in. Dig to a depth of 3 ft. 4 in. keeping the top soil on one side for final topping off later. Ram 4 in. of clinker or cinders in the bottom of the holes. Put each upright in position, level and ram the sub-soil in layers 4 in. deep (Fig. C394). The last 4 in. will be the top soil.

Similarly, fix the second upright in position, after checking with the headpiece that the uprights are the correct distance apart. To fix the headpiece in position, drill two holes through upright and headpiece at each end and insert greased bolts.

Find the centre of the headpiece and mark off 1 ft.

Fig. C394. Joints or uprights, stays and headpiece.

4 in. each side, drill two holes, then insert hook-bolts. Alternatively hook-screws can be screwed into the head-piece. If the former type is used, cut a small recess in the capping piece for each nut. Paint the capping piece on the underside and place over the headpiece, then screw down.

The seat should be about 2 ft. long by 12 in. wide and 1 in. thick. The underside should have two battens, 12 in. × 4 in. × 1 in. thick, secured by means of screws. The diameter of the rope will govern the size of the holes to be drilled in the seat. A metal ring should be used between the rope and hooks to minimise rope wear; a small amount of grease on the hook will keep it free from rust. The rope should be firmly lashed beneath the hooks and just above the seat; the lashing must be uniform, otherwise the seat will not remain level. Rub all the wood down with sandpaper to clear away splinters, plane all sharp corners away, and give a final coat of paint to the whole structure.

COMBINED SWING AND SLIDE

A combined swing and slide is an interesting and novel out-of-doors project for the garden which will provide endless amusement for the children all the year round (Fig. C395).

The construction is simple, the only tools required being those generally found in the average household. Redwood is a suitable timber, and should be bought planed.

Figs. C396 and C397 show a front and side elevation respectively; Fig. C398 shows an elevation of the frame A. For strength, all the main parts should be bolted together.

Frames

Commence by preparing the frames A, B and C. Dealing with frame A (Fig. C398), the uprights are 10 ft.×3 ft.× 2in.,with two stretchers D and E, of 3 in. × 2 in. which are bolted to the two uprights with ⅜ in. diameter bolts. To construct the frame, lay the uprights on the ground with the lower ends 7 ft. apart and with a space of 2 in. at the upper ends to take the top crossbar. Bore ½ in. holes through the top ends of the uprights and ⅜ in. holes in the uprights to take the bolt securing the crossbar and stretchers D and E respectively. Frames B and C (Fig. C397) are prepared in the same way. Note that the stretchers F and G, which are 3 in. × 2 in., are bolted to the inner faces of the uprights, all others being bolted to the outside of the frames.

Crossbar

The crossbar, 4 ft. 4 in. × 4 in. × 2 in., is bolted with ½ in. bolts between frames A and B. Two braces 3 in. × 1½ in. are screwed to the crossbar and uprights. Stiffen frames B and C with a diagonal brace 4 in. × ¾ in. screwed to the inner faces of the uprights as shown in Figs. C395 and C396. To keep the three frames alike it will be necessary to bolt a 4 in. × 2 in. packing piece be-

Fig. C395. The completed swing and slide.

Fig. C396 (*above, left*).   Front elevation.
Fig. C397 (*above, right*).   Side elevation.

Fig. C398 (*above*).   Elevation of frame 'A'.

Fig. C399 (*below*).   Section through slide.

Fig. C400 (*right, centre*).   Suspension hooks.

Fig. C401 (*right, bottom*).   Seat details.

tween the top of the uprights of frame C. Fix a 3 in. × 2 in. stay at the end of the swing frame as shown in Fig. C396.

Stringers for Steps

The stringers for the steps are 2 in. × 1 in., screwed to the inner sides of the frames; the fillets for supporting the steps are 3 in. × 1 in. × 1 in., screwed to the stringers; and the steps are 1 ft. 5½ in. × 4 in. × ¾ in., nailed or screwed to the fillets.

The platform boarding which rests on stretchers F is formed of 4½ in. × ¾ in. slats screwed to the stretchers.

The frame for the slide has 4¾ in. × ¾ in. sides rounded on the top edges and is bolted to the inner faces of the uprights with ⅜ in. diameter bolts. Fillets, 1 in. × 1 in., are screwed to the sides of the slide, as illustrated in Fig. C399.

The bottom, which is a piece of ¾ in. external grade plywood, is screwed to the fillets. A section through the slide is shown at Fig. C399. Legs, 2 in. × 2 in., driven into the ground are screwed to the bottom ends of the slide.

Swing Hooks and Seat

The suspension hooks for the swing (Fig. C400), are ½ in. diameter and should be obtained from a local blacksmith. The hooks are fixed to the crossbar with nuts and a good-sized washer.

The seat can be a piece of shelving ⅞ in. thick with holes bored in the ends for the ropes (Fig. C401). Strong manilla rope is required to suspend the seat and care should be taken with the knots which should be non-slipping and neatly tied or securely bound.

Bedding the Frames

The frames are let 18 in. into the ground, and the ends should be bedded in concrete composed of 1 part cement, 2 parts sand and 4 parts broken brick. Before filling in the concrete, see that each frame is plumb and the heads of the frames are level.

Temporary struts will be required to keep the frames in position until the concrete is set. The legs of the frames which are under the ground should be tarred or treated with a wood preservative, and all woodwork above ground should be given two or three coats of good quality paint.

An ordinary door mat could be used to form a pad at the bottom of the slide.

MATERIALS

Uprights 6 off 10 ft. × 3 in. × 2 in.
Stretchers, 3 off 5 ft. 8 in. × 3 in. × 2 in.
Stretchers, 3 off 3 ft. 3 in. × 3 in. × 2 in.
Stretchers, 2 off 2 ft. × 3 in. × 2 in.
Crossbar, 1 off 4 ft. 4 in. × 4 in. × 2 in.
Braces, 2 off 2 ft. × 3 in. × 1½ in.
Brace, 1 off 3 ft. × 4 in. × ¾ in.
Step stringers, 2 off 5 ft. 6 in. × 3 in. × 1 in.
Step fillets, 8 off 3 in. × 1 in. × 1 in.
Steps, 4 off 1 ft. 5½ in. × 4 in. × ¾ in.
Slats, 8 off 1 ft. 7½ in. × 4½ in. × ¾ in.
Slide sides, 2 off 10 ft. 6 in. × 4¾ in. × ¾ in.
Fillets, 2 off 10 ft. 6 in. × 1 in. × 1 in.
Legs, 2 off 1 ft. 6 in. × 2 in. × 2 in.
Stay, 1 off 10 ft. 6 in. × 3 in. × 2 in.
Ply bottom, 10 ft. 6 in. × 1 ft. 6 in. × ¾ in.

GARDEN OR CAMPING TABLE

The big advantage of this sturdy table is that it will not tip over, no matter where the load is placed on its surface.

The time required to pull out the legs and lock them in position is a mere five seconds. When closed the overall size is 32¼ in. × 22¾ in. × 1¾ in., which means there is virtually no storage problem. The table is shown in Fig. C402.

Fig. C402 (*above and below*). Top and bottom views.

The table can be made in an attractive hardwood for interior use, or, if required chiefly for outside use, a somewhat cheaper (but tough) timber may be substituted.

Faced plywood of approximately ¼ in. thickness is suitable for the table top or, where intended principally for open-air use, hardboard is lighter and makes for easy portability. In either case the wooden frame adds strength and finish. The four lengths of ⅝ in. square material should be rebated to the full thickness of the top surface

Fig. C403.   Layout of legs, stays and blocks.

Fig. C404.   Locking mechanism and anchor block details.

MATERIALS

Table top (faced plywood or hardboard), 1 off,
  32 in. × 22½ in.
Table top frame, 2 off, 32¼ in. × ⅝ in × ⅜ in.
Table top frame, 2 off, 22¾ in. × ⅝ in. × ⅝ in.
Legs, 4 off, 28 in. × 1 in. × ½ in.
Leg supports, 4 off, 14½ in. × 1 in. × ½ in.
Leg rails (dowel), 1 off, 17½ in. × ⅝ in. dia.
Leg rails (dowel), 1 off, 16½ in. × ⅝ in. dia.
Leg strengtheners, 1 off, 17 in. × ¾ in. × ¼ in.
Leg strengtheners, 1 off, 17½ in. × ¾ in. × ¼ in.
Leg strengtheners, 1 off, 18 in. × ¾ in. × ¼ in.
Leg strengtheners, 1 off, 18½ in. × ¾ in. × ¼ in.
Corner blocks, 4 off, 3 in. × 1 in. × ½ in.
Anchor blocks, 2 off, 7½ in. × 1½ in. × ⅝ in.

and mitred on, allowing ⅛ in. border to lie flush with the top.

The corner blocks (Figs. C402/3) and anchor blocks (Figs. C403/4) are glued-and-screwed to the underside of the table top. For the plywood article they would need to be well countersunk and finished off with woodfiller.

The 28 in. leg pieces are all drilled on one side ⅝ in. diameter and ¼ in. deep at a centre point ¾ in. from the end. Into these recesses the dowels are glued and secured crosswise by panel pins, to give two pairs of legs 18 in. and 17 in. wide respectively. The strengthening pieces are cut, drilled and screwed home a few inches from the extremity of the opposite ends.

Ordinary woodscrews, at least 1¼ in. long, are used for the pivots, the surplus end being removed with a hacksaw and filed clean. Insert thin washers in each joint.

The locking mechanisms are of 18- or 20-gauge mild steel strip ½ in. wide. Two 3 in. lengths and four of 2½ in. are needed, the latter being slotted as shown in Fig. C404. They are drilled and riveted, and each mechanism is fitted through the operating lever to its anchor block with a roundhead japanned screw, using a small washer under the operating lever. Use roundhead screws through the slots of the arms to obtain a sliding fit, so that when the arms are pushed home they will retain the dowels in their respective recesses.

The list of materials shows the finished planed sizes of the various members—any variation would need to be

strictly in the same ratio. Accuracy in cutting, finishing and assembly will ensure sturdiness and rigidity in use.

FLOWER BARROW

The barrow in Fig. C405 is a floral display cart which will bring a touch of Olde Worlde charm to porch or patio. When filled with potted flowering plants, the cupid design barrow makes a colourful centre-piece—but it can also be used as a novel service trolley for tea on the lawn.

The front board of the barrow is heart-shaped and the pot shelf is fixed by small blocks and bent iron scrolls. The cupid motif is further emphasised by the use of arrow legs and a painted scroll effect on the 15 in. diameter wheel.

Two pieces of ¾ in. board measuring 20 in. × 9 in. are needed for the big heart. A grid of 2 in. squares is lightly pencilled on one board as shown in Fig. C406, and the half shape is copied by reference to the sketch. Mark out the small decorative heart and the slot to accommodate the wheel and then saw out the parts. A jig-saw attachment on the power drill makes short work of this task, which can be finished with a handsaw.

Use the half-heart shape to mark out the second piece. Then cut and fasten the two with a couple of cross bars 2 in. × 1½ in., which are cut on the slant to suit the inward taper of the barrow body sides. The top cross bar is 14½ in. measured along its top edge and the bottom bar is 13½ in. long. Screw them to the heart with six screws apiece about 2 in. apart.

Four blocks made of 1 in.-square wood make the axle housings and are screwed behind the wheel slot. Leave a 1 in. gap between the top and bottom blocks to take the axle dowel. Complete the heart board by making the pot shelf from a 14 in. × 4 in. × ¾ in. board. Round off the front corners, then screw the shelf to the front of the heart with 1½ in.-square wood blocks fixed underneath. The metal scroll brackets are added later.

The barrow body sides, of 6 in. × ¾ in. board, measure 20 in. across the top and taper to 17 in. along the bottom edge (Fig. C407). Each end slopes inwards an equal 1½ in. from top to bottom. The back end board is also from 6 in. × ¾ in. board and is 14½ in. at the top and 12½ in. at the base. Screw the end board between the side pieces as

Fig. C405. The finished barrow.

Fig. C406 (*right*). The heart-shaped wheelboard.

FRET OUT SMALL HEARTS

2"x1½"x14½" LONG

SCREWS

POSITION OF CROSS BRACES

9"

2"

6"

20"

2"x1½" x13½"

WHEEL SLOT 9"x 2"

HEART MADE FROM TWO 9" WIDE BOARDS

1½"

1"

1"

4"

14"

10" BETWEEN SCROLLS

¾"

FIX SHELF WITH SMALL BLOCKS

Fig. C407 (*below*). Details of body and arms.

20"

3"

6"

6"

1½"

17"

1½"

AXLE TURNS IN BLOCKS

11½"

14½"

5"

12½"

6"

LEGS SET SAME ANGLE AS HEART BOARD

LEGS ¾" THICK

¾" THICK END BOARD

MARK OUT ON 1" SQUARES

ARMS ¾" THICK

BARROW ARMS 2 OFF

¼" DIA. HOLES

SCROLLS BENT FROM $\frac{3}{4}$"×$\frac{1}{8}$" STEEL STRIP 14" LONG

2"

6"

3"

Fig. C408 (*above and right*). Bending the metal scrolls. Either a vice or two metal bars held vertical make a good bending jig.

Fig. C409 (*right*). Barrow wheel details.

1$\frac{1}{2}$" No.10 SCREWS HOLD WHEELBAND IN POSITION

CROSS BEAMS 15"× 3"×1"

15"DIA. $\frac{1}{4}$" PLY OR HARDBOARD DISCS SCREWED TO EITHER SIDE

HALF JOINT HERE

C/S HOLES

SAW ENDS TO SUIT RADIUS OF DISCS

1" DIA. HOLE FOR AXLE

ALUMINIUM STRIP WHEELBAND 50"×1$\frac{1}{2}$"

1" DIA. WOOD AXLE 5"LONG

GLUE INTO WHEEL HOLES

$\frac{1}{2}$"

2"

$\frac{1}{4}$" HOLES

7 BASE RAILS WITH $\frac{1}{2}$" SPACINGS

HEART FRONT

IRON SCROLL BRACKETS

SHELF 4" WIDE

PLY KEEPER PLATES 1"SQUARE

1"DIA AXLE

22$\frac{1}{2}$"

ARROW LEGS

2$\frac{1}{2}$"× $\frac{1}{4}$" COACH-BOLTS

Fig. C410 (*left*). Putting the barrow together.

Fig. C411. Plywood keeper plates hold the wheel axle into the housings; attach with small screws.

show. Seven base rails, 14 in. long of 2 in. × ½ in. wood, are screwed to the bottom of the body with ½ in. spacing between.

Mark out the two arm pieces on 10 in. × 3 in. × ¾ in. wood strips and saw out to the contours given in Fig. C407. Smooth the edges with plane or rasp then drill two ¼ in. holes for mounting to the body sides. The arrow-shaped legs are marked out to the dimensions shown in Fig. C407—once again using 3 in. × ¾ in. strips, but measuring 22½ in. overall in this case. The feathered flight at the top of each arrow is shaped to a depth of 6 in. and the arrow point measures 5 in. up from the ground. The remaining shaft is reduced to 1½ in. width between flight and point. Smooth the edges and drill two fixing holes to take ¼ in. dia. coachbolts. Whether you wish to use two coachbolts for each arrow and arm, or only one as was used in the prototype (Fig. C405)—or whether you prefer to simply screw these parts in place—will depend upon the strength you require in the finished barrow.

The bent iron metal scroll brackets are 14 in. lengths of ¾ in. × ⅛ in. mild steel strip. Bend the scrolls to the general dimensions given in Fig. C408, using suitable pieces of round steel bar held in the vice as bending formers. This size of metal strip is easily bent cold and there should be no difficulty in obtaining even flowing curves. Drill two small holes in each bracket and screw the scrolls to the barrow front and shelf in the positions indicated.

The 15 in.-diameter wheel is a built-up sandwich assembly—Fig. C409—with a central X-frame and ply or hardwood facing discs. If the barrow stands in a reasonably-sheltered spot, hardboard construction is quite suitable provided it is kept well painted; otherwise external-quality ply should be used for the discs. If the barrow is to stand out in all weathers, a brass or aluminium strip is recom-mended for the wheel tread, but a hardboard strip will give durable and adequate service on a covered terrace or patio.

Half-joint two 16 in. pieces of 3 in. × 1 in. timber leaving the ends square. Glue-and-screw the joint but leave the centre free for the axle hole which is drilled later. Mark out and saw the two 15 in.-diameter discs and put a ¼ in. drill through the centre of each to act as guides for the 1 in. drill. Screw the discs to the frame and countersink the heads flush with the surfaces. At this stage, the end of the X-frame arms can be sawn off on the curve to match that of the discs. Open out the axle hole to full size and insert a 5 in. length of dowel. Glue the axle permanently in place.

The wheel band is a strip approximately 48 in. long, but cut this on the actual job to get a good butt fit. The brass or aluminium strip should be purchased 50 in. long and cut to size. If ¼ in. ply has been used for the discs the strip will be 1½ in. wide. A hardboard wheel strip on hardboard discs will be a little under this width. Secure the band with countersunk screws put into the ends of the X-frame.

Fit the body to the heart board with screws going through the barrow sides into the ends of the heart cross bars. Bolt or screw the arms to the rear, making sure that they are parallel with each other (Fig. C410). The arrow legs are fixed to the sides at an angle equal to that of the heart-board, both sloping backwards to the same degree. Bolt up with 2½ in.-long ¼ in. coachbolts, having washers and nuts on the inside—or screw them with 1½ in. × 10 r.h. screws.

The wheel with its axle fits into the wheel slot and axle blocks. The keeper plates—3 in. × 1½ in. × ¼ in. ply—are screwed behind the blocks to keep the axle in place and the wheel should turn easily without much slack (Fig. C411).

Brush at least two coats of wood primer to all the woodwork and a metal primer to the bolts and scrolls. Paint the body (inside and out), the wheel and arrow shafts white. The arrow flights and points, scrolls and pot shelf, handles, and body edges could be black or red. Paint wheel rim black or leave bright metal, according to taste.

MATERIALS

Barrow Sides and Back; 2 pieces 20 in. × 6 in. × ¾ in.; 1 piece 14½ in. × 6 in. × ¾ in.
Heart Board; 2 pieces 20 in. × 9 in. × ¾ in.
Pot Shelf; 1 piece 14 in. × 4 in. × ¾ in.
Arrow Legs; 2 pieces 22½ in. × 3 in. × ¾ in.
Arms; 2 pieces 10 in. × 3 in. × ¾ in.
Body Base Rails; 7 pieces 14 in. × 2 in. × ½ in.
Heartboard Cross Bars; 1 piece 14½ in. × 2 in. × 1½ in.; 1 piece 13½ in. × 2 in. × 1½ in.
Pot Shelf Blocks; 2 pieces 3 in. × 1½ in. × 1½ in.
Wheel X-Frame; 2 pieces 16 in. × 3 in. × 1 in.
Axle Blocks; 4 pieces 1½ in. × 1 in. × 1 in.
Wheel Discs; 2 pieces 15 in. × 15 in. × ¼ in. ply;
Keeper Plates; 2 pieces 3 in. × 1½ in. × ¼ in. ply.
Wheel Rim; 1 piece 50 in. × 1½ in. (× 16 gauge, if metal).
Wheel Axle; 1 piece 5 in. long, 1 in. dowel.
Mild Steel Scrolls; 2 pieces 14 in. × ¾ in. × ⅛ in. mild steel.
Coachbolts; 8 off 2½ in. × ¼ in. Nuts and Washers.
Woodscrews and Paint; as required.

GARDENING BARROW

This barrow is within the constructive powers of any amateur woodworker, and will be found most useful either in the large or small garden. Fig. C412 shows the general idea.

In the main it is constructed of half-inch deal and ex. 2 in. × 1 in. battens. ⅜ in. waterproof plywood can be substituted for the ½ in. deal, if preferred. The handles are of 2 in. × 1 in. and the handrail is a length of broomstick about 1½ in. in diameter.

Making the Body

Two four-foot lengths of the nominal 8 in.-wide board will, when placed edge to edge, give an approximate width of 15½ in. which is near enough to the 1 ft. 3 in. measurement given on A. There is no point in gluing the edges since glue will not stand up very well against the elements, but they might well be secured at, say, one-foot intervals by means of corrugated steel joint fasteners obtainable at most ironmongers and general stores. Cross-cut at 45° to the measurements given and then trim the other half of the joined board to make an exact match. The battens, mitred at the corner, are then screwed on ½ in. in from the bottom and back edges. The bottom and the back are next cut to size, using two joined 9 in. boards, and screwed to the outer edges of the battens. A little trim up here and there and a good glasspapering completes the main body.

Tool Rest and Tool Box

As will be seen from the diagram B, the tool rest has no bottom and is for the storage of small-handled tools such

Fig. C412. Functional, yet easily-built this light gardening barrow has a place in any garden. Diagrams A to D show constructional details.

as trowel, small fork, dibber, etc. The view of the rear of the barrow gives details of its assembly which is extremely simple. The tool box is triangular in shape and its back is slightly less wide than the length of the longest side of the triangular end pieces; the narrow space thus left prevents water and dirt accumulating. The larger tools such as shears, pruners, etc., and tying-up twine may be kept in this lower container for easy access. The end pieces are best fastened with a 2 in. csk screw near the bottom (or narrow) end and either with a well-sunk long screw near the top or a small repair bracket.

Wheels

These should be approximately 6 in. in diameter and about 20 in. apart, and a suitable length of $\frac{5}{8}$ in. $\times \frac{5}{8}$ in. iron or mild steel bar also needed. The ends can quickly be rounded on a lathe or filed. Two $\frac{1}{4}$ in. holes are drilled through the bar—about 2 in. from the inside of the wheels —and corresponding holes bored in the bottom of the barrow. The axle is fastened with the two Whitworth bolts and nuts with their heads inside the barrow.

The leg may now be made—see the small diagram C for approximate measurements. This should preferably be of hardwood and be of such a depth that the barrow rests horizontally. It is fastened to the front of the barrow from the inside with two $1\frac{1}{4}$ in. csk. screws.

Handles

The slope of the handles is such that the rail is brought about 2 ft. 6 in. from the ground—about 45° will be found suitable. Each is screwed from the inside of the barrow with three or four screws—take care that both slope at exactly the same angle so that the handrail will lie parallel with the back of the barrow. Before fixing, the handles should be bored near the top (which should be rounded) to take the handrail. This latter is shouldered as shown at D to a depth of $\frac{7}{8}$ in. and leaving a $\frac{1}{2}$ in.

MATERIALS	
Sides (2)	These may be cut from 8 ft. of 8 in. $\times \frac{1}{2}$ in.
Bottom	Cut from 4 ft. 6 in. length of 9 in. $\times \frac{1}{2}$ in.
Back	Cut from 2 ft. 6 in. length of 9 in. $\times \frac{1}{2}$ in.
Tool Rest	One piece 18 in. $\times$ 2 in. $\times \frac{1}{2}$ in. Two pieces each 2 in. $\times 1\frac{1}{2}$ in. $\times$ 1 in.
Tool Box	One piece 18 in. $\times 4\frac{1}{2}$ in. $\times \frac{1}{2}$ in. Two pieces (triangular) ex. 4 in. $\times 2\frac{1}{2}$ in. $\times$ 1 in.
Centre Leg	Ex. 8 in. $\times$ 4 in. $\times$ 1 in. preferably hardwood
Wheels	One pair 6 in. rubber-tyred, and axle
Batten	Two pieces 2 ft. 3 in. $\times$ 2 in. $\times$ 1 in. Two pieces 1 ft. 3 in. $\times$ 2 in. $\times$ 1 in.
Handles	Two pieces about 3 ft. 4 in. $\times$ 2 in. $\times$ 1 in.
Handrail	20 in. length of $1\frac{1}{4}/1\frac{1}{2}$ in. broomstick
About 2 doz. $1\frac{1}{4}$ in. No. 8 csk. screws and 2 Whitworth bolts 2 in. $\times \frac{1}{4}$ in. with nuts and washers.	

---

dia. peg. The peg should be a tight fit and, for additional strength, may be pinned through the handles.

Finish

First apply a coat of good priming, then, when dry, putty all countersunk screw holes and fill in any irregularities or cracks in the wood. Next apply a good, lead-based undercoat, and finish in hard gloss of the desired colour—a medium or dark green is best. If storage presents a problem and the barrow has to be left in the open throughout the year, apply a fresh coat of paint each season and give the wheels a touch of oil.

When using, lift the front of the barrow slightly from the ground to prevent the curved leg from scraping.

DUSTBIN HIDEAWAY

The unit consists of an easily-built timber cupboard which is improved in appearance by the addition of a flower box on the top (Fig. C413). The box can either be filled with earth and planted flowers, or filled with peat and embedded pot plants. No dimensions are given. They depend on the size of the bin to be hidden. Planed red or white pine would be suitable.

Start by attaching 2 in. $\times$ 2 in. posts to the house wall either with spikes or wall plugs, countersinking the heads. The corner posts are 2 in. $\times$ 2 in. with 2 in. $\times$ 2 in. top and bottom rails. These bottom and top rails are half lapped at the corners, as detailed in diagram A. Note there is no bottom rail between the posts fixed to the wall. The top is a piece of $\frac{3}{4}$ in. plywood screwed to the framing. The two sides are covered with $\frac{5}{8}$ in. grooved-and-tongued matching. The door is framed up with 4 in. $\times \frac{3}{4}$ in. ledges and brace covered with $\frac{5}{8}$ in. matching. Fix $\frac{5}{8}$ in. $\times \frac{1}{2}$ in. stops to the inner edges of the door posts and hinge the door to the outer post with strap hinges. A turnbuckle will keep the door closed.

The flower box consists of $\frac{3}{4}$ in. exterior-grade plywood sides bevelled on the lower edge, butt-jointed and nailed at the corners and screwed along the front and sides to the top rails. The interior of the box is lined with thin sheet copper and two short pieces of copper tube are inserted through the side of the box to drain away any surplus moisture.

For handling the bin, a trolley will be found useful and labour-saving. It is made from a piece of $\frac{3}{4}$ in. plywood fixed to four rubber-tyred castors. Cleats $1\frac{1}{2}$ in. $\times$ 1 in. thick are screwed to the plywood, one on each of the four sides, the distance between these being the diameter of the bottom of the bin (see diagram at B).

Coat the bottom rails and inside woodwork with a wood preservative and finish the outside with one coat flat and one coat gloss paint.

EXTERIOR ATTRACTIONS

The ideas shown here can enhance the appearance of the front of the house or can be used to make an attractive sitting-out place at the rear.

Window Boxes

These make very effective window dressing. The boxes are easy to make and can be of any size and style; for a permanent display, pot plants are desirable since you

A

Plan of alum. nium liner.

Bend on dotted lines

Rivets

Drainage holes

Metal liner corners are rivetted and sealed with mastic

Timber 3/4" thick

Slatted base should line up with slots

Fig. C414. Window box construction.

Fig. C413. Dustbin hideaway.

B

Sides ends and base from 3/4" timber

Legs from 1" thick timber screw to sides

Note: notches cut in base to accommodate legs

Drainage holes

Fig. C415. Long trough construction.

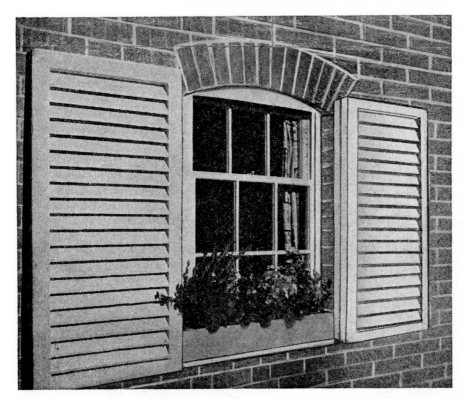

Fig. C416–C418. More exterior attractions.

Plant Troughs and Shutters

The long trough shown in Fig. C415 is simply a variation of the window box idea—again plants in pots are the answer if blooms are wanted all the summer. They are the ideal way of livening up a courtyard or an over-shadowed front entrance where real gardening is not

can change them and keep up a succession of blooms, and you avoid the weight of a full trough of earth. Details for construction are given in Fig. C414.

feasible. Troughs without legs can be used as window boxes or stood outside on stands as shown.

The shutters are not intended to work, only to be an ornament (Fig. C416). Paint in a contrasting colour to the wall behind them, e.g. white on a red wall, blue or grey on a white or pink wall, pink or blue on a grey wall. Constructional details for two designs are given in Fig. C417.

The circular trough shown in Fig. C418 was originally built round one upright of a porch, but it can be adapted to stand on a short pedestal or even on the ground.

GARAGE DOORS

New garage doors are likely to be expensive to buy, but making them reduces the cost to that of the materials only.

The timber for the pair of doors shown in Fig. C419 consists of 4 in. × 2 in. for the uprights and cross pieces, beading for the glazed section and three sheets of three-ply for facing, as can be seen from the exploded view of the door components in Fig. C420.

The main frames of 4 in. × 2 in. are mortised-and-tenoned with two uprights in each frame and two cross pieces as framing for the glass—as can be seen in Fig. C421. (A mortise attachment for a power drill is well worth having

and soon pays for itself in time and money saved.)

The three-ply is pinned to either side of the centre aperture as well as at the top and bottom, thus leaving space for the beading and glass. A suitable beading is then pinned to the two centre uprights and cross-pieces. The glass is secured with panel pins and putty.

Two portions are marked out for the hinges and cut away. After hanging, the hinges are covered by specially-shaped wood sections. These are then screwed through the hinges to the main frame.

The doors require a priming coat of paint, followed by two undercoats and two top coats, rubbing down, of course, between each coat.

Fig. C420. Exploded view of door components.

WOOD FACING

HINGE

3 PLY FACING

GLASS

MAIN FRAME

BEADING

Fig. C421. Dab the wedges with resin glue. Use weather-proof (resin-bonded) plywood.

Fig. C419. The new garage doors.

JOINTING AND REBATE FOR GLASS

'WENDY' BUNGALOW

The playhouse shown in Fig. C422 was designed with an up-to-date look to please the modern child. The 'Wendy' bungalow has several novel features including a picture-window with a miniature flower-pot rack, roof lights in the ceiling, side chimney unit and a carport to house a pedal car or tricycle.

The method of construction is straightforward, with hardboard panels fixed to a light, folding frame enabling the structure to be packed away fairly flat. The roof is hinged and bolted to the main frame for separate stowage and the chimney unit and carport are also easily removable. Windows may be either left unglazed or covered with transparent plastic sheeting—glass is not recommended. Dimensions of the bungalow—6 ft. × 4 ft. with a ridge-height of 5 ft.—give a good-sized playhouse that will be reasonably weatherproof through the summer months if well painted. A timber floor could be built as an extra.

The general dimensions are shown in Fig. C423.

Folding Frame

The main frame of the bungalow comprises a front and back frame with inward folding ends (Fig. C424). The entire framing is of 1½ in. square-section softwood half-jointed throughout and screwed for strength.

Front and back frames are plain rectangles 6 ft. × 4 ft. but the front frame has extra pieces let in to hang the door and make the windowframe opening. End frames—there are four of them—are 2 ft. wide and slope from a wall height of 4 ft. to the apex of 5 ft. Six pairs of brass butt-hinges are used to assemble the body frame but those hinges on the outside—the two pairs on the centre line of each end—cannot be fixed before the hardboard covering has been added.

Cut the window opening out of the front hardboard panel—2 ft. 6 in. wide by 2 ft. deep—and nail some extra framing round the inside of the opening to stiffen up the cut edge; also cut the door opening to suit the hanging posts. Completed, the main box for the bungalow should fold into a 6 in.-thick package and yet open up quite easily when required.

Roof frames measure 6 ft. × 3 ft. and have a pair of hinges under the ridge at each end for folding. Build a frame for the skylights to the dimensions given and mount it on a couple of extra downrights in the forward facing frame (Fig. C424). Clad the frames with hardboard sheet and fix pieces round the skylight frame too. Fix the roof to the main frame with four 4 in.-long coach bolts, which not only mount the roof but also lock the folding ends in an opened position.

Door and pot rack

The door for the bungalow is a wood frame made to fit the door opening, covered with a hardboard panel and hinged into the structure. A handle, door-knocker and latch complete this item. Make the flower-pot holder from a piece of 6 in. board ⅝ in. thick and 27 in. long. Draw a centre line along the length of the board and mark out the 3 in. holes leaving 2 in. spacings between the ends of the board and holes.

Mount the rack to the window front with a pair of scroll brackets bent from 14 in. lengths of mild steel strip ⅛ in. × ½ in. This section of steel strip can easily be bent cold round a bit of suitable bar held in the vice Drill a couple of screw holes in each scroll and fix beneath the pot rack.

Carport

The frame for the roof of the carport measures 4 ft. by 2 ft. 6 in. and has a pair of angle blocks fixed in the far corners to house the dowel support columns which are 1½ in. dia. by 4 ft. high. This frame is bolted to the bungalow body with a pair of ¼ in. dia. bolts put through the

Fig. C422. This little playhouse needs no foundations and folds away for winter storage.

5'-0" HIGH TO RIDGE

CAR PORT BOLTS ON

GREEN

RED

10" 6"

TOP BOXED IN

RED

2'-0"

4'-0"

HINGES ON THE OUTSIDE

DOOR ON TIMBER FRAME

CHIMNEY, HARDBOARD ON 1½" SQ. FRAME DETACHES FOR STORAGE

2'-0"

2'-6"

RED

BROWN

CREAM

9" 1'-2"

WALLS FOLD IN FOR STORING

6'-0"

FLOWER RACK TO HOLD 3" POTS

Fig. C423 (*above*).   Bungalow dimensions.

Fig. C424 (*below*).   Frame details.

SUPPORTS FOR ROOF LIGHT

ROOF LIGHT FRAME

12"

12"

12"

3'-0"

BOLT ROOF TO WALL FRAME

2'-6"

DOWEL SOCKETS

HINGES FITTED ON UNDERSIDE OF ROOF

4'-0"

1½" DIA. DOWEL 4'-0" LONG

1½" SQ. TIMBER

2" BUTTS

3" HOLES 2" APART

1'-8" 9"

6" 2'-3"

HALF JOINTED THROUGHOUT

main frames. Roof the car port with a single sheet of hardboard.

Chimney Unit

The tall tapering chimney adds considerably to the contemporary appearance of the bungalow. It is 6 ft. tall and tapers from 14 in. × 9 in. at the base to 10 in. × 6 in. at the top. Box the frame from more 1½ in.-square wood and cover with hardboard strips. It is advisable to fill the top of the chimney with a covering sheet. Fix the chimney to the bungalow with a pair of coachbolts permanently anchored into the chimney framing and simply requiring internal wingnuts and washers.

Finish

Hardboard is very durable providing it is kept well painted on the outside. Apply a suitable undercoat to the whole structure, then finish with a good gloss paint.

There is a range of small fittings—porch lamps, house number and name plates, fancy brasswork, etc.—suitable for fixing to the bungalow which may be obtained from most handyman stores.

KENNEL FOR TWO DOGS

The traditional dog-kennel is quaint rather than useful. Like a miniature house with its ridge roof and an access hole at the front, the shelter it provides is inadequate.

Any dog will spend all day out-of-doors if it has some-where dry and draught-free in which to avoid the worst of the weather.

In devising and building a day kennel for two dogs, cost is an important consideration. Hardboard over a sawn timber frame is practical so long as the exterior surface is painted thoroughly.

In order to assess the material required for the design shown in Fig. C425 make rough sketches of the basic frame, with notes of the types of joint to be used. Keep the number of joints as few as possible to save labour and maintain strength while keeping the weight of the timber to a minimum. It is important to remember the extent to which a mortised or half-lapped joint can weaken a timber, often just at the point where strength is needed.

The dimensions have to be generous to allow for two dogs to settle in with comfort. To avoid the worst of the draughts, it is best to recess the front of the kennel so that the entrance has a porch with closed sides. This is to prevent wind and rain beating into the living quarters. A lean-to type of roof is easiest to make. The following dimensions are adequate but they can, of course, be altered if required: overall length 6 ft.; overall height 3 ft. 4 in.; height at eaves 2 ft. 8 in.; width 2 ft. 2 in.

Use sawn timber of 2 in. × 2 in. section for the main uprights of the frame and for the two longitudinal members. For the remainder of the frame use 2 in. × 1 in. section.

No cross-members are needed at the base of the frame, since 5 in. × ¾ in. tongued-and-grooved floorboards are

Fig. C425. Warm cosiness and reliable shelter for two dogs.

HARDBOARD ROOF

ROOFING FELT

$1'' \times \frac{3}{4}''$

HARDBOARD WALL

Fig. C426.   These are the simple joints required.

Fig. C428.   Method of securing felt.

Fig. C427.   The completed framework.

used for the floor. This may appear extravagant, but running the boards transversely saves the use of any other crossties at the lower part of the frame. Also, many dogs are reluctant to walk over a surface which is in any way unsteady or yields to their weight; and good, sound flooring is, therefore, called for. In addition, tongued-and-grooved boards are almost entirely draught-proof if fitted properly and that, too, is important if the dogs are to be persuaded to use the kennel in bad weather.

In the entire construction there are only six joints to make, and these are of the simplest kind. They occur at the points where the longitudinal base timbers intersect with the 2 in. × 2 in. uprights. See Fig. C426.

The completed framework is shown in Fig. C427. At this stage of the work it is time to think about the weather-proofing.

The feet of the kennel, which hold the floor some 4 in. from the ground, might have to stand in rainwater, and the underside of the floor itself could become damp due to splashing. Therefore apply creosote liberally to the feet and all exposed underparts of the floor and frame before fitting the hardboard cladding.

To secure the hardboard to the timber frame, use nails rather than hardboard pins. These should be driven in obliquely at about 5 in. intervals to resist their being pulled from the timbers in the event of a heavy dog leaning against the inside surface of the hardboard.

Covering the hardboard roof with felt is simplified by using waterproofing compound where the felt overlaps. The adhesive properties of the compound make it unnecessary to employ battens to hold the felt down—which sometimes can prove troublesome because of the need to drive nails through the felt.

The felt is secured at the edges as shown in Fig. C428 and it should be noted that the 1 in. × ¾ in. battens which secure the felt also support the top edge of the hardboard walls. While this requires nails to be driven outwards from within the kennel, other methods demand more joints to be made at the top intersections of the frame. With the size of kennel described, working from within is not difficult but would be difficult if the design were scaled down to suit smaller dogs.

A coat of gloss paint over undercoat on all exposed surfaces completes the work which should serve for years.

INDEX